POLITICAL DEVELOPMENT
AND THE NEW REALISM
IN SUB-SAHARAN
AFRICA

POLITICAL DEVELOPMENT AND THE NEW REALISM IN SUB-SAHARAN AFRICA

Edited by
David E. Apter and
Carl G. Rosberg

University Press of Virginia

Charlottesville and London

The University Press of Virginia
Copyright © 1994 by the
Rector and Visitors of the University of Virginia
First published 1994

Library of Congress Cataloging-in-Publication Data
Political development and the new realism in Sub-Saharan Africa /
edited by David E. Apter and Carl G. Rosberg.
    p. cm.
    Includes bibliographical references and index.
    ISBN 0-8139-1479-5 (cloth). — ISBN 0-8139-1480-9 (paper)
    1. Africa, Sub-Saharan—Politics and government—1960–   .
    2. Political development.   I. Apter, David Ernest, 1924–   .
    II. Rosberg, Carl Gustav.
    JQ1879.A15P62   1994
    306.2'.0967—dc20   93-2428
                                    CIP

Printed in the United States of America

In honor of
James Smoot Coleman
1919–1985

More than most area or regional studies, the field of African studies has been deeply concerned with not only what happens politically, but how what happens can best be analyzed. While it is true that to a considerable extent different theoretical approaches have a life of their own, sharing in and being influenced by more general paradigm shifts, the social sciences more than other fields have been preoccupied with how to apply theory to empirical problems. For this reason African studies has been characterized by great intellectual intensity both among scholars and practitioners. Indeed, not infrequently both tendencies are combined in the same person.

James S. Coleman was perhaps the most remarkable representative figure in African studies. A scholar deeply concerned with the impact on theories on practice and practices on theory, he left his institutional imprint on the African Studies Center at UCLA that bears his name and his policy imprint on the programs he shaped and implemented for the Rockefeller Foundation. Among the more enduring consequences of his concerns have been the advancement and encouragement of African scholarship. Michael Chege, one of the contributors to this volume, put the matter very well. "Those who had the good fortune to be taught by him or to work with him, will recall his capacity to tolerate and deliberate on views which span the ideological spectrum from left to right, with unusual ease. His own teaching was a model in exposing students to a wide variety of ideas and interpretations and in challenging them to reflect before taking a position. His working life was suffused with humane qualities and the right balance between cynicism and wit" (Nairobi *Daily News,* May 13, 1985).

It is in the spirit of theory and practice that these essays are presented.

D.E.A.
C.G.R.

CONTENTS

Acknowledgments   ix

1

DAVID E. APTER AND CARL G. ROSBERG
Changing African Perspectives   I

Part I: Ideology, Society, and Social Groups

2

CRAWFORD YOUNG
Evolving Modes of Consciousness and Ideology:
Nationalism and Ethnicity   61

3

JOEL D. BARKAN
Resurrecting Modernization Theory and the Emergence of Civil
Society in Kenya and Nigeria   87

4

RICHARD L. SKLAR
Social Class and Political Action in Africa:
The Bourgeoisie and the Proletariat   117

Part II: State, Society, and Development

5

MICHAEL F. LOFCHIE

The New Political Economy of Africa 145

6

THOMAS M. CALLAGHY

State, Choice, and Context: Comparative Reflections on Reform
and Intractability 184

7

COLIN LEYS

Learning from the Kenya Debate 220

Part III: Rulership, Leadership, and Development

8

MICHAEL CHEGE

Swapping Development Strategies:
Kenya and Tanzania after Their Founding Presidents 247

9

ROBERT H. JACKSON AND CARL G. ROSBERG

The Political Economy of African Personal Rule 291

Contributors 325

Index 329

ACKNOWLEDGMENTS

This volume has been a collective endeavor of the editors and contributors to analyze and develop themes, concepts, and theoretical positions that have been concerns of political science in the exploration of the new realities of African politics. Our endeavor is not exhaustive in discerning the contours of postwar African politics. Our contributors have graciously responded to the many unusual demands made upon them in the preparation of this volume. Each of them, of course, remains responsible for his own essay. We are also most grateful for the assistance of many others whose knowledge and insights have greatly added to the quality of this work. We would particularly like to thank Nadine Zelinski for her superb and efficient secretarial assistance and would like especially to express our gratitude for the helpful comments of our anonymous reader. David Apter would like to acknowledge the support of the Institution for Social and Policy Studies and the Council on African Studies, Yale University. Carl Rosberg wishes to express his appreciation to the generous assistance of the Institute of International Studies, University of California, Berkeley. Lastly, we are particularly grateful for the encouragement and assistance of Richard Holway, our acquisitions editor at the University Press of Virginia.

POLITICAL DEVELOPMENT
AND THE NEW REALISM
IN SUB-SAHARAN
AFRICA

1

CHANGING AFRICAN PERSPECTIVES

DAVID E. APTER AND CARL G. ROSBERG

EVENTS HAVE A WAY of upsetting theories about them. The best-laid analyses, especially those claiming to unmask realities hidden or disguised by powers that be (whether by design or default), turn out, at best, to have only a moment of truth. As that moment fades events and perspectives appear quite differently, and especially in retrospect (indeed if remembered at all). As for theories that once aroused great political passion, one tends either to look back in anger or (as with failed religions) to wonder what the fuss was about.

Africa—or, more precisely, Sub-Saharan Africa—has been particularly subject to such fluctuating truths and flights of interpretative fancy. This is not surprising. No other continent has been heir to so many judgments and speculations about its very nature, i.e., "Africanness." In no other continent have so many layers of power and prejudice been imposed from the outside. Today everything is subject to controversy; race, ethnicity, language, religion, ideology, all heated up by severe economic decline and long-standing and unresolved difficulties of state formation.

By the same token no continent has been the subject of more yearning, or wishful thinking. An intense desire to catch up has been linked to the exorcising of self-doubts that, originally fostered by a colonial mentality, continue to inhibit individuality and prejudice political freedom, so much so that when someone like Fanon speaks of the need to purge African self-doubts by violence, it strikes a responsive chord even among those who passionately favor peace.

When did the yearning begin? Probably with the missionaries and their salvationalism. It was intensified by merchants and traders who saw civilization in the commercialization of African life. Superimposed on both were successive and subsequent redeeming projects, each imposed from the outside, each creating its own pathos. Even colonialism, rooted as it was in

I

hard-nosed commercial endeavor, cast its role in the form of moral uplift. "Responsibility" was the centerpiece of the colonial enterprise, especially in its last and tutelary stages when it defined its legacy in the idealized terms of Western institutional democracies and was embodied in the practice of the constitutional lawyers. And, despite its formidable vocabulary, in modernization theory, too, and only thinly disguised, there was yearning, indeed, intensified in the radical post-Marxist transformationalism that succeeded it.[1]

Superimpose all these different kinds of yearning on nationalism and mobilize the clienteles each represents around a common objective, getting rid of colonial authorities territory by territory, case by case, and an apparent unity is constructed out of diversities. No obstacle seems too great to tackle. There was an explosion of texts explaining each anticolonial project as an intrinsic part of a larger historical process. Yearning became the basis of truths simultaneously personalized and universalized in the texts of radical cosmocrats like Sékou Touré or Kwame Nkrumah or in the somewhat more modest offerings of Nyerere, and for every Pan-African activist, Nkrumah's aphorisms were embodied in the little black book of axioms à la Mao.[2] The most cosmocratic political leaders placed themselves in a linear progression from Lenin through Mao, hoping to leap historical periods and jump stages of development by the collectivization of the people through the mobilization of the party.

The difficulty of yearning is in the hope it engenders, the innocence it produces, and the political dangers that arise when it is extinguished. When the great expectations imposed on political leaders decline, too much yearning imposes not practical realism but barriers to it. Every form of local parochialism revives. New and old boundaries of territory, of belief and behavior, of power and ideas, work at cross-purposes. Rather than facilitating change one finds conditions in which risk, danger, uncertainty grow and with them corruption, patronage, violence, and manipulation. Those in positions of responsibility despair of relying on conventional forms of political power or normal expectations of social responsibility. The different expressions of yearning impose too many burdens and yield to power based on wishful thinking. It becomes far easier to blame others for failure, those in political opposition, foreigners, particular ethnic groups, etc. No matter how much change may be desired, the more it is imposed, the less people favor it. Political leaders who come to power on a wave of popular enthusiasm discover that the public is the source of their problems rather than the solution.

Nor should it be surprising that so many hopes and doctrines are so quickly exploded on the hard rocks of economic decline. Social conflict is one consequence. Coups and civil wars are another. No one agrees on solutions. Given such vicissitudes, it is no wonder that power quickly becomes arbitrary and rule personalized. People who lose their innocence become cynical, their despair often punctuated by violence.

What is true of events also has been the case with preferred modes of interpretation. Theoretical systems used to analyze the complexities of African life began to seem too simple and verging on overkill. Some theories, in the guise of explaining what goes wrong, were little more than thinly disguised efforts to assign blame, identify culprits, all in the name of objectivity. Not that this would matter except that as claims, theories often wound up as ingredients in concrete struggles for power, a kind of truth radiating ideological tension around basic issues of race, culture, and nationality and defining friends and enemies, imperialist, tribalists, Marxists, and quite easily picked up by the local general, colonel, brigadier, or sergeant who, taking over power, thereby cast himself in the role of savior.

In many countries those who came to power ringed themselves with advisers able and willing to substantiate their claims no matter how flamboyant, absurd, or outrageous. Drawn from these different yearning communities were floating groups of intellectuals composed of West Indians, Europeans and Americans, South African exiles, black and white. They moved about depending on the vicissitudes of politics, first in Ghana and Guinea, then in Tanzania, later in Burkina Faso, wherever it was possible to promote preferred theories as guides to action, an elite professing to speak for Africa in the name of the mass. Often caught by shifting realities in the ballet of power, what began on the left could wind up on the right, for each had a way of turning into the other. To be attracted by power was to attach oneself to any kind of authoritarianism affording access, as those around Sékou Touré, or Nkrumah, or Amin quickly discovered.

Under these circumstances no historical recounting of events and no interpretation of them can be innocent. Each historical period in the political evolution of colonial and postcolonial Africa is associated with certain changes in styles and insights according to the different doctrines and political ideologies that accompanied those events. The danger is that in the recounting of them one is likely to impute too much significance to theories about African politics embodied at any moment in the practice of it. However, if it is true to say that in many African countries advisers and intellectuals have had uniquely privileged political significance, it is also correct that their ideas had unduly significant consequences for how African political leaders perceived what it was they were doing.

Most bread-and-butter politics is, of course, reflex response to immediate problems. But a good deal of African politics, precisely because it wanted more, because it was engaged in exorcising the larger uncertainties of blackness, Africanness (yearning again), was never just bread-and-butter politics. It was about a future that had to be drastically reshaped if Africans were to play a significant role in it. Hence, doctrine, even when thin, shrill, and rhetorical, or perhaps because thin, shrill, and rhetorical, could count for a great deal. In this respect theory has been at times important, especially when advisers and their ideas have been plunged into the realities of African politics by leaders desperate for solutions (and mostly to the detriment of those who have had to confront the consequences). One should quickly add that to the extent that this was so, theory has more to answer for in Africa than in most places, not so much for trying, but for serving power better than understanding it.

The essays in this volume represent efforts to confront some of the consequences, which occurred under circumstances vastly different from the so-called development decades. More than three decades have passed since most African territories became independent, and conditions are very different from then. The polarization between East and West that led to North-South confrontations has come to an end. The human costs of catastrophe, natural disasters, drought, erosion, the mass migrations of the starving, not to speak of corruption, mismanagement, and the failures of autocratic rule and civil wars, while they may not have brought an end to the illusions and delusions of power, have in Africa as elsewhere in the world intensified the desire for greater responsibility and accountability of leadership and indeed in several instances stimulated a return to democratic practices.

Perhaps one might add, more tentatively than hopefully, that it is also time for a new round of conceptualizing, one more fitted to the even more tentative efforts to revive democracy itself. It is in this spirit that we attempt a partial review of some of the events and lines of inquiry that characterized African politics and scholarship since independence. Our discussion centers around three interrelated problems: state formation and efficacy, the integration and evolution of society, and the sources and effectiveness of authority and power.

Most African territories became independent by means of populist nationalist movements. These were substitutes for civil society. After independence such nationalism tended to break up into a variety of parochialisms, ethnic, linguistic, religious, ideological, or combinations of all of these.[3] The common postindependence predicament was how to develop forms of civil society capable of supporting state structures. But the more the state tried to alter and modify civil society for this purpose, the more vulnerable it became to former supporters turned enemies. Not only did people rapidly become withdrawn, insular, parochial, and cynical; but as political leaders discovered very quickly, change from the top is quite different from struggles from below aimed at toppling foreign or alien powers.

The common response was to eliminate the opposition and to liquidate enemies. In one African country after another where constitutional governments had been instituted, they were quickly dismantled in favor of arbitrary rule. The postindependence period in Africa is a history of coups, military rule, one-party regimes, civil wars, personal rule. Localism and ethnicity have served as a main line of defense against the capricious exercise of power at the center, not in some traditionalistic revivalism but as a modern form of coping, of resistance, (including the uses of ritual power against corrupt politicians). Hence, under the surface of national power are other forces which, even if they do not confront the center directly, erode its power.

It was such circumstances that opened the way for justifying the exercise of power by means of doctrinal prescriptions that would discredit rival claims. During the transition from colonialism, political leaders took their administrative style and textbook applications of institutional democracy from Western theorists, using democratic theory itself in principle to support the drive to independence. In the immediate postindependence period, modernization theory of the American variety became the framework within which those inheriting power established programs of aid, infrastructure development, and social mobilization. The radical rejection of modernization theory coincided with the assertion of greater independence by African states and justified radical poles, vanguard parties, and African socialism. In this sense theories became complicit in politics. The debates they sponsored served as substitutes for the realities of governing.

This suggests the structure of the present discussion. We want to play back and forth between events and theories. We do not assume any one-to-one relationship between them. Each follows its own rhythm. But each also had relevance for the other. We also try to suggest where theory is at the moment in light of what might be called the new realism of today's politics.

The Colonial Legacy

We begin with the colonial period in part because interest in it is reviving at a time when most of those who remember it are dying off. Today it is being reinterpreted according to present requirements through the recuperation of texts rather than the immediacy of experience. Revisionism of course has a significance of its own. But it reinvents the past better than it restores it to view. Hence we comment in some depth on colonialism both as a legacy and also as a fugitive phenomenon and hold up to the light a few photographs and snapshots, some now pretty faded.

Both colonialists and their adversaries are rapidly disappearing from the scene, taking with them both their memories of events and the discourses in which they described them. One forgets the curious relationships between both sides. They knew each other well, despite differences. Most nationalist leaders were educated under colonial auspices, some imprisoned under them and freed under them, and in the end colonial officials and militants fought and compromised each other. Of the original generation of founder / scholar / warriors, activists, and thinkers whose portraits stare down from the wall in the main hall of the Organization of African Unity in Addis Ababa, some of the most famous like Modibo Keita, Kwame Nkrumah, Sékou Touré, and Jomo Kenyatta are dead. Nnamdi Azikiwe, Léopold Sédar Senghor, and Julius Nyerere have stepped down. Kenneth Kaunda was voted out of office after twenty-six years in power. Only Hastings Banda and Félix Houphouët-Boigny are still in power. The rest are gone, prey as often to coups and rebellions as to old age.[4]

Their common object was the formation of mass nationalist parties. They sought appropriate political outlets, mostly but not always by constitutional means, and not because of principle but of necessity. But they also represented that moment of innocence when everything could be tried and there were few penalties for failure. Experimentalism was the order of the day, and exorcising colonialism seemed a relatively cost-free exercise.

They soon discovered that they had inherited a complicated developmental process, which especially in British and French Africa had begun just before and after World War II. As well, they discovered that the mass nationalism, populist in character, which they helped to foster could only paper over the cracks in the societies they inherited, cultural, ethnic, religious, not to speak of class, rural versus urban, etc. In many instances after independence these cracks became more visible, plaguing those in power so that conflicts between state and subunits of society became common and gave frequency to the generic term *ethnic conflict*. This is, of course, in hindsight. Prospects and processes looked somewhat different at the time.[5]

Apart from colonies with relatively large settled European populations, prying loose from colonial authorities was less difficult in English-speaking Africa than in francophone areas. In the latter, strenuous efforts were made by the authorities to slow nationalism down and prevent it from breaking up the two colonial confederations, the eight territories of French West Africa and the four of French Equatorial Africa, into politically autonomous states, under the guise of preventing Balkanization. More generally one might say that colonial reactions varied from crackdowns and violent civil war (as with the Mau Mau in Kenya) to compromises. Nevertheless, after independence in the Sudan in 1956, the Gold Coast (Ghana) in 1957, and Guinea in 1958, such nationalism spread rapidly to French West and Equatorial Africa, Nigeria, Zaire, East and Central Africa, and to Portuguese dependencies. It would not stop until the entire subcontinent was independent of colonial rule in 1990 with Namibian independence.

Near the end there was a sudden rush to institution building. The view from the metropole was how best (during the last dying kick of colonialism) to prepare the way for a self-government few had anticipated and even fewer thought desirable.

During the interwar period it has been said that two opposite colonial ideological tendencies developed. French Africa was assimilationist, with a focus on the metropole and power radiating downward through the African territories via Dakar and Brazzaville. British Africa, following the Lugard syndrome, sought to integrate "traditional" and "secular" systems in a seamless web of administration which allowed for the slow devolution of power to local legislative bodies under the rubric of indirect rule, quickly made obsolete with the rush toward independence. But while there is great difficulty in using these terms, they have left in place legacies that are still working their way through contemporary African politics.[6]

In turn, in the French colonial assimilationalist tradition we can trace two contrasting tendencies, both of which had long-term effects on postindependence regimes. One, the Jacobin emphasis, represented a kind of post-1792 Rousseauism which traced its historical origins to the freeing of slaves (later reversed until 1848). It represented the principle of universalism, the common humanity of black and white, who, becoming involved, would be personified by a kind of Greek-inspired classicism in which all men could find their place if properly integrated with France. Their common inspiration was embodied in the principles of revolutionary enlightenment.[7]

Guinea under Sékou Touré and Mali under Modibo Keita might be said to have represented this tradition after independence.

By the same token one can speak of a conservative military tradition within the French concept of empire. Roman in inspiration, its emphasis was on order. This military character imposed itself on the civil structure of administration, the inspiration for which derived from the conquest and administration of Algeria and Indochina. The military structure was more important in the French colonial administration than in the British case.

Moreover, many of these military-style administrators had contempt for the bumpy pattern of French politics in the metropole, the revolutions, upheavals, and especially the politics of the Third Republic, particularly during the Popular Front under Léon Blum, attitudes which extended well into the Fourth Republic. They regarded with horror the introduction of democratic politics in Africa and did their best to impede it, not least of all by imprisoning and exiling more radical African leaders.

Whatever their real differences on the ground, both the Jacobin and the military traditions had one feature in common. Both emphasized a centralizing pattern of politics and administration. This in the end undermined the conservative position, for what began as a method of centralized rule in which basic statutory instruments laid down by the colonial administration in Paris were effected simultaneously in all French West and Equatorial African territories eventually came to favor the Jacobins. African politics in Paris accomplished major reforms by increasing the significance and scope of both interterritorial and territorial councils. The result was the localization and territorialization of political parties, which nevertheless did not lose their links to one another. As French parliamentary and party politics were opened up to substantial African representation, assimilationist politics became more lively and significant.

The reforms of most significance occurred during the Fourth Republic. Then Lois Cadres embodying reforms were fashioned in part by African parliamentary coalitions. The result was a phased pattern of decolonization in which organization below affected politics at the top and reform leaps by means of administrative ukases. It was thus a method of political advance which at its inception was quite the opposite of the British pattern. Political change in French Africa, beginning with only a small cadre of political elites at the center, widened their base. These elites first organized interterritorial coalitions composed of territorial branches. Later these branches became real parties still linked to interterritorial ones.

To a significant extent, and especially within the territorial parties of the

Rassemblement Démocratique Africain (RDA), the revolutionary tradition was an important influence. Moreover, a political figure from one territory could be elected to office in another. A Guinean politician, for example, might hold a ministerial position in Senegal or Mali. This circulation of radical elites was facilitated by the interterritorial politics of, for example, Houphouët-Boigny's RDA, itself for a time affiliated with the French Communist party in the National Assembly in Paris. The pattern affected the organization and ideology of local territorial party organizations, of which two territorial branches of the RDA, the Union Soudanaise under Modibo Keita in Soudan and the Parti Démocratique de Guinée under Sékou Touré were among the most militant.

There were of course other tendencies, especially associated with tradition of Catholic socialism. These were best represented by Léopold Sédar Senghor's Independents d'Outre-mer (IOM), which in 1957 changed its name to the Convention Africaine (CA). The relationship between the RDA and the IOM was one of intense ideological conflict. Each maintained very different parliamentary party links in Paris.

Whatever else might be said about the pattern of interterritorial party competition, it found its outlets in a proliferating body of institutional and representative bodies (up to and including the French parliament and the assembly of the French Union). The effect was to make territorial politics more important. It meant also an ever-enlarging political class, less elite and closer to rural and village life. Its job was the basic mobilization of popular support so that at a certain point the centralized administrative structures became subordinated to more territorial elective bodies. What evolved might be called a circular political flow. The initial political momentum was to push politics upward to the metropole. The effect was to return politics downward from the metropole to the territories. In this process the first initiatives came from African politicians engaged in parliamentary activities in Paris, i.e., from above, and by and large they were resisted by colonial officials below. This resistance intensified the significance of territorial politics and favored the mobilization of Jacobin tendencies in radical mass parties, which increasingly made use of national territorial assemblies and other councils at a subterritorial level.

As to British "empiricism" (as Thomas Hodgkin described British colonial practice), one might say it was manifested in economic terms, i.e., a politics of pay as you go. Colonies were worth it if they could be made to pay their way. Since some were in that sense worth more than others, one treated each colonial territory case by case. But there was principle involved as well (to which Hodgkin's own Quaker ancestors would no doubt have attested). For example, there was a strand of colonialism based on antislavery movements and followed by Wilberforce and Buxton, not to speak of the Evangelicals, which insisted that to end slavery one had to administer the source, i.e., the hinterland of a territory where such commerce flourished, and not simply patrol the seas or administer the coastal forts and factories.[8] There was also a considerable concern in early colonial policy with how to deal with matters of race, religion, and culture. What might be called a politics of cultural hierarchy began very early on in India. For example, Robert Clive, one of the earliest representatives of the British East India Company who had fought the French in Madras and won the battle of Plessey in 1757, took the view that one had to have a dual government in India, a hidden one (British) and a public one (Indian). This was not the view shared by his immediate successors who saw the need to put an end to a culture that James Mill considered "hideous" and "disgusting" among other things. Establishing the rule of law, an independent Supreme Court, and a "disinterested civil service" was one way (Macaulay's) by means of which Indian culture could be first modified through education and then provided outlets through local government and the civil service.

When Lord Lugard went to India as a young man, all the arguments over "traditional institutions" and their place in British civil administration were already made, and his later "dual mandate" was a refinement in an African context of principles (more than practices) well debated in India. He moved them one step further into the principle of the "seamless web" of Native African and British administration. There was empiricism here, but lots more.

In the British case we find a flow of politics but oriented territorially rather than toward the metropole. It took the form of constitutional-institutional reforms according to precedents first established in the white dominions, then adapted to India as the first nonwhite case, and only lastly to African territories; namely, the transformation of the executive and legislative council systems into a "phase movement" stimulated by African protests and demands. These phases were marked by a changing proportion of ex officio and appointed members in executive and legislative councils to unofficial and elected representatives and eventually a shift toward parliamentary government, pushed from below by mass nationalist parties. Here the circular flow refers to a shifting pattern of nationalism in which colonial administrators first favored chiefs and chiefs' nationalism, which in turn, with educational reform, led to elite nationalism that was often anti-chief and eventually to mass nationalism which was antielite and occasionally in alliance with chiefs or opposed to them, depending on which leaders and parties they backed. The phase movement of constitutional-institutional reform went hand in hand then with shifting nationalist clienteles, and from narrow to broadly based, first chiefs on the basis of ethnicity, then elites on the basis of occupation and education, and eventually populist politicians favoring mass parties based on omnibus class clienteles. Each shift that broadened the base moved constitutional reform through the cycle more quickly. Each shift of the cycle helped stimulate the organization of mass nationalism. But each territory had to go through its own struggle. Timing varied greatly, especially when it came to devolution. Where there were white communities, as in parts of East Africa or Central Africa, the job was how to keep it from favoring whites at the expense of blacks. It was here that violence accompanied the process, as with Mau Mau in Kenya and the war in Zimbabwe.[9]

Furthermore, notions like Cartesianism or empiricism ignore a more fundamental aspect of colonialism, what might be called its discourse of "positive" obliteration. This saw "native" cultures as morally flawed. It was common to identify some "barbarous" practice, elevate its significance, and use it to demonstrate how "debased" that society was, whether the suttee in India, human sacrifice in Ashanti, or clitoridectomy in Kenya. These identifying characteristics were juxtaposed with commerce, Christianity, and colonialism, as the foundation stones of moral uplift.[10] Moreover, if properly administered these changes would simultaneously whet the appetite of Africans for European goods and weaken their desire to pursue "barbarous customs." Colonialism in this sense parodies history and on its own terms starts it all over again as the extension of empire, imposing what Christopher Miller has called "blank darkness" in place of a recognized past.[11] Even today a politics of memory, of retrieval, goes along with the mobilization of anger and yearning that began with bitter attacks on the tyranny of Eurocentrism and colonial practices.[12]

As to the strategy of colonial resistance to nationalism, one might say that as protest occurred and became formed into coherent nationalist ideologies and organizations, it was itself transformed from a rather torpid authoritarianism not so different from Mary Kingsley's original characterization, "a coma punctuated by fits," to a last-ditch transformationalism.[13] High on the list of priorities was the construction of new educational facilities, especially universities modeled after their metropolitan counterparts.[14] The French West African (AOF) counterpart was the University of

Dakar (now known as Université Cheikh Anta Diop de Dakar), an integral part of the state-run French university system. In both British and French Africa there was as well a virtual explosion in teacher-training colleges, administrative training institutes, and community development and other crash programs sponsored by both governmental and nongovernmental agencies, not to speak of the expansion of training and educational facilities in Europe.

Education was part of a larger strategy to channel nationalism into Western-style conciliar institutions in the name of democratization, the latter now viewed as the chief bulwark and defense system against radicalism and possibly communism. Democracy was both a goal and a legacy, providing the necessary hubris for a process which to more radical nationalists only thinly disguised the interests of the metropole in the name of the periphery. If they went along, it was because they had no choice.

It was a game in which both sides were coconspirators. Nationalist political leaders were anxious to get the colonial authorities off their backs as quickly and painlessly as possible. Colonial officials were concerned to lock into place institutional links with the metropole (especially economic ones) in the name of future growth and development. On the whole even those most willing to cooperate with African politicians had the deepest of reservations.[15]

There were, of course, many well-intentioned individuals involved in the process. During the period of the Lugard syndrome, functionalist anthropologists helped to associate African traditional politics with British civil administration. There was a close if uneasy intellectual relationship between scholars and administrators. Some officials following in the tradition of indirect rule and the principles of Lord Lugard's dual mandate were influenced by official anthropologists like R. S. Rattray, C. K. Meek, or M. M. Green. Others like Robert Delavignette or Lord Hailey wrote extensively on colonial administration, local government reforms, expansion of the franchise, the transition from indirect to direct electoral methods, the evolution of national assemblies and other legislative and executive institutions, the co-optation and election of African officials, the translation of a colonial service into national civil services, and eventually the way that electoral reform would convert confrontational nationalism into competitive party politics and, on occasion, even deal with "peasants."[16]

Serious homage was rendered to local cultures, seeing them in a rather different light than the primitive and nasty or the romantic and exotic. Suddenly African culture had intrinsic merit, artistic rather than intellectual, vibrant and vibrating, and from masks to dance, festival to theater, with traveling troupes putting on performances at the Paris Opera and study sessions at the Institute of Colonial Studies at Oxford or the sacred precincts of the Royal African Society in London.

After the war when colonialism became a domestic political issue and the Labour party became involved, a parade of Bloomsbury intellectuals and Fabians, an occasional sympathetic Colonial Office official like Sir Andrew Cohen, a ranking Labour party politician like Arthur Creech Jones, the odd parliamentary leftist like Fenner Brockway, and some Pan-Africanist figures like George Padmore, T. Ras Makonnen, Kwame Nkrumah, and Jomo Kenyatta threw themselves into the process.[17] Their equivalents in France included leftist Catholic intellectuals around Alioune Diop and *Présence Africaine,* radical economists like Jean Suret-Canale, Charles Bettelheim, and others from the French Communist party or the Confédération Générale des Travail (CGT) (with its links to African nationalist trade unionists like Sékou Touré), as well as such intellectuals as Jean Paul Sartre, Aimé Césaire, and Frantz Fanon.[18] There was a rush to build museums, to establish archives, and to enlarge and expand the scope of embryonic research institutes like the Institut Française Afrique Noir (IFAN), the West African Institute of Social and Economic Research, the East African Institute of Social Research, and the Rhodes Livingston Institute whose research endeavors came to include everything from anthropological studies of change to demographics and the search for appropriate infrastructures to facilitate economic growth from above as well as below in conjunction with colonial instrumentalities.[19]

If late colonialism was tutelary (especially in the stages leading to constitutional negotiations preceding transfers of power) where previously it had been autocratic, for a few brief years colonialism was able to present itself as benign, sheltering under its political umbrella those ordinary people likely to be victims of the vicissitudes of populist and nationalist politics. From this perspective what was going on in Africa, albeit very unevenly, was a race between devolution and radicalization (and well before the Belgians and Portuguese had even entered the race).[20]

Strenuous efforts were now made to cultivate and recruit new African political elites who, upstanding in demeanor and acceptable in public utterance, would be responsible to their clienteles. These twin emphases, higher education and administration, were designed as buffers against the populist politicians claiming to represent the people, not to speak of troublemaking ex-servicemen, trade unionists, and intellectuals who were regarded as responsible for unrest, strikes, and political turbulence.[21] To the colonial gaze these upstarts had little pretense of education and even less gainful employment except as second-rate journalists, nonpracticing lawyers, and the occasional medical doctor. Adept at organizing movements that called themselves parties, or parties that called themselves movements, they were forcing the officials to march to a quicker tune by engaging in misguided efforts to politicize a public ill equipped to participate in politics. But they were unreliable even to each other, the young trying to displace the old and the old to manipulate the young-pied pipers who had to be put on a proper road before they led their followers astray.

Given a choice, even the most enlightened colonial administrator would have argued for a longer maturation period to nurture and better prepare people for independence. Indeed in some cases in British Africa, those on the ground saw the haste with which independence came as a kind of plot hatched by Colonial Office and Colonial Ministry officials to hand over power before people were prepared to receive it, knowing the results would be a shambles. Among the debates of the day was whether a territory could be prepared for independence and self-government by means other than actually becoming independent and governing oneself.[22] The matter too often was resolved mainly by considerations of cost and political expediency.

In the end all sides recognized that economically as well as politically it was financially impossible to maintain the colonial connection in the face of mass nationalism. (How many equivalents of the Algerian conflict could the French afford, and how many equivalents of the Malaysian and Kenya's Mau Mau rebellions could the British be responsible for quelling?) If colonial good intentions were in large part a consequence of the momentum of nationalism, so the response varied less in terms of how prepared or ready a territory was for self-government than how divided or unified was the nationalist movement (and whether these were resident white settlers). From the perspective of post–World War II colonials, there were only two basic alternatives: (1) to incorporate African elites into newly improvised institutions, administrative and political, and when push came to shove hand power over to them, or (2) if such elites were thrust aside by ruder and semiradicalized politicians (backed up with some kind of nationalist party or movement), to try to channel these movements into party and parliamentary institutions which would "civilize" them in the ways of governing according to metropolitan models. By means of councils, legislative bodies, parliaments, and interest group and party politics, colonial authorities hoped there would be created self-reinforcing networks that might become self-validating in principle and reinforcing in practice. Their vitality would depend on crosscutting ethnic, class, religious, and other interests, both within and between newly formed political parties.

Whatever their particular points of view about decolonization, the major premise (articulated or silent) was largely a face-saving embellishment of a process which could be neither reversed nor resisted. Since replacing a no longer workable colonial authoritarianism with a more workable political alternative was now a project of considerable urgency, late colonialism became politically tutelary where in its earlier incarnations it had been frankly hegemonic. One might also say that while colonial officials were not unconcerned with preventing local dictatorships, they were more anxious to prevent what they feared most—the radicalization of nationalist movements and mobilizing parties, especially those with Jacobin tendencies and revolutionary ambitions, led by radical intellectuals of the sort that had been associated with the founding and evolution of the Pan-African movement.

Hence the strategy: if power could not be handed over to the elites, then it would be necessary to respect rival claims, ethnic or religious, within institutions purporting to represent people according to more traditional claims to power, thus challenging the right of nationalist leaders to speak for all. Among the political issues behind the complex political maneuvers and constitutional engineering that these issues engendered was the question, What constitutional safeguards would best protect local and regional autonomy from too much power at the center and dilute centralizing forces by the protection and promotion of ethnic, religious, and linguistic interests?

Indeed, most nationalists opposed "tribalism" in the name of unity and democracy while colonial authorities supported ethnic claims, also in the name of unity and democracy. In Nigeria, for example, power sharing between the predominant Northern Emirates of the Northern Region, the Yoruba in the Western, and the Ibo in the Eastern not only left an inheritance of conflict between the three but also opened the way for ethnic parochialism within each region and disputes over minorities problems.[23] So great was the variety of groups competing for power and so intense the conflicts both between and within political parties that there was little effective power at the center. Not surprisingly, opposition was increasingly ethnic.

Whatever else they were, colonial officials were not apologetic about their record. They believed that on close inspection they would come off, if not as well their most ardent protagonists claimed, at least better than their enemies allowed. After all, there was a record of accomplishment without huge resources or large corps of expatriates. Whether the method of rule was direct, as in the French case, or largely indirect, as in the British, on the ground one often could not tell them apart; and despite the depression and war that preceded late colonialism, there had been considerable developmental accomplishment. Even in most rural areas there was provision for local services, courts combined traditional customs with Western legal codes, schools combined teaching in local languages with English or French, local government facilities incorporated chieftaincy and traditional authority in some degree (not to speak of the provision of at least rudimentary medical services), and agricultural policies involved famine protection, conservation, increasing the fertility of the soil while preventing erosion, etc., all concerns of a sort which would today be called environmental. Accompanying these large concerns were, on the ground, an enlarging of practical down-to-earth reforms—well digging in the villages, piped water stands, latrines, the provision of midwives, etc.

As for balancing local customs and native laws with those of a more universalized and "enlightened" kind, this included a variety of accommodations, from so-called animism to the Muslim *sharia*. Hence to a young and largely postwar generation of colonial officers—themselves a very different kettle of fish from their prewar predecessors (more enlightened, flexible, etc.)—the idea of independence was, if not desirable, certainly not unthinkable, as it had been a generation earlier. Moreover, if colonialism polarized, distanced, and emphasized the differences between races and cultures—the one representing enlightenment, the other a negative pole to be transcended, there was also a certain pull between these poles and a curious kind of intimacy. District officers and commandants du cercle knew local languages and were on tour in their districts a good part of the time, and not a few of them did "ethnographic" studies on various aspects of "tribal customs," land tenure, chieftaincy, etc. In this sense, difference was diluted by direct contact and intellectual curiosity, so much so that one could call late colonialism a period of intimate differences.

Otherness or difference, for all the mutual misunderstandings which resulted, also enabled officials to avoid taking sides or being drawn into highly complicated internal conflicts and factionalism of the sort in which their African successors quickly became embroiled. Standing both outside as well as inside their local fiefdoms, colonial officials on the whole were not easily manipulated, bribed, or corrupted.

In their franker and more private moments, a good many colonial officers basically agreed with their critics that the process of devolution was a bamboozling game in which the odds were determined by how quickly and effectively the authorities could establish institutional networks with the sticking power to entrap politicians and their clienteles in the web of their own self-interests. The point was to transform political struggles from the plane of confrontation over principles into negotiable interests, rendering ethnic, religious, and class conflict into political party competition, and in the process reducing the rhetoric and the pious posturing of politicians into some reasonable facsimile of recognized parliamentary debate. The gamble was that devolution through such networks would provide sufficiently attractive distributive payoffs that even radical and transforming political ambitions would be rendered nugatory.[24]

For all its manipulative trials and errors, late colonialism was not quite able to control the process, but it was less for lack of trying than because it was "too little and too late" (and with too few resources). Efforts to secure power for replacing elites were not unsuccessful; elites were not swept away by mass mobilizing movement/parties. On the whole the last-ditch efforts to establish European-style institutions of higher education (for the most part more designed to create cadres of civil servants than agronomists) were also successful, forming the nucleus for more diverse types of instructional programs and universities after independence. Less successful were the attempts to direct the transition to independence by means of electoral geometries, phased enlargement of the franchise, and grudging extension of conciliar government from local to national levels. On balance, mass political parties were the beneficiaries of such constitutional engineering, since each election, each expansion of territorial legislative and executive power provided new grounds for recruitment, mobilization, and indoctrination in party ideologies. Far from isolating radical troublemakers, all these different venues helped to breed more by providing more opportunities for their followers.

These results left a legacy of institutional indigestion, insufficiently trained cadres, poorly entrenched but with great power, and a host of developmental problems that quickly overwhelmed nationalist political successors. On all sides, colonial and nationalist, the concern was more for the form than the substance of democracy. In the sense that no one knew whether the institutional graft would actually take root, democracy was a venue for transition rather than a genuine concern. There were of course other views of the decolonization process. For a distinguished scholar like Margery Perham, the process of devolution was not a Colonial Office plot but the following through and institutional recapitulation of what happened en route to democracy in Britain itself.[25] The tutelary tradition was thus a natural historical and evolutionary process, although in this case within a compressed time frame. For people like Perham, decolonization basically involved the transformation of legislative and executive councils (largely ex officio and officials) to nonofficials and elected officials, turning them into parliaments and establishing cabinet responsibility and accountability, side by side with the growth of a modern political party system and the extension of the franchise to the lower orders by means of successive reform acts.

There were similar views among the French, although historical parallels were a bit less comfortable given the French record of domestic political instability, the rapid rise and fall of governments, not to speak of the frequency of revolutions. Indeed, so unprepossessing was politics in the third and fourth republics as a model that the colonial officials preferred to emphasize the universality of French culture—a politics of culture preceding a politics of devolution within a tradition of assimilative centralization. To the end, French administrators in overseas territories remained hardly enamored of metropolitan democracy in France, let alone in the colonies. Few could be called democrats, although there were a few remarkable leftist French colonial officials and socialist governors. Whether left or right, they still tended to see colonialism as a more rationalized and enlightened form of rule than any party politics. If devolution meant grafting to the original militarized administrative structure a hierarchy of local, regional, and eventually metropolitan councils, their hope was that it would not weaken centralized power as much as broaden its base.[26]

On the other hand, when the base was indeed broadened by means of crosscutting mass parties, it was possible to speed up the process because of that same centralized method of control. Pressures from the left in the National Assembly favored political reforms leading to the passage of constitutionally critical Lois Cadres that resulted in major changes throughout French Africa and at one stroke, in contrast to the piecemeal, territory-by-territory pattern in British Africa. The Loi Cadre of 1956, for example, provided for a political great leap forward in the system of territorial councils and elections simultaneously in the eight territories of French West Africa and all four in French Equatorial Africa, opening the way simultaneously for greater territorial and interterritorial party participation up and down the line, from each territory, then to Dakar or Brazzaville, then to participation in the French parliament and cabinet.[27]

For the French left the political process facilitated a closer association between radical African intellectuals and elites and politicians rather than separating them, as tended to be the case in British Africa. The more radical political parties, cross territorial in character and affiliated with French metropolitan political parties, organized around such political figures as Senghor who followed in the socialist tradition of Lamine-Gueye, while Houphouët-Boigny's Rassemblement Démocratique Africain was associated with the Communists in the immediate postwar years.

Engaging Americans

For the first post–World War II generation of American political scientists working in Africa three perspectives came together. One was a recognition of the significance of race and the impact that African independence would have on the American black experience. The second was a view of what was going on Africa as part of a larger transformation from a world of empires to a world of nations. The third, which belonged to the "behavioral revolution" in political theory, considered the actual processes of such transition so complex that modes of thought and analysis characteristic of conventional political science would be inadequate. One had to study society as well as the state and culture as well as institutions. Hence the American study of African politics was interdisciplinary from the start.

To most American political scientists interested in Africa, then, the sudden rush to establish democratic institutions represented a remarkable opportunity for studying whether or not democracy could be exported and made to work. Their main point of entry was African nationalist movements rather than administrative devolution. Their studies included leadership, the social composition of new African states, African unity, one-party states, and parties and elections more generally. They were also concerned with how to make developmental projections and ascertain economic trends.[28] Influenced by functional anthropology, they were interested in seeing how more "traditional" African institutions accommodated to mass nationalism, the growth of a popular press, and the organization of movement-parties, what happened to the authority systems and participation, and how the transfer of political institutions from metropole to periphery proceeded.

Such perspectives were quite different from British scholarly work, which emphasized parliamentary institutions, the fashioning of civil service establishments out of colonial services, and how best to extend the Commonwealth formula from the original white dominions to all members of the former empire. They differed, too, from those of the French scholars among whom a more legal and constitutional method prevailed within a rather hastily improvised and unsuccessful French Union fashioning its own institutions and assembly.[29]

Americans were also interested in political development as a common phenomenon found elsewhere—India, Indonesia, Latin America—so that one might say their interests were both broadly comparative and developmental, on the one hand, and field oriented on the other. Taking as their modus operandi field study techniques pioneered by anthropologists, they also examined the "interiority" of African politics, bringing into immediate focus such broad themes as nationalism, sociopolitical movements, cultural separatism and integration, political stability and instability, and the structural tendencies of newly independent states. Most had methodological and empirical interests quite different from their European colleagues. Methodologically and theoretically oriented, their scholarship put a greater stress on how to reconceptualize "system change," a concern which derived from the larger pedigrees of historical sociologists like Emile Durkheim and Max Weber, functionalists like Bronislaw Malinowski and A. R. Radcliffe Brown, and the structural-functionalism of Talcott Parsons.

American Africanists who began their work at the point where behaviorialism had already begun to attack the conventional study of politics were able to apply to empirical questions matters appropriate to the psychology of politics, with its emphasis on socialization processes, political learning, the internalization of norms, relations between mass and leadership, the role of the media, etc. Their emphasis was less on formal institutions of political power than on the connections between state and society. Some were also concerned with variable analysis in operational and quantitative terms. Most used cases for comparisons deriving general hypotheses about political change by the deployment of interdisciplinary theories, approaches, and procedures. They were on the whole less interested in the political realities of transition in descriptive terms than the theoretical problems such realities posed. Hence transition was defined less in terms of a demarcation

the imposition on those systems of colonialism, say English or French. The different colonial systems could thus also be compared synchronically. Putting together synchronic and diachronic analysis allowed the study of (a) the differential variation of different traditional systems and (b) the differential patterns of innovation imposed by different colonial systems. One then might be in a position to identify what mutual accommodations would be necessary in these different combinations in order to induce more newly minted alternative postcolonial solutions, liberal or radical, etc. Depending on the precise character of the transposed sets, some traditional systems would be more resistant to change, and some would adapt more easily and at different component points—normative, behavioral, or structural adaptation or resistance. One central problem might be how to analyze the way new authority patterns evolve out of a combination of traditional and modern norms and whether or not political solutions are forthcoming that resolve political conflicts.[41]

Within these abstract formulations it is possible to organize highly complex masses of data around a host of subsidiary variables. Hence it is possible to use case methods for both time and sequence studies in terms of system change and comparisons between cases to see variations in relationship, with a view to making theoretical generalizations. One can more or less arbitrarily make any one dimension the independent variable and make the others intervening or dependent (although in general the tendency is to give precedence to the normative factor insofar as norms are related to legitimacy and legitimacy to power).[42] As a general model of modernization, structural-functional analysis assigns a mediating and/or controlling role to the state, which has special responsibilities for maintaining stability.

There is a clarity to this framework and, if it is used with a certain austerity, a theoretical power lacking in some of the work of those who attacked it. Certainly it favors a liberal orientation and stability as a moving equilibrium. Although pluralistic, it rejects marketplace models based purely on rationalities of self-interest. It deals with networks of class and role and as much in terms of conflict and competition as cooperation and integration. Indeed, with a little imagination the same framework can be made to analyze revolutionary movements seeking to transform state and society according to more radical change. In short, there is no reason why an equilibrium focus cannot be used for the analysis of disjunctive change as well as stability and democracy.[43]

But there are also some fundamental flaws in the modernization paradigm, flaws which on the ground would come to haunt it and open the way for attacks, root and branch, by dependency theorists, Marxists, neo-Marxists, and others. Functionalism and modernization theory share an emphasis on system and crisis, i.e., systems crisis. Resolving crises means to establish systems capable of mediating conflict and generating stability, social integration, and political development. In practice, this model works best for examining the successful transition to self-government and independence. But it tends to be too generalized to deal with the practical problems that African nationalism has had to confront.

For one thing, it has within it certain unilinear assumptions of developmental progress, in which economic growth would result in new forms of social differentiation, greater complexity, and a politics of pluralism, mediation, and coordination. It assumed that developmental aid from metropole to periphery would be benign and would not introduce contradictions of class, of urban-rural imbalances, and it virtually ignored the possibility of corruption. In fact, it could not cope substantively with the difficulties that Africans met when they tried to form viable states.

Useful for examining the changing authority relationships between Europe and Africa, functional theories of modernization were no more successful than nationalist ideologies as normative systems. Even where colonialism left in place stabilizing institutions that in principle should have worked, these after independence quickly became vulnerable to unforeseen political conditions. And as institutions began eroding, so, too, theories were polarized between radical and liberal solutions.

The Personalization of Power and Authority

A continuous succession of crises in virtually all African states followed independence. As nationalism withered as a force capable of shaping postindependence politics and territorial consciousness, intensified parochialism, ethnicity, and the conditions leading to civil war increased. The institutional void often was filled by authoritarian solutions, bureaucratic and military, or more radical mobilization.

Performing at low levels of efficacy, leaders quickly sought to concentrate power by controlling whatever levers of power might be available, a situation leading more or less inexorably to the evolution of personalized and authoritarian regimes.

In the absence of viable political institutions, most African states came to be ruled by authoritarian civilian or military leaders.[44] Indeed, about half of the political rulers of African states in the 1980s were soldiers. In those

Changing African Perspectives

African states which came to independence complete with formal constitutions, most were quickly breached. For the most part, and despite some notable exceptions such as Julius Nyerere, African politicians, and their cadres of close and trusted associates established their links to centralized elites and urbanized populations. Those in the rural sectors were increasingly residualized. To realize political stability and development would have required exceptional commitment, skill, and ability to govern fractious parties and deal with difficult oppositions. Virtually everywhere a politics of personal rule replaced institutional politics, so much so that we can say that personal rule in Africa had the effect of reversing Montesquieu's dictum that "in the birth of societies it is the leaders of the state who create the institutions; afterward it is the institutions that shape the leaders."

In case after case power was concentrated in individual political leaders who both symbolically and instrumentally became responsible for law and order and, in the face of various ethnic, religious, and other forms of revivalism, came to represent the state itself. If personal rule is the hallmark of postindependent Africa, few rulers have conceded much to institutionalized forms of power. However, this has not stopped them from building up enormous patronage networks, not to speak of huge bureaucracies whose cost has been among the highest in the Third World.[45] The sheer weight of such clienteles, and party and particularly state bureaucracies (state and parastatal), results in a huge tax on the rural sectors, not to speak of petty tyranny and massive corruption. As a consequence ethnic interests and conflicts have become exacerbated, with factional alliances operating more and more like Mafia activities. Personalism, plus clientelism, plus bureaucratism, intensifies a politics of political survival rather than the advancement of civil and socioeconomic goals.

To maintain power in an environment of conflicting factions and plotting, personal rulers require support. They rely heavily on the loyalty of key military, state, and ethnic leaders whose loyalties are always in doubt and whose appetites are infinite. In such circumstances there is little trust. Coercion is endemic. Secrecy thrives. Political opposition goes underground. Not surprisingly many rulers have made special military arrangements to enhance their security, sometimes going abroad for mercenaries. Moroccan soldiers served as presidential guards in Equatorial Guinea. They also replaced Cubans who had served for years in faction-ridden Congo. French forces are stationed in several francophone states—Senegal, Côte d'Ivoire, Cameroon, Gabon, the Central African Republic, Chad, and Djibouti.[46] Despite these and other measures, only a dozen or so African presidents have had a sufficient concentration of power and authority to ensure lengthy tenure and stability for their regimes.[47]

Nor does personal rule inspire a commitment to the national political community (the rare exception perhaps being Tanzania). There is no way to produce a genuine consensus on goals and practices of government. This condition often provides the opening for ethnic revivalism. Indeed, ethnicity has remained a latent and powerful political resource for opposition parties forced to go underground. In a number of countries with autocratic regimes, ethnicity has bolstered power where the regime has elevated the interests of one ethnic group over others. Mauritania has maintained its dominance of Arab-Berber Moors over black Africans. In the past in Burundi a small ruling Tutsi minority has conducted pogroms against the Hutu. The control by the Djerma-Songhai minority over the Hausa majority in Niger is similar.[48]

There are, of course, different kinds of personal rulers. Those which have brought the greatest deterioration to the quality of life include Idi Amin in Uganda, Francisco Macias in Equatorial Guinea, and Jean-Bédel Bokassa in the Central African Empire in the 1970s. Essentially amoral regimes, based on the exercise of pure power, coercion, and violence, all three regimes were overthrown in 1979.[49] Similarly, Mobutu's Zaire, despite its remarkable economic potential, has steadily declined throughout the past decade. Mobutu remains an autocrat who has held on to power despite widespread protest, rioting, and opposition as well as international criticism. So, too, in many other countries, Siaka Stevens's Sierra Leone, Paul Biyas's Cameroon, Moussa Traore's Mali, Mathieu Kerebou's Benin, Denis Sassou-Nguesso's Congo, Samuel Doe's Liberia, Gnassingbé Eyadema's Togo, Siyad Barre's Somalia, and Kenneth Kaunda's Zambia. So much have mismanagement and corruption compromised African political systems that it is estimated that $40 billion in African private assets are held in industrial states.[50]

Does it make a difference whether a state favors socialism? Virtually all experiments in African socialism have ended in failure.[51] There are many reasons, including lack of organizational and managerial skills, know-how, and resources. Even the most committed socialist cadres quickly lose their convictions, and in many instances it is difficult to distinguish socialism from state capitalism. For the most part advancing socialism has led to declining economic conditions. For example, the founding president of Mali, Modibo Keita, set out in 1960 to transform his country's economy radically by nationalizing trade and harnessing peasant agriculture. The

result was economic disaster. Even the successful cotton-growing cooperatives established under the French were destroyed. He was overthrown in
1968 by a military leader who ruled until his own downfall in 1991. Kwame
Nkrumah, who shortly after independence in 1957 launched an ambitious
program of industrialization, established state farms and state enterprises
and drained the rural sectors of capital. The economy stagnated while
Nkrumah tried to transform Ghana into a base for African independence.
Not surprisingly, he alienated members of his own party, drove the opposition underground, and made the country dependent on external sources of
food, a situation only very recently reversed under Flight Lieutenant Jerry
Rawlings.[52]

In Guinea, also a country with considerable resources, Sékou Touré, one
of the most militant radical independence leaders, who had the courage to
refuse de Gaulle's offer to remain within a French confederation, went
from populist radical to despotic dictator. When he died in 1984, the legacy
he left was twenty-six years of economic stagnation, a third of the population including most of the educated elites in exile, and some of his most
outstanding associates like Diallo Telli, the former head of the Organization
of African Unity, dead in prison of the "black diet" (starvation).

One could of course go on. Even Tanzania's Julius Nyerere in his determination to replace rural poverty with agrarian socialism, which commanded broad support from overseas donors, failed to win Tanzanian peasants over to his vision of Ujamaa, a rural communal society. He favored a
one-party state with elections, and there were marked increases in literacy
and life expectancy. Nevertheless, the economy declined seriously in the
latter part of the 1970s, and living standards for Tanzanians continued to
drop in the 1980s.[53]

As for those countries with greater economic success, like Kenya and
Côte d'Ivoire, substantial advancement in socioeconomic development has
occurred at the expense of democratic institutions. Both have seen growth
in agricultural and industrial capability. They have invested heavily in education, health, and physical infrastructure and maintained a reasonable
degree of political stability. Kenya in particular was able to build upon a relatively well developed colonial state. The Kenyatta government expanded
the economic infrastructure and supported competitive elections for legislative representatives. However, the economic and political accomplishments of the Kenyatta era (1963–78) have been undermined and compromised by the more autocratic and less politically secure regime of President

Daniel arap Moi. Michael Chege's analysis in this volume compares and analyzes the policies and actions of Kenya's different regimes with those of Nyerere and Ali Hassan Mwinyi in Tanzania.

In Côte d'Ivoire, Félix Houphouët-Boigny, the autocratic president for over three decades, gave economic growth the highest priority. Agricultural production was diversified. Drawing heavily on French expertise and organized around a highly centralized bureaucracy, Côte d'Ivoire experienced one of the highest rates of growth during the first two decades of independence, while in the last it has faced severe problems resulting from falling international commodity prices and the burden of heavy capital debts. At the same time, challenges to Houphouët-Boigny's rule became sufficiently strong so that competitive elections were permitted in 1980, leading, a decade later, to a rather reluctantly accepted multiparty competition in general elections. In the fall of 1990 he easily retained the presidency, his party keeping control over the National Assembly.

In general one might say that near the end of the 1980s the tendencies toward liberal solutions accelerated. Characterized by greater openness and market-driven growth, liberalization of trade, and multiparty elections, the tentative return to democracy is anxiously being watched by many observers.[54]

Radical Critiques and Critical Theories

The emphasis of the original late colonialist regimes was on institutional change, whether cast in the form of building new democracies or democracy as a form of political entrapment, or both. If the postwar American emphasis was on theories of nationalism and state formation and on modernization, deteriorating conditions in the postindependence period stimulated sweeping critiques of both in the form of more radical types of system theories, particularly Marxist and neo-Marxist. These were aimed at showing what went wrong systemically, i.e., as a consequence of advanced capitalism locked into metropole-periphery relations. So regarded, events in Africa were determined not by internal decisions made by African leaders but by external forces imposing political systems foreign to African experience and economic systems favorable to imperialism. In this sense both the economic decline of the state and personal rulership are to be explained more as inevitable consequences of neocolonialism and imperialism and less by defects in leadership and political actions by Africans themselves. Insofar as Africans were guilty, it was the compradors of capitalism who were to blame, and those who insinuated into African social life divisions of class and social hierarchy that did not exist in earlier times. Importing class struggle into Africa, such compradors and their associates perpetuated not only external exploitation but internal corruption, "big man" politics, and the victimization of both leaders and led. The radical critique, especially by later generations of scholars, would emphasize not the need for socialization into democratic niceties but the hegemonic consequences of trying to do so. Required was not the socialization into civility so dear to democratic theorists like Edward Shils but a more fundamental transformational rupture with the entire colonial past (with its determining tutelary-pupillary characteristics) in favor of some version of a Marxist / Fanonist disjunctive break, orchestrated by means of a mobilizing and ideologically oriented political movement.[55] Those elites who had emerged from the colonial experience, even if they did not share the colonial viewpoint, tended to speak for, rather than represent, African perspectives and African points of view.

Some scholars like Thomas Hodgkin argued that only Africans were properly qualified to speak on such matters. Others, like Gervase Mathew and Basil Davidson, tried to rewrite conventional African history in order to emphasize African perspectives.[56] One danger in such efforts was a certain romanticization of both an African past and the prospects of a revolutionary future. Another was the danger of reifying the categories for analyzing both the colonial experience and its impacts in terms of an African bourgeoisie or a peasantry, making them into undifferentiated class categories with the force of their European historical counterparts while ignoring the interactions of their component parts, the diluting effects of kinship, clanship, extended family, not to speak of affiliations in both urban and rural settings more or less simultaneously. Indeed, such politically charged categories became hegemonic in their own way by ignoring the complexity and density of African social life. They projected radical outcomes that did not and could not occur. Moreover, ignoring concrete variations in practice because of a too analytically compressed dialectic regard for a totalizing impact of the colonial legacy on a generalized negative "other," the analytical arguments for the necessity of revolutionary outcomes remained interesting mainly to radical elites, the latter forming into "discourse communities" talking largely to each other. One could convince oneself that only a profoundly disjunctive rupture could negate the effects of neocolonialism and imperialism and develop elaborate theories to prove it.[57]

Seen in this light, an emphasis on democratic politics characteristic of

European and British institutionalism and American modernization theory appeared not only obsolete but positively sinister. Moreover, since functional analysis was considered integration rather than conflict oriented, it was regarded as a form of mystification disguising the concrete struggles going on. Those favoring a more radical version of dependency theory found that even African socialist countries were wanting. Reviewers like Bob Fitch and Mary Oppenheimer found that in Nkrumah's Ghana much that passed for socialism was only a principled name for a state capitalist practice.[58] Indeed, some of the most interesting analysis by Charles Bettelheim and other Marxist advisers to African governments dealt with differences between state capitalism and socialism—differences which otherwise might evade the eye of the beholder.

What began as a critical view was quickly transformed into the larger perspective of dependency theory itself. Such theory was always a composite representing a confluence of ideas emerging from the work of the dependency theorists specializing in development in Latin America, the post-1968 radicalization of student movements, and more explicit neo-Marxist analytical approaches.[59] In turn, when used in fieldwork the results not only drastically altered many of the assumptions on which the modernization paradigm was based but opened up a range of entirely different questions about social formations, perhaps the most outstanding example being Colin Leys's discussion of the contradictions of neocolonialism.[60]

The analytical shift toward Marxist and dependency theory drastically reinterpreted the colonial legacy. However, it suffered from the same overkill tendencies of the theories it displaced, scooping up and dumping in the same categories international or world-system economic tendencies, metropole-periphery relations, and, as in the work of Walter Rodney and John Saul, the theme of underdevelopment by external design.[61]

Among its defects was a too simple conception of class. African cultivators became "peasants," implying a kind of peasant radicalism associated with the Chinese revolution or more radical Latin American guerrilla movements. There is substantial disagreement among scholars about differences between African cultivators as "economic men," entrepreneurial and market oriented, and as Africans peasants locked into some kind of pseudofeudatory relationship. Similarly with urbanization, where class becomes more easily distinguishable. The enemy, aside from neo-imperialists of one sort or another, is in particular an African bourgeoisie, whether compradors or participants in commercial enterprise or for that matter as civil servants. There is no doubt that class is an important category for analysis but one which in many African contexts is diluted by competing affiliations, ethnic, kinship, etc. For example, in Ghana or Nigeria, on closer inspection, a proper "bourgeois" family might include civil servants, teachers, business persons, a taxi driver, farmers, i.e., virtually a mirror image of the entire range of the occupational and role structure of the society within one extended kinship unit. Difficulties arise if one wants to connect "bourgeois" class relations with property ownership. The owners of, say, a boat on the Niger might effectively be several hundred kin members even though legally it is the property of one or two persons. Hence the implication that class leads to power relations based on class interests may be correct for some purposes but not for others, depending on situation and circumstances.[62]

Faulty imposition of Western categories of class failed to produce the appropriate dynamics. Yet there was plenty of polarization that occurred through rural and agricultural decline, the growth of urban marginality, etc. Similarly, there were simplistic associations about African wealth and exploitable surpluses. Foreign enterprise in particular was charged with siphoning off great wealth (one model being perhaps the Union Minière du Haut Katanga), leading to disastrous schemes of nationalization that in the name of socialism produced vast opportunities for private plunder and corruption.

Moreover, such views easily lent themselves to conspiracy theories. The major American philanthropic foundations, the United States government, the American academic establishment, the CIA, the Council on Foreign Relations, and the Brookings Institution came under particular scrutiny. Lumped together, they revealed the hegemonic intents of American scholarship and the subversive intents of programs of aid and assistance. Not surprisingly, a body like the African Studies Association came to be regarded not as a center of scholarly work on Africa but as an instrument of domination by the United States. Representative of influential scholars and major research universities with African studies programs funded by the foundations, the association was considered to be the nuclear center of an extended imperial family. Purporting to set standards of objectivity and appropriate styles of empirical research, it was above all dominated by white males. Hence, African studies was now regarded as a screen for the perpetuation of racist and American hegemonic controls over African studies and, where possible, over African politics.[63]

Although attacks of this kind depended a good deal on guilt by association among what was after all a not very large group of people or cluster of institutions, the more serious issue was not only politics but the larger question of objectivity in political research. It raised the question of how neutral analytical categories could be. Depending on what categories one deployed, it was possible to show "objectively" how necessary were links between developed metropoles and underdeveloped peripheries, or precisely the opposite, how these links were a cause of the problem of underdevelopment.

One can see how objectivity received different definitions in the context of a political polarization between left versus right theories of political economy. Among the significant members of the former were such figures as Charles Bettelheim, Samir Amin, Claude Meillassoux, Claude Ake, Colin Leys, Timothy Shaw, Irving Markovitz, Immanuel Wallerstein, John Saul, Reginald H. Green, and Ann Seidman, whose work was reinforced by similar theoretical work going on elsewhere, particularly in Latin America.[64] Among the latter were such reliable figures as Sir W. Arthur Lewis, Douglas Rimmer, Elliot J. Berg, Andrew Kamarck, L. H. Samuels, P. T. Bauer, and Robert Bates.[65]

On the whole these emphases in political economy have had an enormous impact on the shape of African studies, squeezing out earlier structural and functional concerns and promoting either a reductionist class and power analysis or a market and trade approach. What was dependency from one point of view became interdependency from the other. Not surprisingly, with the failure of various experiments in socialist alternatives (the political and economic disaster of Guinea under Sékou Touré, the failure of even modest and down-to-earth experiments like Ujamaa in Tanzania, not to speak of Angola and Mozambique), the political economy of the right prospered, and not a few who began on the left eventually moved to the right.[66]

With respect to the state, radical theorists varied widely from the more Marxist assumption of the state as a ruling class derivation, with the ruling class perhaps outside the country but acting through its compradors, to elaborate theses of state power deriving from the influence of Louis Althusser and Nicos Poulantzas.[67] A very large body of neo-Marxist literature was employed in analyses of African class, worker formations, and, following post-Mao interpretations of peasant society, the role of African peasants in the productive process.

As with modernization theory before it, these emphases have all but disappeared as part of the more general trend. As the deplorable state of agriculture and industry, not to speak of civil society itself, in the former

Soviet Union and Eastern European countries has become visible, and countries like China struggle with a socialist inheritance, the old solutions seem useless. Nor has experience in Africa proved otherwise, Ethiopia, Angola, and Mozambique being the last to make the transition from socialism. (Not that resolution of problems of decline under capitalism are likely to be resolved soon.)[68]

If radical tendencies have been reversed by current realities, the radical thrust has now taken a very different tack. Neo-Marxist formalism, ideas of dependency, and the emphasis on Africans as victims of imperialism, colonialism, and postcolonial practices have shifted attention from the political economy to moral and intellectual matters. Retrieving the tradition of critical theory (which has its roots in the Frankfurt School and neo-Marxist literary criticism and also in postmodernism and deconstruction), many of those following a radical line of critical inquiry have attached themselves to a larger corpus that includes women's studies, diaspora studies, and the analysis of suppression and oppression more generally. This raises two kinds of questions: first, the nature of the discourse on Africa and, second and in a new form, the question of objectivism. Not only are there concerns about appropriate categories but also about the texts, the writing, the representation of Africans, their portrayal as a result of fieldwork. Challenging the ethnographic position in favor of a phenomenological one, some scholars are concerned with the "interpretation of the interpretation" or "discourse on the discourse," treating the actual productions of African scholarship, i.e., its writings, as the focus of analysis. Writing then is both a key to discourse and the hegemony of that discourse. It also shifts the emphasis from what happens on the ground to thought and analysis itself. But what happens on the ground poses questions of a magnitude and significance that no current developmental theories can cope with. Before going on to discuss this newer radical perspective, it will be useful to review what has indeed been happening.

The Breakdown of Authority—Some Cases

Modernization theory coincided with the creation of new African states. Radical dependency theories coincided with the emergence of personalized rulership and one-party states. Neither has been able to confront or deal comprehensively with the consequences of political fragmentation, and none are adequate to explain the complete breakdown of authority that has occurred in major African countries and the bitter internal conflict and civil

a breakdown has induced. In some instances the conflicts have
been a great persistence, as in Sudan, while in others they exploded in bitter
ethnic conflict, only to recede, so much so that in the ensuing civil society
the war appears to have left few festering political sores. Despite its ethnic
ferocity and large number of casualties, not to speak of long-standing ethnic
tensions between Ibo and Hausa Fulani, it is quite remarkable how amica-
ble is the political solution that has been achieved in the wake of the Biafran
War of 1967–70 in Nigeria.[69]

While there are several ways to describe such breakdowns of authority,
most of the major civil wars of the last decade exhibited two tendencies,
ideological and ethnic. That there is a great overlap between the two goes
without saying, so that what may appear to be ethnic conflict may be not
only ideological but the result of class distinctions or other forms of discrimination. Ethnicity elevated to the level of principles rather than interests in a political context becomes nationalism. On the other hand, such
conflicts over political ideology in Angola between the Popular Liberation
Movement of Angola (MPLA) versus the National Union for the Independence of Angola (UNITA) happen also to coincide with bitter conflicts over
power between competing ethnic groups, not to speak of rivalry between
their two dominant political leaders, José Eduardo dos Santos and Jonas
Savimbi. As in more than a few instances, the conflicts became internationalized because of larger East-West tensions, with Cuba and the Soviet
Union supporting Santos's MPLA and the United States and South Africa
supporting UNITA.

We can say, albeit with considerable caution, that in Sudan, Somalia, and
Chad ethnic civil wars predominate, with differences including religion,
race, ethnicity, and language. Predominantly ideological (cum ethnic) conflicts have occurred in Angola, Mozambique, and Ethiopia. The Ugandan
conflicts are long-standing, some going as far back as precolonial times. In
1978–79 they involved the armed incursion of Tanzanian forces.

Other civil wars have also become supraterritorial in part. Within Africa,
Libya became directly involved in Chad. Tutsi soldiers from the Ugandan
army invaded Hutu-ruled Rwanda in an effort to restore Tutsi rights. In
Liberia the Americo-Liberian oligarchy, descendants of freed slaves who
created the Liberian state in the early 1800s and ruled for more than century
and a half, was overthrown in April 1980 by privates and noncommissioned
officers led by Master Sergeant Samuel Doe. The president, William Tolbert, a reformer who believed in the incorporation of indigenous Africans
into the modern order, was assassinated along with several leading mem-

bers of his regime. As President Doe's rule became more ruthless, corrupt, and oppressive, he relied on his ethnic kinsmen for support. In December 1989 civil war broke out and became both internationalized and regionalized, with Libya, Burkina Faso, and Côte d'Ivoire assisting the rebel forces of Charles Taylor's National Patriotic Front of Liberia (NPFL). As the civil war intensified, the Economic Community of West African States (ECOWAS) intervened with a West African peacekeeping force. Since August 1990 the Economic Community Monitoring Group (ECOMOG), composed of several thousand troops, has kept Taylor's NPFL at bay while supporting the interim government of Amos Sawyer in Monrovia. However, it has not been able to challenge Taylor's control of the rest of the country or disarm his forces, frustrating the aim of ECOWAS, which is to hold multiparty elections.[70]

African mediating interventions sometimes have occurred to prevent African civil wars from becoming surrogate occasions for East-West conflicts, as happened in Ethiopia, which shifted from an American to a Soviet surrogate, or Angola, which became a Cuban surrogate. External influences, which by feeding the contestants and providing weapons and logistical support perpetuate conflict, have been responsible for massive destruction and death. Angola's MPLA government was dependent on Soviet and Cuban military support even before independence. Its territorial authority was challenged by the guerrilla forces of UNITA dominating the southern third of the country. At first UNITA received support from the South African Defense Force, and then after 1985 the United States gave it military aid. In the thirteen years of conflict, the entire economic infrastructure was seriously damaged and the toll in human casualties and lives immense.[71]

In Mozambique, which only gained its independence in 1975 after a long and bitter guerilla war against the Portuguese, Frelimo (the Mozambique Liberation Front) had no competitors in the early days of rule, unlike Angola. Like the MPLA, however, it was deeply committed to developing a socialist state and society, a goal which turned out to be more easily stated than accomplished. President Samora Machel's attempts to socialize agricultural production failed. The country lacked educated managers, skilled technicians, and necessary resources. Instead, an anti-Frelimo terrorist movement, Renamo, supported by South Africa, became a major force and by the end of the 1980s was responsible for the deaths of hundreds of thousands of peasants and the destruction of untold numbe
while over a million people became refugees and untold othe
vation. As Soviet support waned, and after the death of 1

airplane crash, the crippled Frelimo government, now led by Joaquim Chissano, in December 1990 accepted the principles of competitive multiparty national elections, a free press, and an independent judiciary.[72]

In Ethiopia a coup against Emperor Haile Selassie in 1974 established a leftist military regime, the Derge. In 1977 Lieutenant Colonel Mengistu Haile Mariam seized power, and a neo-Stalinist Marxist-Leninist regime was established. Soviet military and economic support replaced American aid. Efforts to mobilize the country and socialize agriculture resulted in eroding agricultural productivity during a period of rapid population increase. The famine that followed threatened the lives of millions of people. Installing socialism at home while engaging in a long-standing major civil conflict with Eritreans effectively ruined the economy. The conflict went on for three decades, involving Ethiopian Amhara civilian and military rulers who controlled the highlands of the country in wars with Eritreans, Muslim and Christian, fighting for independence of their lands adjacent to the Red Sea and with Tigreans of the northern highlands of the country who demanded self-determination and the reorganization of the state. Despite the cost in lives and resources, the civil war defied a military solution until the Tigre People's Liberation Front allied with the Eritrean People's Liberation Front (EPLF) and other groups under the designation of the Ethiopian People's Revolutionary Democratic Front (EPRDF) marched on and captured Addis Ababa in May 1991. Mengistu, losing Soviet military assistance, resigned and fled to Zimbabwe. In July a transitional coalition government was established headed by Meles Zenawi, the Tigrean leader of EPRDF. It has had the primary task of creating a democratic constitutional order, balancing the demands for national stability and unity and at the same time accommodating the interests of Ethiopia's main ethnic groups. National multiparty elections in Ethiopia were scheduled for 1993. The new Ethiopian government reluctantly accepted the de facto separation of Eritrea, which was confirmed by an Eritrean referendum in April 1993,[73] and Eritrea was formally declared independent in May.

Perhaps the most tragic case of the total disintegration of the state into warring clans is Somalia, a country formed out of a former Italian colony in the south and British Somaliland in the north. Arid and poor, a pastoral country whose population is mostly nomad or seminomad, it nevertheless shared a common language, religion (Islam), and cultural identity. The paradox is that while the Somalis constitute one of Africa's most homogenous populations, they are bitterly divided by clan and lineage affiliations. After independence in 1960 Somali was governed by a parliamentary democracy until it was overthrown by General Mohamed Siyad Barre in 1969. In a campaign against ethnicity and tribalism in politics, the new regime proclaimed itself in favor of programs promoting national values, adult literacy, rights of women, and equality through the attainment of socialism. Siyad created the Somali Revolutionary Socialist party in 1976, developed an army with Soviet aid, and fought the Ethiopians in 1977–78 in support of the Ogaden Somali of Ethiopia in order to create a Greater Somalia. When the Ethiopians defeated Somali, its nationalism quickly unraveled in favor of clan and lineage politics. In northern Somalia (former British Somaliland), a civil war broke out between the Somali National Movement of the Isaaq clan and Siyad's military forces. Siyad, increasingly isolated and his authority dwindling, was driven from power in January 1991 by the United Somali Congress, consisting mainly of the Hawiye clan. With the capital, Mogadishu, devastated and Siyad routed, rival factional forces and warlords in armed and bitter opposition to one another have continued to add to the human and material losses, and an interim government for national reconciliation failed to establish a new political framework. Indeed, Somalia was soon without civil order or government, and anarchy reigned with untold numbers at risk of starvation. Former British Somaliland declared itself independent in May 1991, although its future remains very problematic.[74] To ensure and protect international food relief reaching starving Somalias, the United Nations authorized armed intervention by the United States in early December 1992. This unprecedented action appears to be the beginning of an international effort to restore political order to Somalia.

Chad is still another example of civil war based on internal ethnic division and external involvement, in this case by Libya and France. Until 1978 Chad was ruled by southerners, mainly agriculturalists and with a large Christian contingent. However, the northern two-thirds of the country was inhabited by pastoral and nomadic Arabic-speaking Muslim population. Under French colonial administration little progress toward unification had been achieved and a general condition of warlordism prevailed. The French military continued to administer northern Chad until 1965. A civil war broke out, eventually putting an end to southern political hegemony in 1978. In June 1982 the capital, Ndjamena, was captured by the leader of a northern army, Hissene Habré, who not only tried to promote unification by a mixture of military action, repression, and conciliation but also drove the Libyans out of the Aouzou strip in northern Chad that they had occupied for many years. In April 1989 one of Habré's leading commanders, Iris Deby, revolted and with Libyan support defeated Habré, with France, a supporter of Habré against the Libyans, refusing to get involved. Deby approved the restoration of political parties in January 1992 and promised to promote constitutional government in place of the warlordism of the past.[75]

We cite these specific events to remind ourselves of the differences between the discourse on Africa and what in fact Africans themselves have confronted and still have to confront in their daily political lives. These distinguish a different order of realities from what can be described as the more intellectualized discourse of some contemporary theorists. The fact is that several of the states in Africa, apart from Ethiopia, now face the prospect of being divided by partition. Civil wars in Africa might be said to represent the negative pole that virtually all African political leaders have feared. They suggest the terrible realities in human costs and resources that lie behind such abstract terms as *ethnicity* and *ideology*. With virtually all African countries vulnerable, Africans themselves, with their underdeveloped states, have had to confront both the costs of personal rule and the disasters of civil conflict. But they also pose once again the formidable challenge that theorists cannot duck. How can these realities become the basis for new ideas about what went wrong and how to put things right, the unending task of those concerned with how to think one's way past current difficulties to possible solutions?

Any such reconstruction of theory ought to begin by recognizing what the others lacked and where they failed, conceptually. Some like formal choice theories provide answers so simple they cannot be wrong, except that people always find ways of confounding what they are supposed to do rationally by what they actually do, ways that from their point of view perhaps are equally rational. Modernization and functional theory have no way of dealing with development that leads to contradictions, polarization, and an intensified search for local solutions, which in turn may engender mutual hostilities and localized conflicts, with clan, ethnic, class, religious, linguistic, male / female, etc., divisions. Radical theories that identify polarities fail to recognize how easily they fragment, breaking up larger solidarities into smaller ones, prejudicing power as well as creating opportunities for it.

One promising line of inquiry which some formal theorists working on Africa have examined in the case of farmers is how people try to minimize risk while living under conditions of high uncertainty.[76] A more general way to put the problem is how to restore values to a universe of chance. One way has been a return to fundamentalisms, religious, ethnic, or other (including political fundamentalisms), and to evoking different boundaries and affiliations that seem to draw the circle around groups of people whose actions are mutually responsive, responsible, and predicable. The rationality behind fundamentalism in this sense is to reduce randomness. Such problems are, of course, universal.

Is There a New Realism?

If our assumptions are correct, and no matter how it evolves, present-day theory will have to confront the kind of political and social realities that it has shied away from, either because of wishful thinking, the desire to fix responsibility on external political and economic forces, or the effort needed to think up new alternatives, none of which have worked. But just as institutionalism, modernization, and dependency theories derived from elsewhere and were applied to African settings, so with most present-day efforts to unmask and demystify. Modernization theory made too many optimistic assumptions about societal change and the roles of elites vis-à-vis the state. Dependency theory was good at showing how Africans became victims of imperialism but gave useless advice on how they were to extricate themselves from such conditions.

One thing is clear: the more institutional politics decayed, the more the negative and unforeseen consequences of modernization took the form of ethnic nationalism, separatism, and parochialized conflicts. And as well, the more dependent Africa became on metropole-periphery relationships on the one hand and personalized rulership on the other, from protomonarchies to radical one-party regimes, the greater the threat of outside intervention and civil conflict. The result has been an actual or incipient neo-Hobbism.

Moreover, it should be recognized that of course Africa is by no means unique in this situation. Even a quick glance at Latin America would show that given variations of time, place, manner, and cultural specificity, the poverty / personalized rulership connection is a common one. So, too, in their own ways in Eastern Europe, not to speak of the rapidly disintegrating former Soviet Union where conditions are so bad that at least some African countries look in contrast like lands of opportunity. The reality is that massive developmental change is extremely difficult to realize under acceptable political conditions, and such circumstances predispose one to reconstitute power by authoritarian and coercive means.

Some things do change, however. When one-party regimes and personalized rulership took hold in Africa, claims of sovereign inviolability were magnified. It became a delicate matter to criticize publicly even the worst regimes, and external efforts to influence African governments were met with charges of neo-imperialism. Outsiders went along. In the United States the region never had a very high priority except in terms of cold war politics. Dominating United States policy from the start were two main concerns, stability and the prevention of communism.[77] Today, the former Soviet Union is out of the picture. The economic erosion of Africa after the early 1970s, combined with massive corruption and the accumulation of vast foreign debts, has made African countries far more vulnerable to outside pressure. Insofar as there is a growing desire for another try at democracy on the part of many Africans fed up with the legacy of the postindependence years—not to speak of a decline in influence of left or left-leaning intellectuals—Africa is becoming more susceptible to outside pressures for democratization.

There is a good deal of scholarship presently dealing with this problem, not only in Africa but elsewhere. The new realism has been in part defined by harsh economic conditions that have stimulated such international agencies as the World Bank to establish stringent terms based on market conditions and especially structural adjustment programs (SAPs) aimed at increasing overall productive efficiencies. Belt tightening, control of credit, elimination of bureaucratic controls, in short doing everything possible to stimulate African entrepreneurship, remain the primary concerns.[78] The idea is simply to get African economies moving again so that they might reach the levels they were at independence and immediately after.[79] These are among the conditions defining the new realism. As well these concerns include the changing character of the state itself. Increasingly they are being addressed in analytical as well as policy terms. The model remains a multiparty electoral system, coalitional politics, free markets, and a capitalist or mixed economy based on a market system. One representative of such thinking applied to African politics is Robert Bates's *Markets and States in Tropical Africa,* but there are other interesting treatments as well.[80]

At the same time an alternative theoretical direction in African studies is away from such empirical matters and toward such concerns as the re-creation of African history, its historicity and pedigree, and with it a politics of memory and retrieval, often the basis for new projective affiliations and ideological solutions.[81] Some would charge that this represents a flight from economic and political realities.

One might also call it critical realism. Picking up where radical political economy and dependency theory left off, it drastically shifts the focus from economy to discourse and meaning, as well to more general questions about knowledge and the categories of knowledge appropriate to Africa. This tradition, which incorporates on the one hand the Frankfurt School and, on the other, more French structuralist renditions of social philosophy, pays little attention to what happens to Africa on the ground. Rather it uses Africa as a way of challenging the entire corpus of past writings, texts, and theoretical perspectives that have evolved over the years. Above all it questions the ethnographic authority of those who do fieldwork and write about Africa. From the perspective of what might be called radical criticism, the new realism is applied to exploding the ethnographic authority of the old, including its claims to scientific validity, which now appears, to use James Clifford's picturesque phrase, as "ethnographic surrealism."[82]

This not only turns attention away from events, circumstances, and conditions of African life or practical politics but endows the discursive context in which they are to be understood with particular significance. Critical realism directs attention to what Africanists write, the discourse they create, revealing what Africanists come to represent as a body, i.e., as a discourse community. This includes the entire intellectual establishment, its research centers, professorships, professional associations, and their domination of not only how one thinks about Africa but how Africans think about themselves.

The main focus of critical realism is on inversionary themes.[83] The tradition followed was originally that of Hegel's master and slave and Marx's inversionary class struggles. It was Sartre who used the thief who becomes the redeemer, while Foucault uses the madman or the homosexual to reveal the domination of discourse by means of expertise, knowledge itself. As a form of new realism, for example, it reveals the revolutionary texture of sexuality—the woman who reveals the power of the male—or race—the black who refracts the image of the white—redefining the kind of oppression described in Fanon in terms of languages of power.

It also attacks the overkill character of structural and configural theories left and right (overdetermination and disjunctive theories like those of Althusser and Poulantzas, theories of myths and the symbolic like Lévi-Strauss or Barthes) in favor of more phenomenological and hermeneutical approaches. And the work of Anthony Appiah and others imports the postmodern critiques of Frederic Jameson, Jean-François Lyotard, and Jean

Baudrillard to what might be called the magic realism of African political life.[84] The common theme running through these works is difference and what difference difference makes.

In this regard perhaps three general works have been particularly influential: Edward Said's *Orientalism;* Clifford Geertz's devastatingly funny portrayal of one of the icons of African studies, "Sir Edward Evan Evans-Pritchard; E.P."; and James Clifford's *The Predicament of Culture.*[85] Said attacked the exoticizing superiority of Western views of orientalism. Geertz went after the presumptuous "witnessing," the conspiratorial "we" and the false familiarity of the "they" enthusing E.P.'s writings, which, brilliant in their self-assurance and the effortless superiority of their style, imply, too, a crushing superiority of English culture, demonstrating indeed how authorial authority becomes magisterial. Such ethnographic witnessing has its own kind of magical power, defining what a people "are." Puncturing "E.P.," Geertz raised the question not only of writing but of ethnographic validity.[86] Once raised, it does not go away.[87]

All challenge objectivism in research, the tradition of science, and, indeed, the ideal of ethnographic integrity. Under attack are canons that research workers have long regarded as the very basis of their professionality. Clifford showed them up as disguises in the name of values, as principles of superiority and domination. He suggested that the canon implies at best a kind of political acculturation which leads to false projects, prime candidates being institution building, education, and administration.[88] Critical realists, often under the more general rubric of cultural studies, challenge the entire conceptual legacy of social engineering that replaced the colonial legacy. For even if one does not see the world in tutelary-pupillary terms, there are deeper problems of the need for totalized upending experiences which break the psychic filaments of postcolonialism, perhaps even requiring violence as O. Mannoni and Fanon asserted.

But is this kind of critical realism realistic? One difficulty with it is that the reality it designates is a text about an African case, or an author and his or her authorial language. It can never apprehend the original authorial experience. Hence the claim to a new realism may well be simply parasitic. It makes no effort to establish conditions, contexts, meanings as they were. Indeed, the subject status of the ethnographic objective, its subordination by examination, defines a political problem in the minds of those lacking any substantive knowledge. In the end they make theory less powerful in terms of understanding events or giving prescriptive advice while holding out as a political project the destruction of interpretative ideas.

Another difficulty is that they produce a strange mixture of pious posturing and the kind of bacchanalia described by a bemused editor of the journal *African Arts* commenting on the 1990 meetings of the African Studies Association, where few attended panels on moral aspects of African crisis or listened to the rather sober remarks of scholars like Adu Boahen on political ethics, in favor of the postmodernism of Anthony Appiah. "Their discourse was absolutely *comme il faut:* Baudrillard, the Epcot Center, *Heart of Darkness,* Papa Wemba, Flaubert a / o Finkielkraut in Kinshasa, fashion discourse—it looked and sounded like the Zaire edition of *Spy* magazine."[89]

If this is the new realism, it will bring little comfort to those desperately trying to pick up the pieces of a shattered continent where, as in the former Soviet Union and elsewhere, realities overwhelm possibilities. Moreover, radical criticism applied to Africa makes suspect not only the kinds of theories we have discussed but theory itself, which at least in its social science modes becomes an incubus, less legacy than sheer weight, a burden upon the Africa of today. It might be politically correct that what is necessary is to "rethink Africa" in order to lift all those intellectual impositions from the outside which continue to "figure" African thought according to external views, thereby trapping Africans in the role of the "negativized other," a self-reinforcing condition. But it is also the case that something more is needed in the wake of all those overturned African regimes where each successive political generation finds itself overwhelmed by insoluble problems.

If, indeed, there is to be a new realism, must it be on the basis of African analysis made on African terms by Africans themselves? Does one require theoretical discourses different from those which have evolved outside the continent, liberal or Marxist, European, Latin American, American, etc. The question is an old one, especially in ethnographic circles. To what extent is it necessary that the concepts employed for the analysis of African political and social life be uniquely African? Or, to put it the other way around, to what extent should universal concepts be employed regardless of their place of origin. The first view has been subscribed to in various ways by scholars as diverse as Paul Bohannan vis-à-vis African law and Janheinz Jahn, Father Tempels, and Alexis Kagame on "Bantu philosophy," to the writings of Senghor on negritude, Nkrumah's on "consciencism" and African personality, and the variety of local versions of African socialism from Nyerere's Ujamma to Cabral's agrarianism. Here again, the interior view embodies a good deal of yearning with its emphasis on the unique moral and intellectual qualities of African cultures, some of it pandering to black-white differences in a relatively sentimentalized way not so different from the more rhapsodic "black and white keys" notions of early colonial officials who saw harmony as racial complementarity on which happy tunes could be played.[90]

On the other hand, there is now a much more tough-minded group of scholars like Abiola Irele and Paulin J. Hountondji who will have none of it. In Irele's introduction to Hountondji's *African Philosophy*, he wrote: "But perhaps the most significant aspect of Senghor's theory of negritude is that it contains within it a theory of knowledge, indeed an epistemology. The key notion in Senghor's theory is that of *emotion*, which he virtually erects into a function of knowledge and attributes to the African as a cardinal principle of his racial disposition."[91] Hountondji himself wrote, "The Africanness of our philosophy will not necessarily reside in its themes but will depend above all on the geographical origin of those who produce it and their intellectual coming together."[92]

In this sense any return to theory in Africa is political. But the term includes philosophy and literature as well as political economy. Among those involved in theoretical work of significance are Ali Mazrui, J. E. Wiredu, H. Odera, Niamey Koffi, and Paulin Hountondji, to name only a few.[93] Perhaps the most significant is the work of V. Y. Mudimbe, whose book *The Invention of Africa* applies French structuralism, an emphasis on language and the inversionary discourse of Foucault, and draws on the contributions of diverse African scholars, applying them to problems of African self-discovery.[94] In these terms the old questions are newly relevant. Africans are wrestling with these larger analytical concerns in the context of educational reform, of how to square effective administration and the recruitment of cadres with competitive parties, so much so that the time is long since past for changing lenses and peering at faded snapshots. For now the entire field of view is being reformulated, and in terms of an interior history less penetrable by the outsider looking in than ever was the case in the past.

In this discussion we have only touched on some of the kinds of questions challenging African scholarship. There are problems specific to Africa and indeed Africans. But insofar as the issue is how to make the final break with colonialism, many of these problems connect to the broader black experience (including the entire black diaspora). Indeed, from this standpoint it may well be true that the first generation of Africanists actually perpetuated the "colonial gaze" under the smoked glasses of abstract theories, while maintaining Africans in the role of the "negative other" and the "subaltern." Today's critical theory in African studies challenges the imposition of functionalist, structural-functionalist, multivariate, institutionalist, Marxist theories, etc., on grounds that these are all overkill, superimposing on Africans conditions to which people on the ground aspire. The danger is that it can degenerate into a kind of narcissism, more of an intellectual's pastime than a way of grappling with concrete problems. Perhaps its best consequence would be to reinforce an ethnography from inside, indeed, from below, a phenomenology of African intentions.[95]

There has been a tendency, too, for proponents of each mode of analysis to try to displace the other in terms of retrospective pieties, each change of the lens being as well a turn of the political screw. It may now be time to assess the whole panoply of original contexts, remedial solutions, and the different questions and methodological criteria involved.

Perhaps it would be well to pay more attention to the caveat of O. Mannoni years ago: "The problem must therefore be tackled from the bottom and not from the top: the people as a whole, and not just the elite, must be helped forward and they must go forward alone and not in the wake of guides, for that would but perpetuate their psychological dependence."[96]

One can, however, begin again. One of the crucial original questions was about democracy and how it could be achieved in an African setting, the main emphasis of modernization theory. It was knocked into a cocked hat by dependency theory with socialism of some variety as the preferred solution. Today socialism is everywhere discredited. Democracy is coming back. Whether it will do any better in its reincarnation will, to some considerable extent, depend on what can be learned from past experience.

Some things have indeed changed. Despite the deterioration in African life, there is now a lively discourse within African scholarship by Africans in most fields, including philosophy, political science, history, literature, and the arts.[97] The proportion of contributions by Africans is growing so rapidly that it is a proper subject for another analysis. Hence, if the political wheel has in some instances turned full circle and some original political concerns have returned, this time it is in a context of African rather than outside tutelage and as a result of bitter experiences rather than either the decolonization game or the wishful thinking of particular rulers. Democratic pressures or pressures for democratization are underway in places as diverse as Benin, Côte d'Ivoire, Gabon, Zaire, Kenya, Ghana, Nigeria, Congo, Niger, and Mali. Botswana and The Gambia have had democratic government ever since independence. Zambia has moved back to multiparty government with President Kaunda replaced in the 1991 election. Senegal moved from multiparty democracy to one-party dominant rule and then returned to a form of multiparty politics in which power has been shared with the opposition. Namibia has become a virtual model constitutional democracy, and South Africa, despite ethnic conflict, is in search of a democratic polity which would embrace all of its peoples.[98] In political terms one can say that these tendencies have three different strands. One is that democracy has been stripped of its earlier romanticism, the symbolism of fresh starts and rebirths. It starts from the experience of failed chances and lost opportunities. A second is a methodological moment in which philosophers and literary people have as much to do with the search for new political theories as social scientists. A third, an ongoing project in a world where racism is on the increase rather than in a decline, is how to come to grips with racism and in practical terms render it nugatory.

The new emphasis then is on the terms of political order in a context of democracy. Today's concerns will have to deal with the big and universal questions of democracy in an African setting.[99] How much libertarianism and how much egalitarianism should there be, how much private enterprise and how much public, not to speak of the matter of regionalization, changing jurisdictions, etc. These are the same concerns facing Europe, Eastern Europe, the former Soviet Union, and other parts of the world. One might say that with them, African exceptionalism comes to an end. Grappling with these universalized problems of democracy in effect defines the new realism. With these general considerations in mind, we now turn to the case studies themselves.

The Essays

The contributions in this volume deal with the historical realities of African politics since independence. Crawford Young examines the role that nationalism played in the political awakening of Sub-Saharan African, exploring as well the pioneering contributions of James Coleman to an understanding of nationalism and the importance of ethnicity in African politics. Young is concerned with ethnicity as a possible resource rather than an obstacle to state formation. Joel D. Barkan identifies the new and emerging issues in civil society and the revival of modernization theory in a context of accountability. Richard Sklar argues the inadequacies of conventional notions of markets and of bourgeoisie and proletariat and shows that neither capitalism nor socialism alone can serve as solution.

Michael Lofchie, Thomas M. Callaghy, and Colin Leys are concerned with the forms of political economy that have manifested themselves in a context of developmentalism. Lofchie examines the reassertion of neoclassical economic theory in the case of Africa and evaluates new policy alternatives designed to correct distortions in African economies. With respect to problems of state formation and development, Thomas Callaghy's analysis draws attention to the underdeveloped and weak character of the state and its inability to promote economic development, advocating in the contrast to the more neoclassical approaches a new balance between the needs of the state for stability and the developmental need for a market-driven economy. Leys reviews the arguments for dependency and classical Marxism in the context of Kenya and is concerned with whether or not, however defined, the Kenyan bourgeoisie can engender capitalist growth.

Finally, in a concluding section, Michael Chege and Robert M. Jackson and Carl G. Rosberg focus on questions of rulership and leadership. Chege examines the contrasting patterns of capitalist and socialist orientations in development in both Kenya and Tanzania under their respective presidents. Jackson and Rosberg conclude with an analysis of the importance of leadership in determining political and economic development. More specifically, they examine how the political dyseconomy of personal rule, with its tolerance of corruption and clientelism, has undermined the viability of most new African states.

Notes

1. Among the redemptive strands associated with various African nationalist movements were the black Zionism and black capitalism of the Garvey movement, memorialized by Nkrumah in Ghana in the black star in the Ghanian flag, Black Star square, and the Black Star steamship line; Pan-Africanism and socialism as represented by W. E. B. Du Bois and perhaps best exemplified in George Padmore's *Pan-Africanism: The Coming Struggle for Africa* (London: Dennis Dobson, 1956); and the emphases on a historic past embodied in the work of such figures as Cheik Anta Diop, Senghor's negritude and Nkrumah's "African personality." Each of these linked up with wider and increasingly politicized communities: Garvey and the African diaspora; an emphasis on radical transformationalism separate from communism and closer to Gandhi and nonviolence; the acceptance and rejection of European cultural universalism, especially French, in which key figures like Aimé Césaire, Franz Fanon, and of course Jean-Paul Sartre played important parts.

2. See Kwame Nkrumah, *Axioms of Kwame Nkrumah* (London: Thomas Nelson, 1967).

3. See chap. 2 below.

DAVID E. APTER AND CARL G. ROSBERG

4. See Harvey Glickman, ed., *Political Leaders of Contemporary Africa South of the Sahara: A Biographical Dictionary* (Westport, Conn.: Greenwood Press, 1992). See also W. H. Morris-Jones and Georges Fischer, *Decolonization and After* (London: Frank Cass, 1980); Prosser Gifford and William Robert Louis, eds., *Decolonization and African Independence: The Transitions of Power, 1960–1980* (New Haven: Yale Univ. Press, 1988); D. A. Low, *Eclipse of Empire* (Cambridge: Cambridge Univ. Press, 1991).

5. We focus mainly on French and British colonialism, excluding Belgian, Portuguese, and Spanish Africa in part because none had a theory of the state or made plans for a smooth transition of power to Africans. See Crawford Young, "Decolonization in Africa," in *Colonialism in Africa, 1870–1960*, vol. 2, *The History and Politics of Colonialism, 1914–1960*, ed. L. H. Gann and Peter Duignan (Cambridge: Cambridge Univ. Press, 1970), pp. 450–502, and his "The African Colonial State and Its Political Legacy," in *The Precarious Balance: State and Society in Africa*, ed. Donald Rothchild and Naomi Chazan (Boulder, Colo., and London: Westview Press, 1988), pp. 25–66.

6. Of course these distinctions, like many others common made, were commonly wrong in practice. So, too, with Thomas Hodgkin's description of French Cartesianism and British empiricism. Both make their points. See Thomas Hodgkin, *Nationalism in Colonial Africa* (London: Frederick Muller, 1956), pp. 29–59.

7. The incorporation of the four communes of Dakar, Rufisque, Goree, and St. Louis as parts of France was perhaps one consequence of such thought.

8. The question of how much responsibility colonial authorities would accept for freeing slaves who had escaped from the hinterlands to one of the administered coastal areas touched off great debate on what the colonial enterprise was all about. See the various minute papers and dispatches on the subject in Colin W. Newbury, *British Policy towards West Africa* (Oxford: Clarendon Press, 1971).

9. See Carl G. Rosberg, Jr., and John Nottingham, *The Myth of "Mau Mau": Nationalism in Kenya* (New York: Praeger, 1966).

10. See in these connections Paul B. Rich, *Race and Empire in British Politics* (Cambridge: Cambridge Univ. Press, 1986), and Lance E. Davis and Robert A. Huttenback, *Mammon and the Pursuit of Empire: The Political Economy of British Imperialism, 1860–1912* (Cambridge: Cambridge Univ. Press, 1986).

11. Christopher L. Miller, *Blank Darkness: Africanist Discourse in French* (Chicago: Univ. of Chicago Press, 1986).

12. See Aimé Césaire, *Discours sur le colonialisme* (Paris: Présence Africaine, 1955).

13. See Mary H. Kingsley, *West African Studies* (London: Macmillan, 1899), p. 330. See also Robert Rotberg and Ali A. Mazrui, *Protest and Power in Black Africa* (New York: Oxford Univ. Press, 1970).

14. In the British case standards were maintained by a system of external degrees, with examinations set in London or other British universities and recruitment a function of various interuniversity Commonwealth consortia.

15. In 1952 David E. Apter interviewed Sir Charles Noble Arden Clarke (then governor of the Gold Coast) on his views of the future for an independent Ghana. He replied that "it would be one cut above a banana republic."

16. See Sir F. D. Lugard, *The Dual Mandate in British Tropical Africa* (Edinburgh and

London: Blackwood, 1922); M. M. Green, *Ibo Village Affairs* (London: Sidgwick and Jackson, 1947); R. S. Rattray, *Ashanti Law and Constitution* (London: Oxford Univ. Press, 1929); C. K. Meek, *Law and Authority in a Nigerian Tribe: A Study in Indirect Rule* (London: Oxford Univ. Press, 1937); Lord Hailey, *An African Survey* (London: Oxford Univ. Press, 1937; rev. ed., 1957); Robert Delavignette, *Freedom and Authority in French West Africa* (New York: Oxford Univ. Press, 1950).

17. See, for example, Arthur Creech Jones, ed., *New Fabian Colonial Essays* (London: Hogarth Press, 1959). See also Padmore, *Pan-Africanism*.

18. See, for example, the extremely influential pamphlet of Césaire, *Discours sur le colonialism*, in which he wrote: "Colonisation et civilisation? La malediction la plus commune in cette matière est d'être la dupe de bonne foi d'une hypocrisie collective, habile a mal poser les problèmes pour mieux légitimer les odieuses solutions qu'on leur apporte" (p. 8). See also Frantz Fanon, *Les damnés de la terre* (Paris: Maspero, 1961) with its preface by Sartre; Jean Suret-Canale, *French Colonialism in Tropical Africa, 1900–1945* (London: C. Hurst, 1971); Charles Bettelheim, *Planification and croissance accélérée* (Paris: Maspero, 1954).

19. See, for example, Ursula K. Hicks, *Development from Below: Local Government and Finance in the Developing Countries of the Commonwealth* (Oxford: Clarendon Press, 1961).

20. A good example of high thinking in high places is Sir Andrew Cohen's *British Policy in Changing Africa* (London: Routledge and Kegan Paul, 1959).

21. In the colonial view transition involved the establishment not so much of political but administrative bodies. These would provide the steel frame to hold these countries together after independence. Educational facilities were equally important not only for the usual purposes, of transforming ignorance into knowledge, poverty into wealth, but also for the creation of elites who could combat both populist nationalists and prevent as well an inevitable resurgence of ethnic parochialism. The problem was to enlarge the proportion of educated elites until they provided a thin social veneer in the face of nationalist leaders inclined to the volatile and dangerous game of politics.

22. See the Hansard Society, *Problems of Parliamentary Government in Colonies* (London, 1953). See also the Hansard Society, *What Are the Problems of Parliamentary Government in West Africa* (London, 1958).

23. See James S. Coleman, *Nigeria: Background to Nationalism* (Berkeley and Los Angeles: Univ. of California Press, 1958). For a comparative study of several national party systems at independence, see James S. Coleman and Carl G. Rosberg, eds., *Political Parties and National Integration in Tropical Africa* (Berkeley and Los Angeles: Univ. of California Press, 1964).

24. The intensification of the cold war politics of the Soviet Union and the United States imposed its own reality, deeply affecting official attitudes and processes of political change that had begun not in Africa but in other British territories—Burma, Ceylon, and India. Fear of radicalism and communism often led to strenuous efforts by the metropolitan powers to hang onto certain territories even as they let go of others.

25. See Margery Perham, *The Colonial Reckoning* (London: Collins, 1961). See also Michael Crowder, "Whose Dream Was It Anyway? Twenty-five Years of African Independence," *African Affairs* 86, no. 342 (Jan. 1987): 7–24.

26. See, for example, Virginia Thompson and Richard Adloff, *French West Africa* (Stanford, Calif.: Stanford Univ. Press, 1958) and *States of French Equatorial Africa* (Stanford, Calif.: Stanford Univ. Press, 1960). We have already suggested that for French administrators colonialism, then, represented precisely that rationality of modernity missing at home, where party politics was destructive and destabilizing.

27. See Kenneth Robinson, "Senegal: The Elections to the Territorial Assembly, March, 1957," in *Five Elections in Africa,* ed. William J. M. Mackenzie and Kenneth Robinson (Oxford: Clarendon Press, 1960), pp. 281–390.

28. See, for example, on one-party states, Gwendolen M. Carter, ed., *African One-Party States* (Ithaca, N.Y.: Cornell Univ. Press, 1962); her ed., *National Unity and Regionalism in Eight African States* (Ithaca, N.Y.: Cornell Univ. Press, 1966); and her ed., *Five African States: Responses to Diversity* (London and Dunmore: Pall Mall Press, 1964).

29. It was of course the dramatic no vote of Guinea under the Parté Démocratique de Guinée (PDG) and Sékou Touré to the de Gaulle referendum on independence in 1958 that destroyed both the idea of an effective French Union and, as well, a continuing legal association with France of the former territories of the Afrique Occidentale Française (AOF). It is interesting to recall the fury with which this was met by de Gaulle, who reacted by stripping Guinea of virtually anything movable, pulling out all support, cadres, etc. For the classic study of the period, see Ruth Schachter Morgenthau, *Political Parties in French-Speaking West Africa* (Oxford: Clarendon Press, 1963).

30. See Lloyd A. Fallers, *Bantu Bureaucracy: A Study of Integration and Conflict in the Political Institutions of an East African People* (Cambridge: Heffers, 1956); Georges Balandier, *Political Anthropology* (New York: Random House, 1970).

31. See Gabriel A. Almond and James S. Coleman, eds., *The Politics of the Developing Areas* (Princeton, N.J.: Princeton Univ. Press, 1960).

32. See David Easton, *The Political System: An Inquiry into the State of Political Science* (New York: Knopf, 1953), and *A Systems Analysis of Political Life* (New York: Wiley, 1965). The model of the political system used by Easton was taken from general systems theory involving inputs and outputs following feedback loops, i.e., a politics of moving equilibrium.

33. Almond and Coleman, *Politics of the Developing Areas*, p. 17.

34. Still other versions of functionalism used specific indicator variables to compare countries in terms of development syndromes. Heuristic functionalism paid particular attention to political socialization, schooling, the family, peer groups, etc. In the context of the modernization paradigm, it also emphasized links to social psychology; in political learning, the relation between learning and norms and their motivational consequences in terms of people's capacity to perform their roles, as in Alex Inkeles's *Becoming Modern*. See Alex Inkeles and David H. Smith, *Becoming Modern: Individual Change in Six Developing Countries* (Cambridge: Harvard Univ. Press, 1974). See also Karl W. Deutsch, *Nationalism and Social Communication: An Inquiry into the Foundations of Nationality* (Cambridge: MIT Press, 1953).

35. See David C. McClelland, *The Achieving Society* (Princeton, N.J.: Van Nostrand, 1961), and Robert A. LeVine, *Dreams and Deeds: Achievement Motivation in Nigeria* (Chicago: Univ. of Chicago Press, 1966). In both books there is a search for the functional

equivalents of that Weberian holy grail—the Protestant ethic. If one could not expect this worldly asceticism, one could see in budding political parties and organizations the political stimuli for innovative action.

36. See Samuel Huntington, *Political Order in Changing Societies* (New Haven: Yale Univ. Press, 1968).

37. See James S. Coleman, ed., *Education and Political Development* (Princeton, N.J.: Princeton Univ. Press, 1965).

38. James S. Coleman, "The Development Syndrome: Differentiation-Equality-Capacity," in *Crises and Sequences in Political Development,* ed. Leonard Binder et al., (Princeton, N.J.: Princeton Univ. Press, 1971), pp. 73–100.

39. See David E. Apter, *The Politics of Modernization* (Chicago: Univ. of Chicago Press, 1967).

40. See, for example, Bronislaw Malinowski, *The Dynamics of Culture Change* (New Haven: Yale Univ. Press, 1945).

41. In Africa, for example, the work of David Apter focused on "political institutional transfer," i.e., the superimposition of secular and parliamentary institutions on accommodated but still "traditional" ones by means of nationalism and the mediation of a populist political party. See David E. Apter, *Ghana in Transition,* 2d rev. ed. (Princeton, N.J.: Princeton Univ. Press, 1972). See also Apter, *The Political Kingdom in Uganda: A Study in Bureaucratic Nationalism,* 2d ed. (Princeton, N.J.: Princeton Univ. Press, 1967).

42. This in contrast to more radical followers of the dependency paradigm, which privileged structural factors, particularly class, and posited the need for normative transformation and behavioral alteration.

43. See David E. Apter, *Choice and the Politics of Allocation* (New Haven: Yale Univ. Press, 1971) and his *Rethinking Development* (Beverly Hills, Calif.: Sage Publications, 1987). See also Aristide Zolberg, *Creating Political Order: The Party States of West Africa* (Chicago: Rand McNally, 1966); Stanislav Andreski, *The African Predicament: A Study in the Pathology of Modernisation* (London: Joseph, 1968); Crawford Young, *Ideology and Development in Africa* (New Haven: Yale Univ. Press, 1982).

44. See Robert H. Jackson and Carl G. Rosberg, *Personal Rule in Black Africa: Prince, Autocrat, Prophet, Tyrant* (Berkeley: Univ. of California Press, 1982). See also chap. 9 below.

45. See Robert M. Price, *Society and Bureaucracy in Contemporary Ghana* (Berkeley: Univ. of California Press, 1975); David B. Abernethy, "Bureaucratic Growth and Economic Stagnation in Sub-Saharan Africa," in *Africa's Development Challenges and the World Bank: Hard Questions, Costly Choices,* ed. Stephen K. Commins, (Boulder, Colo., and London: Lynne Rienner, 1988), pp. 178–209. See also Richard A. Joseph, "Class, State, and Prebendal Politics in Nigeria," in *State and Class in Africa,* ed. Nelson Kasfir (Totowa, N.J.: Frank Cass, 1984), pp. 21–38.

46. See Francis Tony McNamara, *France in Black Africa* (Washington, D.C.: National Defense Univ., 1989).

47. Perhaps the only political leader in Africa in 1991–92 without an organized political opposition is H. Kamazu Banda, life president of Malawi. See Samuel Decalo,

DAVID E. APTER AND CARL G. ROSBERG

"Modalities of Civil-Military Stability in Africa," *Journal of Modern African Studies* 27, no. 4 (1989): 403–35.

48. See Ron Parker, "The Senegal-Mauritanian Conflict of 1989: A Fragile Equilibrium," *Journal of Modern African Studies* 29, no. 1 (1991): 155–71.

49. See Samuel Decalo, *Psychoses of Power: African Personal Dictatorship* (Boulder, Colo., and London: Westview Press, 1989).

50. See *African Confidential* 32, no. 21 (Oct. 25, 1991): 2, in which is mentioned a New York University study by Kevin Chang and Robert Kumby showing that African individuals have about $40,000 million in industrial countries. See also Larry Diamond, "Political Corruption, Nigeria's Perennial Struggle," *Journal of Democracy* 2, no. 4 (Fall 1991): 73–85.

51. See Charles F. Andrain, "Democracy and Socialism: Ideologies of African Leaders," in *Ideology and Discontent*, ed. David E. Apter (New York: Free Press, 1964), pp. 155–205; Carl G. Rosberg and Thomas M. Callaghy, eds., *Socialism in Sub-Saharan Africa: A New Assessment* (Berkeley, Calif.: Institution of International Studies, 1979); Young, *Ideology and Development in Africa*; Helen Desfosses and Jacques Levesque, eds., *Socialism in the Third World* (New York: Praeger, 1975); Edmond J. Keller and Donald Rothchild, eds., *Afro-Marxist Regimes: Ideology and Public Policy* (Boulder, Colo.: Lynne Rienner, 1987); Marion and David Ottaway, *Afrocommunism*, 2d ed. (New York and London: Africana Publishing Co., 1986).

52. See Elliot Berg, "Structural Transformation versus Gradualism: Recent Economic Developments in Ghana and the Ivory Coast," in *Ghana and the Ivory Coast: Perspectives on Modernization*, ed. Philip Foster and Aristide R. Zolberg (Chicago: Univ. of Chicago Press, 1971), pp. 187–230, and Donald Rothchild, ed., *Ghana: The Political Economy of Recovery* (Boulder, Colo., and London: Lynne Rienner, 1991).

53. Nyerere was one of the few African leaders to give up power voluntarily. In 1985 the new president, Ali Hassan Mwinyi, reoriented Tanzania toward recovery with assistance from the IMF, the World Bank, and external donors. But he has faced stiff opposition within the party from those who favor socialism even if it prejudices growth.

54. See chaps. 5 and 6 below.

55. See Edward Shils, *Political Development in the New States* ('S-Gravenhage: Mouton, 1962). See also Fanon, *Les damnés de la terre*.

56. See, for example, Basil Davidson, *Old Africa Rediscovered* (London: Victor Gollancz, 1959), which is dedicated to Gervase Mathew and Thomas Hodgkin.

57. Perhaps the best example of this kind of thinking elevated to a very abstract level is Giovanni Arrighi's *The Geometry of Imperialism* (London: New Left Books, 1978).

58. See, for example, Bob Fitch and Mary Oppenheimer, *Ghana: End of an Illusion* (New York and London: Monthly Review Press, 1966).

59. A good deal of radical dependency theory owes for its inspiration the work of four figures, Paul Baran, André Gunder Frank, Ernest Mandel, and Fernando Henrique Cardoso. See, in particular, Paul Baran's *The Political Economy of Growth* (New York: Monthly Review Press, 1962); Fernando Henrique Cardoso and Enzo Faletto, *Dependency and Development in Latin America*, tr. Marjory Mattingly Urguidi (Berkeley: Univ. of

Changing African Perspectives

California Press, 1979). See also Immanuel Wallerstein, *The Modern World System: Capitalist Agriculture and the Origins of the European World Economy in the Sixteenth Century* (New York: Academic Press, 1980).

60. See Colin Leys, *Underdevelopment in Kenya: The Political Economy of Neo-Colonialism, 1964–1971* (Berkeley: Univ. of California Press, 1975), pp. 254–75, and chap. 7 below. See also Paul M. Lubeck, ed., *The African Bourgeoisie: Capitalist Development in Nigeria, Kenya, and the Ivory Coast* (Boulder, Colo.: Lynne Rienner, 1987).

61. See Walter Rodney, *How Europe Underdeveloped Africa* (London: Bogle-l'Ouverture, and Dar-es-Salaam: Tanzania Publishing House, 1972), and John Saul, *The State and Revolution in Eastern Africa: Essays* (New York: Monthly Review Press, 1979). See also Giovanni Arrighi and John Saul, *Essays on the Political Economy of Africa* (New York: Monthly Review Press, 1973).

62. See Kasfir, *State and Class in Africa,* Gavin Kitching, *Class and Economic Change in Kenya: The Making of an African Petite Bourgeoisie 1905–1970* (New Haven: Yale Univ. Press, 1980); Leonard Markovitz, *Power and Class in Africa: An Introduction to Change and Conflict in African Politics* (Englewood Cliffs, N.J.: Prentice Hall, 1977). See also Leonard Markovitz, ed., *Studies in Power and Class in Africa* (New York: Oxford Univ. Press, 1987); Michael G. Schatzberg, *Politics and Class in Zaire: Bureaucracy, Business, and Beer in Lisala* (New York: Africana Publishing Co., 1980); Peter C. Gutkind and Peter Waterman, eds., *African Social Studies: A Radical Reader* (London: Heinemann, 1977); Lionel Cliff and John Sauls, eds., *Socialism in Tanzania,* vol. 1, *Politics,* vol. 2, *Policies* (Nairobi: East African Publishing House, 1972, 1973).

63. In a bitter article by David Horowitz for the African Research Group (translated into French as "Les études africaines en Amérique: La famille étendue"), reference is made to "the Rockefeller Foundation (James Coleman and Company)," with Coleman himself described as one of the mandarins extending American influence in Africa. The document also includes the manifesto of the African Heritage Studies Association, a black organization which attacked the African Studies Association at its Montreal meetings. See Maurice Godelier, ed., *Anthropologie et imperialisme* (Paris: Maspero, 1975), p. 162.

64. See in particular Claude Ake, *A Political Economy of Africa* (Harlow: Longman, 1981). See also Samir Amin, *Neo-Colonialism in West Africa* (New York: Monthly Review Press, 1973).

65. See Sir W. Arthur Lewis, *The Theory of Economic Growth* (London: George Allen and Unwin, 1955); Andrew Kamarck, *The Economics of African Development* (New York: Praeger, 1967); P. T. Bower, *Equality, the Third World, and Economic Delusion* (Cambridge: Harvard Univ. Press, 1981); Douglas Rimmers, *The Economies of West Africa* (London: Weidenfeld and Nicolson, 1984); Elliot J. Berg, "The World Bank Strategy," in *Africa in Economic Crisis,* ed. John Ravenhill (New York: Columbia Univ. Press, 1986), pp. 44–59. See also the World Bank, *Accelerated Development in Sub-Saharan Africa* (Washington, D.C., 1981), of which Berg is the principal author. For a more anthropological perspective, see Keith Hart, *The Political Economy of West African Agriculture* (Cambridge: Cambridge Univ. Press, 1982).

66. Terms like *left* and *right* are perhaps misleading. Right in this context means

liberal approaches both to politics and development with market principles at the center. It includes a small number of scholars working in the general area of formal choice theory such as Robert H. Bates, *Markets and States in Tropical Africa: The Political Basis of Agricultural Policies* (Berkeley: Univ. of California Press, 1981).

67. See Louis Althusser, *For Marx*, tr. Ben Brewster (New York: Vintage Books, 1970), and Louis Althusser and Etienne Balibar, *Reading Capital* (New York: Pantheon Books, 1970). See also Nicos Poulantzas, *Political Power and Social Classes*, tr. Timothy O'Hagan (London: New Left Books, 1973), *Classes in Contemporary Capitalism*, tr. David Fernback (London: Verso, 1974), and *State, Power, Socialism*, tr. Patrick Camiller (London: Verso, 1978).

68. See chap. 4 below.

69. See John J. Stremlau, *The International Politics of the Nigerian Civil War, 1967–1970* (Princeton, N.J.: Princeton Univ. Press, 1977).

70. It should also be noted that although the United States was a longtime patron and major donor of economic aid to Liberia, it refused Doe's call for intervention on behalf of his regime. Doe was assassinated by rebel forces who had broken away from Charles Taylor's guerrillas. An interim government was established by ECOWAS headed by Dr. Amos Sawyer, an exiled leader. For a background to Liberian politics in the 1980s, see J. Gus Liebenow, *Liberia: The Quest for Democracy* (Bloomington: Indiana Univ. Press, 1987).

71. Not until 1988 were the Soviets, the Americans, the South Africans, the Cubans, and the MPLA able to agree on the terms of a settlement (which included the independence of Namibia in 1990). Cuba began a two-year withdrawal of some 50,000 troops. South Africa agreed to remove its forces from Angola and accepted the independence of Namibia. Having given up the principle of a vanguard party and abandoning its Marxism-Leninism, the MPLA signed an agreement with UNITA (mediated by the former colonial power, Portugal), sponsored by the United States and the Soviet Union, which ended the civil war in May 1991. The agreement provided for competitive multiparty national elections that were held under United Nations supervision in late September 1992. While Santos's MPLA retained control of the government, Savimbi's UNITA refused to accept electoral defeat and resumed fighting, making the political future of Angola problematic. See *Africa Research Bulletin, Political Series* 28, no. 6 (June 1991): 10170–71; John A. Marcum, "Angola: Twenty-five Years of War," *Current History* 85, no. 511 (May 1986): 193–96, 229–31; Linda M. Haywood, "UNITA and Ethnic Nationalism in Angola," *Journal of Modern African Studies* 27, no. 1 (1989): 47–66; Anthony G. Pazzanita, "The Conflict Resolution Process in Angola," ibid., 29, no. 1 (1991): 83–114; Prexy Nesbitt, "U.S. Foreign Policy: Lesson from the Angola Conflict," *Africa Today* 39, nos. 1 & 2 (1992): 53–71.

72. After two years of negotiations a cease-fire signed between the Frelimo government and Renamo in October 1992 paved the way for Mozambique's first multiparty national elections. See Martin Lowenkopf, "Mozambique: The Nkomati Accord," in *Reassessing the Soviet Challenge in Africa*, ed. Michael Clough (Berkeley, Calif.: Institute of International Studies, 1986); pp. 48–68; Glenda Morgan, "Violence in Mozambique: Towards an Understanding of Renamo," *Journal of Modern African Studies* 28, no. 4

(1990): 603–19; Robert T. Huffman, "Colonialism, Socialism, and Destabilization in Mozambique," *Africa Today* 39, nos. 1 & 2 (1992): 9–27.

73. *African Research Bulletin, Political Series* 28, no. 5 (May 1991): 10135; ibid., no. 7 (July 1991): 10209–11. See Christopher Clapham, *Transformation and Continuity in Revolutionary Ethiopia* (Cambridge: Cambridge Univ. Press, 1988), and Edmund J. Keller, *Revolutionary Ethiopia: From Empire to the People's Republic* (Bloomington: Indiana Univ. Press, 1988). See also Martin Doornbos et al., eds., *Beyond Conflict in the Horn* (London: James Currey, 1992).

74. See *African Research Bulletin, Political Series* 28, no. 1 (Jan. 1991): 9737–39. See also I. M. Lewis, "The Ogaden and the Fragility of Somali Segmenting Nationalism," *African Affairs* 8, no. 253 (Oct. 1989): 573–84; Rakiya Omaar, "Somalia: At War with Itself," *Current History* 91, no. 565 (May 1992): 230–34; Ahmed I. Samatar, *Socialist Somalia: Rhetoric and Reality* (London: Zed Books, 1988).

75. See Virginia Thompson and Richard Adloff, *Conflict in Chad* (London: C. Hurst, 1981). See also William J. Foltz, "Chad's Third Republic: Strengths, Problems, and Prospects," *CSIS Africa Notes* 77 (Oct. 30, 1987): 1–8.

76. See Robert H. Bates, *Beyond the Miracle of the Market: The Political Economy of Agrarian Development in Kenya* (Cambridge: Cambridge Univ. Press, 1989).

77. See Michael Clough, *Free at Last: U.S. Policy toward Africa and the End of the Cold War* (New York: Council on Foreign Relations, 1992); Robert M. Price, *U.S. Foreign Policy in Sub-Saharan Africa: National Interest and Global Strategy,* Policy Papers in International Affairs, no. 8 (Berkeley, Calif.: Institute of International Studies, 1978); Gerald J. Bender, James S. Coleman, and Richard L. Sklar, eds., *African Crisis Areas and U.S. Foreign Policy* (Berkeley, Los Angeles, and London: Univ. of California Press, 1985).

78. See Bjorn Beckman, "Empowerment of Repression? The World Bank and the Politics of Adjustment," in *Authoritarianism, Democracy, and Adjustment: The Politics of Economic Reform in Africa,* ed. Peter Gibbon, Yusuf Bangura, and Arge Ofstad (Uppsala: Scandinavian Institute of African Studies, 1992), pp. 83–105; World Bank, *Sub-Saharan Africa: From Crises to Sustainable Grown* (Washington, D.C., 1989).

79. Included among the approaches applied to an African setting is formal choice theory which has the advantages of simplicity, methodological elegance, and a kind of realism which focuses on economic matters, individual rationality, and the politics of interest calculation, which follows from these. What it leaves out or regarded as extraneous is the diversity of cultural factors, contingencies, situations, and circumstances under which people act, often in ways that confound the models.

80. See Zaki Ergas, ed., *The African State in Transition* (London: Macmillan, 1987), and Rothchild and Chazan, *Precarious Balance.*

81. The question of African history has been examined in many different contexts. One interesting one is the UNESCO *General History of Africa.* See, in particular, Joseph Ki-Zerbo, "General Introduction," in *Methodology and African Prehistory,* vol. 1, ed. Joseph Ki-Zerbo (UNESCO: Paris, 1981), pp. 1–23. See also G. N. Uzolgwe, "European Partition and Conquest of Africa: An Overview," in *Africa under Colonial Domination,* vol. 1, ed. A. Ada Boaden, (UNESCO: Paris, 1985), pp. 19–44; Terence Ranger, "African Initiatives in the Face of Partition and Conquest," ibid., pp. 45–61.

82. See James Clifford, *The Predicament of Culture: Twentieth-Century Ethnography, Literature, and Art* (Cambridge: Harvard Univ. Press, 1988).

83. See David E. Apter, "Democracy and Emancipatory Movements: Notes for a Theory of Inversionary Discourse," *Development and Change* 23, no. 3 (1992): 139–73.

84. See, for example, Fredric Jameson, *The Political Unconscious: Narrative as a Socially Symbolic Act* (Ithaca, N.Y.: Cornell Univ. Press, 1982); Jean-François Lyotard, *The Postmodern Condition: A Report on Knowledge* (Minneapolis: Univ. of Minnesota Press, 1984); Jean Baudrillard, *For a Critique of the Political Economy of the Sign,* tr. Charles Levin (St. Louis: Telos Press, 1981).

85. See Edward Said, *Orientalism* (New York: Pantheon Books, 1978); Clifford, *Predicament of Culture.*

86. See Clifford Geertz, "Slide Show: Evans-Pritchard's African Transparencies," *Works and Lives: The Anthropologist as Author* (Stanford, Calif.: Stanford Univ. Press, 1989), pp. 49–72.

87. See, for example, the search for "deeper understanding" in the work of Renato Rosaldo, especially his *Culture and Truth: The Remaking of Social Analysis* (Boston: Beacon Press, 1991).

88. See, for example, V. Y. Mudimbe, *L'autre face du royaume* (Paris: L'Age d'Homme, 1973).

89. See Donald J. Cosentino, "First Word" in *African Arts* 24, no. 2 (April 1991): 6.

90. See Paul Bohannan, *Justice and Judgment among the Tiv* (London: Oxford Univ. Press, 1951); Janheinz Jahn, *Muntu: An Outline of Neo-African Culture,* tr. Marjorie Grene (London: Faber and Faber, 1961); Robin Cohen and Harry Goulbourne, eds., *Democracy and Socialism in Africa* (Boulder, Colo.: Westview Press, 1991); R. P. Placide Tempels, *La philosophie bantoue* (Paris: Présence Africaine, 1949), with an introduction by Alioune Diop; and Alexis Kagame, *La philosophie bantou-ruandaire* (Brussels: Academie Royale des Sciences Coloniales, 1956). See also Sir Gordon Guggisberg, *The Future of the Negro* (London: Student Christian Movement, 1929).

91. See Abiola Irele, "Introduction," in *African Philosophy, Myth, and Reality,* ed. Paulin J. Hountondji (Bloomington: Indiana Univ. Press, 1983), pp. 18, 53.

93. See, in particular, ibid.

94. See V. Y. Mudimbe, *The Invention of Africa: Gnosis, Philosophy, and the Order of Knowledge* (Bloomington and Indianapolis: Indiana Univ. Press, 1988). It is of interest that this book is dedicated to James S. Coleman.

95. See, for example, John Van Maanen, *Tales of the Field* (Chicago: Univ. of Chicago Press, 1988).

96. See O. Mannoni, *Prospero and Caliban* (New York: Praeger, 1956), p. 176.

97. See, for example, in political science, Walter O. Oyugi et al., eds., *Democratic Theory and Practice in Africa* (Nairobi: Heinemann, 1988), and Peter Anyang' Nyong'o, ed., *Popular Struggle for Democracy in Africa* (London: Zed Press, 1987).

98. See Robert M. Price, *The Apartheid State in Crisis: Political Transformation in South Africa, 1975–1990* (New York: Oxford Univ. Press, 1991). See also Donald L. Horowitz, *A Democratic South Africa?: Constitutional Engineering in a Divided Society* (Berkeley: Univ. of California Press, 1991).

Changing African Perspectives

99. See Goran Hyden and Michael Bratton, eds., *Governance and Politics in Africa* (Boulder, Colo., and London: Lynne Rienner, 1992); Larry Diamond, Juan Linz, and Seymour Martin Lipset, *Democracy in Developing Countries,* vol. 2, *Africa* (Boulder, Colo.: Lynne Rienner, 1988). See also Richard Joseph, "The Rebirth of Political Freedom," *Journal of Democracy* 2, no. 4 (Fall 1991): 11–26, and Peter M. Lewis, "Political Transition and the Dilemma of Civil Society in Africa," *Journal of International Affairs* 46, no. 1 (Summer 1992): 31–54.

PART I

IDEOLOGY, SOCIETY, AND SOCIAL GROUPS

2

EVOLVING MODES OF CONSCIOUSNESS AND IDEOLOGY: NATIONALISM AND ETHNICITY

CRAWFORD YOUNG

During the 1950s, nationalism, parties and elections, and ideology figure prominently; during the early 1960s, political modernization had an evanescent appeal, but in the later part of the decade issues of military intervention, ethnicity, and intra-African relations increasingly commanded the spotlight; in the 1970s, political modernization lost its vogue, intractable military rule and ethnicity continued their insatiable claims to attention, and issues of class, dependency, and "political economy," the emerging omnibus code words of the new epoch, asserted their primacy.—James S. Coleman and C. R. D. Halisi, "American Political Science and Tropical Africa"

IN THEIR MASTERFUL summation of a quarter century of the intellectual history of Africanist political science, "American Political Science and Tropical Africa: Universalism vs. Relativism," James S. Coleman and C. R. D. Halisi elegantly mapped the trajectory from the "unbounded optimism" of the 1950s to the "deep pessimism" emerging in the 1970s. This pathway, strewn with discarded paradigms, winds between the magnetic fields of universality, embedded in the "evangelical, American-dominant discipline of political science," and particularity, rooted in the historical-cultural specificities of Africa. The incorrigible disposition of the field to compress the inherent complexity of large political fields into a handful of master variables continues unabated, from structural-functionalism to dependency, mode of production, or rational choice. One might add that recently an additional important genre has emerged, doubtless with the same liabilities as its predecessors: state / civil society models.[1]

In this essay I extract from the broader corpus of Africanist political science two central themes, nationalism and ethnicity. Pursuing with this narrowed focus an endeavor parallel to the Coleman-Halisi article, I examine the evolution of perspectives concerning these intertwined forms of ideology and consciousness. The first major author to explore systematically the juxtaposed forces of nationalism and ethnicity was Coleman; I use his early works as a point of departure. Crucial to an appreciation of the first stages in this debate are the blank tablets upon which the first generation of Africanist political scientists inscribed their understandings; there was literally nothing in accumulated colonial knowledge to guide their intuitions on prospective itineraries of either nationalism or ethnicity.[2]

When Coleman set forth to seek out the sources, dynamic, and prospective pathway for nationalism in Nigeria in 1951, to the colonial official mind this irritating doctrine was recognized as a troublesome fact of imperial life but only loosely understood; like the classical American judicial definition of pornography, one could recognize it on sight but could not clearly state what it was. Lord Hailey, a central figure in terminal colonial policy thought in Britain, wrote at that time (1952) that "Africanism" was the driving idea behind anticolonial agitation: "For the most part [territories] represent only geographical units and not communities with any such natural ties or affinities as can form a basis for nationhood. . . . People who are brought together by fate into one governmental unit—generally as a result of outside action—can of course be welded into something like nationality by the force of circumstances. . . . But it is an historical process . . . a matter of time, often of very considerable time."[3]

In the 1956 edition of his epic *Africa Survey*, Hailey clung to this definition, insisting that anticolonial sentiment should not be termed nationalism: "In Europe nationalism is a readily recognizable force, even though it may not be easily definable, but as a concept it has associations which make it difficult of application in the conditions of Africa."[4] At that time colonial officialdom still tended to see African nationalism as above all a West African (and Arab) phenomenon. The ultimate aim of "self-government," a notion incompletely defined, was officially stated by 1938, but many of the colonial officials Coleman encountered in Nigeria still shared the sentiments expressed in a 1942 Colonial Office memorandum: "We all know in our heart that most Colonies, especially in Africa, will probably not be fit for complete independence for centuries."[5] David Apter, arriving in Ghana on a similar quest in 1952, was told by officials that "it would be a long time before African territories would become independent."[6] Indeed, nationalism as topic of inquiry was viewed with suspicion; as Coleman wrote in 1955, the very word "tended to be treated as the equivalent of sedition, or even treason."[7]

Nonetheless, in 1951 the existence of a swelling demand for African rights, an intensifying cry for liberation from European rule, was obvious enough in Nigeria and most other parts of Africa. Much less self-evident was the precise nature of nationalism, both as ideology and consciousness. Those who fashioned its thought at the time were preoccupied with the pragmatics of liberation, and not the definition of their doctrine. The imperatives of praxis drove the emergent political leaders whose unfolding discourse of struggle cumulatively constituted nationalism in directions determined by successive circumstances of terminal colonialism. Nationalism in Africa evolved above all as a set of ideas fashioned in the heat of political action. The requirements of anticolonial combat differed widely from one setting to another, which helps explain what seemed to the first generation of analysts the elusiveness and diversity of African nationalist thought.

In British West Africa nationalists faced foot-dragging from colonial bureaucracies and ambivalent response from indirect rule elites (and the Freetown Creoles in Sierra Leone) whose intermediary standing was threatened by mass politics and universal suffrage elections. In eastern, central, and southern Africa, initial colonial decolonization schemes presumed multiracial constitutional schemes, conceding exorbitant group rights to small European and Asian minorities. A "Eurafrican" state was also the initial Belgian objective. In French-ruled Sub-Saharan Africa, political advance through claiming full prerogatives as French citizens and participating in parliamentary politics in France competed with independence as motivating vision. These factors explain the diversity of nationalist thought and the stress placed by Coleman in his classification of these differences in his early writing.

Most fundamental of all, nationalism implies nation; yet in Africa at the beginning of the 1950s the territorial frame of African liberation was far from clear. Much earlier African nationalist thought was expressed within the framework of Pan-Africanism; the 1945 Manchester conference denounced the artificiality and illegitimacy of the territorial partition of the colonial domain. Within given colonial zones, the precise frame for eventual African sovereignty, if achieved, was still undefined. The various administrative federations (Afrique Occidentale Française, Afrique Equatoriale Française) or colonially sponsored interterritorial groupings (East Africa,

Central Africa, High Commission territories) remained possible frameworks for political evolution. In some instances historical states (Buganda, Barotseland) or ethnoregional collectivity lurked—usually below the surface—as potential bases for solidarity. Accordingly, the negative "other" for nationalism—the specific occupying power—was clearer than the human or territorial boundary of the "nation" whose rights were asserted.

Thus Coleman and his contemporaries faced the challenge of defining nationalism in Africa before it had fully defined itself. In this respect one can understand the timely but ultimately unsatisfactory choice of Thomas Hodgkin, in his immensely influential 1956 monograph on African nationalism, for equating the phenomenon with protest.[8] Nationalism was to be sought in its organizational forms above all (urban associations, unions, prophetic movements, especially political parties). Organized protest, whatever its form and content, provided only that African rights were asserted; it pegged the capacious tent sheltering nationalism. Thus conceptualized, nationalism was implicitly tied to the colonial phenomenon; with the achievement of independence, the analytical clarity of the original Hodgkin perspective vanished. Indeed, closely examined, an intriguing paradox may be discerned in this work. The focus upon nationalism as political action meant that classic texts played relatively little role in the Hodgkin exegesis; only a dozen African writings were cited as sources of the nationalist idea, and of these, nearly half are really ethnic charters.[9]

One may detect strains of indeterminacy in the first published Coleman definition of nationalism. He distinguished its "modernity" from "traditionalist" and "syncretistic" protest movements, linking organized nationalism with "Western ideas of democracy, progress, the welfare state, and national self-determination."

> It aspires *either:* (a) to create modern independent African nation-states possessing an internal state apparatus and external sovereignty and all of the trappings of a recognized member state of international society (e.g., Sudan, Gold Coast, Nigeria, and possibly Sierra Leone); *or* (b) to achieve absolute social and political equality and local autonomy within a broader Eur-African grouping (e.g., French and Portuguese Africa) or within what is manifestly a plural society (e.g., except for Uganda, the territories of British East and Central Africa).[10]

In his 1958 Nigerian monograph, Coleman devoted a definitional appendix to the quest for clarity. While demurring from a notion so broad as to include all sentiment or activity opposed to alien rule, he now identified nationalism as the aspiration for independent statehood on the part of a human collectivity of undefined but yet "large" scale believing itself to be a "terminal community," or a territorially defined group claiming the vocation of becoming a nation. Thus specified, nationalism in Africa might pertain to Pan-Africa, extant colonial territories, regions within such territories, or large (but not small) ethnic groups.[11]

Hodgkin, one may add, amended his concept of African nationalism in 1961, to tie it much more explicitly to the territorial frame that ultimately shaped decolonization. The "common political language" of nationalism now identified a nation as a given colonial territory subordinated to an imperial power, whose subjects have an inalienable right to rule themselves, under the guidance of a "national liberation movement" capable of mobilizing mass resistance to colonial subjugation and defeating the internal enemies of "tribalism" and "feudalism" (chiefs).[12] The myriad forms of protest now coalesced into a distinctive ideology.

Yet understandings of nationalism, at the hour of its greatest triumph, remained rooted in the observation of political action. In a revealing paragraph Coleman stressed that the study of African nationalism "is concerned mainly with the attitudes, activities, and status of the nationalist-minded Western-educated *elite.*" Above all by direct interview and close observation "can one get a partial glimpse into the depth of nationalist feeling, the sources of inspiration and ideas, and the key elements in nationalist motivation."[13] Crucial to grasping this construction of the idea of nationalism was the intimate symbiosis between the independence generation of African leaders and the scholars who served as amanuenses for their political thought. Coleman, Hodgkin, Apter, Immanuel Wallerstein, Ruth Schachter Morgenthau, Basil Davidson: these interpreters of African nationalism enjoyed privileged access to the leaders of the independence struggle, shared their aspirations, and supplied faithful synthesis to their thought.

In this period African nationalism gave rise to relatively few classical texts. Its expression occurred above all through the speeches of political leaders, resolutions of party congresses, and polemics of tracts and newspapers. It was especially after independence that the more historically conscious leaders—Kwame Nkrumah, Leopold Senghor, Julius Nyerere—began to assemble their thoughts in printed form.[14] A broader realm of anti-imperial thought germinating in other parts of the Middle East and Asia, at the left end of the Western ideological spectrum, or in the "camp of socialism" as a common pool of shared discourse had some influence; however, evidence of detailed study of major works in radical anti-imperial nationalism from other regions appears far less often than the more diffuse impact of common ideas expressed in international forums and through the global-ized media.

Nor was the study of African nationalism strongly shaped by the intellec-tual history of nationalism more generally. Hodgkin wrote that "African nationalism, in its many manifestations, [is] an historical movement, neces-sarily and characteristically African, yet revealing definite points of resem-blance to the nationalisms that have emerged in other parts of the world."[15] However, his own work does not pursue these parallels, nor does his bibli-ography suggest that they strongly influenced his analysis.[16] Coleman made passing reference to Karl Deutsch's work *Nationalism and Social Communica-tion,* but this is the only bibliographic entry drawn from the general pool of nationalism studies.[17] His work does, however, bear the imprint of his Harvard mentor, Rupert Emerson.[18]

In his retrospective Coleman reflected upon the "elite-centrism" of the first wave of Africanist political science. Nationalism was perceived as the quintessential creation of the modern elite, in simultaneous revolt against the dead hand of tradition and the live weight of alien rule. What character-ized the nationalist leadership was its origins in the Western school system, its links to Christian missions, and its ties to the urban sector. This strate-gically located category, fashioned by the apparatus of ideological hege-mony of the colonial state, possessed the unique capacity to grasp the multiple grievances that alien rule engendered at all levels of civil society and to formulate them in a discourse of universal resonance. Hidden for future discovery was the inarticulate major premise of an identity of inter-est between an elite not yet stigmatized as a petite bourgeoisie on the road to class power and the mass of the populace.

Nationalism in Africa was thus constituted, in this symbiosis between its practitioners and its scholars, as triumphant discourse of political decolo-nization and as ascendant paradigm for an emergent Africanist social sci-ence. Although the moment of African independence is frequently cited as the apogee of "modernization theory" or "structural-functionalism" in American political science, close inspection of the actual pattern of African-ist scholarship reveals the inadequacy of this notion.[19] The Coleman-Halisi survey of journal articles published by American political scientists between 1953 and 1982 in five major journals shows that only 3.6 percent were devoted to "political development" or "modernization" theory.[20] The more powerful model shaping scholarship was simply nationalism. The corpus of colonial knowledge, so deeply burdened by the overpowering assumption of European rule as the highest evolutionary stage, required deconstruction. Historians, armed with oral methodologies, sought to rediscover the African past and validate the African cultural heritage. Anthropologists turned from the standard ethnography, with its suddenly troubling axiom of an "anthropological present" extending backward and forward, to seek out social change. And political scientists, for a generation, clamped onto the political party as a privileged object of inquiry.

The logic of this elective affinity of the discipline and the movement corresponded to the impact of nationalism as paradigm. The most fundamental vector driving political change was nationalist protest; its organizational vehicle was the political party. Appearing simultaneously with African independence was a generation of monographs devoted to political parties, many of admirable quality.[21] Parties were thus historically the chosen instrument for understanding African reality. But not all parties equally expressed the progressive purposes of history; the chosen carrier of destiny was the mass single party whose transformational potential and democratic possibilities, however contradicted by subsequent performance, were eloquently argued at the time by Hodgkin, Wallerstein, and Morgenthau in particular.[22]

Nationalism as the ideology of anticolonial struggle followed the pathway of liberation around the continent to the final bastions of intransigent imperial resistance and white minority domination, in the former Portuguese territories, Zimbabwe, Namibia, and South Africa. In the process the doctrine acquired enhanced sophistication from some of the lessons of the initial decolonizations, first drawn by Frantz Fanon in his biting polemic *The Wretched of the Earth*,[23] where he argued that a petite bourgeoisie might appropriate the benefits of independence. The most subtle and profound of the later contributors was doubtless Amilcar Cabral, whose class and ethnic analysis was far more penetrating than any of the earlier texts. His summons to the petite bourgeoisie to "commit class suicide," however unrealistic, was nonetheless a clear-sighted recognition of the deepening gap between the state class and civil society in independent Africa.[24]

At the very moment of its greatest triumph—the liquidation of European empire in Africa—the talismanic force of nationalism began to ebb away. Little by little, its commanding role as prime mover of historical process and shaper of scholarly paradigms eroded. To some extent its seeming success made the nationalist perspective less imperative. Struggle against colonially constructed knowledge no longer seemed urgent; as Catherine Coquery-Vidrovitch playfully observed, in explaining her abandonment of her earlier theory of an "African mode of production," such a notion no longer had the pertinence it enjoyed when the "affirmation of the very existence of African societies and history" was crucial.[25] But the phenomenal intellectual distance traveled in the three decades since independence goes beyond the simple loss of standing of a discourse. Emblematic of the long journey between African nationalism as expressed by the independence generation and portrayed by Coleman, Hodgkin, and others and the present is the 1990 cri de coeur of Basil Davidson, scholar-activist whose career has been devoted to the cause of African liberation, whose successive struggles he has so eloquently chronicled. Nationalism, in the form that it took, was at bottom a "mystification" which arose "from the delusions of its ideologues: delusions transformed into realities which, when examined, transform themselves back into delusions." In this dispiriting metamorphosis the idea of nationalism changed from icon of liberation to captive doctrine of an African nation-state which, Davidson continued, "has become a lifeless shell of bureaucratic or personal tyranny, corruption and defeat."[26] Equally symbolic of profoundly altered circumstance was the 1990 Algerian election, which saw the historical nationalism incarnated by the Front de Liberation Nationale, architect of the independence war which contributed so much to African liberation, sent to stunning defeat by the Front Islamique de Salut, bearer of a very different vision. So radical a change summons our contemplation.

Davidson identified one important factor: "This nationalism, alienated from its peoples' history in order to adopt another history, a European history, emerged as the opposite of its legitimating self." The idea of nationalism that was constructed borrowed too heavily from an alien text in tying its liberation project to conquest of the central institutions of colonial power and seeking their legitimation as nation-state. Because, as a tactical necessity, independence could only be efficaciously pursued through the territorial frame of the colonial partition, the weapon of history, so critical to the nationalist *mythomoteur* elsewhere, was a two-edged sword for African nationalists. The contemporary emissaries of the African past were the chiefs and religious notables for the most part effectively co-opted as colonial intermediaries, a group the nationalist generation generally viewed as adversaries. The other face of history was etched in the ethnocultural diversity of the territorial units seeking independence. Thus African nationalists readily absorbed European stereotypes about historical heritage as stagnant tradition. "They presented themselves as the instruments of dynamic change, but on the basis of an inert or useless past," Davidson noted, "an alienation from history . . . that was to hamstring their democratic aspirations."[27]

Historical heritage was at times invoked, but in highly generalized fashion. Cheikh Anta Diop proposed a global reinterpretation of history, suggesting Africa as source of civilization with a Black Egypt as center of diffusion. Aimé Césaire and Léopold Senghor deduced from a common African heritage the theory of negritude, arguing that a unique set of naturalistic, nonmaterial values suffused African culture. The exegesis of African religious beliefs, arguing a common philosophical culture, by Franciscan missionary Placide Tempels supplied useful themes for nationalist thought, which were appropriated by Nkrumah among others.[28] Past glories of historical African states were invoked, but especially those safely in the past: the medieval kingdoms of Ghana and Mali, for example, were exhumed by new states unconnected by lineage with these empires as legitimating designations. But none of this selective use of the past invalidates Davidson's point: "Africa's past achievements could be useful as food for anti-colonial argument—essentially . . . anti-racist argument—but could offer no useable design for political action. . . . Hence the African past was not to be remodelled and reconstructed, but utterly renounced as being, in sorrowful fact, useless to the future and obstructive in the present."[29]

The marriage of nationalism to the postcolonial state, ineluctable but no less fateful, emptied the doctrine of much of its populist content over time. The abiding fear of ruling classes of politicized ethnicity—however much they might employ ethnic security maps in the inner corridors of power—dictated unitarian versions of nationalism, and generalization of the single-party system was intended to institutionalize this image of society. The essential mission of nationalism was now to legitimate state power and those that exercised it. As the expectations created by the promises of militant nationalism gave way to disappointment, disillusionment, and—by 1990 in much of Africa—despair, state-based nationalism had a hollow ring. The idea, of course, remains as an available component in a populist critique of incumbents or as an element in the resentment directed at alien forces partly responsible for Africa's distress. But the exhilarating sense of future promise contained in the nationalist idea of the 1950s is denatured by its association with patrimonial autocracies ruling states viewed by their societies as predators.

The obsessive concern with "national integration" as the fulfillment of nationalism that has been common to the postcolonial state has had some effect. William Miles and David Rochefort have presented fascinating data showing that Hausa villagers on either side of the Niger-Nigeria frontier each attached much more significance to their national identity than to their shared ethnicity (at least in response to survey questions).[30] Africa is unique in the degree to which ethnicity has been successfully stigmatized as tribalism and rejected as a legitimate basis for making formal claims upon the political system. On a regional level the superior claims of the territorial state are reflected in quickly asserted norms of the African international system. The Pan-African idea itself was domesticated by the state system through its institutionalization in the Organization of African Unity (OAU). The 1963 OAU Charter enshrined territorial integrity and the inviolability of frontiers as a foundational principle of the African state system. Its 1964 summit went further to assert defense of territorial integrity principles as a basic obligation of African states, a position which goes well beyond global doctrines of the law of nations.[31] But not only is ethnic self-determination categorically excluded; equally proscribed is the overt use of ethnicity as a basis for political organization. As African states come to terms with their own social environments, the view so widely held in the original version of nationalism equating ethnicity with backwardness has doubtless softened. But wherever multiple parties are contemplated, ethnic, regional, or re-ligious labels are invariably prohibited (in Nigeria, Guinea, Senegal, for example). Such policies evoke no protest; on the contrary, opposition intel-lectuals applaud these measures. The contrast with Asia and Europe, in this respect, is striking. Yet another illustration of the impact of African na-tionalist thought upon generalized social understandings is the lexicon employed for cultural pluralism; with the sole exception of Ethiopia, which was influenced under Mengistu by Soviet nationality theory, everyday dis-course labels cultural solidarities as ethnicity (or tribalism), almost never as nationalism.

Nationalism, in its marriage with the state, wed at the same time the state class. A class dimension to the idea of nationalism is one of its uni-versal properties. Marx was perhaps the first to discern a relationship be-tween class and nationalism, in reaching the conclusion, as Walker Connor has summarized it, that "nationalism is everywhere a bourgeois ideology pressed into service by that class in order to divert the proletariat from realizing its own class consciousness and interests."[32] While greatly under-estimating the potential of the doctrine to acquire a mass following, Marx pointed in the right direction in identifying the source of the idea. The rise of nationalism from the French Revolution onward is intimately associated with the emergence of a new commercial, industrial, and professional middle class, from whose midst the intellectuals who fashioned the ideology emerged.[33] In Africa their counterparts were the "modern elites" identified by Coleman as carriers of the nationalist idea. In different terms, in their role as activists leading the political parties, they were characterized by Richard Sklar as a "rising class."[34] Subsequently, as the configuration of postcolonial politics became clearer, Sklar argued—and most analysis since has followed—that in Africa "class relations, at bottom, are determined by relations of power, not production."[35] The dominant class, thus, is determined by its hold on state power; in turn, this class becomes the principal advocate and main beneficiary of the idea of nationalism, as it has been appropriated as state ideology.

Finally, in looking backward at nationalism as it seemed to its first students, one need note the difference in intellectual conjuncture. The classical studies of nationalism—Carleton Hayes, Hans Kohn, Alfred Cobban, and others[36]—adopted a historical and philosophical approach; they had, as subliminal problematic, a sense of the pathology of the nationalisms that provoked repeated Balkan crises and triggered the two world wars. Rupert Emerson and others, in their exegesis of Asian and African nationalism, sought to draw a distinction between aggressive and destructive nationalism in Europe, which deserved its reputation as "the last refuge of scoundrels," and a liberating nationalism in the Third World, which "intrudes itself not only with an aura of inevitability but also as the bearer of positive goods."[37]

Strikingly different is the intellectual gestalt of the most influential recent studies of nationalism, such as those of Ernest Gellner and Benedict Anderson. Influenced by recent currents in neo-Marxist and poststructuralist debate, these works reflect upon the cultural determinants shaping the idea of nationalism, located in contemporary macrohistorical context. For Anderson, the phenomenal political power of nationalism as idea contrasts strangely with its "philosophical poverty and even incoherence . . . nationalism has never produced its own grand thinkers: no Hobbeses, Tocquevilles, Marxes, or Webers." The nation, for Anderson, is an "imagined community," a cultural creation, defined by its boundedness, faced with the "other," and by its inherent sovereignty. The conditions for its emergence, unique to the modern era, are print capitalism, with the vast anonymities through which collective imagination can be communicated, and the decline of religious dominance over consciousness formation. A dynamic was thus unleashed in which, argued Gellner, the very notion of a "man without a nation" strains "the modern imagination . . . defies the recognized categories and provokes revulsion. . . . A man must have a nationality as he must have a nose and two ears; a deficiency in any of these particulars is not inconceivable and does from time to time occur, but only as a result of some disaster, and it is itself a disaster of a kind." Further, Gellner added, "nations, like states, are a contingency, and not a universal necessity." Yet nationalism holds that states and nations "were destined for each other; that either without the other is incomplete, and constitutes a tragedy."[38]

From this perspective the troubled trajectory of nationalism in postcolonial Africa becomes clearer. "Nation" as an imagined community of anticolonial combat, to whose creation scholars as well as activists contributed, was relatively unproblematic, even if its precise definition was elusive. But "nation," once independence was won, required the postcolonial state as vehicle: thus its imperative of "national integration." However, the mood of disengagement that progressively permeated civil society eventually drove the popular imagination in new directions deeply subversive to the imagined community of liberation struggle. The state as bearer of the idea of nation takes refuge in what Achille Mbembe has labeled a *principe autoritaire*. In response, the citizenry flees into an astonishing assortment of religious and other shelters: "Bref, l'indigène recourt, comme à l'époque coloniale, a toutes les ressources de ce qu'il faut bien appeler sa *capacité historique à l'indiscipline*. . . . *Partout, la délinquance d'Etat a produit une culture de débrouillardise et de sauve-qui-peut et un déclin de l'identité citoyenne*."[39]

This leads us to the other potent form of consciousness in contemporary African politics, ethnicity. Here the contrast in perspective is even more dramatic than with respect to nationalism. Particularly striking is the simultaneous, though sometimes reluctant, recognition that ethnicity existed as a problem and the absence in most works by the nationalist apogee of any sustained reflection upon its nature. The corpus of Coleman writings stands out as an important exception. His initial steps toward conceptualization of ethnicity, even if incompletely developed, were a major intellectual accomplishment, all the more impressive because they swam against the theoretical currents of the time.[40]

More characteristic was the dismissive view of Colin Leys, in explaining why in a long treatise on Kenyan politics, composed in the "dependency theory" phase of his intellectual journey, he chose to largely ignore so central a factor in Kenyan politics. "So far," he wrote, "nothing has been said about 'tribalism.' It is tempting to leave it that way." Invocation of this variable, he suggested, reflects an ideological bias on the part of its analysts, akin to earlier racialist arguments that Africans had "smaller brains."[41] This profoundly revealing passage supplies much of the explanation for the banalization of ethnicity in many works of the nationalist conjuncture. The lexical choice is itself consequential; *tribalism* carries connotations of backwardness, traditionality, and illegitimacy that are purely intentional. The imputation of ideological motivation to those who might examine the phenomenon here refers not simply to the normative dimension ineradicable from social science but to a more malicious form which is the special property of "bourgeois" or "neocolonial" analysis, contaminated by racism.

At the time of independence struggle, excessive preoccupation with ethnicity indeed risked playing into the hands of the imperial enemy, fond of invoking cultural divisions as a pretext for prolongation of colonial rule. Nationalist leaders at that moment, while fully cognizant of the phenomenon, for the most part shared a sublime faith in the progressive capacity of nationalism to transcend it. Sékou Touré spoke for a generation in 1959 when he said, "In three or four years, no one will remember the tribal, ethnic or religious rivalries which, in the recent past, caused so much damage to our country and its population."[42]

The powerful grip that the idea of progress then held upon the scholarly as well as the popular mind enters in.[43] This evolutionary perspective engendered the pervasive modern / traditional dichotomy basic to all paradigms of the day, drawing upon the classical texts of historical sociology: status versus contract (Henry Maine), community versus society (Ferdinand Tönnies), organic versus mechanical solidarity (Emile Durkheim). In this implicit social Darwinism, modernity was both imperative norm and historically determined outcome. In the field of consciousness, nationalism necessarily represented the progressive side of the dichotomy, with ethnicity deconstructed as tribalism the retrogressive side. The beneficent determination of macrohistorical process, with nation and state as prime agents, might be delayed or even derailed by the forces of reactionary tribalism in particular circumstances: all the more reason for the scholar to give it no analytical quarter.

But more was involved than the simple hegemony of particular paradigms at one moment in intellectual history. The world of states, in their unfolding dialectic with the cultural plurality of the great majority, stood at a remarkable conjuncture where the nation seemed to enjoy unparalleled ascendancy. World War II—and in a different way perhaps the Great Depression that preceded it—had a deeply unifying effect on those polities most directly involved. The postwar settlement, with its large-scale redrawing of the European political map and its demographic redistributions through large-scale deportations and resettlements, had produced a historically unprecedented degree of cultural homogeneity in the European state system. Anticolonial nationalism in Asia and Africa, though at times divided by communalism, as in India, nonetheless was predominantly unitarian in appearance. If the creole elites in Latin America who led the nineteenth-century revolt against Spain had created nations of Spanish administrative subdivisions, why could not Afro-Asian nationalists do the same?

The voice of revendicative cultural pluralism was remarkably still. In the United States the 1924 immigration act had shut off sources of Euro-ethnicity for four decades, and effective politization of the minority voice was yet to occur; meanwhile the highly assimilative pedagogy of the state through its socialization apparatus worked effectively. The Soviet Union persuaded itself and others that the "nationality question had been solved" by astute ideological dialectics, co-optive opportunities for collaborative non-Russian party elites, and the formidable coercive apparatus of state socialism. The seductive force of this myth misled even such canny politicians as Michael Gorbachev.[44] In Western Europe ethnonationalism was perceived as the folkloric retreat of small-town antiquarians, clerical reactionaries, and unreconstructed royalists. In this setting national integration as midwife of progress seemed so natural as to be beyond discussion.

Thus some of the pacesetter studies of liberation politics in Africa virtually ignored ethnicity; such, for example, was the case with Hodgkin in his masterful monographs on nationalism and political parties.[45] Apter, although constructing an elaborate theory of political change based upon comparison of Ashanti and Buganda, viewed them exclusively as political structures bearing broadly categorized value systems, and not as forms of consciousness.[46] Aristida Zolberg noted the importance of ethnicity as a structural basis for the organizational dynamic of the Parti Démocratique de la Côte d'Ivoire (PDCI) but did not explore the sources of consciousness. Wallerstein in a discerning analysis recognized the new dynamic of ethnic consciousness formation in the urban crucibles but remained enclosed within a vision of nationalism as progress; the new urban ethnicity is explained as a step in "detribalization," through its displacement of presumptively real traditional consciousness with an artificial and transitional form, destined for transcendance by a yet higher evolutionary form of identity, the nation and its mass single party.[47]

Here one must again stress that there was virtually no body of theory concerning ethnicity upon which this generation of studies might have drawn. "Colonial science" constructed a wooden and unusable model of "tribal man" in Africa. There existed, for purposes of drawing administrative subdivisions within colonial territories, a normative map in the alien mind, into which discrete ethnic units could be distributed, with due regard for colonial security calculus. Thorough administrative inquest and competent bureaucratic sifting and winnowing of ethnographic data would permit successful tribal cartography. A similar subliminal perspective shaped colonial anthropology, eloquently denounced by Aidan Southall.[48] The classical anthropological demarche began by assuming the unit, looking to its central zone for a site for participant observation, then monographically projecting the findings from the village upon an entire "tribe."

Only in the 1950s did more subtle analyses appear, most notably from urban Zambia.[49] Paul Mercier pursued a similar line of analysis in examining urban ethnicity, viewed as "retribalization" or "supertribalization."[50] Important insights into the contemporary dynamic of identity formation are found in these studies, although they remained rooted in the premise of the modern / traditional dichotomy. More broadly, the inventory of comparative studies offered virtually nothing on which to build an understanding of ethnicity in Africa. Older studies of nationalism had focused upon the ideological and philosophical dimensions and the political history of nationalist movements. Studies of ethnicity and cultural pluralism focused upon assimilation,[51] examined forms of prejudice and stratication in racially divided societies,[52] or postulated a rigid and hierarchical array of self-enclosed cultural units.[53] None of these approaches yielded much that could be applied to the dynamics of ethnicity in Africa; there should be no surprise in noting their absence from the bibliographies of the first-generation studies of African nationalism.

The originality of Coleman's effort to achieve conceptual purchase on ethnicity becomes the more noteworthy set against this analytical void. He identified several important sources of ethnic consciousness. Urban environment was one; the new social requirements of the city induced the creation of ethnic associations to serve a multitude of purposes: self-help, rite de passage assistance (birth, marriage, funeral), mutual aid, communal representation and voice. The political structuration of ethnic units (real or imagined) for purposes of colonial local administration, particularly within the indirect rule doctrine, embedded identity within an institutional frame, especially in historically centralized African states. In African responses to colonial oppression, the drive to validate African culture as refutation of European racism partly stimulated the creation of ethnic charters. Finally, political competition played a crucial role; "new élites tend to gravitate to their ethnic or racial group of origin as a base and springboard from which to assert their leadership in the larger political order." In so doing, "they are . . . in a better position to manipulate and control the unaccultur-ated masses of their own group through the adaptation or perversion of traditional magico-religious symbols and sanctions with which they are familiar."[54]

Coleman's choice of Nigeria for his study of nationalist politics admit-tedly compelled analysis of the ethnic factor. In his Nigeria study Cole-man—to my knowledge alone of Africanist scholars at this time—referred to the large ethnoregional clusters as "nationalities" and the crystallization of ethnic political competition in the 1950s as the "regionalization" of na-tionalism. This clearly separated his conceptualization from the restrictive modern / traditional distinction between nationalism and ethnicity that characterized virtually all other works at the time. Although Coleman occasionally characterized "tribe" as "traditional," he also insisted that eth-noregionalism was driven by the "same passionate quest for modernity and equality which formed so crucial an ingredient in the motivation of Nige-rian nationalists."[55] Differing rates of success in this quest were identified as a key driving factor in mobilizing ethnic consciousness. Some ethnic com-munities—the Ibo were the paradigmatic example—by the 1950s had ac-quired a highly visible strategic lead in "modern" roles, whether by cultural propensity, psychological predisposition to change, or fortunate access to mobility opportunities.[56] In his final contribution on this subject, Coleman added the situational dimension: the ebb and flow of ethnic consciousness in function of social circumstance, the critical impact of political context in defining ethnic response.[57]

Three decades later a vast corpus of ethnicity literature has emerged; comparative ethnicity has become a recognizable interdisciplinary subfield, with its own array of journals, none of which existed at the time Coleman was laying the foundations (for example, *Ethnic and Racial Studies, Plural Societies, Canadian Review of Studies of Nationalism, Journal of Ethnic Studies*). I have no intention of undertaking a comprehensive review of the Africa-focused segment of this material but wish to extract from what Coleman and Halisi termed its "insatiable claim" to analytical attention three ma-jor themes—instrumentalism, primordialism, and constructivism—which emerged in the three postindependence decades.[58]

This cumulation of knowledge concerning ethnicity in action draws upon the political events of the postcolonial era, when the ethnic factor was less submerged, empirically and normatively, by the imperatives of anti-colonial struggle. It bears the imprint of a global conjuncture far different from that of the first generation of African political studies. "Melting pot" theories of ethnicity have long outlived their credibility as well as their utility, as Nathan Glazer and Daniel P. Moynihan observed pointedly in the American context.[59] The delusion that Lenin and his heirs had solved the Soviet nationality problem that captured not only the USSR ruling class but also most external observers began evaporating in the face of the new transparencies of *glasnost* and utterly vanished in the spectacular 1991 collapse of the Soviet Union as created by Lenin and Stalin. The cultural plurality of the overwhelming majority of sovereign entities in the world system of states has become newly apparent, as the limitations of nation-state ideologies of national integration stand revealed. Ethnicity can no longer be viewed as a transitional problem awaiting final solution by nationcraft; in most polities it is an enduring element of the social environment, calling for creative formulas of civil coexistence. The powerful tides of democratization and liberalization that began to flow throughout the globe in the 1980s altered in fundamental ways the arena of ethnic conflict and breathed new life into the explosive doctrine of self-determination. The remarkably long era of stability of the territorial basis of the world state system after World War II seemed to come to an end at the beginning of the 1990s, with the breakup of Ethiopia, Yugoslavia, and the USSR; a number of long-standing states in their present form are also now problematic (Canada, Sri Lanka, Sudan, Cyprus, and Somalia, to name but a few). These broader forces necessarily impinged upon the process of the "invention of Africa," in the scholarly mind.

The first stage was dominated by a perspective toward ethnicity retrospectively labeled instrumentalism. Building upon the insights of Coleman and others, its contributors privileged the uses of ethnicity as a weapon in political combat and social competition.[60] Ethnicity was contingent, situational, and circumstantial; it was an available identity in a repertoire of social roles for use in the pursuit of material advantage. Such a conceptualization beckoned exploration of the political factors that might induce its activation, the cultural entrepreneurs who supplied its doctrine, and the activists who exploited these solidarities.[61] The instrumentalist school of analysis achieved a substantial audience in part because its stress upon material factors rendered it compatible with important paradigms exerting a powerful influence upon Africanist political science that were emerging at the same time as ethnicity was emerging as a subject: neo-Marxism and rational choice. For the neo-Marxist the centrality of class could be affirmed while according recognition to ethnicity as a subsidiary vector through the mediation of instrumentalism. Ethnicity, from this perspective, could be seen as a form of consciousness, if not false at least not fundamental, available for manipulation by petit bourgeois politicians pursuing class interest.[62] For the rational choice theorist, the view that, as Charles Keyes expressed it, "ethnicity is salient only insofar as it serves to orient people in the pursuit of other interests vis-à-vis other people seen as holding contrastive ethnic identities"[63] serves as a password opening the door to its analytical appropriation.[64]

The sheer fluidity and flux of ethnicity in Africa lent powerful support to the instrumentalist premise. Yet something important was missing in this perspective, an element which the primordialists sought to supply. A. L. Epstein, whose early Copperbelt inquiry provided building blocks for instrumentalist analysis,[65] pointed to "the powerful emotional charge that appears to surround or to underlie so much of ethnic behavior; and it is this affective dimension of the problem that seems to me lacking in so many recent attempts to tackle it."[66] Freud, in reflecting upon his own Jewish cultural identity, described it in evocative words as "many obscure emotional forces which were the more powerful the less they could be expressed in words, as well as a clear consciousness of inner identity, the safe privacy of an inner mental construct."[67] Harold Isaacs, in an influential comparative essay, gave systematic exposition to the primordialist perspective in its psychological guise, stressing the "ineffable significance" and "peculiarly coercive powers" of an identity search seen as "a desperate effort to regain the condition of life in which certain needs were met, to get behind walls that enclose them once more, if only in their minds, in a place where they can feel they belong, and where, grouped with their kind, they can regain some measure of what feels like physical and emotional safety."[68]

Cultural anthropologists followed a different pathway to primordiality. Geertz, a major contributor, stressed the culture-creating disposition of our species. Humans, born as incomplete animals, complete themselves through the culture they create, which then becomes a primordial given of social existence.[69] For Keyes, ethnicity as primordiality "derives from a cultural interpretation of descent."[70] For Fredrik Barth, the essence of identity lay in the array of symbols, cues, and basic value orientations by which groups recognize themselves and perceive their distinctiveness from "the other."[71] The boundary is the essence, not a trait list or a set of instrumental uses.

The most extreme version of primordialism was contributed by the sociobiologists. Pierre van den Berghe argued that ethnicity is, at bottom, "an extended form of kin selection" and thus related to elemental instinctual urges of the species. R. Paul Shaw and Yuwa Wong went further to argue that the capacity to recognize members of the kindred was critical to survival in the early evolution of the species; thus, a consciousness of group affinity is not just socially learned but imprinted in the genetic code.[72]

Primordialism, thus, completed instrumentalism by explaining the power of the "affective tie" through which interest is pursued.[73] It captured the passionate dimension latent in ethnic conflict, its capacity to arouse deep fears, anxieties, and insecurities and to trigger collective aggression inexplicable in terms of simple material pursuit of interest. The synthesis with instrumentalism which the primordialist perspective invites is reflected in recent work.[74]

The third, and most recent, orientation one might label constructivist. The interrogation proposed by constructivists adopted the same point of departure as the "imagined communities" notion in the Anderson explication of nationalism.[75] Jean Loup Amselle summoned us to "deconstruct ethnicity," to invert the démarche of the instrumentalists and the primordialists, whose pattern of explanation either takes ethnic unit for granted and unravels its mobilization or defines the unit in terms of a set of cultural givens. Instead, ethnic group itself should be seen as the problematic entity: "Rather than beginning with given ethnonyms, as empty notions which requiring filling with economic, political and religious structures, it would be preferable to demonstrate how a term located in time and space acquires progressively a multiplicity of meanings, in sum to establish the genesis of symbols in the realm of ideas."[76] Thus, the essence of the problematic is the creation of ethnicity.

The constructivist inverts the logic of the instrumentalist and primordialist, both of whom presume the existence of communal consciousness, either as weapon in pursuit of collective advantage or as inner essence. The constructivist sees ethnicity as the product of human agency, a creative social act through which such commonalities as speech code, cultural practice, ecological adaptation, and political organization become woven into a consciousness of shared identity. Once a threshold is reached, the consciousness may become to a degree self-reproducing at a group level but continue to be contingent for the individual, who remains engaged in an ongoing process of transacting and redefining identity. The constructivist thus places higher stress on contingency, flux, and change of identity than the other two major approaches would concede.

Leroy Vail, in his introduction to a seminal collection of essays, well summarized the approach:

> The creation of ethnicity as an ideological statement of popular appeal in the context of profound social, economic and political change in southern Africa was the result of the differential conjunction of various historical forces and phenomena. It is the very unevenness of their co-appearance and dynamic interaction that accounts for the unevenness of ethnic consciousness in the region. One may discern three such variables in the creation and implanting of the ethnic message. First, as was the case in the creation of such ideologies elsewhere, for example in nineteenth century European nationalism, it was essential to have a group of intellectuals involved in formulating it—a group of culture brokers. Second, there was the widespread use of African intermediaries to administer the subordinate peoples, a system usually summed up in the phrase "indirect rule," and this served to define the boundaries and texture of the new ideologies. Third, ordinary people had a real need for so-called "traditional values" at a time of rapid social change, thus opening the way for the wide acceptance of the new ideologies.[77]

The nub of the matter, then, was to grasp ethnicity "as manufactured rather than as given, as innovative rather than as atavistic."[78] The multiple mechanisms by which it evolved and redefined itself were located at all levels of state and society; ethnicity was an unfolding manipulation of social space by both dominators and dominated. Consciousness over time tended to project itself upon larger social spaces, widely employing the metaphor of kinship. In Peter Ekeh's view, ethnicity as collective imagination was above all the "crystallization of kinship systems into ethnic groups," driven by distrust and insecurity engendered by successive political instances: slave-raiding mercantile states, the colonial state, and its post-colonial successor.[79]

Applied to a given case—let us take the Igbo in Nigeria—the instrumentalist perspective leads to a focus upon identity politics in what Nigerians often describe as "slicing the national cake": the struggle to ensure that the Igbo community receives a serving of national resources commensurate with its size and worth. The primordialist inquiry might search for innate cultural properties—for example, the oft-cited argument that Igbo customary values and structure predisposed the group for competitive success in a market economy—of the psychic vectors of ethnic consciousness that bred the deepening fears and insecurities leading to the 1967 secession effort. The constructivist analysis queries how Igbohood became an active and power-ful form of collective consciousness, when a century ago it clearly was not.

In so doing, constructivism superimposed a new and promising analyt-ical overlay upon the emergent synthesis of instrumentalism and primor-dialism. Cumulatively, these three approaches offer a rich array of intel-lectual resources for conceptualizing ethnicity. Further, they measure the distance traveled beyond the virtual theoretical void confronting Coleman in exploring the "regionalization of nationalism."

The very vacuum—conceptual and empirical—at the point of departure created an intellectual moment when exhilarating dreams of a liberated tomorrow could mold perceptions of the social forces of today on the threshold of a brilliant destiny, the vision of a nationalism triumphant. Reality has progressively intruded into the reflections of political activist and academic analyst alike. Nationalism has vanished as paradigm and bears more subdued hues as ideology. Ethnicity—as ideology and con-sciousness—acquires a deference as intellectual object which corresponds to its transparent impact in the real world of empirical events.

Notes

1. James S. Coleman and C. R. D. Halisi, "American Political Science and Tropical Africa: Universalism vs. Relativism," *African Studies Review* 26, nos. 3 / 4 (Sept. / Dec. 1983): 25–62. See also, for example, Jean-François Bayart, *L'état en Afrique: La politique du ventre* (Paris: Fayard, 1989); Donald Rothchild and Naomi Chazan, eds., *The Precarious Balance: State and Society in Africa* (Boulder, Colo., and London: Westview Press, 1988); Achille Mbembe, *Afriques indociles: Christianisme, pouvoir et état en societe postcoloniale* (Paris: Karthala, 1988); Thomas Callaghy, *The State-Society Struggle: Zaire in Comparative Perspective* (New York: Columbia Univ. Press, 1984); Crawford Young and Thomas Turner, *The Rise and Decline of the Zairian State* (Madison: Univ. of Wisconsin Press, 1985); Naomi Chazan, *An Anatomy of Ghanaian Politics: Managing Political Recession, 1969–1982* (Boulder, Colo.: Westview Press, 1982); Zaki Ergas, ed., *The African State in Transition* (New York: St. Martin's Press, 1987); Nelson Kasfir, ed., *State and Class in Africa* (London: Frank Cass, 1984); Joel S. Migdal, *Strong Societies and Weak States: State-Society Relations and State Capabilities in the Third World* (Princeton, N.J.: Princeton Univ. Press, 1988).

2. The early Coleman writings upon which I draw include above all his magistral work *Nigeria: Background to Nationalism* (Berkeley: Univ. of California Press, 1958); other important articles and essays include "Nationalism in Colonial Africa," *American Politi-cal Science Review* 68 (1954): 404–26; "The Problem of Political Integration in Emergent Africa," *Western Political Quarterly* 8, no. 1 (March 1955): 44–57; "The Emergence of

African Political Parties," in *Africa Today,* ed. C. Grove Haines (Baltimore: Johns Hopkins Univ. Press, 1955), pp. 225–56; "The Politics of Sub-Saharan Africa," in *The Politics of the Developing Areas,* ed. Gabriel A. Almond and James S. Coleman (Princeton, N.J.: Princeton Univ. Press, 1960), pp. 247–368.

3. Quoted in R. D. Pearce, *The Turning Point in Africa: British Colonial Policy, 1938–1948* (London: Frank Cass, 1982), pp. 42–67.

4. Lord Hailey, *An African Survey,* rev. ed. (London: Oxford Univ. Press, 1957), p. 251.

5. J. M. Lee and Martin Petter, *The Colonial Office, War, and Development Policy* (London: Maurice Temple Smith, 1982), pp. 115–42.

6. David E. Apter, *Ghana in Transition* (New York: Atheneum, 1963), p. x.

7. Coleman, "Nationalism in Colonial Africa," p. 424.

8. Thomas Hodgkin, *Nationalism in Colonial Africa* (London: Frederick Muller, 1956).

9. Sir Apolo Kagwa (Buganda), Alexis Kagame (royalist Tutsi), Samuel Johnson (Yoruba), J. M. Serbah (Fanti), J. B. Danquah (Ashanti).

10. Coleman, "Nationalism in Tropical Africa," p. 407.

11. Coleman, *Nigeria,* pp. 419–27.

12. Thomas Hodgkin, "A Note on the Language of African Nationalism," in *African Affairs,* ed. Kenneth Kirkwood (London: Chatto and Windus, 1961), reprinted in William John Hanna, ed., *Independent Black Africa: The Politics of Freedom* (Chicago: Rand McNally, 1964), pp. 236–37.

13. Coleman, "Nationalism in Tropical Africa," p. 425.

14. For example, Kwame Nkrumah, *I Speak of Freedom: A Statement of African Ideology* (New York: Praeger, 1961), and his more pretentious, ghosted philosophical text, *Consciencism: Philosophy and Ideology for Decolonization and Development with Particular Reference to the African Revolution* (London: Heinemann, 1964); Léopold Sédar Senghor, *On African Socialism* (New York: Praeger, 1964); Julius K. Nyerere, *Ujamaa: Essays on Socialism* (London: Oxford Univ. Press, 1968).

15. Hodgkin, *Nationalism in Colonial Africa,* pp. 16–17.

16. The sole citations to studies of nationalism elsewhere are to G. Antonius, *The Arab Awakening* (1938; rept. New York: Capricorn Books, 1965), and George M. Kahin, *Nationalism and Revolution in Indonesia* (Ithaca, N.Y.: Cornell Univ. Press, 1952).

17. Karl W. Deutsch, *Nationalism and Social Communication: An Inquiry into the Foundations of Nationality* (Cambridge: MIT Press, 1953).

18. The magnum opus by Rupert Emerson, *From Empire to Nation: The Rise to Self-Assertion of African and Asian Peoples* (Cambridge: Harvard Univ. Press, 1960), on which he had labored for many years, was published after Coleman's work on nationalism.

19. As one of innumerable examples which might be cited, see Goran Hyden, "Governance: A New Approach to Comparative Politics," paper presented to the 31st annual meeting of the African Studies Association, Chicago, Oct. 28–31, 1988. Ironically, Hyden's own first major study, *TANU yajenga nchi: Political Development in Rural Tanzania* (Lund, Sweden: Bokforlaget Universitet och Skola, 1966), while employing the categories of structural-functionalism, is above all shaped by the commitment to the nationalist paradigm.

20. Coleman and Halisi, "American Political Science and Tropical Africa," pp. 28–29.

Certainly a larger fraction were influenced by the analytical categories supplied by structural-functionalism, but I believe this figure does reflect the fact that the Social Science Research Council Committee on Comparative Politics, primary sponsor of the structural-functional model, had greater impact on seminar discussions than empirical research.

21. Among the most influential were Thomas Hodgkin, *African Political Parties: An Introductory Guide* (Harmondsworth, Middlesex: Penguin Books, 1961); James S. Coleman and Carl G. Rosberg, eds., *Political Parties and National Integration in Tropical Africa* (Berkeley: Univ. of California Press, 1964); Richard Sklar, *Nigerian Political Parties: Power in an Emergent African Nation* (Princeton, N.J.: Princeton Univ. Press, 1963); Ruth Schachter Morgenthau, *Political Parties in French-Speaking West Africa* (Oxford: Clarendon Press, 1964); Immanuel Wallerstein, *Africa: The Politics of Independence, an Interpretation of Modern African History* (New York: Vintage Books, 1961); Aristide R. Zolberg, *One-Party Government in the Ivory Coast* (Princeton, N.J.: Princeton Univ. Press, 1964); René Lemarchand, *Political Awakening in the Congo* (Berkeley: Univ. of California Press, 1964); Henry Bienen, *Tanzania: Party Transformation and Economic Development* (Princeton, N.J.: Princeton Univ. Press, 1970).

22. Hodgkin, *African Political Parties;* Wallerstein, *Africa: The Politics of Independence;* Morgenthau, *Political Parties in French-Speaking West Africa.*

23. First published in French as Frantz Fanon, *Les damnés de la terre* (Paris: Maspero, 1961).

24. Amilcar Cabral, *Revolution in Guinea, an African People's Struggle: Selected Texts* (New York: Monthly Review Press, 1969).

25. Catherine Coquery-Vidrovitch, "Reflexions d'historienne," in Bogumil Jewsiewicki and J. Letourneau, eds., *Mode of Production: The Challenge of Africa* (Ste-Foy, Quebec: SAFI, 1985), p. 13.

26. Basil Davidson, "The Challenge of Comparative Analysis: Anti-Imperialist Nationalism in Africa and Europe," paper presented to conference on state crisis in Eastern Europe and Africa, Bellagio, Italy, Feb. 1990, pp. 4, 13.

27. Ibid., pp. 15, 9.

28. Cheikh Anta Diop, *Nations nègres et culture* (Paris: Présence Africaine, 1965); Aimé Césaire, *Cahier d'un retour au pays natal* (Paris: Présence Africaine, 1956); Leopold Senghor, *On African Socialism;* R. P. Placide Tempels, *La philosophie bantoue* (Elisabethville, Belgian Congo: Lovanie, 1945); Nkrumah, *Consciencism.* Willie Abraham, who worked closely with Nkrumah in drafting this work, intended to serve as major synthesis of nationalist thought, also draws upon the Tempels theses in *The Mind of Africa* (London: Wisedenfeld & Nicolson, 1962).

29. Davidson, "The Challenge of Comparative Analysis," p. 8.

30. William F. S. Miles and David Rochefort, "Nationalism versus Ethnic Identity in Sub-Saharan Africa," *American Political Science Review* 35, no. 2 (June 1991): 393–404; Miles, "Self-Identity, Ethnic Affinity, and National Consciousness: An Example from Rural Hausaland," *Ethnic and Racial Studies* 9, no. 4 (Oct. 1986): 427–44.

31. Onyeonoro S. Kamanu, "Secession and the Right of Self-Determination: An O.A.U. Dilemma," *Journal of Modern African Studies* 12, no. 3 (1974): 355–76.

32. Walker Connor, *The National Question in Marxist-Leninist Theory and Strategy* (Princeton, N.J.: Princeton Univ. Press, 1984), p. 10.

33. On the abundant literature tracing the rise of nationalism, see especially Ernest Gellner, *Nations and Nationalism* (Ithaca, N.Y.: Cornell Univ. Press, 1983); Benedict Anderson, *Imagined Communities: Reflections on the Origin and Spread of Nationalism* (London: NLB, 1983); Anthony Smith, *Theories of Nationalism* (New York: Harper & Row, 1971), and *The Ethnic Origins of Nations* (Oxford: Basil Blackwell, 1986); John A. Armstrong, *Nations before Nationalism* (Chapel Hill: Univ. of North Carolina Press, 1982); K. Minogue, *Nationalism* (New York: Basic Books, 1967); Boyd C. Shafer, *Nationalism: Myth and Reality* (New York: Harcourt, Brace & World, 1955); Hans Kohn, *The Idea of Nationalism* (New York: Macmillan, 1943).

34. Sklar, *Nigerian Political Parties.*

35. Richard L. Sklar, "The Nature of Class Domination in Africa," *Journal of Modern African Studies* 17, no. 4 (1979): 537.

36. Carleton Hayes, *The Historical Evolution of Modern Nationalism* (New York: Richard R. Smith, 1931); Kohn, *The Idea of Nationalism;* Alfred Cobban, *The Nation State and National Self-Determination* (New York: Thomas W. Crowell, 1970).

37. Emerson, *From Empire to Nation,* p. 379.

38. Anderson, *Imagined Communities,* p. 14; Gellner, *Nations and Nationalism,* p. 6.

39. Mbembe, *Afriques indociles,* pp. 148–49.

40. The most systematic formulations of Coleman's thought on this issue are found in "The Problem of Political Integration" and *Nigeria: Background to Nationalism.*

41. Colin Leys, *Underdevelopment in Kenya: The Political Economy of Neo-Colonialism, 1964–1971* (Berkeley: Univ. of California Press, 1975), p. 198.

42. Sékou Touré, *Toward Full Reafricanisation* (Paris: Présence Africaine, 1959), p. 28.

43. See the various essays in Gabriel A. Almond, Martin Chadorow, and Ray Harvey Pearce, eds., *Progress and Its Discontents* (Berkeley: Univ. of California Press, 1982).

44. For a useful history of Soviet nationality theory, see Connor, *The National Question in Marxist-Leninist Theory and Strategy.* Among the flood of works triggered by the dissolution of this myth, I find particularly valuable Lubomyr Hajda and Mark Beissinger, *The Nationalities Factor in Soviet Politics and Society* (Boulder, Colo.: Westview Press, 1990).

45. Hodgkin, *Nationalism in Colonial Africa; African Political Parties.*

46. See especially Apter's very influential article, "The Role of Traditionalism in the Political Modernization of Ghana and Uganda," *World Politics* 13 (1960): 45–68. See also Apter's two excellent monographs, *Ghana in Transition* and *The Political Kingdom in Uganda: A Study in Bureaucratic Nationalism* (Princeton, N.J.: Princeton Univ. Press, 1961). One may note the equation of "traditionalism" and attachment to Ashanti or Buganda as orienting focus.

47. Zolberg, *One-Party Government in the Ivory Coast;* Immanuel Wallerstein, "Ethnicity and National Integration in West Africa," *Cahiers d'Etudes Africaines* 2, no. 1 (Oct. 1960): 129–39. One may note the significant lexical distinction proposed by Wallerstein; *tribe* refers to rural (thus backward and traditional) identity, while *ethnic group* denominates urban (progressive) consciousness.

48. Aidan Southall, "The Illusion of Tribe," *Journal of Asian and African Studies* 5, no. 1 (1970): 28–50.

49. See especially A. L. Epstein, *Politics in an Urban African Community* (Manchester: Manchester Univ. Press, 1958); J. C. Mitchell, *The Kalela Dance: Aspects of Social Relationships among Urban Africans in Northern Rhodesia* (Manchester: Manchester Univ. Press, 1956).

50. Paul Mercier, "Remarques sur la signification du 'tribalisme' actuel en Afrique noire," *Cahiers Internationaux de Sociologie* 31 (1960): 61–80.

51. For example, Milton M. Gordon, *Assimilation in American Life* (New York: Oxford Univ. Press, 1964).

52. See, for example, George E. Simpson and J. Milton Yinger, *Racial and Cultural Minorities*, rev. ed. (New York: Harper & Row, 1958); Brewton Berry, *Race and Ethnic Relations*, 3d ed. (Boston: Houghton Mifflin, 1965).

53. J. S. Furnivall, *Colonial Policy and Practice* (London: Cambridge Univ. Press, 1948).

54. Coleman, "Political Integration in Emergent Africa," p. 52.

55. Coleman, *Nigeria: Background to Nationalism*, p. 330.

56. See the Coleman discussion of Ibo uplift, ibid., pp. 332–43.

57. James S. Coleman, "Tradition and Nationalism in Tropical Africa," in *New States in the Modern World*, ed. Martin Kilson (Cambridge: Harvard Univ. Press, 1975), pp. 3–36. This work was long delayed in publication; most of the articles, including, I believe, the Coleman chapter, were first drafted in the middle 1960s.

58. For more extensive surveys of this literature, see my two review articles, "Nationalism, Ethnicity, and Class in Africa: A Retrospective," *Cahiers d'Etudes Africaines* 26, no. 3 (1986): 421–95, and "The Temple of Ethnicity," *World Politics* 35, no. 4 (July 1983): 652–62.

59. Nathan Glazer and Daniel P. Moynihan, *Beyond the Melting Pot: The Negroes, Puerto Ricans, Jews, Italians, and Irish of New York City* (Cambridge: MIT Univ. Press and Harvard Univ. Press, 1963), p. v.

60. Among the influential studies reflecting this perspective, see Nelson Kasfir, *The Shrinking Political Arena: Participation and Ethnicity in African Politics, with a Case Study of Uganda* (Berkeley: Univ. of California Press, 1975); Robert Melson and Howard Wolpe, eds., *Nigeria: Modernization and the Politics of Communalism* (East Lansing: Michigan State Univ. Press, 1971); Crawford Young, *The Politics of Cultural Pluralism* (Madison: Univ. of Wisconsin Press, 1976); Joseph Rothchild, *Ethnopolitics: A Conceptual Framework* (New York: Columbia Univ. Press, 1981).

61. See, for example, the engaging delineation of "language strategists" as cultural entrepreneurs by Brian Weinstein, *The Civic Tongue: Political Consequences of Language Choices* (New York: Longman, 1983).

62. This argument is developed with particular skill by John Saul, *State and Revolution in Eastern Africa* (New York: Monthly Review Press, 1979), pp. 394–98. This premise also underlies the analysis of the leading African political scientist focusing upon ethnicity, O. Nnoli, *Ethnic Politics in Nigeria* (Enugu, Nigeria: Fourth Dimension Publishing Co., 1978).

63. Charles Keyes, ed., *Ethnic Change* (Seattle: Univ. of Washington Press, 1979), p. 10.

64. See the most enthusiastic practitioner of rational choice in Africanist political science, Robert Bates, "Modernization, Ethnic Competition, and the Rationality of Politics in Contemporary Africa," in *State versus Ethnic Claims: African Policy Dilemmas,* ed. Donald Rothchild and Victor Olorunola (Boulder, Colo.: Westview Press, 1983), pp. 152–71.

65. Epstein, *Politics in an Urban African Community.*

66. A. L. Epstein, *Ethos and Identity: Three Studies in Ethnicity* (London: Tavistock, 1978).

67. Quoted in Harold R. Isaacs, *Idols of the Tribe: Group Identity and Political Change* (New York: Harper & Row, 1975).

68. Ibid., p. 24.

69. Clifford Geertz, "The Integrative Revolution: Primordial Sentiments and Civil Politics in the New States," in Geertz, ed., *Old Societies and New States: The Quest for Modernity in Asia and Africa* (New York: Free Press, 1963), pp. 105–57, and *The Interpretation of Cultures* (New York: Basic Books, 1973).

70. Charles F. Keyes, "The Dialectics of Ethnic Change," in Keyes, ed., *Ethnic Change* (Seattle: Univ. of Washington Press, 1981), p. 5.

71. Fredrik Barth, ed., *Ethnic Groups and Boundaries: The Social Organization of Culture Difference* (Boston: Little Brown, 1969), p. 12.

72. Pierre van den Berghe, "Race and Ethnicity: A Sociobiological Perspective," *Ethnic and Racial Studies* 1 (1978): 401–11; R. Paul Shaw and Yuwa Wong, *Genetic Seeds of Warfare: Evolution, Nationalism, and Patriotism* (Boston: Unwin Hyman, 1989).

73. To paraphrase the deft aphorism of Daniel Bell, attributing the ubiquity of ethnicity to its capacity to "combine an interest with an affective tie"; "Ethnicity and Social Change," in *Ethnicity: Theory and Experience,* ed. Nathan Glazer and Daniel P. Moynihan (Cambridge: Harvard Univ. Press, 1975), p. 169.

74. For example, the monumental comparative work by Donald Horowitz, *Ethnic Groups in Conflict* (Berkeley: Univ. of California Press, 1985), combines these perspectives.

75. Anderson, *Imagined Communities.*

76. Jean-Loup Amselle, "Ethnies et espaces: pour une anthropologie topologique," in Amselle and Elikia M'bokolo, *Au coeur de l'ethnie: Ethnies, tribalisme, et état en Afrique* (Paris: Editions la Decouverte, 1985), p. 44.

77. Leroy Vail, ed., *The Creation of Tribalism in Southern Africa* (Berkeley: Univ. of California Press, 1989), p. 11.

78. See the brilliant essay by Terence Ranger, "Ethnicity and Nationality in Southern Africa: Eastern European Resonances," paper presented to conference on state crisis in Eastern Europe and Africa, Bellagio, Italy, Feb. 1990, p. 2. See also, from the same conference, Peter P. Ekeh, "The Kin-Construction of the State in Nigeria: Aspects of the Political Sociology of Nigeria."

79. Ekeh, "Kin-Construction of the State in Nigeria," pp. 5–6.

3

RESURRECTING MODERNIZATION THEORY AND THE EMERGENCE OF CIVIL SOCIETY IN KENYA AND NIGERIA

JOEL D. BARKAN

The Resurrection of Modernization Theory

MODERNIZATION THEORY may be making something of a comeback among students of African politics, albeit under a new rubric—the quest for civil society, effective governance, and the accountable state. Dismissed by critics in the late 1960s and 1970s as Westerncentric, static, ahistorical, and elitist in approach, modernization theory ceased being the dominant paradigm among students of political change in the Third World. However, the decline of political authority and economic stagnation in Africa since the late 1970s suggest that at least three of the assumptions on which the modernization approach was based might not be as "wrong" as its critics supposed.

The first assumption is that the integration of the plural and agrarian societies which constitute the Third World into viable political and economic systems is fundamentally a process internal to society, rather than a process driven by external forces. The second is that in the long run, if not the short,[1] viable rule and economic performance are mutually reinforcing.[2] The creation of viable political institutions is contingent on a measure of economic growth and a just distribution of society's wealth. Conversely, economic growth and a just distribution of wealth are most likely to occur where political institutions are regarded as responsive to societal interests. The third is that effective governance—that is to say, the exercise of political authority that is regarded as predictable and legitimate by those who are subject to it—is associated with democratic rule or, at a minimum, with the existence of institutions, both public and private, that are accountable to the people they purport to serve.

While these assumptions were challenged vociferously by critics of the modernization approach, especially neo-Marxist scholars, the counterassumptions that they advanced have not led to satisfactory explanations of, or solutions to, the intractable problems of Africa's underdevelopment. Exogenous factors resulting from Africa's dependent position on the periphery of the world capitalist system certainly impinge on the process of political integration and economic performance, but in the final analysis the institutions that speed or retard these dimensions of development are the institutions (or the lack of such) within individual countries.

World prices for Africa's principal export commodities have fluctuated greatly since 1970, but changes in export prices and the external terms of trade have not been good predictors of economic performance.[3] In most African countries those in positions of political authority have failed to balance the many claims for the consumption of export earnings with the need to invest and provide incentives for raising production, especially in agriculture.[4] Countries committed to both capitalist and socialist conceptions of development pursued policies that resulted in a swollen and over-centralized state, overvalued exchange rates, adverse internal terms of trade for farmers, declining production in both agriculture and state-owned industries, and an overall lowering of the quality of life, especially among the rural population.[5]

In the political domain the emergence of regimes of personal rule has resulted in a crisis of political authority whereby those who govern find it increasingly difficult to obtain compliance from the populations they formally rule.[6] Because the state is not accountable to the governed yet extracts resources from them, the governed, being rational actors, are increasingly distrustful of the state. Where possible, particularly in the rural areas, where the burden of the state is usually heaviest (as a result of adverse internal terms of trade) but where most people have access to land, the governed may withdraw into subsistence.[7] Rural dwellers may also drop out of the national political system altogether.[8] Where these "exit options" are not feasible, they adopt other defensive strategies, including self-help,[9] passive resistance, foot-dragging, feigning ignorance, etc., to keep the state at bay.[10] In either case, the social base of support for the state, from which it derives its legitimacy, contracts.

This disjuncture between state and society in Africa has led in recent years to an interest in what is loosely termed governance and the search for civil society.[11] Stated simply, this is a concern with the institutionalization of legitimate and accountable political authority[12] as the sine qua non of African development—the necessary condition without which economic development, whether capitalist or socialist, and the creation of viable political systems cannot occur. This concern with the institutionalization of accountable authority marks a return to the modernization paradigm of the 1960s. It is a permutation of the modernization paradigm, however, that places less emphasis on central institutions and the elites that control them than the original formulation of three decades ago and more emphasis on how organized interests in society seek to establish linkages with the state to make it more responsive to their needs.

In their earliest articulations of the modernization paradigm in the late 1950s, Gabriel Almond, David Apter, and James Coleman explicitly or implicitly equated political modernization with the replication of Western democratic systems in the non-Western societies emerging from colonial rule. Apter was the most unambiguous in this regard in his initial study of the Gold Coast (Ghana), where he examined the attempt to transfer British parliamentary institutions to African soil.[13] Coleman's study of Nigerian nationalism took a similar approach, though he did not pose his research question explicitly in terms of institutional transfer.[14] By the early 1960s Almond in his introductory chapter to *The Politics of Developing Areas* sought, as Coleman later observed, "to liberate comparative analysis from the ethnocentric bias in Western culture-bound structural categories. However, the dominant impression . . . was that culturally relative [American] categories were being proposed [imposed?] as universal."[15]

In an effort to break free from the critique that modernization was simply a code word for Westernization, and the related charge that the concept posited a unilineal model of change, Samuel Huntington argued in 1968 that "the most important political distinction among countries concerns not their form of government, but their degree of government."[16] Huntington argued that the former Soviet Union, then in its heyday as a Communist state, and China had achieved a significant measure of political modernity. Moreover, political modernization in the developing areas was most likely to occur where the regimes in power had established and institutionalized strong party organizations to contain the demands of primordial subnational interests. Put differently, ruling elites at the center of the political system would achieve a measure of political modernization by establishing their power over the hinterland.

We now know from the experience of the Third World (including China) during the 1980s, and especially from events in Eastern Europe and the former Soviet Union since 1989, that one-party regimes do not, indeed cannot, wield the degree of authority they claim when such authority is based mainly on their capacity to coerce the governed rather than on their capacity to be held accountable by the governed. The experience of the last decade also suggests that regimes whose authority is based mainly on the capacity to coerce do a poor job of managing their countries' economies. Centralized authoritarian rule and economic decline appear to be linked when a feature of the former is state ownership of the principal means of production.[17] In the late 1960s, however, students of political modernization became increasingly concerned with what they perceived as the need in the new states to establish strong centralized authority at the same time as they sought to wiggle free from the charge that modernization was an inherently Westerncentric concept.

In his contribution to *Crises and Sequences in Political Development,* published in 1971—the last exploration of the modernization paradigm by the members of the Social Science Research Council Committee on Comparative Politics—James Coleman continued the search for a non-Westerncentric model of political development by arguing that political development is "the continuous interaction among the processes of structural *differentiation,* the imperatives of *equality,* and the integrative, responsive and adaptive *capacity* of a political system." Like Huntington, Coleman emphasized the capacity of central institutions—that is to say, ruling elites, including senior civil servants, educated in a secular (i.e., Western) tradition—"to contain the participatory and distributive demands generated by the imperatives of equality." Drawing on Weber, Coleman argued that the

> scope and effectiveness . . . of a developing polity's performance, are directly dependent upon . . . the predominance of rationality in governmental decision-making. . . . The peculiarly modern feature of this development is not the existence of centralized bureaucracy. Rather it is the predominance, pervasiveness, and institutionalization of a rational-secular orientation in political and administrative processes. This orientation is an absolutely indispensable ingredient in the creative capacity of a developing polity.[18]

But if Coleman was perceptive in recognizing that the existence of a centralized bureaucracy without a "rational-secular orientation" would not lead to political modernization, it is also clear that he and his collaborators regarded the state and its bureaucratic institutions as the principal repository of rationality in the Third World. It was the state and the ruling and bureaucratic elites which controlled it that would be the primary agents of both political and economic development by containing the diverse interests, especially ethnic and regional interests, in these societies. Central elites were likewise viewed as the principal bearers of modernization and development to the peoples on the rural periphery of society by penetrating the periphery and by integrating its diverse communities into a single political system.[19] Development, in short, was to be a center-out and top-down process.

In their effort to escape the charge of Westerncentrism, the modernization theorists became elite-centric and hence state-centric in perspective, with the result that their original concern for political accountability and participation as critical components of modernization got lost in the shuffle. The decline of effective political authority in Africa, however, suggests that top-down approaches to both political and economic development have failed, and that there is a need to return to the early concept of political development that included the exercise of accountable (read "democratic") authority. It is in this context, therefore, that one can call for the resurrection of the initial version of modernization theory, albeit in terms of the quest for civil society and the accountable state.

State Accountability and the Expansion of Civil Society

If the establishment of accountable authority is the bottom line of African development, how might it be achieved? How might the rulers of African states become more accountable to the populations over which they claim authority? What mechanisms might facilitate a relationship of bargaining through which the interests of the state and those in society can be adjusted to each other so that the exercise of state power might be regarded as legitimate by those subject to it? This chapter explores one answer to these questions by examining the proliferation and function of rural voluntary associations and the state response in Nigeria and Kenya.

The argument presented is straightforward and derived from Alexis de Tocqueville's observations of over a century ago that there is an inverse relationship between the state's capacity to coerce the governed and the extent to which local interests organize themselves to advance their objectives. The more the members of society organize themselves into groups to advance their particular interests, the less likely the state can function in an autonomous and unaccountable manner. The proliferation of organized interests is thus a bulwark against unbridled state power.[20] Put positively, the more the members of society organize themselves to advance their interests, the more likely they can make claims on the state and ensure that the state will respond to their needs. The existence of a robust civil society—that area of organized human activity concerned with the exercise of state authority which functions between the state and the family—is thus essential for a responsive and accountable state. This view of civil society is, of course, the basis of the pluralist conception of democracy that dominated American political science in the postwar era.[21]

Though the argument is an old one, the significance of civil society for nurturing democracy in Africa has been embraced only recently by students of African politics. Two reasons explain their previous reluctance to appreciate the significance of civil society. First, because interests on the continent are often organized on the basis of ethnic and / or regional affinities, students of political development and African leaders have often viewed organized interests as forces that exacerbate societal cleavages and retard the process of political integration. Second, it has been assumed that the number of organized interests is very small and growing slowly—especially the number based on functional affinities, such as occupation, that cut across ethnic and regional cleavages to reduce the salience of these divisions. In the context of peasant societies, distinctions of ethnicity and language, regional loyalty, religion, and even economic interest, when it is tied to a particular commodity produced in a single region, have been viewed as sources of social cleavage that are superimposed upon each other. African societies are thus invariably defined as plural rather than pluralistic in structure.[22] Viewed in this context, civil society has been regarded as a threat—the source of excessive and divisive demands leading to conflict—rather than as a contributor to the establishment of a stable and accountable political order. State and civil society exist in an adversarial relationship to each other, which necessitates that the major task of the former is to regulate rather than to reflect the latter.

This view of Africa is too simple. While the conditions of industrial and postindustrial society that gave rise to pluralism in the West do not obtain in Africa, it does not follow that civil society does not exist on the continent, or that it cannot have a salutary effect on the political process and the process of economic development. One should remember that the civil society described by Tocqueville did not emerge as a reflection of the highly differentiated array of nonterritorially defined interests found in industrial society. Nor was Tocqueville's civil society pluralistic in structure. More-

over, the structure of organized interests in civil society and their relationships to the state as found in the advanced industrial democracies do not
necessarily conform to the pluralist model.[23] The basic question for those
wishing a democratic order is not whether civil society is pluralist, but
whether and how it contains state power and legitimizes state authority.

In a thoughtful article which marks one of the first attempts to explore
systematically the significance of civil society in Africa for establishing
accountable and democratic political order, Michael Bratton has argued
that "political scientists should devote more research attention to the associational life that occurs in the political space beyond the state's purview.
Far from being stunted in sub-Saharan Africa, it is often vibrant." Bratton
noted the wide variety of associational life found on the continent, including ethnic and village development associations, farmers associations, religious groups (Christian, Islamic, and separatist), urban traders (market
women), taxi drivers, urban welfare associations, labor unions, and professional associations (educators, journalists, lawyers, physicians). Bratton further observed that the relationships between state and civil society need not
be adversarial:

> A broader implication of this sketch of state-society relations is that interaction
> need not always be confrontational but, under certain circumstances, may be
> complementary. Civic organizations can never completely replace the state in
> all its manifold functions; nor should they attempt to. Instead, they are well
> placed to exhort and assist political elites to adapt the state's actions to accord
> more closely with interests expressed by groups in society. I take issue with the
> view . . . that state-society relations are always a zero-sum-game in which the
> holders of state office necessarily weaken themselves if they share power with
> other organized social interests.[24]

It is from this perspective that an analysis of one type of voluntary
association—the rural community development association—is instructive
for understanding the dynamic between civil society and the state and for
showing how the vibrancy of the former legitimizes rather than under-
mines the latter. By considering the operation and political significance of
associational life that is local in geographical setting and scope but often
links rural communities to central institutions (including, but not limited
to, the state), we can better appreciate how the flourishing of such groups
strengthens the center as well as the periphery. An examination of this
particular form of associational life also enables one to test and, as demon-

strated here, reject the long-held assumption that in plural societies local associational life often leads to severe political cleavages of an ethnic and regional nature.

Local Voluntary Associations and State Response in Kenya and Nigeria

Kenya and Nigeria have a rich tradition of rural associational life which dates back to the period before independence and, in the case of the Nigeria, to the period before colonial rule. While there are some significant differences between the two countries with respect to the organization and leadership of associational life, the overall manifestation of civil society in the rural areas and its relationship to the state are remarkably alike. This in turn suggests that while the intensity of rural associational life in Kenya and Nigeria is probably the highest in Africa, the replication of this activity and its impact on state-society relations is possible elsewhere on the continent.

Kenya's Harambee Movement

The principal vehicle of rural associational life in Kenya is the Harambee[25] self-help development organization, which exists in almost every rural community for the purpose of providing basic social welfare services and infrastructure to the local population. It is estimated that there are now over 15,000 Harambee organizations in Kenya.[26] These organizations are responsible for the construction and operation of most of the primary and secondary schools established in Kenya since independence, as well as the construction of rural health clinics, small-scale water systems, cattle dips, feeder roads, and bridges. Most Harambee organizations function as autonomous groups at the level of the local community. A minority, perhaps as many as 20 percent, operate with some assistance from the government or other external agency such as a nongovernmental organization (e.g., CARE or the National Council of Churches of Kenya). Almost all seek state assistance. In the process many organizations, particularly those involved with large projects such as secondary schools that serve catchment areas beyond the local community, become the subject of local politics.

The distinguishing feature of Harambee organizations is that they are groups which operate on the basis of collective action to provide collective goods to members of the local community. In principle the services provided by Harambee are available to all members of the community, but an increasing number of groups find it necessary to limit the provision of services (e.g., a place in a primary or secondary school or the use of a cattle dip) to those who have contributed to its development or who can pay a user fee to cover recurrent costs. Thus, the collective goods produced by Harambee are not necessarily public goods, because the potential beneficiaries of many projects can be excluded from the services these projects provide. A minority of Harambee organizations, moreover, have become involved in efforts to produce goods for sale on the open market. Usually organized by women, these groups make handicrafts, raise poultry, or grow vegetables or other cash crops on a collective basis. Generally speaking, these efforts to produce and market goods have not been as successful as those to provide social welfare services.

Self-help development organizations first emerged in central Kenya during the 1930s as part of the nationalist movement. Their initial purpose during the period before independence was to provide needed services to rural communities that the colonial regime would not provide, or would provide only under conditions that were unacceptable to the rural population—in this case, the Kikuyu people of Central Province. The particular need at the inception of self-help was for Western education, which was obtainable only from missionary schools. The missionaries, however, as well as the colonial government, were strongly opposed to the Kikuyu practice of female circumcision—a practice defended by the emergent nationalist movement as an inherent part of African culture. The response by the Kikuyu was to organize their own network of schools known as the Kenya Independent Schools. These schools were viewed by nationalist leaders and the local population as a way to meet a basic need on their own terms.[27] The independent schools were a means by which a segment of civil society could resist the colonial regime that it regarded as illegitimate. Early manifestations of self-help were thus part of a larger process through which the nationalist movement organized civil society in the rural areas and sought to create a more accountable and legitimate state.

Building upon this tradition, Harambee self-help development projects began to proliferate across Kenya in the years after independence as it became clear that the recently installed government of Jomo Kenyatta could not provide rural communities with the full array of social welfare services they hoped to receive. The proliferation of Harambee groups was orchestrated by Kenyatta, who encouraged the movement throughout his tenure as Kenya's president, and who viewed Harambee an integral part of his regime.[28]

By the mid-1960s Kenyatta regularly made speeches that exhorted Kenyans to engage in self-help and also urged members of Parliament to assist their constituents in these efforts. In making these exhortations Kenyatta sought to solve two problems. The first was to deflect and contain popular demands for social welfare services that exceeded the capacity of the Kenyan state to provide. The second was to shift the arena of parliamentary activity from the Kenya National Assembly, where MPs often subjected Kenyatta's policies to intense review, to the countryside. Just as Kenyans had engaged in self-help development in the era before independence, so, too, should they engage in it now. "God," Kenyatta liked to remind his audiences, "helps those who help themselves." His government would do the same by directing its resources to those areas which demonstrated local initiative.

By stressing that MPs should engage in constituency service, Kenyatta also succeeded in changing the rules of the game of Kenyan politics. Instead of emphasizing the debate of national policy, as would be expected in a parliamentary institution inherited from the British, Kenyatta's call for constituency service was closer to the norms of American legislative practice. Kenyatta also institutionalized two practices that forced MPs into more constituency service and that were to have profound implications for self-help and the proliferation of associational life. First, and perhaps most significant, despite the establishment of a de facto one-party state by 1969, Kenya maintained a relatively free and competitive electoral system through 1983.[29] Second, he instituted a system of patronage which greatly rewarded MPs who played by the new rules.

Under this system competitive elections were held in Kenya in 1969, 1974, 1979, and 1983 that resembled primary elections in American congressional districts. With few exceptions, any individual who met the minimal legal requirements for office and proclaimed loyalty to Kenyatta and the ruling party, the Kenya African National Union (KANU), could stand for office. Under this system up to a dozen candidates would stand for office and campaign on their records of constituency service. Elections became referendums on the level and effectiveness of support by incumbent MPs for self-help in their districts. Had the incumbent contributed an appropriate amount of money to self-help projects within his district? Had he or she encouraged other prominent individuals to contribute? Had the MP lobbied government agencies to assist projects where such assistance was provided on a discretionary basis? Where voters perceived the MP's record to be poor, the number of challengers rose significantly, and the vote share garnered by the incumbent fell sharply.[30] Between 1969 and 1983, the last year competitive and honest elections were held in Kenya under a one-party format, 38 to 54 percent of all incumbents who ran for reelection were defeated.[31]

The second factor that pushed MPs to spend more time responding to the needs of Harambee organizations was Kenyatta's system of patronage. By expanding the number of ministers and assistant ministers to roughly one-third of all MPs, Kenyatta greatly increased the number of parliamentarians who were rewarded for tending to their home areas. MPs who were reelected once were invariably appointed assistant ministers. Those reelected two or more times were given ministerial portfolios. With each promotion, the access to patronage that MPs could funnel back to their districts grew. Not surprisingly, MPs who survived the first test for reelection stood a much greater chance to survive the second and the third. Whereas up to 65 percent of incumbent backbenchers went down to defeat, only 40 percent of assistant ministers met the same fate, while the average for ministers was 23 percent.[32] In the process MPs who rose to ministerial status also became the regional political bosses in their home areas, while assistant ministers became district bosses.

In Kenyatta's Kenya the combination of Harambee, regular elections, and liberal patronage was used to establish a clientelist system that was both stable and accountable in terms of state responsiveness to rural civil society. Under this system rural dwellers and local elites felt that they had opportunities for making claims on the state, while the weaker members of the Kenyatta regime were periodically purged, thereby deflecting any significant challenge to the regime from below. This system also promoted a process of bargaining between civil society and the state that was positive-sum rather than zero-sum in nature, and that derived support from a broad segment of the peasantry.

This process of bargaining between rural civil society and the state extended beyond self-help. During the Kenyatta era large farmers usually were successful in securing high producer prices for maize and wheat because of the pressure they could put on the government through the Kenya Farmers Association (KFA). Although the KFA was formed in the colonial period to advance the interests of white settler farmers, the organization became a vehicle for African farmers after independence, and one which benefited smallholders, albeit indirectly, as well. Smallholder producers of tea also have secured high prices for their product through participation in the programs of the Kenya Tea Development Authority, a parastatal agency which has often functioned as an interest group for the farmers it serves.

Harambee organizations are found in almost every rural community in Kenya. Initially formed in Central Province, these organizations spread first to other rural areas that were more densely populated and more developed in terms of the practice of cash-crop agriculture. Conversely, the number and success of self-help organizations have been lowest in the arid and semiarid areas of northern and northeastern Kenya, which are sparsely populated by poor and seminomadic peoples and are remote from the country's principal cities. Harambee thus has been concentrated geographically in those areas which are relatively rich and most incorporated into Kenya's capitalist economy. Although the Kenyan economy remains primarily agrarian in structure, the correlation between the extent of associational life and economic development, as measured by economic growth and the degree of capitalist penetration of the rural areas, is unmistakable. This relationship is consistent with Bratton's observation that associational life in Africa is most extensive in those countries where the level of capitalist industrialization is highest,[33] as well as with the original argument made by the modernization theorists that the probability for democratic (i.e., accountable) government rises with the level of economic development.

Notwithstanding these variations in the geographic distribution of Harambee and the emergence of class interests in the areas where capitalist penetration was highest, a distinctive feature of self-help was its broad social base. Case histories of seventy-six self-help organizations and survey data from more than 2,000 respondents about the nature of their participation in self-help indicate that almost 90 percent of all rural dwellers were involved in Harambee.[34] Those who participate in self-help became involved in an average of 3.9 separate projects—projects which were frequently mounted by different organizations, though many of the most successful self-help organizations sponsored multiple projects. Perhaps most significant, participation in self-help was highest among small and middle farmers who owned from one to five and from five to twenty acres respectively, and who together comprised 72 percent of all rural dwellers. Participation by the landless and by large farmers, who owned more than twenty acres, was only slightly lower.[35]

For most of those who joined Harambee organizations, participation did not involve leadership but the contribution of personal resources to support projects and consumption of project services once the project was up and running. Only 20 percent of the respondents surveyed reported having been an officer of a Harambee organization, and unlike the rates of other forms of participation in self-help, the incidence of leadership was positively correlated with the amount of land owned.[36] Because they were more numerous, however, small farmers led more Harambee organizations than any other category of rural dwellers. Thus, while large farmers were more likely to become leaders than small, leadership was drawn from a wide spectrum of the population.

Turning to the questions of who financed self-help and who benefited from the services it provided, the data indicate that in relative terms, the landless and small farmers contributed the least yet were more likely to believe that they benefited than middle and large farmers. Individual contributions to self-help took two forms that were derived mainly from two sources. Most projects functioned autonomously from the state because they were financed entirely by project members. Contributions were made to self-help in cash or in kind—or in labor when the project involved the construction of a facility (e.g., a school building or an addition to an existing building). Contributions in cash or kind (usually farm produce or animals that could be sold for cash) were made by community members at levels that were usually scaled to their ability to pay. In this regard, the survey data indicate that the annual amount of contributions was strongly correlated with the amount of land owned. On a per capita basis, large farmers contributed two and one half times the average amount given by the landless and 52 percent more than the average amount contributed by small farmers. It is problematic, however, whether local contributions to Harambee were a progressive tax on rural dwellers in terms of their ability to pay. Middle and large farmers, for example, paid a much smaller proportion of all funds contributed than the proportion of land they controlled; it is doubtful whether their marginal rate of contribution was higher than that of small farmers. As for contributions of labor, the pattern was even less progressive, as labor contributions was mostly made by the landless and the rural poor.

A second and major source of funding for self-help came from contributions solicited in the urban areas by and from members of the local community who lived and worked in Kenya's cities on a permanent or semipermanent basis—civil servants and those with salaried positions in the private sector. It is impossible to determine the absolute magnitude of these solicitations or accurately estimate the percentage of all funds raised through these remittances. A rough guesstimate would be in the range of 10 to 40 percent, with the percentage rising with the size of the project being financed. Generally speaking, the more elaborate and technically complex the project, the greater the proportion of financing provided by members of the community who now resided in the urban areas. Such financing, however, was most likely to be available to communities and regions that were already relatively more developed in terms of existing social infrastructure (especially education), for it was the migrants from these areas who were most likely to occupy salaried positions in the towns.

More significant than the actual amounts remitted is the fact that remittances for Harambee were transfer payments from the center to the rural periphery and from those who were relatively well-off to those who relied on self-help to meet their basic needs. It is also clear that these transfer payments would never have been made in the absence of the proliferation of Harambee organizations. Although this discussion is concerned mainly with how a robust civil society pressures the state to become more responsive to group interests, the indirect impact of associational life through the pressure it places on central elites and subelites, in both the private and public sector, is noteworthy.

Turning lastly to the question of who benefits from Harambee, three observations are particularly germane. The first is that the overwhelming majority of rural dwellers believe they benefit from self-help. Whereas 60 percent of the respondents said they had benefited "a great deal" from self-help, only 12 percent indicated that they received "very few benefits," while less than 1 percent said they had received "none." This balance of opinion varied little by the different categories of landowners, indicating again the broad support for self-help. For example, 65 percent of the landless believed they had benefited "a great deal."

The spread of social infrastructure across Kenya also reflects the extent to which Harambee organizations became an institutionalized feature of Kenyan rural life under Kenyatta and the extent to which both politicians and bureaucrats responded to its presence. Though only a minority of projects, and hence a minority of Harambee organizations, receive direct and formal assistance from the government of Kenya, MPs as well as centrally based bureaucratic elites monitor self-help closely.

The proliferation of self-help organizations and projects forced the Kenyan state to make a formal response in the form of a program called District Focus. In 1983 Kenyatta's successor, Daniel arap Moi, announced that Kenya would decentralize rural administration to the district level to improve development planning and project implementation. As self-help spread willy-nilly across Kenya, many projects were ill conceived and not completed, while others became a burden on the country's recurrent budget. Expenditures on education, for example, now constitute over 30 percent of the annual recurrent budget,[37] because thousands of Harambee schools have succeeded in persuading the Ministry of Education to provide one or more certified teachers whose salaries are paid by the ministry. By decentralizing aspects of rural development planning and finance to the districts and raising the level of coordination among members of the district administration, the Kenyan government hoped to improve the quality of its technical support to self-help. At the same time, the government sought to contain what it regarded as excessive and runaway growth in some areas of self-help such as education. It would also appear that District Focus was pursued as a mechanism to reduce substantially the measure of political authority that MPs and regional leaders have historically derived from their involvement in self-help.[38] The extent to which politicians are free to engage in entrepreneurial activity on behalf of projects of their choosing has been greatly limited. All projects, regardless of whether they receive state funding, must now be approved by the District Development Council (DDC), a body dominated by members of the district administration, although MPs are prominent members. The use of the DDC to determine which projects shall receive state assistance and which shall not is a further brake on the activities of elected officials on behalf of self-help.

Regrettably, the containment of self-help by District Focus in combination with two other changes suggests that the high-water mark of Harambee, and with it the vibrancy of associational life in Kenya, may have passed. Since succeeding Kenyatta as Kenya's president in 1978, Moi has sought to control self-help and manipulate the movement to strengthen his own political base. Whereas during the Kenyatta era Harambee was defined as a series of local arenas within which MPs and senior politicians could do good works to renew their electoral mandate, under Moi Harambee has become a highly centralized and two-tiered process in which the upper tier is the domain of the president and the lower tier is subject to increasing regulation. During the Kenyatta era fund-raising for self-help was largely a local affair with the exception of occasional rallies to collect money for pet projects of the president (i.e., the Gatundu Hospital). Under Moi the number of fund-raisers for presidential projects has increased dramatically. Vast sums are raised at these events, which are highly publicized in the press and attended by the president and most members of the cabinet. Civil servants are expected to make regular donations to such projects, thereby reducing the money they can give to self-help in their home areas.[39] Rural dwellers are likewise forced to make contributions to projects of the president that otherwise would support local efforts at self-help within their communities.[40] Both civil servants and rural dwellers have, in effect, become subject to a Harambee tax.

The authority of individual MPs and their support for Harambee have also been weakened by changes in the electoral system, though the long-term effect is unclear. New rules adopted for the parliamentary elections of 1988 and intimidation of voters, plus widespread rigging by Moi and his cohorts to ensure desired outcomes, greatly reduced the extent to which voters were free to evaluate candidates on the basis of their records on self-help. However, the legalization of opposition parties and the advent of multiparty elections in December 1992 have created a new opportunity for Kenyan voters to evaluate candidates in terms of constituency service, including self-help. Perhaps for this reason, more than 70 percent of the incumbent MPs contesting the 1992 elections were defeated in their bids for reelection.

The sum of these changes has significantly deinstitutionalized the political process in Kenya and reduced the breadth of rural associational life, at least in the short term. In addition to the containment of Harambee organizations, the independence of other organized interests also was seriously curtailed between 1986 and 1991. In 1986 the Kenya government forced the Kenya Farmers Association to restructure itself as the Kenya Grain Growers Union, a move intended to reduce the influence of Kikuyu farmers, and in 1989 the government announced establishment of Nayao Tea Zones in an effort to weaken the Kenya Tea Development Authority. The government also fought a running battle with various church organizations, particularly the National Council of Churches of Kenya, over a range of issues, especially the question of whether Kenya should remain a one-party state. The national women's organization, Maendeleo wa Wanawake, was brought under the direct control of the ruling party, as was the Central Organisation of Trade Unions (COTU), although both were subsequently "delinked" in 1991. In the same year, however, the government passed the Non-Governmental Organization Registration Act to restrict severely the autonomy of the NGO community, particularly Kenya-based NGOs.

Civil society in Kenya is not as healthy as it was at the end of the Kenyatta era. Despite the proliferation of Harambee organizations and the survival of other associations that articulate the interests of rural Kenyans, the determination of the Moi regime to contain and suppress autonomous associational life continues. Such containment reduces both the accountability and the legitimacy of the regime and eventually may lead to the regime's demise. The widespread unpopularity of the regime as measured by the results of the presidential and parliamentary elections of December 1992 suggests the extent to which the curtailment of associational life is a counterproductive strategy for those wishing to maintain their political authority. Were it not for the fact that the opposition split its vote among three parties, the regime of Daniel arap Moi and the ruling party, KANU, would be history.

Hometown Development Associations in Nigeria

Nigeria's equivalent of Harambee is the hometown development associations that exist in most towns and some villages[41] in the southern half of the country, especially in the areas inhabited by the Yoruba- and Igbo-speaking populations. As in Kenya, the principal purpose of these community-based organizations has been to provide through collective action social welfare services which the state has not supplied. While a tradition of communal self-help among the Yoruba predates the colonial era,[42] the organization of self-help in its current form emerged, as in Kenya, during the early 1930s as a reaction to the perceived failure of the colonial state to meet local community needs. Some of these organizations were formed ten to twenty years earlier as cultural associations and later added development work to their activities. The construction of schools and other basic infrastructure has been the primary activity of these groups. In recent years some hometown associations have branched out into a variety of rural enterprises as the needs for infrastructure and social welfare services have been met. This change in objective at times has led to changes in the internal structure and legal status of hometown associations; some groups have reorganized themselves into private corporations.

The most distinctive feature of hometown development associations is the extensive and sustained involvement by members of the local community who have migrated to Nigeria's urban areas on a permanent or semi-permanent basis but who frequently visit their hometowns. Most hometown associations were started by the first or second generation of such migrants, who usually held low-level positions in the colonial state (e.g., teachers, health inspectors, railway clerks). Although the literature on urbanization in West Africa has discussed the organization of voluntary associations by migrants in the city to help them cope with urban life,[43] the extent and history of migrant participation in hometown life through the formation of hometown associations has not been documented.[44]

The description which follows is based on a modest field study of three hometown development associations and local government conducted in three towns of approximately 25,0000 to 50,000 inhabitants in Western Nigeria in 1989.[45] Two of these associations were established as community development associations in the early 1930s by townspeople who were educated in local missionary schools and then left to seek employment in Nigeria's cities, usually Lagos. The third began as a cultural association in 1912 but expanded into community development in the 1930s. Despite the missionary presence, all three towns were regarded as settlements of minor importance by the colonial government, with the result that little or no infrastructure or social services were provided to them. Once exposed to these amenities in the cities, some migrants determined that their kinsmen back home could enjoy the same services through self-help. Returning home for periodic visits, these migrants helped organize community development associations for this purpose or encouraged existing associations that were not engaged in development projects to add them to their programs. Many migrants became the leaders of these associations and / or recruited local notables to serve in this capacity.

The first area of focus for hometown development associations was invariably education. Both migrants and nonmigrants understood that in the colonial order educational qualifications were the main determinant of individual advancement. The expansion of primary education and, after that, secondary education thus preoccupied these organizations during the first two decades of their existence. In contrast to the independent school movement in Kenya, self-help activities to expand education in Western Nigeria were efforts in which the local residents often worked closely with missionary groups and sought their support. By the 1930s the local missionary clergy had been substantially Africanized, and the expansion of missionary schools was not viewed as antithetical to African interests. Members of the local community were organized by the hometown association to contribute cash or labor to construct schoolrooms or buildings for missionary schools; the missionaries would then recruit additional teachers. By the mid-1950s all three associations included in this study had succeeded in establishing one or two secondary schools under missionary auspices that were open to children of all faiths. At this point the hometown associations turned to other projects.

In the three decades since Nigeria's independence in 1960, the three hometown associations have engaged in a wide range of projects, including the construction of roads, town meeting halls, post offices, local water systems, public toilets and sanitation facilities, electric and telephone systems, and health clinics and hospitals. One organization has now moved into productive enterprise and activities in support of production, including a poultry farm, a demonstration farm with supporting staff of field extension agents, and a tractor service for local farmers.

Participation by town residents is broad. Most residents are expected to contribute cash or labor to these projects, and they do. As in Kenya, members of the community who are relatively well-off financially are expected to contribute more than those who are not. Those who are very poor are not forced to contribute and often enjoy project benefits as free riders.

Three related aspects of these projects should be noted because they affect the overall position of hometown associations within the local community and their relationship to the state. First, over time the projects mounted by hometown associations tend to become more complex and costly. Once these groups have completed the building of schools and other basic infrastructure, the remaining needs of the local community, particularly in the areas of health, water, and electrification, require a level of investment and technical support that can only be obtained from sources outside the community. Depending on the project, these sources have consisted of one or more of the following: (1) the present generation of migrants to Nigeria's cities, especially professionals, leading businessmen and other members of the urban middle class; (2) the relevant bureau (or parastatal) of the state or federal government; and (3) a foreign donor of development assistance.

As in Kenya, transfer payments by migrants living in the major urban areas have grown in importance. Unlike fund-raising in Kenya, these funds are collected by the urban branches of the hometown association, which are assigned quotas (based mainly on the number of branch members) by the parent organization. Between 70 and 90 percent of the funds raised by hometown associations from their members are now raised in this manner, and it is not unusual for an association to have up to two dozen branches working on its behalf. The result is that the residents of the home community contribute a relatively small and declining proportion of project costs—a situation which may lower their sense of having a stake in the project.

The proportion of project costs that are borne by the state or parastatal agencies is also rising. The electrification of a town, for example, is impossible without the participation of the electric company, which must wire and connect the town to the regional power grid. The establishment of a hospital, as occurred in one town, would never have taken place without the active cooperation by the Ministry of Health of Oyo State, which has recruited the senior hospital staff and provides the hospital with most of its supplies and recurrent budget. The hospital is also an example of a project which would not have come to fruition without foreign donor assistance— in this case, the World Health Organization, which provided equipment for the operating theater.

Projects of increased complexity and cost have also altered the internal structure and, in some cases, even the legal status of hometown associations. These changes have occurred at the same time as the founding leaders of these associations have grown older, retired from public life, or died. A common pattern of the organizations followed for this study was the longevity of the founding leaders, not merely with respect to age but in tenure in office. The men (never women) who founded these organizations in the 1930s continued to lead them thirty and, in some cases, forty years later.

As voluntary associations, all three organizations are theoretically open to all members of the local community. All residents of the community can join and are encouraged to do so. In contrast to Harambee organizations in Kenya, most hometown associations in Nigeria have a written constitution or bylaws which specify the structure of internal governance. In all cases these include a formal provision to ensure that the organization's leadership remains accountable to the rank and file—usually via an annual or semiannual meeting of the membership. Some associations also reserve places on their executive committees for women.

In practice, the leadership of hometown associations usually has been limited to an oligarchy of local notables and prominent migrants who return home on a regular (e.g., monthly) basis. The oligarchy forms the executive committee or board that directs the day-to-day operations of the organization and determines what projects the organization will pursue. By the 1960s and 1970s the hometown associations included in this study were faced with two related challenges—the need to recruit a new generation of leaders and the need to pursue more complex projects once basic needs had been met.

These challenges evoked three different responses that are probably typical of all hometown associations. In one association the original generation of leaders slowly co-opted men who were only somewhat younger than themselves to join the leadership group. As the oldest of the original leaders became infirm or died, younger men took over, but the founding oligarchy was perpetuated. Men in their late sixties to late seventies were replaced by men only ten years their junior. The professional skill level of the current leadership and their network of contacts with outside agencies remained largely the same as that of their predecessors.

The second association experienced a more abrupt change in leadership when the founding oligarchy was overthrown in the early 1980s by a group of highly educated professionals in their late thirties and early forties. These men, most of whom lived outside the community, but who maintained close ties to local businessmen and the headmaster of the town's secondary school, had become increasingly frustrated by the aging of the founding oligarchy and a concomitant decline in the 1970s of the association's activities. Since taking over they have reinvigorated the association and implemented a series of complex projects that have required outside assistance to complete. Because these men are prominent professionals and businessmen based in the urban areas, they have been able to secure such assistance through their contacts with government and other centrally based organizations. They have also raised the level of support derived from the association's urban branches and have become increasingly involved in lobbying local government authorities, who now receive substantial block grants from the Federal Military Government.[46] Though more aggressive and knowledgeable about the possibilities for rural development than its predecessor, the current leadership functions as much as an oligarchy as the group it replaced. Indeed, in a pattern consistent with Robert Michels's "iron rule of oligarchy,"[47] the current leadership functions as an oligarchy precisely because its members possess the high measure of expertise that is necessary to pursue the current development objectives of the association.

The third and most sophisticated response to the twin challenge of leadership change and the need to pursue different types of development projects occurred in the association that began as a cultural association and then added development activities in the 1930s. Because these two areas of activity are in fact very different, and because the younger generation of leaders recognized them as such, the solution was to create separate organizations for each. In 1982 the existing town voluntary association thus reverted to its original purpose of perpetuating the local chieftaincy and other cultural practices, while a new organization was established as a nonprofit corporation to oversee the development of the town. This arrangement has resulted in the continued leadership of the cultural association by an older group of locally based leaders of long standing, while a younger group of urban-based professionals comparable to the group that overthrew the old guard in the previous example determines the policies of the corporation. This arrangement has facilitated a working relationship between two different generations of leaders while providing a leadership cadre and division of responsibility appropriate to the activities of each organization. Strictly speaking, the corporation is not a hometown association based on the principle of collective action. Residents of the town are members of the cultural association but not the corporation. Town residents, however, are expected to support projects organized by the corporation. Most financing of corporation projects is thus raised by the cultural association, especially its urban branches, and then transferred to the corporation in the form of periodic grants.

The corporation has its own salaried and volunteer staff that enables it to run a poultry farm and demonstration farm on a profit-making basis. The corporation seeks to disseminate improved methods of farming and services to local farmers through a two-tiered extension organization. The information flow through this organization is strictly top-down, though the farmers have established a separate communitywide forum to provide feedback to the corporation's leaders. The corporation also has supported the farmers by constructing and operating a market and by providing tractor services on a subsidized basis. To finance and organize these services, the directors of the corporation regularly approach relevant agencies of the local, state, and federal governments as well as foreign assistance agencies.

As the efforts required for economic development have shifted from activities that provide towns with basic infrastructure to activities that raise production, the transformation of the hometown association from a voluntary association to a corporate entity is appropriate to the new ventures. The long-term impact of this change on state-society relationships, however, is unknown. On the one hand, the emergence of a well-organized corporate body has increased the capacity of town leaders to lobby state agencies. On the other hand, these corporate entities are run largely by urban-based elites and no longer depend on mass participation by town residents (other than their cash contributions) to realize their objectives. The evolution of hometown associations into corporate bodies may thus result in greater transfers of state resources to rural communities and greater accountability by state officials to the elites who run these communities. At the same time the level of accountability by state officials to ordinary citizens may be reduced. If this is true, state accountability will depend increasingly on the extent to which the elites who run hometown associations remain sensitive to local public opinion and seek to obtain public support.

Although hometown associations in Western Nigeria are more dominated by an alliance of local notables and urban elites than Harambee
organizations in Kenya are, it would appear that these organizations are
also more powerful and autonomous vis-à-vis the state. Indeed, it is because of extensive elite involvement that these organizations are able to
press their claims effectively on state agencies. For the same reason, these
organizations are difficult for the state to control. Hometown organizations
in Nigeria, moreover, are subject to fewer constraints than Harambee organizations in Kenya. The Nigerian state has not intervened in the process of
fund-raising for community development as in Kenya. Nor has it sought to
subject all new projects proposed by hometown associations to government review or to reduce the influence and independence of other types of
interest groups by restructuring their organizations and / or bringing them
under direct state control. Professional associations such as the Nigerian
Bar Association and teachers unions operate with remarkable independence in Nigeria. The existence of a free and diverse press in Nigeria also
enables interest groups to make their voices heard to a degree not possible
in Kenya before the return to multiparty politics in 1992. Although Nigeria
remains under military rule, civil society is alive, resilient, and growing.

Community Associations and Modernization Theory

The experience of Kenya during the Kenyatta era and Western Nigeria
indicates that voluntary associations can flourish at the local level in Africa
without being a divisive force or destabilizing the political system. On the
contrary, where such organizations flourish, the state is more likely to be
held accountable to rural interests than where such organizations do not
exist. To the extent that a proliferation of rural community organizations
raises the prospects for state accountability, it can also be argued that the
pluralist model of democracy remains relevant for Africa—indeed more
relevant than was supposed a few years ago. It is also clear that organizations of this type are most likely to emerge in areas where there has already
been some significant measure of economic growth and where educated
elites have become involved in these organizations. This pattern validates
another basic argument of the modernization approach—that economic
and political development are positively correlated.

While the theoretical significance of community associations is best
captured by the modernization approach, the original theory said little
about how the process of building civil society and an accountable political

order might be encouraged. Modernization theory was largely silent with respect to individual behavior and organizational change on the periphery of the new states, other than contending that change would occur as a result of the penetration of the periphery by central institutions and their agents. More troublesome was the implicit assumption that individual actors on the periphery, particularly peasant farmers, did not count in the developmental process until mobilized from outside the local community. Mired in "tradition," these individuals were not deemed capable of creating new forms of organization within the local community to provide for their needs or capable of making claims on the state on their own.

As the microlevel literature on African peasant economy has shown convincingly, residents of local communities are rational actors who carefully devise both individual and collective strategies to advance and defend their interests. The formation of community-level associations in Kenya and Nigeria is best understood in these terms. Their history and the activities in which they are engaged suggest that the relationship between local communities and central institutions is more dynamic and two-way in both structure and outcome than the modernizationists assumed. Thus, while the modernization approach captures part of the theoretical significance of these organizations, it must be amended to capture all.

Lastly, it must be asked how civil society, including the organization of rural communities, can be encouraged in Africa given the uneven distribution of associational life across the continent? How might the types of associational life found in Kenya and Nigeria be replicated in other countries? To observe that associational life is most developed in countries and regions of countries which are most economically developed is not very helpful for a continent struggling to avert further economic decline, let alone grow. Can associational life be stimulated in regions of economic stagnation, and if so, how?

Definitive answers to these questions are beyond the scope of this chapter and the data on which it is based. It is nonetheless apparent that communities that are very poor, though not the poorest, can and will organize themselves for self-help development provided the political climate does not discourage them from doing so and provided they can do so free of state regulation. It is also clear that rural communities are capable of generating a substantial amount of resources to support their development from within the local community as well as from outside. Where this process is linked to a system of open elections, as was the case in Kenya, associational life in the rural areas becomes an integral part of the political process. But

Resurrecting Modernization Theory

even where electoral politics has been an intermittent phenomenon as in Nigeria, community associations will proliferate, if permitted to do so, and have a salutary effect on state-society relations.

The relationship between civil society and the state in Africa as elsewhere is reciprocal. On the one hand, the existence of associational life raises the level of state accountability by subjecting the state to pressures from societal interests, including interests in the rural areas. On the other hand, the growth and good health of associational life are unlikely unless those in control of the state conclude that it is in their interest—that it will enhance the legitimacy of their rule—to give associational life free rein. State accountability, in short, depends greatly on a willingness by those who rule to be held accountable by the populations they purport to serve and to tolerate public expressions of opposition to their rule.

Given the record of most African leaders since independence, the prospects for the growth of associational life may seem dismal. Two factors, however, suggest that the prospects in the 1990s are the brightest since independence. Both are responses to the overall decline of political authority and economic performance across the continent. The first is that a growing number of African leaders have begun to realize, albeit grudgingly, that the exercise of state authority must be transformed into a more accountable process if the state itself is to avert total collapse. The decision by President Kenneth Kaunda of Zambia in October 1990 to change his country's constitution to permit the existence of opposition parties and competitive elections, and the actual holding of such elections in November 1991, is perhaps the most explicit example of this thinking. Other examples include Julius Nyerere's statements in 1990 and 1991 that Tanzania should not remain a one-party state and the subsequent decision by the country's ruling party to transform Tanzania into a multiparty democracy; the overwhelming vote by the politburo of the ruling party of Zimbabwe in August 1990 to draw back from its long-standing policy of establishing a one-party state in that country; and Daniel arap Moi's announcement in December 1991 that Kenya would permit opposition parties to contest the next parliamentary elections. In all of these cases, African leaders have begun to modify their approach to the exercise of state authority in the face of growing internal opposition to unaccountable rule.

The second factor enhancing the prospects for autonomous associational life is the growing external pressure by the international donor community on African leaders to democratize their regimes. The end of the cold war and the democratization of Eastern Europe, coupled with the genuine steps toward political reform in South Africa, have led members of the donor community to demand similar reforms throughout Africa. The United States and other bilateral donors as well as the World Bank now make the continuation of economic assistance conditional on the evolution of more open political systems. The donors increasingly articulate the view expressed at the outset of this essay—that economic development is impossible in societies where the state is unaccountable for its actions.[48]

Faced with growing internal and external pressure, African leaders may be reluctant to create an atmosphere where associational life can flourish. Yet as Kenyatta recognized two decades ago, associational life can strengthen a regime by providing it with an organized social base. Perhaps it is in this regard that those portrayed as "modernizing elites" in the literature on modernization will now assume their appropriate role.

Notes

1. Mancur Olson, "Rapid Growth as a Destabilizing Force," *Journal of Economic History* 23 (Dec. 1963): 529–52, reprinted in Jason L. Finkle and Richard W. Gable, eds., *Political Development and Social Change* (New York: Wiley, 1971), pp. 557–68; Samuel P. Huntington, *Political Order in Changing Societies* (New Haven: Yale Univ. Press, 1968), pp. 39–59.

2. For one of the clearest articulations of the relationship as measured by the association between the average per capita income in a country and the nature of its political system, see S. M. Lipset, "Economic Development and Democracy," *Political Man* (New York: Anchor, 1963), pp. 27–63. Lipset's argument, however, was based solely on a cross-sectional analysis of data from fifty countries for a single time period (the 1950s) and not on a longitudinal analysis of these same countries over the period of their economic development. Drawing on Lipset, James S. Coleman also discussed this relationship in his concluding chapter to *The Politics of the Developing Areas,* ed. Gabriel Almond and James S. Coleman (Princeton, N.J.: Princeton Univ. Press, 1960), pp. 532–76. For a more recent observation of the relationship in the context of Sub-Saharan Africa, see Michael Bratton, "Beyond the State: Civil Society and Associational Life in Africa," *World Politics* 41, no. 3 (April 1989): 407–30.

3. Although prices of Africa's principal agricultural commodities dropped precipitously after 1977, they are at roughly the same level as they were in 1970. Prices for nonoil primary commodities from Africa, moreover, have dropped less than the prices of similar commodities from other developing countries. The external terms of trade for non-oil-producing countries is significantly lower than in the early 1970s, but the terms of trade for oil producers such as Nigeria are higher. See World Bank, *Sub-Saharan Africa: From Crisis to Sustainable Growth* (Washington, D.C., 1989), p. 32, and World Bank and UNDP, *Africa's Adjustment and Growth in the 1980s* (Washington, D.C., 1989), pp. 1, 11.

4. The best example is Nigeria's mismanagement of its earnings from oil exports through the mid-1980s and the subsequent decline of the Nigerian economy in the second half of the decade.

5. This rather harsh generalization holds for Angola, Ethiopia, Mozambique, and especially Tanzania. See E. Wayne Nafziger, *Inequality in Africa: Political Elites, Proletariat, Peasants, and the Poor* (New York: Cambridge Univ. Press, 1988).

6. Robert H. Jackson and Carl G. Rosberg, "Why Africa's Weak States Persist: The Empirical and the Juridical in Statehood," *World Politics* 35, no. 1 (Oct. 1982): 1–24.

7. Goran Hyden, *No Shortcuts to Progress: African Development Management in Perspective* (Berkeley: Univ. of California Press, 1983), p. 71.

8. One indication of dropout is the declining turnout rates for parliamentary elections in countries where voters no longer have a meaningful choice. Turnout in the 1988 elections in Kenya was approximately 24 percent of those eligible to vote, the lowest in Kenya's six elections since independence. Following a campaign of intimidation by the ruling party, turnout in the 1990 parliamentary elections in Zimbabwe dropped to 54 percent of those eligible compared to over 80 percent in 1980 and 1985.

9. Frank Holmquist, "Defending Peasant Political Space in Independent Africa," *Canadian Journal of African Studies* 14 (1980): 157–68.

10. For an instructive review of such passive resistance by rural dwellers, albeit in Southeast Asia rather than Africa, see James C. Scott, *Weapons of the Weak* (New Haven: Yale Univ. Press, 1986).

11. See Goran Hyden "Governance and the Study of Politics," in *Governance and Politics in Africa,* ed. Goran Hyden and Michael Bratton (Boulder, Colo.: Lynne Rienner, 1991), pp. 4–26. For a review of the importance of civil society, see Bratton, "Beyond the State," and Naomi Chazan, John Harbeson, and Donald Rothchild, *Civil Society in Africa* (Boulder, Colo.: Lynne Rienner, forthcoming, 1993).

12. For the purpose of this discussion, *accountable authority* is defined as authority exercised by those in control of the state within boundaries established through periodic expressions of consent, support, or criticism by those subject to such authority. Under this definition, the holding of competitive elections is only one procedure of establishing such boundaries. The existence of a free press, for example, is another.

13. David E. Apter, *The Gold Coast in Transition* (Princeton, N.J.: Princeton Univ. Press, 1958), chap. 1.

14. Coleman was concerned with the quest for self-rule in Africa rather than the form of government such rule would bring. Like Apter, however, he assumed that the political structures would be those inherited from the British and modeled on the Westminster model of parliamentary democracy. See *Nigeria: Background to Nationalism* (Berkeley: Univ. of California Press, 1958), introduction.

15. James S. Coleman and C. R. D. Halisi, "American Political Science and Tropical Africa: Universalism versus Relativism," *African Studies Review* 26, nos. 3/4 (Sept./Dec. 1983): 41.

16. Huntington, *Political Order in Changing Societies,* p. 1.

17. Where the state does not own the means of production, as in Southeast Asia, the relationship between authoritarian rule and economic stagnation may not be valid. It is

interesting that this relationship, stated in the negative, is the obverse of Lipset's original observation that economic development and democratic rule go hand in hand.

18. James S. Coleman, "The Development Syndrome," in *Crises and Sequences in Political Development,* ed. Leonard Binder et al. (Princeton, N.J.: Princeton Univ. Press, 1971), pp. 74, 78–79, 80.

19. Ibid., p. 74.

20. Alexis de Tocqueville, *Democracy in America,* ed. J. A. Mayer and Max Lerner (New York: Harper and Row, 1966), p. 177.

21. See, for example, William Kornhauser, *The Politics of Mass Society* (London: Routledge and Kegan Paul, 1960), and David Truman, *The Governmental Process: Political Interests and Public Opinion* (New York: Knopf, 1971).

22. See Leo Kuper, "Plural Societies: Perspectives and Problems," in Leo Kuper and M. G. Smith, eds., *Pluralism in Africa* (Berkeley: Univ. of California Press, 1969), pp. 7–26.

23. See, for example, Theodore Lowi's critique of pluralism in his classic study of American politics, *The End of Liberalism* (New York: Norton, 1968). Students of corporatism in the context of Western Europe, such as Philippe Schmitter, have also demonstrated that civil society in the context of the advanced industrial democracies and pluralism do not necessarily go hand in hand. See Philippe C. Schmitter and Gerhard Lehmbruch, eds., *Trends towards Corporatist Intermediation* (Beverly Hills, Calif.: Sage Publications, 1979).

24. Bratton, "Beyond the State," pp. 411, 428.

25. *Harambee* is the Kiswahili word for "to pull together"; as Kenya's national motto it appears on the country's coat of arms.

26. This estimate is based on a review of district registration rolls of self-help organizations conducted in 1979. At that time, Kenya was divided into forty administrative districts with an estimated average of 375–500 self-help groups in each.

27. Carl G. Rosberg and John Nottingham, *The Myth of "Mau Mau": Nationalism in Kenya* (New York: Praeger, 1966), pp. 103–35.

28. See Frank Holmquist, "Implementing Rural Development Projects," in *Development Administration: The Kenyan Experience,* ed. Goran Hyden, Robert Jackson, and John J. Okumu (Nairobi: Oxford Univ. Press, 1970), pp. 201–29; Holmquist, "Defending Peasant Political Space"; Frank Holmquist, "Class Structure, Peasant Participation, and Rural Self-Help," in *Politics and Public Policy in Kenya and Tanzania,* ed. Joel D. Barkan (New York: Praeger, 1984), pp. 171–97; and Joel D. Barkan and Frank Holmquist, "Peasant-State Relations and the Social Base of Self-Help in Kenya," *World Politics* 41, no. 3 (April 1989): 359–80.

29. Kenya did not become a one-party state by law until 1982 when the country's constitution was amended to permit the existence of only the ruling party, the Kenya African National Union (KANU). This section of the constitution was repealed in December 1991 to set the stage for the formation of opposition parties and Kenya's first multiparty elections since independence in December 1992.

30. For a statistical model demonstrating these relationships as well as the rationality of Kenyan voters, see Joel D. Barkan, "Reassessing the Conventional Wisdom," *American Political Science Review* 70, no. 2 (June 1976): 451–54.

31. The 1988 elections are generally regarded as rigged and therefore do not provide valid data on how voters evaluated incumbents who stood for reelection. Because many "elected" in 1988 were regarded as having obtained office through fraudulent means, more than 70 percent of the incumbent members of the National Assembly were defeated in the party primary elections and the multiparty general elections held in November and December 1992.

32. Joel D. Barkan, "Legislators, Elections, and Political Linkage," in Barkan, *Politics and Public Policy in Kenya and Tanzania,* p. 94.

33. Bratton, "Beyond the State," p. 427.

34. I collected these data in 1979 and 1980 in collaboration with Frank Holmquist, David Gachuki, and S. E. Migot-Adholla. Case histories were compiled of ten to fourteen Harambee organizations in each of seven rural parliamentary constituencies located in the Central, Eastern, Western, Nyanza, and Rift Valley provinces. Sample surveys of between 293 and 300 respondents were conducted in each of the same seven constituencies the year after the case histories were compiled so that the respondents could be queried about their involvement in specific examples of self-help. Interpretation of these data has been informed by follow-up visits to Kenya in 1986 and 1987. For a detailed analysis of the social base of self-help, see Barkan and Holmquist, "Peasant-State Relations."

35. Small farmers join an average of 4.2 projects, middle farmers an average of 4.8, and the landless and large farmers averages of 2.5 and 3.5, respectively (ibid., p. 368).

36. Only 9 percent of landless respondents reported that they had led Harambee projects, while the figure for large farmers was 30 percent and for small and middle farmers 20 and 29 percent, respectively (ibid., p. 369).

37. Republic of Kenya (Office of the President), *District Focus and Rural Development, Revised* (Nairobi: Government Printer, March 1987).

38. Space does not permit a detailed analysis of District Focus and its significance for state-society relations. For an analysis of how administrative procedures have been changed by the policy, see John M. Cohen and Richard M. Hook, "Decentralized Planning in Kenya," *Public Administration and Development* 7 (1987): 77–93. For a discussion of its political significance, see Joel D. Barkan with Michael Chege, "Decentralising the State: District Focus and the Politics of Reallocation in Kenya," *Journal of Modern African Studies* 27, no. 3 (1989): 431–53.

39. For example, on March 23, 1990, Kenya's leading news magazine, the *Weekly Review,* reported (on p. 15) that a record sum of 141.8 million Kenyan shillings (or $7.6 million) was raised at a Harambee fund-raiser led by President Moi. The president "and his friends" were credited with giving K Sh. 485,000. Contributions by civil servants for these fund-raisers are now deducted from their paychecks—in effect, a withholding tax.

40. For a detailed description of how the Provincial Administration was used to extract contributions for presidential projects, see the testimony by Eston Mbajah to the Judicial Commission of Inquiry into the Murder of Robert Ouku as reported in the *Standard* (Nairobi), Nov. 13, 1991, p. 14.

41. Settlement patterns in southern Nigeria are more concentrated than in Kenya. Whereas in East Africa most of the population outside the major cities live on small

household settlements that are dispersed across the fertile areas of the country, in Nigeria people are grouped into villages of up to several hundred residents or into towns of between 25,000 and 50,000 people.

42. N. A. Fadipe, *The Sociology of the Yoruba* (Ibadan: Univ. of Ibadan Press, 1970), p. 243.

43. See Kenneth Little, *West African Urbanization: A Study of Voluntary Associations in Social Change* (Cambridge: Cambridge Univ. Press., 1965), and Claude Meillassoux, *Urbanization in a West African Community: Voluntary Associations in Bamako* (Seattle: Univ. of Washington Press, 1968).

44. Little, *West African Urbanization*, p. 29, and P. C. Lloyd make brief reference to the involvement of migrants in hometown associations, but neither explores the process or its political significance. See P. C. Lloyd, *Power and Independence: Urban African's Perceptions of Inequality* (London: Routledge and Kegan Paul), pp. 130–31.

45. All three associations included in this study are in Oyo state: the Otan-Ayegbaju Progressive Union is located fifteen miles northeast of Osogbo, the Awe Development Corporation is located just east of Oyo, and the Fiditi Progressive Union is located twenty miles north of Ibadan. Except where noted, the organization and activities of the three associations are the same. This study, which also included an analysis of Nigeria's evolving system of local government, was conducted in collaboration with Michael McNulty and M. A. O. Ayeni. Responsibility for the interpretation of the data presented in this essay is solely mine.

46. There are now 500 local government authorities in Nigeria which receive 10 percent of the federal budget and an additional 5 percent of state budgets to run their operations. Local government in Nigeria has grown substantially since 1976 when the present system was instituted and is rapidly becoming a significant arena of local political life. Each local government authority is run by an elected local government council. The present councillors have been elected on a nonpartisan basis, but it is the stated intention of the Federal Military Government to change the system to partisan contests as part of Nigeria's return to civilian rule.

47. Robert Michels, *Political Parties* (1915; New York: Dover, 1959), pts. 1 and 6.

48. *Sub-Saharan Africa: From Crisis to Sustainable Growth*, pp. 60–61. A notable example of donor implementation of this position occurred in November 1991 when the members of the Consultative Group of bilateral donors (CG) informed the government of Kenya that it would receive no additional foreign assistance until it embarked on fundamental reforms. A similar action taken by the CG for Malawi in May 1992 and the suspension of assistance by the United States to the Cameroon following fraudulent elections in October 1992 are further indicators of the intention by members of the donor community to regard accountable government as a condition for aid.

4

SOCIAL CLASS AND POLITICAL ACTION IN AFRICA: THE BOURGEOISIE AND THE PROLETARIAT

RICHARD L. SKLAR

THE CONCEPT of social class is based on the division of labor in society. Theories of class structure teach that the members of a social class are impelled by their common interests to think and act in similar ways. Class theorists attribute social solidarity to the facts of social inequality and domination. Therefore, class analyses of political behavior frequently appeal to scholars who are motivated by moral commitments to the ideal of social equality.

Despite these intellectual and ethical attractions, the discipline of political science has been basically averse to class analysis. One explanation for that attitude draws attention to ideological tendencies in the United States, where most political scientists practice their profession and relatively few of them, or their intellectual compatriots, believe that class structure is the dominant feature of social organization. Another, perhaps more fundamental, explanation is rooted in the disciplinary values of political scientists. In our time the leading theories of class are economistic. They teach that social awareness is determined mainly by the positions that people occupy in the economic structure of society. Yet there is no lack of evidence for the contrary proposition that noneconomic factors are often more potent than economic factors as determinants of social solidarity and political action. Ethnic (including racial), religious, or national sentiments may be overriding; tyrannical government and the desire for liberty also spurs collective action; and there are "silent revolutions," impelled by generational changes, environmental concerns, and new technologies.[1]

What if class analysis were to be liberated from restrictive, economistic preconceptions and refocused on a more realistic, multidimensional conception of social relations? Would that not command the attention of many political scientists and encourage them to address the moral implications of social inequality?

The chief impediment to a breakthrough of that kind in political science appears to be the immense prestige of Marxist theory among scholars who use class analysis. Marxism teaches that societies are divided into classes as a result of their distinctive modes of economic production and property ownership. This economistic doctrine is not realistic for societies at early stages of industrialization. Its perpetuation by Marxist scholars has been detrimental to the development of viable class-analytic approaches to the study of African politics.

In Africa, and other regions of early industrial development, political authority is the primary foundation of social control. Everywhere in Africa it has been used to create new institutions, particularly governmental agencies and parastatal organizations, including public enterprises. All such institutions provide employment for the first few postcolonial generations of educated citizens: in Sub-Saharan Africa today, public sector employment accounts for half of all jobs in the "modern sector."[2] As Larry Diamond has observed, "Given the role of the state as the primary wage employer, it is not surprising that a huge and often staggering proportion of these swelling expenditures are claimed by 'administration'—essentially, the pay and support of state personnel."[3] Hence the public employment sector is a veritable forcing house of class formation.

By itself salaried employment on a massive scale would not produce a modern and stable system of social stratification; there must also be a reasonably open (rather than exclusive and restricted) system of public education, based mainly on the principle of merit. Between 1950 and 1985 basic literacy in Africa rose from 16 percent of the total population to 47 percent. More to the point of class differentiation, in 1976 the ratio of public expenditures on higher education to those on elementary education, per student, was 100.5 to 1 in Sub-Saharan Africa, compared with 17.2 to 1 in the Middle East / North Africa and 9 to 1 in South Asia.[4] The African university student is an arrivé, whether or not he or she "was at first an *arriviste.*"[5]

In Africa today the exercise of political authority and the availability of public education are the principal determinants of social reconstruction. Other determinants, such as the ownership of productive property, do not affect the social positions of nearly as many people or family groups. Since the system of public education itself is a product of the exercise of political authority, it would follow that in African and other societies at early stages of industrialization, "class relations, at bottom, are determined by relations of power, not production." The application of this theorem to societies at more advanced stages of industrialization, on the ground that relations of production, everywhere, are surely relations of power, would be logical but not directly relevant to the matter at hand. However, the conceptual problem that is implicit in a power-based theory of class would be the same for all societies. It may be stated thus: Power is exercised by persons who occupy positions of authority in any of the diverse sectors of society. Is it reasonable to believe that such persons, normally classified by social scientists as "elites," will "identify with one another more firmly and in more ways than they do with their respective institutional bases or organizational activities"? Do they normally "unite and act in concert—consciously so—on the basis of their common interest in social control"?[6] If so, the concept of class, as an explanatory device, supersedes that of the elite, which continues to be important because it signifies the fundamental fact of inequality in human affairs.

Just as dominant-class formation involves a social fusion of institutional elites, so, too, does subordinate-class formation signify a corresponding fusion of nonelites. However, these processes are neither reciprocal nor symmetrical; the fusion of elites does not entail a countervailing fusion of nonelites. Social and political cohesion is the rule for those who attain elite occupations, including business management and finance, administrative rank in the civil service, governmental and political leadership, the learned professions, and other occupations of similar status. This conception of class formation deviates sharply from standard Marxist theory, which identifies the economic order of society as the primary foundation of its social class structure. In modern African societies, it is difficult to resist the conclusion that political organization, broadly conceived to embrace the realm of public administration, is the principal determinant of social stratification.

Indeed, for all societies with state-centered yet business-oriented economic institutions, such as we find in Africa, the orthodox Marxist doctrine of class determination is not realistic. This view has been advanced with reference to corporate-capitalist and bureaucratic-socialist societies alike by Stanislaw Ossowski, whose significant contribution to Marxian sociology broadens the Marxist conception of class to encompass three main determinants, thus: "Means of Production, Means of Consumption and Means of Compulsion."[7] A similarly complex (plural and variable) basis of class determination would enhance the appeal of class analysis to those social scientists who study Africa but are understandably reluctant to venture beyond the image of dominant elites in uneasy control of fragile institutions. To be sure, elite theories of society are realistic since they confirm the common experience of inequality and personal leadership in all walks of life. However, elite analyses deal with the tip of the iceberg and largely overlook what is going on in the underlying mass. Hence they are fairly alleged to yield relatively superficial explanations of social change.[8] Yet elite theories are frequently adopted by professed Marxist scholars, who do not appear to recognize the difference between elite and class analyses. For example, the familiar idea of a bureaucratic class (or bureaucratic bourgeoisie) suggests that a functional elite of administrative personnel is, itself, a social class. Such restrictive conceptions drastically minimize the theoretical richness and explanatory power of class analysis.[9] This one, "bureaucratic class," attributes class domination to the effects of bureaucratic organization despite the fact that bureaucratic methods are essential to ensure reasonably equal and fair (impersonal) treatment of all concerned. Its widespread use to characterize state management of the economy as a form of class rule has often obscured the real political determinants of a society's class structure.

For three decades professed Marxists have oscillated between doctrinaire, economistic theories of social class and un-Marxist elite theories. However, there was always a Marxian alternative, represented by Ossowski's revisionist work, which was published both in Polish in 1957 and in a widely acclaimed English translation in 1963. Looking for ways to broaden the orthodox Marxist conception of class, he quipped, but seriously, that "the witty Warsaw cockneys defined the two classes in socialist countries by the terms 'proletariat' and 'chevroletariat.'"[10] This word coinage anticipated the colloquial term *Wanenzi*—meaning those who either own or have guaranteed use of Mercedes Benz automobiles—in postcolonial Eastern Africa. In Zambia an adviser to the president, the respected French agronomist René Dumont, was reported to have made this trenchant observation: "There is an urban elite of Party officials cruising the road in chauffeur-driven Mercedes and peasants working two days to afford a bag of salt. 20% of Zambia's gross national product goes to the 2% of the population who wield power."[11] Although the "urban elite," in Zambia and elsewhere in Africa, is hardly limited to party officials, his barbed remark hits home. Apart from the sparsely populated oil-rich states of Gabon and Libya, the ostensibly privileged power holders and their immediate families probably make up between 2 and 4 percent of the population in most African countries.

Do such high-income and elite-occupational groups, whose members also control the dominant institutions of their societies, qualify for identification as social classes? The criteria of class identification are both subjective, meaning consciousness of class, and objective, for example, common actions that unite such persons across institutional and other social boundaries. Subjective identification with reference to a dominant class does not appear to have been studied systematically in Africa since the mid-1970s, when the attitudes of university students were analyzed with the help of survey research.[12] The subsequent recession of scientific social, including political, research in Africa reflects an overall decline in the quality of African universities and the related failure of Africa-based scholars, with relatively few exceptions, to produce valid empirical research. In political science this shortcoming is not unrelated to doctrinaire tendencies that actually discourage open-minded inquiry.[13] It may also be a function of the illiberal political climate that prevailed in most African states until the turnabout of 1990–91, since, as W. J. M. Mackenzie has observed, "political science cannot develop except in certain limited intellectual and social conditions; there must be an established practice of debate based on analysis and observation, and it must be accepted that there exist political questions open to settlement by argument rather than by tradition or by authority. In this sense political science is conditioned by political society."[14] In any event, the disappearance of scholarly journals edited and published in Africa—for example, the world-class Zambian journal *African Social Research*—bodes ill for Africa-based social science.

Fortunately, objective measures of class identification can be discovered by various means, including direct observation of collective actions. This chapter considers objective evidence bearing on the identification of two social classes in African societies, specifically, the dominant class and the proverbial working class.

The Bourgeoisie

During the eighteenth century the term *bourgeoisie* was used to specify free citizens of French towns. Gradually it became synonymous with "middle class" throughout the world. In 1888 Friedrich Engels identified the bourgeoisie as "the class of modern Capitalists, owners of the means of social production and employers of wage-labour."[15] During the present century its meaning for Marxists expanded from the core conception of those who practice capitalism to connote the complex dominant class of societies that maintain market economies and allow capitalist accumulation as a consequence of private property in the means of production. Following the Sino-

Soviet split of the early 1960s, Maoists applied the term to allegedly domi-nant classes in Soviet-bloc countries on the ground that they were either backsliding or not really socialist. Currently the term is used by a variety of thinkers to designate the dominant classes of all modern societies regardless of the mode of production in effect. Most of those who use the term in this way still define it narrowly to mean those who control the means of eco-nomic production and gain political dominance by virtue of such control. However, that definition would be misleading if, as I contend, the relations of production are determined by more fundamental relations of power. The broader, noneconomistic version adopted here does diverge from Marxist tradition. Yet my retention of the term *bourgeoisie* to identify the dominant social class of modern society is intended as a tribute to Marxism, which culled it from common usage for promotion to social theory.

In previous works I have suggested the idea of a managerial bourgeoisie, defined as the dominant class in countries at early and intermediate stages of industrial development, where the public management sector predomi-nates while it also nurtures and promotes private enterprise.[16] It is impor-tant to stress that this term does not connote a class of managers; that it is not an occupational or functional concept but a "socially comprehensive category, encompassing the entrepreneurial elite, managers of firms, senior state functionaries, leading politicians, members of the learned professions, and persons of similar standing in all spheres of society."[17] Furthermore, the adjective *managerial* is specifically intended to reflect the spirit of business management.

It is equally important to differentiate my conception of a managerial bourgeoisie from that of a "petite bourgeoisie," which has been adopted by some analysts to identify "ruling" classes in Africa.[18] That term, which properly refers to proprietors of small-scale enterprises and persons of comparable social status, fails to capture the hegemonic tendency of the African bourgeoisie, which derives its power primarily from political orga-nization. Its use to represent dominant classes in African societies signifies continued adherence to the economic basis of class determination by think-ers who resist the broader, power-based conception of class recommended here.

In Africa, as elsewhere in the world today, sustained economic develop-ment depends upon the mobilization of powerful personal incentives to create and conduct profitable enterprises. As in China, Eastern Europe, and the post-Communist Commonwealth of Independent States, so, too, in Africa have *dirigiste* or statist economic policies, based on coercive central direction, been discredited and progressively abandoned. The spirit of capitalism in Africa has now emerged from a long shadow of ideological distrust, attributable mainly to its historic association with colonial rule. Its growth surely will invigorate the African bourgeoisie and shape its nature as African societies begin to free themselves from oppressive statism. Yet social scientists rarely report political activity in opposition to restrictive economic regulation by African governments. Nor, until 1991, did leading political parties in Africa plainly call for reduced governmental intervention in the economy.[19] However, a few analysts have adduced evidence of activities that signify concerted efforts by leading sectors of the African bourgeoisie to establish capitalism on a firm basis in politics and the law as well as economic organization.

Elsewhere, I have used the expression "capitalist movement" to represent "currents of thought and related actions in support of economic enterprise based on the private ownership of productive property." Therein, I cited Goran Hyden's report of a 1986 Conference on the Enabling Environment for Private Sector Contributions to Development, held in Nairobi under the auspices of the Aga Khan Foundation and attended by officials and business executives from various African countries and international organizations.[20] Subsequently, the idea of an "enabling environment" was adopted by the World Bank to designate one part of a dual strategy for "sustainable and equitable growth," reckoned by the bank to be not less than 4 percent per annum. Defined concisely to signify "infrastructure services, and incentives that foster efficient production and private initiative," the enabling environment is coupled in this approach with the idea of "enhanced capacities" for both "people and institutions" to foster the improvement of productivity in Africa.[21]

Enhanced capacity is explained with reference to (1) human development, including education for effective management and planning, (2) institutional development, and (3) constructive, rather than predatory, political governance. While it is necessary to reduce bloated and parasitical public bureaucracies, there is an essential role for government; it must foster and protect private enterprise in order to release latent productive energies and create healthy national economies. The responsibility of public government for economic development is summarized concisely, thus: "The State has an indispensable role in creating a favorable economic environment. This should, in fact, be its primary concern. It is of the utmost importance for the State to establish a predictable and honest administration of the regulatory framework, to assure law and order, and to foster a stable, objective, and transparent judicial system. In addition it should provide reliable and efficient infrastructure and social and information services—all preconditions for the efficiency of productive enterprises, whether private or state-owned." Furthermore, the World Bank's strategy for African development eschews ideological dogmatism: "The division of responsibilities between the State and the private sector should be a matter of pragmatism—not dogma." Three maxims for the maintenance of "an enabling environment for productive activities" are expressed: "removing unnecessary regulations that add to the costs borne by enterprises, keeping exchange rates competitive, and strengthening infrastructure services."[22]

The World Bank itself cites various instances of governmental commitment to both institutional reform and the creation of an enabling environment for private enterprise.[23] These undertakings include civil service reforms that have reduced costs in several countries and lifted the morale of citizens who value efficiency and integrity in public agencies. In a growing number of countries, inefficient bureaucracies are being scrapped or cut back in favor of private services; examples include the provision of drinking water for some 130 towns in Côte d'Ivoire, refuse collection in Togo, and passenger transport in Ghana. In Nigeria a program of economic liberalization, introduced in 1986, "has transformed the incentive structure of the economy." The key provisions are "a market-determined exchange rate system," elimination of import licensing and relaxation of export regulations, and supportive monetary and fiscal policies.

This program is broadly supported by political activists in Nigeria, including most of those who seek office under the constitutional government of the Third Republic, destined for inauguration in 1993. In accordance with a 1987 decision of the Armed Forces Ruling Council to establish a non-doctrinaire two-party system for electoral competition, President Ibrahim Babangida proscribed thirteen aspirant political associations and instructed the National Electoral Commission to establish two national parties of the center-left and center-right, respectively. This unexpected decision, unanticipated at the time of its announcement in 1989, was widely praised for its realism and common sense. It appeared to reflect a national consensus in favor of political moderation, market mechanisms for the allocation of resources, and increasing private participation in all sectors of the economy. Speaking for the Armed Forces Ruling Council, President Babangida has declared and reaffirmed that his caretaker military government "will not impose an ideology on the country": "We [the Armed Forces Ruling Council] realized that most Nigerians tend to feel that unless ideology is stated in terms of isms in a constitution, the constitutional document lacks merit. This is an unfortunate attitude because in most countries of the world today, whether in the developed or developing countries, or in the nations of the East or of the West, the debate on ideology has become irrelevant."[24] The establishment of national political parties on foundations of pragmatism and skepticism, rather than doctrinaire ideologies, attests to the rapid political mobilization of a Nigerian bourgeoisie imbued with liberal sentiments and the values of private enterprise.

Since 1985, public enterprise reforms have been implemented in a substantial majority of the African countries. Such reforms include financial restructuring, agreements to contract for private management services, and the outright sale of state enterprises to private owners.[25] Regrettably, few scholars have chosen to study business interest groups in Africa, although the pioneering work-in-progress of Ernest J. Wilson III, at the University of Michigan's Center for Research on Economic Development, has begun to address that question. Heretofore, most scholarly analysts of business-oriented policies in Africa have traced their origins to the "state." In this way, the theoretical horizons of social scientists are restricted by what they choose to disregard.

Evidence of concerted efforts by business interest groups to foster conditions that would be propitious for entrepreneurial achievements can be gleaned from periodicals that cater to the African business community. For example, the *Southern African Economist,* published in Harare by the Southern African Development Coordination Conference (SADCC), is an important forum for African business and managerial opinion. Thus, Alexander Chikwanda, a chairman of the Zambia Industrial and Commercial Association, joined a debate in that journal to echo the call for creation of "enabling environments" in Africa in order to promote enterprise and combat stagnation. Affirming the duty of governments to be responsible for "social equity" and regional balance in national development, he nonetheless warned against excessive governmental intervention: "Controls imposed from the top through bureaucratic fiats are never salutary. Wherever there are ubiquitous controls, chronic artificial shortages and black markets, not to mention corruption, are the order of the day."[26] These and related convictions are now being propagated vigorously by the continentwide African Business Roundtable, founded in 1987 by Babacar Ndiaye, president of the African Development Bank, "to promote private sector growth and inter-African trade and investment."[27]

Increasingly, proponents of African enterprise turn their attention to the need for trained managers. In addition to overvalued local currencies and other policies that stifle entrepreneurial initiative, business efficiency in Africa is severely hampered by a debilitating shortage of managerial skills. In response to this need, a group of international agencies (the International Finance Corporation, the African Development Bank, and the U.N. Development Program) and transnational corporations have created an African Management Services Company (AmsCo) to train managers for medium-sized companies in countries where governments have agreed to cooperate.

Thus far I have adduced evidence in support of my thesis on the mobilization of an African continental capitalist movement. These citations indicate growing demands for the creation of an "enabling environment" for private enterprise, privatization policies, management training, and a facilitative role for government in accordance with law rather than political caprice. But these topics all relate to behavior within the so-called formal sector, meaning economic activity that is effectively controlled by legally enforceable devices, e.g., contracts and licenses. However, in Africa, as elsewhere in the proverbial Third World, formal-sector employment lags far behind population growth and the need for work. Consequently, a majority of those Africans who will seek regular work during the next few decades must earn their incomes within the "informal" sectors of economic systems, mainly in urban and peri-urban environments.[28] Increasingly, formal-sector firms depend on the informal sector for both market demand and product supply. Clearly, the informal sector is more than an isolated or separate arena of economic activity to which people withdraw in order to survive. On the contrary, it is an integral part of a unified economic system. As I have observed elsewhere, "a symbiotic relationship between formal-sector demand and informal-sector supply may be the fundamental fact of economic life in poor countries."[29]

Based on her study of household expenditures in Zaire, Janet MacGaffey has estimated "the overall size of the real economy [in that country] to be about three times that given in the national accounts." Her conception of the "real economy" is no less valuable for the study of social movements than it is for economic analysis: "Study of the real economy does away with the false dichotomies between formal and informal, official and second, recorded and unrecorded economies, which are, in reality, inextricably interlinked and only distinguishable in analytical terms. Together, they form the total, real economy: their differentiation is a function of political rather than economic factors."[30] The real, unified economy is largely powered by the energies of enterprising men and women who earn incomes by producing goods and providing services beyond the range of public regulation. Their values reinforce the capitalist convictions of entrepreneurs and others who manage public as well as private economic activities in accordance with formal regulations. In addition to their entrepreneurial activities, small-scale traders and producers regularly form and join associations that provide credit facilities and insurance services. For example, informal credit associations, such as the tontine, have operated in the markets of francophone Africa since the seventeenth century.[31] Adapted to the needs of modern enterprise and urbanization, these local credit clubs provide taproots for capitalist activity in an authentically African cultural context.

How does the capitalist movement manifest itself as a social movement based on the aspirations and beliefs of people in small-business occupations? All people crave respect for their talents and accomplishments. There are few, if any, instances in Africa or elsewhere in the world of popular support for doctrinaire political parties that stifle individual initiative. In the event of a truly competitive electoral process, political parties founded on Marxist-Leninist (vanguardist) principles would either liberalize or be swept out of office. Not even the widely respected African National Congress (ANC) of South Africa could expect to gain majority support without first proclaiming its dedication to a mixed economy and a pluralist political system, which it did in 1988 (despite its organic link to the South African Communist party). Since free and competitive elections tend to transform doctrinaire socialist parties into nondoctrinaire populist parties, demands for that basic political freedom actually promote the capitalist movement in Africa regardless of the personal ideological beliefs of individuals who pursue it. Furthermore, small-business elements within the informal economic sector are less likely to support parties with strictly capitalist orientations than populist parties that accommodate their specific interests.

The Proletariat

In all societies at early or intermediate levels of industrial development, the wage-labor class includes a broad spectrum of workers, employed at rates of pay that are computed variably from hourly to monthly periods. This category includes agricultural workers who neither own nor rent land yet live in ways that are similar to those who do so and are therefore identified as peasants. For Africa as a whole, the wage-earning population is probably less than 20 percent of those who are economically active,[32] although it rises above 50 percent in South Africa and Zambia. Approximately half of all wage earners are employed in the public sector; they include civil servants, government employees without the legal status of civil servants, and employees of enterprises owned, wholly or in part, by a government. Employee organizations, i.e., trade or labor unions, are firmly established for purposes of collective representation in the public sector. Hence the relationship between a government and the national, or central, labor organization is normally sensitive, given the high potential for political discord.

For many years, until the liberal turnabout of 1990–91, the industrial and political rights of employee organizations in African countries were severely curtailed by domineering governments and political parties. In a few countries, however, firmly established labor unions were successful in resisting attempts by governments to undermine their independence. One of the most noteworthy examples of determined and effective resistance to a menacing government is the robust labor movement of Zambia, a country of approximately 8 million people, half of whom are urban dwellers. The strength of Zambian labor is rooted in the so-called Copperbelt, a compact conurban region adjacent to a similar mining region in Zaire. Mining development entailed both railway construction, hence railway workers, and urban growth along the crucial rail line from Zaire to Zimbabwe. Zambia's great copper-producing industry, fifth largest in the world, accounts for the relatively balanced (industrial, commercial, transport, and service-sector) composition of its wage-labor force by comparison with other small states in agrarian regions. For this reason, the Zambian experience is important and may even prove to be paradigmatic for rapidly changing African societies.

During the formative years of labor organization on the Copperbelt, the mine workers union interacted regularly with political organizations that had been formed to pursue national independence and racial justice. Before independence, attained in 1964, the two great issues for mine workers were an industrial color bar to advancement within the industry and an attempt by mining companies to divide the union by helping to create a separate organization for supervisorial staff. After independence, the leading issues concerned discriminatory wages and the actual replacement of expatriates by Zambian workers. With the advent of a unified wage scale and a dramatic reduction in the number of expatriate employees on fixed-term contracts, labor relations shifted from national and racial to bread-and-butter questions. Since 1969, when the Zambian government acquired majority ownership of the entire mining industry, the claims of labor have been contested by public officials. As a result of nationalization measures taken in several sectors of the economy between 1968 and 1970, the state itself became the predominant employer of labor; thereafter, collective bargaining became politically hazardous, particularly after the establishment of a one-party state in 1972. In the words of President Kenneth D. Kaunda, "for a union to push a claim against the State is to push a claim against the people."[33]

Over a span of forty years, the mine workers union has fought successfully to maintain its independence of political parties and its autonomy as an industrial organization.[34] Meanwhile, the ethos of an independent labor movement has spread and been generalized far beyond the 60,000 mine workers to other workers throughout society. Some 400,000 wage earners now belong to unions affiliated with the Zambia Congress of Trade Unions (ZCTU). By the early 1980s leaders of the ZCTU were at odds with government over the practice of administered, rather than negotiated, wages. In 1981 several leading trade unionists, including the chairman and secretary general of the ZCTU, were arrested for allegedly plotting against the government and were publicly accused of "capitalist deviations" by President Kaunda. To the amazement of many who were certain of Kaunda's devotion to nondoctrinaire "humanist" socialism, the president suddenly called for the adoption of "scientific" socialism as the official state ideology. Organized labor responded with unwavering opposition; labor activists forged a de facto alliance with organized religion to prevent the formal introduction of scientific socialism. They understood fully that the chief aim of the proposed ideological shift was party (which would have meant government) control of the unions.[35] Whenever that danger appears it is combated by vigilant trade unionists. For instance, in 1986 the ZCTU secretary general warned member unions against propaganda in support of "party-directed trade unionism."[36]

The Zambian workers' struggle against party control has been remarkably tenacious for many years. Until the Movement for Multiparty Democracy (MMD) emerged in 1990, the ZCTU virtually led the opposition to Kaunda's authoritarian government. When party competition was restored in 1991, Kaunda was defeated in a presidential election by Frederick Chiluba, formerly chairman of the ZCTU. Chiluba stands forthrightly for capitalism, multiparty democracy, and free trade unionism. However, there is no inclination on the part of the ZCTU or any of its affiliates in Zambia to control the MMD, which won elections for 125 of the 150 seats in Zambia's National Assembly, or to guide its policies. Nor do unions elsewhere in

Africa display marked tendencies either to direct or displace broadly supported political parties. African unions often assert their political rights as
worker interest groups, but their members appear to have little taste for
independent political action.

The idea of a labor (or worker-farmer) party has been tested in Nigeria,
where party competition is the normal condition for civilian governments.
In 1956 Nigerian trade unionists of socialist persuasion, who also opposed
affiliation with the Western-oriented International Confederation of Free
Trade Unions, created the first Nigerian Labor party. Defunct by 1960, the
year of independence, it was resuscitated by the same faction in 1965 under
circumstances that were thought to be propitious for independent political
action by organized workers. Briefly, the government of the federal republic
had been humbled the previous year by a nationwide general strike, undertaken for economic reasons. As a result of that heady experience, many
socialists, who identified themselves as Marxist and revolutionary, believed
that worker solidarity had overcome competing political tendencies among
wage earners. They were mistaken; an important study of working-class
political attitudes at this time revealed the strength of multiple motivations.
Ethnic concerns, in particular, produced a "cross-pressured" worker, who
would not often support a strictly class-based political party.[37]

Still, the desire for independent political action did not subside among
socialists in the Nigerian labor movement. A Labor party surfaced once
again in 1989 and was selected by the Federal Electoral Commission as one
of six parties deemed worthy of consideration for a two-party system.
However, the caretaker military regime abolished all of the self-organized
political parties and mandated the creation of two new parties—one center-
left, the other center-right. Despite their own party's distinctive, strictly socialist, posture, the laborites lodged no serious protest; indeed, they echoed
the chorus of praise for this rough-and-ready solution to the perennial
problems of sectarian and sectional politics. Whether or not a mandatory
two-party system proves to be viable in Nigeria, the laborites seem to be
edging toward a position that is consistent with the findings of objective
research. In Africa, as elsewhere, wage earners do not wish to be isolated in
political parties based on the premise of worker solidarity. Their interests
and political beliefs are not determined, decisively or uniformly, by imperatives presumed to issue from their occupational status.

These observations on the political histories of labor movements in two
pivotal countries (representing, in the case of Nigeria, the largest national
economy and, in Zambia, the largest mining industry in Africa outside of

South Africa) support a thesis of worker resistance both to party or governmental control of the unions and to the creation of a Labor party for the labor movement. Only rarely is such resistance expressed in the form of overt political protest; for the most part it occurs "silently" because it is contrary to populist politics. In Zambia the ZCTU did not challenge the political authority of the sole legal party until 1990, when it supported the popular demand for restoration of multiparty elections. In Nigeria, Michael Imoudu, the quintessential Labor party unionist, in his eighty-fifth year, is revered by millions of people. The proper study of worker resistance to both external control and Labor party politics begins with those actions of rank-and-file unionists which are self-directed and uncoerced, such as participation in a free election. In South Africa, where the vast majority of black citizens were still disenfranchised in 1992, black working people have resolutely maintained the independence of their unions as industrial organizations.

Capitalism in South Africa has produced an industrial revolution; the black industrial work force is now larger than its rural counterpart. The number of blacks in recognized labor organizations increased from fewer than 20,000 in 1960 to more than 200,000 in 1980 (following the extension of trade union rights to black unions in 1979); today there are more than one million organized black workers. Various accounts indicate that at least 70 percent of them belong to unions affiliated with the Congress of South African Trade Unions (COSATU), a declared ally of the African National Congress. COSATU's formation in 1985 signified an attempt to resolve two basic dilemmas for black unions. One concerned their strategies of political action; the other, their principles of organization.[38]

For millions of black workers and their families, industrial and political actions are coequal and integral parts of the struggle for racial freedom. Since the great majority of black South Africans were barred from participation in legal political parties until 1990, labor unions have voiced far wider black community concerns. However, experienced labor leaders have repeatedly stressed the crucial difference between working-class organizations, on the one hand, and, on the other, multiclass organizations with middle-class leadership. They believe in cooperation with communitywide popular movements short of organizational affiliation, fearing that, in the absence of a strong and self-directed workers' movement, the popular movement and its cause could be usurped by elements that eventually would oppress the workers. Their arguments reveal an intense sensitivity concerning cultural (especially educational and linguistic) cleavages between working people and other social groups. They fear multiclass organizational practices that would undermine the principles of democratic participation and representation upon which the black unions have been founded. And they are wary of middle-class ideological populism when it is asserted at the expense of working-class realism.

These working-class attitudes, identified as "workerist" in the South African debate, were swamped by opposing "populist" views when COSATU was formed, due mainly to the strong commitment of its largest affiliate, the National Union of Mineworkers, to the ANC. However, the strict trade unionists gained a larger organizational objective: agreement on the principle of industrial unionism, as opposed to the organization of general unions with community orientations. The latter are more likely to embrace populist political goals and strategies at the behest of community-based, rather than workplace-oriented, leaders. The deep substance of this issue is revealed by this report of an exchange between a community activist and a unionist: "The unionist listened patiently as the community activist extolled the power of an alliance between political groups and unions. Then he leaned forward. 'We'll work with community organizations,' he said, 'as soon as we find one strong enough to stop workers in the community from taking strikers' jobs.'"[39]

With the gradual conversion of all-purpose general and community-based unions into industrial unions, the main body of the South African labor movement has effectively affirmed its commitment to a separation of powers between itself and political parties. Accordingly, the idea of a Labor party, once urged by dyed-in-the-wool workerists, has become improbable. When COSATU endorsed the ANC Freedom Charter in 1987, it tacitly renounced the path of independent political action. While its all-but-formal alliance with the ANC is still contested by a few influential COSATU unions and personalities, there does appear to be a general consensus favoring the principle of worker participation in multiclass and community-oriented political parties. But there is no discernible disposition on the part of unionists to countenance encroachments on their freedom of action in the field of industrial relations by political party leaders. Indeed, union leaders require independence from external political authorities to tackle the serious problem of conflict among competing central labor organizations. Approximately 25 percent of the organized black work force belongs to unions affiliated with the National Council of Trade Unions (NACTU), a federation dedicated to the black consciousness philosophy, which rejects color-blind tenets of leadership for South Africa and opposes the ANC. The ongoing process of rapprochement among COSATU, NACTU, and smaller segments of the organized labor movement would not be compatible with party control of union affairs. Hence, the process of negotiation for a unified house of labor helps to solidify the basis for free trade unionism in a postapartheid, democratic South Africa.

If rank-and-file workers resist both party or governmental control of their unions and the formation of political parties based on their union organizations, they might also be expected to resist the imposition of abstract ideologies. In fact, there is little reason to believe that working people in any country are, in the aggregate, deeply committed to any specific form of economic organization. Relatively few wage earners are doctrinaire capitalists or socialists. Early in the twentieth century, Lenin described the theory of socialism as an intellectual product of the bourgeoisie, not the proletariat.[40] Needless to say, this is a complicated question. The kernel of truth in Lenin's formulation lies in his understanding that socialist, like capitalist, convictions are rarely, if ever, direct or simple functions of an individual's class origin or position. In our day many labor leaders are persons of bourgeois origin and / or bourgeois-class identity; many of them are socialists by conviction. In some cases labor leaders havve persuaded their unions to identify themselves officially as capitalist or socialist in orientation. Rarely do such initiatives spring from the rank-and-file workers themselves.

Objective and scientifically valid studies of ideological preference among wage earners in Africa are few and far between. In South Africa anticapitalism is a common ground for many unionists who are divided by the issue of black consciousness versus nonracialism. However, the third largest grouping of unions, based in the province of Natal, is procapitalist. In 1984 a well-publicized survey of black working-class opinion produced evidence of strong support for the concept of nonracial capitalism, in addition to overwhelming support for revolutionary political groups known for their opposition to capitalism. That survey was promptly criticized for having drawn conclusions that were alleged to be rebuttable with reference to the evidence presented.[41] Yet it did indicate the futility of any attempt to characterize the ideological tendencies of African wage earners until scientific methods of survey research are widely used in conjunction with systematic studies of demographic and electoral data.

Analysts who simply impose their own ideas about working-class ideology on the subject of African trade unions may be expected to produce ideological tracts rather than reliable guides to the labor movement. In this connection, one must be wary of works that identify the choice between socialism and capitalism as a significant issue for wage earners.[42] The intellectual choice between capitalism and socialism has no more practical meaning for rank-and-file unionists than the choice of alignment with one or another of the rival international labor groupings. Very few workers were touched by the cold war struggle between anti-Communist and pro-Communist internationals that once preoccupied their union leaders in various African countries.[43] As union members wage earners support various political causes that they perceive to affect the conditions of their employment. Such causes include a free market for labor, free trade unions, free collective bargaining, internal union democracy, worker participation in the making of managerial decisions, and union representation on the boards of enterprises. Threats to the established political rights of labor and attempts to win additional rights desired by the working people themselves, often have galvanized mass actions by organized workers.

For example, in both Ghana and Burkina Faso, avowedly revolutionary regimes seized power in 1981 and 1983, respectively. Each tried to undermine the security and independence of organized labor. In Ghana, Flight Lieutenant Jerry J. Rawlings's regime threatened the labor movement by creating Workers' Defense Committees in enterprises and backing an association of local unions opposed to the independent Ghana Trades Union Congress. In Burkina Faso, Captain Thomas Sankara's regime created Committees for the Defense of the Revolution to intimidate and weaken the unions as well as other established interest groups. In each country the willingness and ability of rank-and-file workers to stand by their unions and defend their organizational rights caused the government to back away from its attempt to seize control of the labor movement.[44] Had Rawlings and Sankara been attentive to the postcolonial labor histories of their respective countries, they might have spared themselves much grief—in Sankara's case death— since previous regimes in both countries had incurred high political costs for their vain attempts to subjugate vigorous trade unions.[45]

In Africa, as elsewhere in the world, it is erroneous to identify working-class consciousness with either specific political parties or a specific social philosophy. One hopes that students of African societies will not cling to these dogmas even as they are being discarded by thoughtful students of labor movements in the more industrial societies, East and West alike. Paradoxically, the ideological dogma is more tenacious than the party dogma because it depends almost entirely on cherished suppositions, rather than facts.

Social Class and Political Action

The Complementarity of Classes

The concepts of capitalism and socialism refer, broadly, to alternative sets of social relations, institutions, and values; narrowly conceived, they denote competing theories and types of economic organization. Their applicability to historical development in the late twentieth century can no longer be taken for granted. Indeed, their respective principles have been combined in all modern societies to form durable mixed economies that continue to evolve more readily than either elemental type.

Bourgeoisie and proletariat are traditional names for the principal social classes of industrial society. Their analytical boundaries are indistinct, and the social composition of each has always been subject to serious debate. In our time the bourgeoisie is not necessarily capitalistic; ideologically socialistic bourgeoisies have often privatized the state itself, as described in the classic study by Milovan Djilas[46] and confirmed by recent disclosures in many former Communist countries. For its part, the proletariat is not compelled by a teleological force to strive for socialism. Nor do these complementary classes of industrial society necessarily oppose and combat one another as prescribed by the ideologists of class conflict. It is just as important for social scientists to detach the idea of a proletariat from the objective of socialism as it is to disassociate the idea of a bourgeoisie from the practice of capitalism.

In the present era class relations are profoundly influenced by problems that cannot be solved with the use of theories that propose a choice between capitalism and socialism. One such problem is the urgent need for economic development in countries at early and intermediate stages of industrialization. In those countries wealth creation is far more important than wealth distribution; physical survival and opportunity for improvement in the overall quality of life take precedence over specifically egalitarian goals. Professedly socialist policies concerning distribution often impede wealth creation; in reality such policies are smokescreens that conceal both economic inefficiency and the exploitation of entrepreneurs, farmers, and workers by officeholders.[47] We learn from experience that neither capitalism nor socialism copes effectively with the dual challenges of increasing human misery and insufficient economic growth in poor countries. Hence the gradual emergence of an international consensus on the desirability of experimentation with mixtures of capitalism and socialism pending future discoveries of transcendent economic forms.

The challenges of development in Sub-Saharan Africa are daunting. Its unprecedented rate of population growth, now 3.2 percent a year, imposes an immense burden on the region's forty-seven national economies. As the World Bank has observed: "Africa's situation is unique. Never in human history has population grown so fast. If current trends continue, Sub-Saharan Africa will have nearly 500 million inhabitants by 1990 and more than 1 billion by 2010. Africa will find it increasingly difficult to feed itself, educate its children, or find jobs for the new entrants to its labor force. The absolute numbers are not so worrying in themselves—there are still vast underpopulated regions. But the high rate of growth means that Africa's economies and social services must sprint ahead for living standards even to stand still." By the year 2020 the population of Sub-Saharan Africa will have grown by "at least 600 million persons" beyond the 450 million of 1987. Urban dwellers will constitute nearly 50 percent of the total (up from 27 percent in 1987), and the work force will be more than twice its present size.[48] Survival at a tolerable standard of living for most people, without catastrophic episodes of social destruction, will depend upon the ability of Africans to produce goods and services for more than a billion souls. Necessity ordains cooperation, rather than ideological conflict, between the bourgeoisie and the proletariat. One contributes entrepreneurship and economic management; the other, collective work and a social ethic of collective responsibility to improve the physical quality of life for working people and their families.

Students of African economic development today focus increasingly on the so-called informal sector, where market activities are not regulated by contracts, licenses, and other legal devices. Recently, the International Labor Organization estimated that 59 percent of the urban labor force in Sub-Saharan Africa is employed within the informal sector.[49] For many years to come, the vast majority of shopkeepers, small-scale entrepreneurs, self-employed persons, and nonunionized workers in Africa will be dependent on the informal sectors of urban society for their livelihoods. Entrepreneurial growth within the informal sector is a major aspect, perhaps the brightest beacon of hope, in the World Bank's latest guideline for economic survival in Africa: "Unregulated and largely unrecorded," activities within the informal sector "comprise the most accessible and competitive part of African economies." Informal-sector firms are remarkably adept at product innovation, apprenticeship training, and the creation of credit facilities, often in conjunction with customary institutions.[50] However, the informal economy could not even begin to approach its potential for investment and growth without the stimuli provided by organized labor, a dimension of the development process that has not as yet been acknowledged by publications of the World Bank.[51]

The wage gains of organized workers make two indispensable contributions to entrepreneurial vitality in the informal sector. First, wage earners transfer wealth from the formal to the informal sector whenever their savings are invested by themselves or members of their families in small-scale business ventures. Second, entrepreneurship in the informal sector is powerfully induced by robust growth in the purchasing power of formal-sector workers. So the "symbiotic relationship between formal-sector demand and informal-sector supply," noted previously in connection with the movement for capitalism in Africa,[52] consists largely of market exchanges between organized workers and competitive entrepreneurs who respond readily to community-based economic opportunities. Vigorous trade unionism promotes growth because it increases the flow of wealth from big business, including transnational enterprise, to the small-business sector, where the battle for economic development must be won.

Among the builders of economic capacity in Africa, neither business nor labor has a claim upon pride of place over and above the other. Neither of these interdependent estates of the economic realm is destined by any so-called law of history to become dominant over the other as a result of its superior economic function. I seriously doubt that any respectable proposition of modern sociology is less realistic than the idea (derived fom Marxist thought) that social classes, when they become mature, are unified by political parties that engage in class conflict with one another.[53] Neither the bourgeoisie nor the proletariat has ever displayed a tendency to unite behind any one political party or economic policy. Nor is there any relationship between that strictly ideological notion and the contribution that must be forthcoming from each of these classes in order to attain the goals of development. Few ideas are more remote from the realities of economic progress in Africa than the idealization of revolutionary political struggle.

The complementarity of business and labor—of the bourgeoisie as a whole and its historic counterpart, the proletariat—implies both class collaboration and class conflict; but it is not consistent with the capitalism-versus-socialism perspective on African or world development. However, the idea of a mixed economy, built mainly on foundations of private, corporate, and cooperative enterprise—all of them regulated in accordance with principles of social justice—is logical, practical, and compatible with the wishes of most people. This approach appears to have gained a substantial measure of acceptance in South Africa, where opposing political forces have confronted one another with ideological hostility for the past quarter century. In 1988 two delegations of approximately forty persons each—one consisting mainly of white business leaders, the other representing the United Democratic Front (a legal surrogate for the ANC, which had not as yet been unbanned) and its labor ally, COSATU—tried, with some success, to find common ground for principled cooperation. Near the end, an Afrikaner business executive made this comment: "I'm looking forward to the day when we can come together and stop talking about capitalism and socialism and the free market system, stop talking about Marxism and Leninism and communism, and start talking about a new thing—about an objective economic system which best satisfies the needs of the people in the most effective way."[54] These words do not bespeak a class enemy of the proletariat but a potentially cooperative partner for the difficult passage ahead.

Notes

An earlier version of this paper was prepared for an International Conference on State, Society, and Social Movements in Africa, organized by the Institute of Developing Countries of the University of Warsaw and held at the Institute for PAX, Wikno, Poland, in March 1990. I wish to thank Geoffrey Bergen and John R. Heilbrunn for their valuable research assistance.

1. See Ronald Inglehart, *The Silent Revolution: Changing Values and Political Styles among Western Publics* (Princeton, N.J.: Princeton Univ. Press, 1977).

2. World Bank, *Financing Adjustment with Growth in Sub-Saharan Africa, 1986–90* (Washington, D.C., 1986), p. 21.

3. Larry Diamond, "Class Formation in the Swollen African State," *Journal of Modern African Studies* 25, no. 4 (Dec. 1987): 574. See also the important study by David B. Abernethy, "Bureaucratic Growth and Economic Stagnation in Sub-Saharan Africa," in *Africa's Development Challenges and the World Bank,* ed. Stephen K. Commins (Boulder, Colo.: Lynne Rienner, 1988), pp. 179–214.

4. Sylvie Brunel et al., *Tiers monde* (Paris: Economica, 1987), p. 107; World Bank, *Poverty and Human Development* (New York: Oxford Univ. Press, 1980), p. 14.

5. Adapted from Robert Michels, *Political Parties* (1915; New York: Dover, 1959), p. 206. On the relationship between education and inequality in Africa, see E. Wayne Nafziger, *Inequality in Africa* (Cambridge: Cambridge Univ. Press, 1988), pp. 127–39.

6. Richard L. Sklar, "The Nature of Class Domination in Africa," *Journal of Modern African Studies* 17, no. 4 (Dec. 1979): 537–38.

7. Sanislaw Ossowski, *Class Structure in the Social Consciousness,* tr. Sheila Patterson (New York: Free Press of Glencoe, 1963), p. 185.

8. T. B. Bottomore, *Elites and Society* (Baltimore: Penguin Books, 1964), pp. 32, 37–38.

9. Sklar, "Nature of Class Domination," pp. 544–46.

10. Ossowski, *Class Structure*, p. 137.

11. Quoted in Klass Woldring, "Corruption and Inefficiency in Zambia: A Survey of Recent Inquiries and Their Results," *Africa Today* 30, no. 3 (1983): 56.

12. Joel D. Barkan, *An African Dilemma: University Students, Development, and Politics in Ghana, Tanzania, and Uganda* (Nairobi and London: Oxford Univ. Press, 1975); Paul Beckett and James O'Connell, *Education and Power in Nigeria: A Study of University Students* (London: Hodder & Stoughton, 1977).

13. See the important critique of prevailing trends in Africa-based political science by Otwin Marenin, "Essence and Empiricism in African Politics," in *Political Science in Africa: A Critical Review*, ed. Yolamu Barongo (London: Zed Press, 1983), pp. 211–38. Nearly all of the essays in this volume illustrate the doctrinaire style that he criticized. However, the publication of his essay in this volume was also an encouraging sign of the changing times, as suggested by S. Egite Oyovbaire, "The Tyranny of Borrowed Paradigms and the Responsibility of Political Science: The Nigerian Experience," ibid., pp. 239–54. See also Marenin's elaboration of his critique, "Resolving Epistemological Contradictions in Marxist African Studies," *Journal of Modern African Studies* 27, no. 4 (Dec. 1989), pp. 641–69.

14. W. J. M. Mackenzie, "The Political Science of Political Science," *Government and Opposition* 6, no. 3 (Summer 1971): 278.

15. Note to the 1888 English edition of the *Communist Manifesto* by Karl Marx and Friedrich Engels.

16. Richard L. Sklar, *Corporate Power in an African State: The Political Impact of Multinational Mining Companies in Zambia* (Berkeley and Los Angeles: Univ. of California Press, 1979), pp. 198–99; Sklar, "The Nature of Class Domination," pp. 546–47.

17. David G. Becker and Richard L. Sklar, "Why Postimperialism?" in Becker et al., *Postimperialism: International Capitalism and Development in the Late Twentieth Century* (Boulder, Colo., and London: Lynne Rienner, 1987) p. 7.

18. See Goran Hyden, *Beyond Ujamaa in Tanzania: Underdevelopment and an Uncaptured Peasantry* (Berkeley and Los Angeles: Univ. of California Press, 1980); Gavin Kitching, *Class and Economic Change in Kenya: The Making of an African Petite Bourgeoisie, 1905–1970* (New Haven: Yale Univ. Press, 1980).

19. For a similar observation, see the astute analysis by Robert H. Bates, "Macro-Political Economy in the Field of Development," Duke University Program in International Political Economy, Working Paper no. 40, June 1988, p. 47.

20. Richard L. Sklar, "Beyond Capitalism and Socialism in Africa," *Journal of Modern African Studies* 26, no. 1 (March 1988): 9–10, 12–13; Goran Hyden, "Business and Development in Sub-Saharan Africa," *USFI Reports* (Indianapolis), 25 (1986): Africa / Middle East. For this conception of a "capitalist movement" I am indebted to Martin J. Sklar, *The Corporate Reconstruction of American Capitalism, 1890–1916: The Market, the Law, and Politics* (Cambridge: Cambridge Univ. Press, 1988), pp. 1–40.

21. World Bank, *Sub-Saharan Africa: From Crisis to Sustainable Growth* (Washington, D.C., 1989), pp. 4–5.

22. Ibid., pp. 55, 62.

23. Ibid., pp. 48, 52, 57.

24. *West Africa*, no. 3765 (Oct. 16–22, 1989): 1714.

25. See Thomas M. Callaghy and Ernest J. Wilson III, "Africa: Policy, Reality, or Ritual," in *The Promise of Privatization*, ed. Raymond Vernon (New York: Council on Foreign Relations, 1988), pp. 179–230.

26. Alexander Chikwanda, "The Best of Both Worlds?" *Southern African Economist* 1, no. 2 (April / May 1988): 17.

27. *Africa News* (Durham, N.C.), Dec. 9–23, 1991, p. 19.

28. Since Keith Hart's prescient article ("Informal Income Opportunities and Urban Employment in Ghana," *Journal of Modern African Studies* 11, no. 1 [March 1973]: 51–89) and a follow-up article by S. V. Sethuraman ("The Urban Informal Sector in Africa," *International Labour Review* 116, no. 3 [Nov.–Dec. 1977]: 343–52), the outstanding work on this subject is Janet MacGaffey, *Entrepreneurs and Parasites: The Struggle for Indigenous Capitalism in Zaire* (Cambridge: Cambridge Univ. Press, 1987).

29. Richard L. Sklar, "Developmental Democracy," *Comparative Studies in Society and History* 29, no. 4 (Oct. 1987): 712.

30. Janet MacGaffey, "Perestroika without Glasnost: The Need for a New Approach to the Real Economy of African Countries," in *Beyond Autocracy in Africa*, Working Papers from the Inaugural Seminar of the Governance in Africa Program, the Carter Center of Emory University, Feb. 17–18, 1989, p. 133.

31. Michele O'Deyé, *Les associations en villes africaines: Dakar-Brazzaville* (Paris: Editions L'Harmattan, 1985), p. 77; World Bank, *From Crisis to Sustainable Growth*, pp. 140–41.

32. See Nafziger, *Inequality*, p. 110.

33. Richard L. Sklar, *Corporate Power in an African State*, pp. 103–16, 124.

34. For the independence era and its aftermath, see Robert H. Bates, *Unions, Parties, and Political Development: A Study of Mineworkers in Zambia* (New Haven: Yale Univ. Press, 1971), pp. 126–65.

35. Richard L. Sklar, "Democracy in Africa," *African Studies Review* 26, nos. 3 / 4 (Sept. / Dec. 1983): 16–17, 21.

36. On that occasion he objected to the alleged selection of unionists by the party for training in the USSR (*Africa Contemporary Record, 1986–1987* (New York: Africana Publishing Co., 1988), p. B872).

37. Robert Melson, "Ideology and Inconsistency: The 'Cross-Pressured' Nigerian Worker," *American Political Science Review* 65, no. 1 (March 1971): 167–71.

38. My principal sources for this section on South Africa are Denis McShane, Martin Plaut, and David Ward, *Black Workers, Their Unions, and the Struggle for Freedom in South Africa* (Boston: South End Press, 1984); Steven Friedman, *Building Tomorrow Today: African Workers in Trade Unions, 1970–1984* (Johannesburg: Raven Press, 1987); C. R. D. Halisi, "Dividing Lines: Black Political Thought and the Politics of Liberation in South Africa" (Ph.D. diss., Univ. of California, Los Angeles, 1988). I have also adapted passages from Sklar, "Developmental Democracy," pp. 701–2.

39. Friedman, *Building Tomorrow*, p. 430.

40. V. I. Lenin, *What Is to Be Done?* (1902; New York: International Publishers, 1943), p. 33.

41. Lawrence Schlemmer, "Black Attitudes, Capitalism, and Investment in South Africa," Center for Applied Social Sciences, University of Natal, Durban, August 1984; "Disinvestment and Black Workers: A Critique of the Schlemmer Report," *South African Labor Bulletin* 10, no. 6 (May 1985): 47–53.

42. For a study of African labor from the ideological perspective of socialism versus capitalism, see Bill Freund, *The African Worker* (Cambridge: Cambridge Univ. Press, 1988). This perspective is also adopted by Roger Southall; see his "Introduction" in *Trade Unions and the New Industrialization of the Third World,* ed. Southall (London: Zed Books, 1988), pp. 1–34.

43. Ioan Davies, *African Trade Unions* (Harmondsworth: Penguin Books, 1966), pp. 188–218. For an insider's view of ideological conflict among Nigerian labor leaders, see Wogu Ananaba, *The Trade Union Movement in Nigeria* (London: Hurst, 1969).

44. George Martens, "Beyond Politics: New Trends in African Trade Unionism," Washington, D.C., Nov. 12, 1986. My summary of these two cases of enduring union strength is indebted to this authoritative paper.

45. For an account of trade union involvement in the political history of Burkina Faso, see Claudette Savonnet-Guyot, *Etat et sociétés au Burkina: Essai sur le politique africain* (Paris: Karthala, 1986), pp. 149–91. For Ghana, see Ukandi Godwin Dimachi, *The Role of Trade Unions in the Development Process with a Case Study of Ghana* (New York: Praeger, 1974), chap. 3; Richard Jeffries, *Class, Power and Ideology in Ghana: The Railwaymen of Sekondi* (Cambridge: Cambridge Univ. Press, 1978); Paul S. Gray, *Unions and Leaders in Ghana: A Model of Labor and Development* (New York: Conch Magazine, 1981).

46. Milovan Djilas, *The New Class* (New York: Praeger, 1957).

47. The economic theory of rent-seeking is pertinent to this problem. See James M. Buchanan, Robert D. Tollison, and Gordon Tullock, eds., *Toward a Theory of the Rent-Seeking Society* (College Station: Texas A&M Univ. Press, 1980).

48. World Bank, *From Crisis to Sustainable Growth,* pp. 6, 33, 135, 278.

49. Ibid., p. 138.

50. Ibid., pp. 135, 138–42.

51. For a criticism of the bank's bias against organized labor, see Howard Stein and E. Wayne Nafziger, "Structural Adjustment, Human Needs, and the World Bank Agenda," *Journal of Modern African Studies* 29, no. 1 (March 1991): 183–85.

52. See note 29.

53. Karl Marx and Frederick Engels, *The German Ideology* (1846; New York: International Publishers, 1947), pp. 48–49; Marx and Engels, "Manifesto of the Communist Party" (1848), in *The Marx-Engels Reader,* ed. Robert C. Tucker (New York: Norton, 1972), p. 343; Marx, *The Poverty of Philosophy* (1847; New York: International Publishers, 1963), p. 173. Many sources could be cited.

54. Willem van Wyk of the South African Iron and Steel Corporation, quoted in Max de Preez, Gavin Evans, and Rosemary Grealy, *The Broederstroom Encounter* (Johannesburg: Consultative Business Movement, 1988), p. 91.

PART II

STATE, SOCIETY, AND DEVELOPMENT

5

THE NEW POLITICAL
ECONOMY OF AFRICA

MICHAEL F. LOFCHIE

IDEAS INSPIRE and empower political action. That is the underlying theme of the 1983 article entitled "American Political Science and Tropical Africa: Universalism vs. Realism" by James S. Coleman and C. R. D. Halisi. Here these political scientists chronicled the evolution of African political studies from its initial preoccupation with nationalist movements, galvanized by the principle of self-determination, to its present immersion in political economy, which attempts to discern the ideas as well as the economic interests that have prompted African political leaders in their choice of development policies.[1]

Coleman and Halisi observed that although the term *political economy* was once a euphemism for Marxian analysis, it has recently become a more ecumenical label. Today, the discipline of political economy is ideologically nondenominational and encompasses the entire range of theoretical approaches that interpret the economic activities of governments. If the emancipation of political economy from its Marxian genesis has opened the door to "scholars of divergent ideological dispositions," as Coleman and Halisi believed, there can be little doubt that scholars at the non-Marxian end of the theoretical spectrum have taken greatest advantage of the opportunity or that they have had the greatest impact on the recent study of African development.

No single transformation has so signaled the new ideological diversity of political economy as the dramatic rise of theoretical approaches inspired by orthodox or, as it is sometimes termed, neoclassical economics. During the 1970s and 1980s, orthodox economics brought about a paradigmatic change in our view of the role of government in the process of development. It shifted the discipline of political economy away from a long-standing emphasis on the indispensability of an active developmental role for the state to an opposite conviction: that the greatest benefits of development arise from the dynamism of free markets. Under the influence of orthodox economics, governments have come to be viewed in pejorative terms, as the source of inappropriate economic policy and, hence, as the primary cause of unsatisfactory economic performance. Prescriptively then, the new political economy urges that governments do their utmost to abstain from market interventions.

Within African studies this paradigmatic shift has commonly been identified with the work of two scholars, an economist and a political scientist. Rarely, if ever, have two social scientists become so personally credited with shifting the terms of intellectual debate as Elliot Berg, principal author of the World Bank's *Accelerated Development in Sub-Saharan Africa* (popularly known as the "Berg Report") and Robert Bates's *Markets and States in Tropical Africa*.[2] During 1981, the year these books were published, analysis of African development shifted to a concern with the political reasons why governments had intervened so harmfully (Bates) and the policy measures necessary to free the marketplace from these interventions (Berg).

The New Political Economy of Africa

Theories arise to group together and explain patterns of facts. The fact pattern that inspired the new African political economy was Sub-Saharan Africa's seemingly irreversible economic decline following independence. This decline first became painfully evident during the early 1970s when the conscience-piercing imagery of persistent famine dramatized the inadequate performance of the continent's most important economic sector, agriculture. The details of this performance have been well documented: a steady decline in per capita food production that resulted in increasing food shortages, virtually universal caloric and nutritional deficits, and a disturbing tendency for these phenomena to become commonplace rather than exceptional.[3]

Foremost among the continent's agricultural difficulties, however, was a tendency toward stagnation in the production of export crops. This resulted in a loss of world market share of exportable commodities, sharply declining foreign exchange earnings, and ever-larger deficits in the balance of payments on international trade. This aspect of agricultural performance had ripple effects that permeated every sector of Africa's fragile economies, for these economies are utterly dependent upon the foreign exchange generated by export crops. The casualties of falling hard-currency earnings ranged from government services such as education, health, and infrastructure to manufacturing industries that required imported capital goods and inputs. Low rates of capacity utilization in industry and high rates of urban unemployment were just as much the consequence of poor agricultural performance as rural starvation.[4]

The political outcome of this economic decline was a heightened incidence of corruption, which assumed explosive proportions because of the sheer desperation to maintain a share of ever-scarcer resources and increased civil strife as the struggle for economic goods accentuated the ethnic, regional, and class cleavages that give rise to political conflicts. Political repression inevitably followed as the stakes of the political game came to involve nothing less than who would and who would not have access to ever more meager economic resources. Less visible but more enduring in its long-term consequences was a massive "brain drain" as Africa's doctors, scientists, scholars, and intellectuals sought more lucrative and politically secure employment in other continents.

Poor agricultural performance had a self-reenforcing quality. The decline of earnings from agricultural exports caused a greater and greater scarcity of vital inputs, ranging from chemical fertilizers and pesticides to imported equipment such as trucks, tractors, and processing machinery. Worsening agricultural performance also fed on itself by lowering government revenues and thereby causing further harm to already impaired systems of health, education, and developmental research.

Since the 1970s the principal intellectual challenge for political economists of Sub-Saharan Africa has been to explain why these trends have been so pronounced in Africa and why this region's economic performance has been so poor in comparison to other developing areas. The analyses presented by Berg and Bates concur in assigning causality to the massively interventionist economic policies adopted by practically all of the new African governments following independence. Although individual African governments sometimes varied in their approach to economic affairs, a highly generalized policy framework did emerge. It had the following features.

The Postindependence Policy Framework

1. Industrialization through import substitution (ISI). To stimulate industrial growth, African governments, following their independence, almost universally adopted policies of import substitution. Initially Africa's import-substituting industries were confined to a fairly standardized range of light consumer goods such as textiles, shoes, cigarettes, and soft drinks, sometimes termed easy import substitution. But a number of African governments quickly sought to broaden their industrial base to include a wider range of products, among them construction materials (concrete, galvanized metal roofing, paint, plywood), light manufactured goods (tires, bicycles, and farm implements), and even the assembly of industrial products such as small trucks and automobiles.

2. Protectionism. Protectionism is an inevitable and integral accompaniment to the development strategy of import substitution. To protect their newly established industries from international competition, African governments engaged in virtually every available form of trade restraint, including tariffs, quantitative restrictions (QRs), outright bans, and in many cases combinations of the three. Quantitative restrictions were the generally preferred form of trade restraint not only because these offered more secure protection from competition but because they had the added advantage of offering greater concealment of the level of protection being provided.

3. Fixed exchanged rates and increasingly overvalued currencies. African governments have generally avoided the global tendency, under way since the early 1970s, to allow exchange rates to fluctuate freely. Instead, practically all African governments have continued the long-standing practice of maintaining officially fixed exchange rates for their currencies. These exchange rates were, almost everywhere, set at unrealistically low levels.[5] Overvaluation is closely associated with an ISI strategy. It cheapens the local currency cost of imported goods, including the capital goods and raw materials required by import-substituting industries. To this degree, it provides as much of a subsidy for those industries as protectionism.

The tendency toward overvaluation of national currencies is, beyond any doubt, the most immediately visible of any of Sub-Saharan Africa's postindependence economic practices and the one that has aroused the most bitter disputes between African governments and external donor agencies. Despite this, it is all but impossible to find a political leader or head of state who has sought to defend this policy on developmental grounds. This is undoubtedly because the origins of the practice are not economic but political.

The best way to assess the political basis of an economic policy is to identify the winners and losers it creates. In Africa the losers from overvaluation are readily apparent. Since an overvalued exchange rate cheapens the prices of tradable goods, it produces a pattern of internal economic discrimination against producers of exportable commodities, especially export-oriented farmers. Members of this group find that the prices they receive are artificially lowered by the extent of the overvaluation. Overvaluation also imposes a stiff penalty on the producers of domestically consumed food-stuffs who must compete against artificially cheapened food imports. The winners are generally wage-earning groups who find that the purchasing power of their salaries is artificially heightened by an artificially strength-ened currency.

4. The rationing of foreign exchange through a system of administered allocation. African governments have typically accompanied their commit-ment to import substitution and fixed exchange rates with a system of administered foreign exchange allocation. Foreign exchange is a commod-ity like any other, and when its price is set at an artificially low level (overvaluation), this can be expected to create an excess of demand over supply. African governments have been extremely loath to increase the cost of hard currency by devaluing, for this would increase the costs of opera-tion, in domestic currency, of their import-substituting firms. Rather than do so, they have typically sought to address the problem of scarcity by creating a system of administered allocation: a firm which receives an import license uses it as the basis for a claim on the central bank's foreign exchange reserves.

The reasons are not difficult to discern. To some degree, administered allocation of foreign exchange is an integral and necessary feature of a system of import substitution. It provides a government with an additional means, over and above trade restraints, of conferring special economic privileges on certain selected industries and not on others. Preferred indus-tries are given ready access to a country's stock of hard currency; non-preferred applicants are not.

5. Mandatory sectoral priorities and interest rate ceilings for domestic credit allocation. To ensure that their new industries would have the first claim on bank credit, African governments generally mandated that their banks give highest priority for domestic loans to the industrial sector. Since mandatory credit priorities were intended to abet the process of import substitution, they typically had to be subsector specific and targeted toward those industries which the government was seeking to establish as the basis of the industrialization process. Thus, for example, textiles, cigarettes, and soft-drink production generally received high priority for domestic bank loans whereas such industries as furniture and automotive parts production did not. Sometimes the priorities were even firm specific, as when a government went so far as to designate an individual firm as the basis for development of a particular industry. In almost all cases mandatory priorities were accompanied by interest rate ceilings intended to guarantee that loans and credit allocations were available on a subsidized basis.

Mandatory priorities for credit allocation are the functional equivalent, for domestic currency, of administered allocation of foreign exchange. They eliminate the element of competition for credit from the development process and substitute central planning and administrative controls. For all practical purposes administrative planning nearly excluded agriculture from access to bank credit, thereby contributing to the credit constraint on agricultural production, which was assigned a low priority. Moreover, the interest rate ceilings were often set so low that real interest rates were negative, a factor that encouraged the inefficient and unproductive use of capital.

6. The use of state-owned enterprises (SOEs) as the vehicle for industrial and mercantile development. As it was conducted throughout most of Sub-Saharan Africa, the strategy of ISI has involved the creation and massive proliferation of state-owned enterprises. These enterprises typically enjoyed budget guarantees from the central government; that is, any operating deficits would be made up by an appropriation from the central treasury. For this reason the state enterprises introduced an extreme form of "moral hazard" into the society's fiscal and economic processes, for they combined decentralized authority to spend with central responsibility to provide operating revenues.[6]

7. Control of agricultural prices through state marketing agencies (parastatal corporations). African governments have sought to control the producer prices of their major agricultural commodities through highly statist systems of crop procurement and marketing. These systems are typically characterized by state agencies that have been given legal monopsony over the purchasing and marketing of designated crops.

The near unanimous consensus that this set of economic policies constitutes the root cause of Africa's economic woes is, perhaps, the strongest

The New Political Economy

indicator of the intellectual ascendancy of the new neoclassically inspired political economy. So great has been the triumph of those who find that the basic fault lies with the postindependence policy framework that among scholars of African development, those who hold a different view have become an even smaller and intellectually more marginal minority. To this degree the new political economy has brought a sharper focus to analyses of Africa's development crisis. There is no longer an interminable debate over the reasons why Africa's economies have declined so disastrously. That much, at least, is settled: bad policy produces bad results.

For the new African political economy, attention has shifted to the need to find an explanation for why these policies originated and why they persisted for so long. Robert Bates's oft-quoted question retains its intellectual freshness: "Why should reasonable men adopt public policies that have harmful consequences for the societies they govern?"[7] This question could be further extended: why did African governments remain committed to their policy framework so long after it had been discredited?

The answer that political economy has provided thus far to these questions is political and is suggested largely by the nature of the experience that the continent has had with administratively regulated patterns of trade and industry. Import substitution, combined with the decision to industrialize through state-owned enterprises, provided an economic strategy that enabled governmental leaders to respond to the most eternal of all imperatives, that of political survival. As both students and practitioners of politics have learned from time immemorial, this means that political leaders must build a viable coalition of supporters and reward its members for their loyalty. In Africa, Bates and Berg have shown that the survival imperative quickly gave rise to industries dependent upon state auspices, highly bureaucratized systems of control on agricultural prices (through the parastatal monopolies), regimentation of trade (through the selective allocation of import licenses and hard currency), and governmental determination of capital allocation through the imposition of mandatory sectoral priorities on the banking system.

The overweening bureaucracies that emerged conferred important political assets on the leading and most influential members of the country's political elite: influential politicians and bureaucrats were able to provide jobs or bribes for family members, political friends, and supporters; lucrative subcontracts for political contributors and associates; and opportunities for bribery to political clients who received government positions.[8] Perhaps most importantly, state-managed systems of trade and industry represented vehicles for massive personal enrichment. Through state management of their economies, Africa's leading politicians and bureaucrats and their most important supporters extracted an economic surplus from agriculture, especially export-oriented agriculture, only for the purpose of converting it into a political resource, the financial wherewithal that enabled them to assemble and maintain the coalitions of clients and supporters necessary for political survival.[9]

Once the political basis of resource allocation is understood, the causes of Africa's agricultural and industrial decline are all too easy to identify. Africa's development formula guaranteed economic stagnation and decline. Following independence, the continent's most productive sector, agriculture, was made the object of a gigantic system of economic extraction whose purpose was to provide resources for the political and bureaucratic elites who controlled the continent's administrative and industrial sectors. Africa's import-substituting industries, whose operation was thoroughly pervaded by rent-seeking practices, generally operated at huge economic losses. The resources that were used to sustain Africa's loss-producing industrial enterprises came from the one sector capable of providing them; namely, agriculture and, in particular, export-oriented agriculture. The foreign exchange that sustained Africa's extravagant commitment to overvaluation, that paid for the imported inputs required by the import-substituting industries, and that supplied the wherewithal for its wasteful systems of administered allocation was almost entirely provided by agricultural exports.

The way in which this extractive system worked forms the substantive core of Bates's book. The essential arguments are by now so familiar that they can be quickly summarized. The agricultural sector was subjected to a number of taxes whose cumulative effective was to increase the costs of production while so lowering the prices that producers received as to impose fundamental disincentives on productivity. Agricultural producers were taxed, for example, by currency overvaluation, which lowered the domestic producer price equivalent for their commodities below levels that would have obtained at more realistic exchange rates. They were further taxed through Africa's ubiquitous marketing board systems, which further suppressed producer prices by imposing a wide margin between the world price of exportable commodities and their domestic producer price and which, in numerous cases, also lowered the price levels of domestically consumed food staples in order to provide cheap food for growing urban populations.

Africa's newly independent governments, it would only be fair to add, did not originate the continent's system of monopolistic marketing boards. These were begun during the colonial period and were justified by colonial administrators as a means of stabilizing the producer prices of commodities whose world price tended to fluctuate abruptly from one year to the next. The operative idea was for the marketing boards to build up large cash reserves during periods of buoyant world prices and to use these cash reserves to subsidize agricultural producers during periods when prices fell.

What independent African governments did originate was the practice of using the agricultural marketing board system as the economic launching platform for import-substituting industries. Thus, although African governments have continued to use price stabilization as the justification for their continuation of the marketing board system, their utilization of these boards by governments has been altogether different. The financial resources controlled by the marketing boards, especially the foreign exchange earnings of those that trade in exportable commodities, in fact have gone to provide for numerous expenses associated with the development of import-substituting industries. These included not only the creation of a capital base but ongoing costs such as replacement machinery, spare parts, raw materials, patent and license fees, and often the salary costs of expatriate technicians and managers.

The postindependence policy framework, then, produced a unilateral and unidirectional transfer of wealth: away from the continent's export-oriented agricultural producers and to the political and bureaucratic elites who managed and controlled its predominantly statist industrial sector; away from those who produced foreign exchange and to those who consumed it; away from the continent's most productive sector and to its least productive one. Africa's postindependence economic systems, then, had three especially pronounced features: they were statist, characterized by mistrust of markets as the basis of resource allocation; they were deliberately industrial, based on a conviction that only industry could generate sustained development; and they were overwhelmingly characterized by a powerful antiagricultural bias.

Once the nature of postindependence economic policy is understood, it becomes possible to build on the work of Bates and Berg and to explore further the reasons why this framework became so prevalent and lasted for so long. Why was it that African governments framed policies that compelled their agricultural producers to bear the costs of an imposed redistribution of wealth to inefficient industries, and why was it that the selected beneficiaries were leading politicians, bureaucrats, import-substituting industrialists, and the managers and workers in state enterprises? Why were the winners, winners? And why were the losers, losers?

The Concept of Urban Bias

To begin a discussion of this question, it is essential to turn to the concept of urban bias and to the seminal work of the foremost proponent of that concept, Michael Lipton.[10] His work on the political basis of economic policy in developing countries is of such great importance that it would only be fair to note that the ideas he developed became the intellectual basis for the policy analyses of Bates and Berg as well as numerous other political economists of the developing world. Lipton's basic argument is disarmingly simple: the most potent, demanding, and potentially volatile groups in developing countries are located in the major cities, principally national capitals. Governments that are concerned with their political survival must, therefore, formulate and implement economic policies that provide for the economic interests of these groups.

The reasons for the political power of urban interest groups are readily discernible. Since they are in direct proximity to the seat of political power, they can convey their demands easily and instantly to those who have the authority to formulate economic policy. Urban location, or more specifically capital location, confers upon the interest groups located there vastly greater political access than is available to rural populations. Lipton shows that the leaders of these interests also enjoy a wide variety of informal channels of communication with political and bureaucratic decision makers. They have often attended the same schools, belonged to the same churches, joined the same social clubs, and in many cases linked their fortunes through intermarriage with those of the political elites.

As a result of all these factors, the leaders of urban interests become intimately familiar with the corridors of political power and with the subtle and not so subtle means of attaining political influence. If quiet lobbying efforts fail, they can resort to more forceful forms of expression. By organizing demonstrations, rallies, strikes, factory closures, or other forms of protest, they can not only dramatize the gravity of their discontents but create an immediate threat to the stability of governments that ignore them.[11] With such diversified and effective means of political influence at their disposal, urban groups can almost always expect that their most important demands will be given an immediate and favorable policy response.

The power afforded urban interests by their ready access to leading politicians and bureaucrats and by their capacity to threaten the survival of incumbent regimes stands in sharp contrast to the relative powerlessness of Africa's rural populations. The same set of geopolitical factors that favors urban interest groups with decisive influence over policy presents formidable obstacles to the exercise of political pressure by the continent's rural and agricultural populations. African farmers are generally so distant from the capitals that any form of contact with political decision makers becomes formidably difficult. In addition, rural populations are generally scattered over vast physical distances and thus are inherently more difficult to organize than such physically concentrated urban groups as university students or trade unionists.

The political weakness of Africa's rural populations is further reenforced by a host of additional considerations. Africa's rural populations are typically fragmented along ethnic and linguistic lines, and these divisions have made it even more difficult for them to organize concerted political action. Combine these geopolitical considerations with such socioeconomic factors as generally lower levels of education and hence a lower level of critical organizational skills, and it is not at all surprising that Africa's rural populations have been far less able to influence economic policy than their urban counterparts. In a nutshell, Africa's farmers have been highly vulnerable to economic policies that exploit them because they have been the least capable of any group in society of doing anything about it.

The concept of urban bias as applied to African political affairs has been subject to much misunderstanding. The proponents of this idea do not claim that urban or rural populations, in Africa or elsewhere, share all economic interests in common. Nor do they claim that the political influence of various urban or rural groups is of a relatively uniform character. It would be absurd on the face of it to suggest that such diverse social groups as industrialists, industrial or service workers, students, and bureaucratic elites share mutual economic interests or a similar degree of economic influence. It would be equally absurd to suggest that such highly differentiated rural groups as large farmers, smallholders, and migratory agricultural workers share common economic interests or the same level of ability to articulate them.

The point of urban bias is far more limited in scope. It is intended merely to suggest that urban dwellers as a group have certain quite important interests that separate them politically from the majority of rural residents, the agricultural producers. The most commonly cited of these is food-pricing policy. All urban dwellers regardless of social class can be said to have a common interest in a cheap food policy because this would lower the cost of living for all persons dependent upon cash income. Industrial workers favor cheap food because this frees a greater proportion of cash income for rent, clothing, and other necessities. Industrial capitalists favor cheap food because, insofar as food is a wage, good, cheap food permits a generally lower level of wage remuneration. In contrast, the small and large farmers who produce food staples tend to favor increases in producer prices.

The most consequential policy difference between urban and rural populations, however, has to do with the way in which societies use the foreign exchange earnings from agricultural exports. Urban populations benefit far more than rural dwellers when these earnings are allocated to finance industrial development, for this pattern of utilization provides capital and other resource costs for industrial entrepreneurs and employment opportunities for industrial workers. It is, therefore, favored by capitalists and trade unions alike. To the extent that a nation's industrial development takes the form of state enterprise, it will also provide rent-seeking opportunity for bureaucrats and politicians.

Farmers as a group and export-oriented farmers in particular suffer from this utilization of foreign exchange. The loss to the agricultural sector is a simple matter of opportunity cost. Hard currency that is expended on urban factories is not available to finance rural infrastructure, agricultural research, the importation of vital inputs, or social services for needy agricultural populations. Perhaps most importantly, the share of agricultural value that is taxed to finance urban industrial development is not available as income to individual agricultural producers. Lowered levels of rural consumption in effect have been a form of forced savings to generate the economic wherewithal to finance Africa's urban industries.

In sum, the political pressures exercised by powerful urban interest groups resulted in a policy framework that not only discriminated against the agricultural sector but did so with such aggressivity as to lower agricultural production. Driven by a coalition of urban group pressures, governments formulated trade, industrial, and agricultural policies that make little developmental sense and that ultimately proved ruinous. Not only did the policy framework produce poor agricultural results, it led to the formation of industries that had not the slightest hope of long-term buoyancy. Once the agricultural subsidy was depleted, the industrial sector on which it was based also collapsed.

The Bates-Berg approach, as informed by Lipton's concept of urban bias, offers such a compelling explanation of why African governments behaved in economically inappropriate ways that it has stood for more than a decade as our profession's definitive understanding of the postindependence policy framework. But troublesome questions remain. One of the most troublesome has to do with the interest group approach that forms the common thread linking Bates and Berg with Lipton. Were African political leaders, in fact, as wholly the captives of urban group pressures as this analysis suggests? If not, what other explanations might help shed light on the origins of the postindependence policy framework?

An Alternative Explanation

The answer to the first of these questions is that postindependence group pressures were by no means as unambiguously unidirectional as the Bates-Berg analysis appears to suggest. An alternative point of view has been suggested by Merilee Grindle, a political scientist at the Harvard Institute for International Development. She believes that African political elites were sufficiently popular and well legitimated when independence occurred that they were not the captives of urban interests and in fact enjoyed considerable discretion over their choice of policy. She has described these leaders as "relatively autonomous at the outset." Grindle's observations raise the classic question of direction of causality. Did the interests of urban clienteles create the policy? Or the policy, the clienteles? She argued that the direction of causality may have been contrary to that suggested by Bates and Berg: the policies that African leaders adopted in many cases gave rise to interest groups that then came to demand the perpetuation and enlargement of the policy framework.[12]

An abundance of historical evidence not only supports this line of interpretation but carries it even further. The exact configuration of interest group pressures in newly independent African nations has not been the subject of extensive case study. But there is much reason to believe that at the moment of independence, some of the most powerful interest groups in African societies were associated with the extractive sectors and thus had powerful reasons for supporting relatively open trade policies. Among many African historians, for example, it has become commonplace to suggest that during the colonial period African economies were deliberately structured on the basis of favoritism toward the export sector. Production of exportable commodities was emphasized so that the earnings from these commodities could be used to import manufactured goods from European metropoles. Industry either was neglected altogether or was emphasized only insofar as it contributed to the export sector, for instance, in the preliminary processing and packaging of primary exports.

To the extent that these broad historical generalizations are correct, they portray a very different alignment of interest group pressures at the time of independence than that found in Bates or Lipton. Even if one discounts export-oriented farmers who were, as these authors suggest, politically handicapped by daunting problems of collective action, there nevertheless would have been a formidable array of interests attached to the extractive sectors.

A host of questions, for example, attaches to the politics of the African working class, cited by both Bates and Lipton as one of the important components in the urban coalition. Not only was the African working class relatively small compared to other segments of the population, such as agriculturists, but it was to a large degree composed of workers dependent upon an export orientation: miners, plantation laborers, transportation and dock workers, and workers involved in the processing of primary commodities for export. Workers dependent upon international trade generally formed the core membership of Africa's trade union movements, and their economic interests clearly lay in development policies that would promote the well-being of the export sectors. As a result African trade unions to a very large extent were motivated by an awareness of political and economic interests that were quite distinct not only from those of many other urban dwellers but from those of political elites who rose to national prominence as the leadership of nationalist movements. This helps explain why, during the nationalist and early postindependence periods, union leaders typically sought assiduously to avoid the superimposition of political control by newly independent governments and to maintain free and independent status for their organizations.[13]

On the other hand, there was clearly a substantial array of urban groups that did stand ready to benefit from an economic framework that would transfer economic resources from agricultural export producers to protected urban industries. These included not only government employees and white-collar workers in the private sector (who would benefit from the wage subsidy inherent in currency overvaluation) but the considerable numbers of unemployed and underemployed urban dwellers, Nkrumah's "verandah boys," who would benefit in the short run from industrial job creation.[14] The antiagricultural side of the urban coalition of course also included the rank-and-file party members and supporters who expected government jobs as a reward for political loyalty. In sum, the array of post-independence political pressures was far more complex and variable than can be encompassed in any single unidirectional notion. As Grindle observed, the postindependence political reality was so complex and fluid that political leaders undoubtedly had considerable latitude to pick and choose between highly diverse interests in assembling a coalition that would sustain their long-term incumbency.

The force of these observations is to suggest that the concept of urban bias that forms the core of the work of Lipton, Bates, and Berg reverses the order of cause and effect. Far from urban political pressures giving rise to a set of policies that favored urban social groups, policy choice gave rise to a set of urban political pressures that then came to demand a continuation of the policies. While Bates and Lipton undoubtedly were correct in assigning blame for Africa's postindependence economic decline to its policy framework, they erred in tracing the origins of this framework to the postindependence configuration of interest group pressures.

Far from being an outcome of group pressures, the ISI strategy with its cumbersome administrative baggage of trade restrictions, controlled agricultural pricing, currency management, and wholesale economic discrimination against both producers and workers in the export sectors had to be forcibly imposed against the interests of important social actors. This explains why African governments so often clashed with their trade union movements, and why, in two of the best-documented cases of government-worker relationships, Ghana and Tanzania, the new economic framework involved wholesale repression of reluctant trade union organizations.[15] Indeed, in both those cases worker opposition to the new policy framework was so strong that the two governments eventually nationalized their trade unions, placing them under tight ministerial control.

What, then, does the urban bias–interest group approach explain, and what does it not explain? The answer, in a nutshell, is that it explains the persistence of the postindependence policy framework but not its origin. This is not unimportant, for the persistence of import substitution and trade restrictions may well be the most distinctive feature of African's recent economic history, the distinct factor that sets it apart from other developing regions where the ISI approach has long since been abandoned. Africa is far from unique in having chosen import substitution as a strategy of development. Numerous countries in Asia and Latin America also chose this approach at one time or other. The critical difference between Africa and other regions lies in the fact that so many African countries remained committed to it long after its economic inadequacies had become painfully apparent and after it had been repudiated by most other developing regions and the majority of the economics profession.

As an explanation of why inappropriate policy continued for so long, the urban bias–interest group approach is extremely useful. The otherwise inexplicable tendency toward policy persistence can be fully explained by reference to the demands of the vocal and well-placed urban pressure groups. These included the worker groups and trade union organizations associated with protection industries. But since some of the most important pressure groups that demanded continuation of protectionism were the product, not the cause, of the selection of an ISI approach, and since African leaders in the early postindependence period had considerable discretion in their choice of whether to build a policy coalition composed of groups favorable to openness to trade or one based on industrial protectionism, there continues to be a major missing ingredient in our understanding of Africa's postindependence policy framework. The missing ingredient can be defined as follows: why, despite such a highly complex array of interest group pressures, one that often varied considerably from one country to the next, did African governments chose time after time, with a consistency that is itself one of the most remarkable features of the postindependence political environment, to adopt a development strategy based on import substitution?

Intellectual Origins

The new African political economy finds its explanation for this choice in the intellectual realm, in the field of development economics.[16] This branch of the economics profession, which enjoyed great intellectual stature during the 1950s and 1960s, was emphatic in its distrust of export-oriented strategies of development, and its ideas were highly influential in many developing areas. Two of these ideas, trade pessimism and entrepreneurship pessimism, were so widely accepted throughout independent Africa that they provided the commonplace assumptions of everyday discourse in both academic and political circles. Their influence on policymakers was considerable.

Trade Pessimism

The intellectual common denominator of the otherwise highly diverse group of people who came to be identified as development economists was a rejection of the traditional assumption that international trade could be structured so as to provide mutual benefits for both advanced industrial societies and underdeveloped, primarily agrarian economies.[17] The economists who were most influential during Africa's postindependence decade shared a different view of the relationship between trade and development; namely, a profound pessimism about the extent to which participation in international trade might enable a poor agricultural country to attain economic growth. Such highly prominent scholars as Hollis Chenery, Albert Hirschman, Gunnar Myrdal, W. Arthur Lewis, Raoul Prebisch, Ragnar Nurske, and Hans Singer shared a basic conviction that international trade would not contribute to the development of the world's poorer nations.

Hans Singer and Javed Ansari summarized the dominant viewpoint of that era when they wrote: "There are systematic forces at work in world markets which tend to reduce the gains of the poor countries in international trade; consequently, trade may actually widen the gap between the rich and poor countries. Furthermore, the adverse movement in the terms of trade of the poor countries transfers the benefits of technological innovations from the poor to the rich and, what is more important, acts as an impediment to the development of the poor countries."[18] Throughout this period, there was a vast outpouring of economic research that sought to document the declining terms of trade of the world's developing areas and concluded, on the basis of this research, that an agricultural country could not improve its prospects of economic growth by concentrating its resources on the production of tradable commodities.

The principal target of the trade pessimists was the classical doctrine of comparative advantage, according to which growth is promoted by economic specialization. To understand their assault on this idea, it is essential to begin with the work of Hollis Chenery who was not only among the most highly respected of the development economists but who held an influential position as vice president for development policy at the World Bank. In an article first published in the *American Economic Review* in 1960, "Comparative Advantage and Development Policy," Chenery made a powerful case against the Ricardian view that a country might develop by emphasizing exports it could produce more efficiently than other countries.

His case was based upon a theoretical distinction between trade theory and growth theory. Comparative advantage, he argued, was a theory of trade maximization and, as such, had only limited utility for a country concerned with promoting its overall growth and development. "Growth theory either ignores comparative advantage and the possibilities of trade completely, or considers mainly the dynamic aspects such as the stimulus that an increase in exports provides to the development of related sectors, or the functions of imports as a carrier of new products and advanced technology. With this different point of view, growth theorists often suggest investment criteria that are quite contradictory to those derived from considerations of comparative advantage."[19] Embedded in Chenery's work was a fundamental doubt that market forces alone would allocate a society's economic resources in such a way as to promote long-term economic growth. His skepticism about reliance on markets provided a powerful intellectual case for those who preferred central planning as an approach to development.

In Africa one of the most influential of the development economists was W. Arthur Lewis who for a period in the early 1960s served as an adviser to the government of Ghana. Lewis was among the most outspoken of the trade pessimists. He argued consistently that African countries could not achieve economic growth by seeking to increase their production of tradable agricultural commodities. A fundamental and unavoidable constraint lay in the low demand elasticity for tropical agricultural products. Lewis believed that world markets were simply saturated with the products that African countries were seeking to export. Increased production would only result in a lowering of the world price, thereby eliminating any prospect of gain. "On the demand side, the world just has all the tea, coffee, cocoa and sugar it wants for the time being. . . . The industrial countries have also developed synthetic substitutes for rubber and for cotton which have eaten into the markets for these two. So the countries which specialize in producing tea, cocoa, coffee, cotton and rubber are trying to increase their sales faster than world demand increases."[20] Nor did African countries have the option of shifting out of these low-demand growth commodities into agricultural products for which demand was increasing more rapidly, such as cereals and beef. The world's markets for these commodities were already dominated by temperate-zone countries like the United States.

Lewis concluded that the key to economic growth in Africa lay in industrialization. Much of his economic research was concerned to show that there was an abundant supply of underutilized labor in the rural areas and that the marginal productivity of labor in African agriculture was low relative to that of industry. Adding an additional worker to the agricultural work force did little to increase the value of a nation's output, whereas adding an additional worker to the industrial work force would improve the value of output greatly.[21] The challenge of development, therefore, lay in finding ways to move labor out of the agricultural sector, where there was an oversupply, to the industrial sector, where it would contribute far more to economic growth.

Lewis was a devout champion of import substitution as a means of doing so. The advantages of the strategy seemed utterly compelling. The most important was that it appeared to offer a way for a country to break free of a developmental straitjacket commonly identified as the "low level trap." This trap consisted of a cycle of underdevelopment: low levels of effective demand, the outcome of the low per capita income levels characteristic of predominantly agricultural societies, constrained the possibility of establishing industries. But without industries, per capita incomes and demand would continue to remain low. Through import substitution, a country could break free of this trap and begin to develop an industrial base. The rising incomes of the growing numbers of industrial workers would provide an expanding demand base for additional industries.

To Lewis, ISI seemed to offer further advantages as well, including the possibility that a country might conserve foreign exchange by reducing expenditures on imports. It would provide increased employment opportunity for rapidly swelling urban populations and help to acculturate a traditionally agrarian population into the rhythms of industrial life. Those industries that could begin to produce efficiently eventually might be able to compete in world markets.

The key point in all this merits clarification. The ideas of the development economists reflected a deep skepticism about the economic possibilities of tropical agriculture. Agriculture was considered incapable of providing the engine for economic growth. The only way to attain growth was to transfer productive inputs (capital and labor) out of agriculture into industry. If agriculture had to be subjected to heavy taxation to do so, even this might not be economically harmful. For, in addition to low demand elasticity, tropical agriculture was also assumed to be characterized by low supply elasticity: the lowered producer prices that would accompany higher agricultural taxes would not significantly reduce total agricultural production.

In sum, the antiagricultural bias inherent in the postindependence policy framework had its intellectual genesis in a set of economic ideas that formed the consensus of development thinking during the early postindependence period. The core of this consensus was a conviction that since the agricultural sector could not provide an adequate impetus to economic growth, it should be taxed to finance growth in other sectors. The existential constraints on agriculture were considered overwhelming. These included such seemingly insurmountable problems as the unreliability of market forces, low demand elasticities for tropical agricultural products, declining terms of trade, the low marginal productivity of agricultural labor, overcrowded world markets, and the growing use of synthetic substitutes for tropical commodities. As a result of these factors, societies that remained predominantly agricultural were doomed to low levels of growth and human welfare. Only industry had the capability of reversing this condition, and the state had a major role to play in fostering the emergence of a viable industrial sector.

Entrepreneurship Pessimism

Africa's postindependence policy framework presupposed a highly activist and regulatory state. Government would not only develop infrastructure, expand social services, and provide political security. It would actively nurture the development of a wide range of new industries by establishing state-owned enterprises. It would capitalize those enterprises by imposing high taxes on the agricultural sector, especially agricultural exports. It would protect the new industries from foreign competition by imposing a variety of forms of protectionism that included not only tariffs but various quantitative restrictions that required complex systems of import licensing. It would cheapen the costs of imported inputs to those industries by overvaluing the currency and would help protect them from domestic as well as international competition by carefully administering the allocation of inputs and hard currency.

The notion that government had a central role to play in the development process was partly the result of the sort of doubt about free markets expressed by Chenery. But it was also the product of an additional form of pessimism, doubt as to whether Africa possessed an entrepreneurial class of sufficient size and skill to launch an industrial revolution. This view, entrepreneurship pessimism, was graphically expressed by Barbara Ward, also one of the most influential of the development economists in Africa. "At this stage of development among the poorer communities, it is virtually certain that the state will play a major part in raising more capital for development. This is because in these early days of growth, a large confident business class is simply not available. . . . Throughout most of Africa today, you can count the number of effective African businessmen on two hands."[22] Private entrepreneurship was, in any case, not considered essential to development. The wartime success of the Soviet Union and its seeming emergence as one of the world's great industrial powers were interpreted widely, among both supporters and detractors of that country, as implying that the centrally planned development of a backward economy was by no means impossible.

The development economics of the early 1960s, then, combined two ideas: first, doubt as to whether international trade would be a source of growth for agricultural countries and, second, a conviction that, due to the scarcity of entrepreneurship, state enterprise, rather than private entrepreneurship, would have to provide the major impetus for industrialization. The acceptability of a mjaor role for the state in economic management was given additional validation by the widespread popularity of Keynesian economics, which emphasized the importance of government in stimulating economic growth, especially in societies that suffered high levels of unemployment.

The influence of these ideas, combined with the fact that they had already been highly influential in a number of other developing regions such as Latin America, helps substantiate Grindle's perspective on the factors that led to Africa's choice of a postindependence policy framework. The choice of policy had less to do with clientele demands or urban bias than with the widespread acceptance by the continent's political leaders of the dominant economic wisdom of the period. At the very least there seemed no outstanding economic reason to doubt that ISI would succeed.

Why Did Import Substitution Fail?

Although the collapse of ISI and the collateral damage this has inflicted on other economic sectors represent the most consequential facts of modern African economic life, detailed studies that might illuminate the causes and implications of this failure are strikingly rare.[23] This lacuna in the literature is particularly regrettable in view of the fact that the Economic Commission for Africa, reflecting the views of number of African heads of state, remains committed to import substitution as a viable means of development.[24]

To understand the failure of ISI in Africa, it is essential to begin with the fact that the manner in which it was typically implemented departed widely from the generic theoretical model of import substitution put forward by its proponents in the economics profession. Thus, its failure may reflect less on the soundness of the theory than on the political fact that African governments consistently found it impossible to implement the strategy in the manner that its most prudent academic advocates had prescribed. The differences between theory and practice can be summarized systematically by identifying the key prescriptive features of import substitution and contrasting these with the reality of ISI as it was commonly implemented.[25]

1. *Selection criteria.* Proponents of import substitution stress the need for industrialization to begin with the selection of a small number of industries carefully chosen on the basis of explicit and economically sound criteria. The criteria of selection would include manageable start-up costs, the availability of technical and managerial skills, the willingness of international parent corporations to initiate host country subsidiaries on generous financial terms, and the likelihood that import-substituting firms eventually would be able to develop export markets, at least in nearby regions.

The most widely discussed of the selection criteria had to do with "backward linkages," the principle that industries should be chosen on the basis of their ability to utilize local agricultural inputs. Thus, cotton-producing countries should begin industrialization with textile industries; tobacco producers, with cigarettes; sugar producers, with soft drink and confectionary industries. The underlying belief was that in this way import substitution would impart a stimulus to the agricultural sector, and the cost of imported inputs would be minimized.

In a number of African countries, however, the number and range of industries chosen for protection were so vast that it quickly became all but impossible to discern an economic criterion for selection.[26] Industries producing a wide assortment of consumer goods often were developed alongside those producing intermediate goods and construction materials. The number and range of industries were so great that they frequently had to compete with one another for foreign exchange to procure inputs, for scarce managerial and technical expertise, and even for physical space in which to operate. And, contrary to the principle of backward linkages, a country's own agricultural specialization generally bore no relationship whatsoever to the industries selected for development.

2. *Form and level of protection.* Advocates of import substitution also stipulated the need for protection to be transparent and limited in both degree and time. Protection, it was generally felt, should be achieved through tariffs, rather than quantitative restrictions, and these should be relatively uniform and limited to the minimal amount of protection necessary to compete with imports. Tariffs offer important advantages over other forms of protection: their price effects are easily measured, they impose an outer

boundary on the margin of inefficiency between domestic and international firms, and they are relatively easy to reduce gradually. By making tariff barriers as uniform as possible, governments would, in effect, create something of a competitive environment under the protectionist umbrella.

Protection in countries such as Ghana, however, typically involved a potpourri of trade limitations that combined tariffs with quantitative restrictions, outright bans on imported goods, and import licenses that could sometimes be arbitrarily issued or withheld. Leith expressed his frustration with the outcome in the understated terms:

> The protection of Ghanaian industrial establishments appears to be largely random. When set against the declared policy of simply promoting industrialization per se, the rationale for this apparently random dissemination of protection is not at all obvious. . . . This protective structure was developed over several years . . . with a complexity that both researchers and policy-makers would find difficult to sort out. . . . we conclude that the variability and randomness of the protection of Ghanaian industrial activities was largely unintended.[27]

By the end of the period of import substitution, it would have been practically impossible for even the most astute Ghanaian administrator to discern precisely which industries were being protected, in what way, and to what degree.

3. Ownership of industrial enterprises. The development economists who advocated import substitution assumed that the new industries would be privately owned. This form of ownership would impose a natural limit on costs by imposing hard budget constraints: companies that operated at a loss, even under the cocoon of protection, could not long remain in business.

The vast majority of African governments, however, sought to industrialize through the mechanism of state-owned enterprises. This form of ownership operated in a manner that tended to eliminate budget constraints, since governments, as owners, typically assumed the responsibility to make up any operating deficits. The problem of moral hazard created by the SOEs was glaring. By divorcing the authority to disburse funds from the responsibility for providing them, the SOE system introduced a built-in incentive to overspending and inefficiency. Since the managers of the state-owned firms knew that their operating losses would be provided for in the annual government budget, there was no effective constraint on such wasteful practices as overstaffing, extravagant employee benefits, or misuse of inputs.

By the end of the 1970s, the operating deficits of SOEs in many countries had become so large that they accounted for a substantial and growing proportion of government budgets. Indeed, SOE deficits alone help explain a part of the pressure toward deficit budgeting at the national level, the tendency to monetize these deficits, and hence high rates of inflation.[28]

4. *Allocation of capital and credit.* One of the central generic ideas of import substitution is that it be industry specific, not firm specific. Industries were to be identified for protection, not particular companies. Proponents of ISI generally assumed that individual firms would be required to compete for capital and credit and that the allocation of these resources would occur through the private banking sector. Like private ownership of enterprise, the idea of private capital allocation carried the implicit notion of financial constraint on the ISI strategy. For it gave critical discretion over capital allocations to bank officials who would have authority to withhold funds from financially unsound ventures. Capital and credit would flow to successful firms and away from those which were poorly managed.

The widespread utilization of SOEs defeated this constraint. It was typical for Africa's SOEs to be given governmentally guaranteed credit lines at private banking institutions. This practice deprived bank administrators such as loan officers of the discretion to withhold funds from SOEs that were performing poorly and encouraged the tendency for SOEs to accumulate massive debt burdens that would then have to be financed from government budgets.

5. *Concern for intersectoral effects.* Even the most enthusiastic proponents of ISI assumed that the outer parameters of this approach would be determined, in large part, by a concern for its effects on other economic sectors such as agriculture. Lewis, for example, believed that because the marginal productivity in agricultural was close to zero and because agricultural supply elasticities were low, ISI could be achieved with minimal or negligible effects on the level of agricultural production. This was essential if agricultural export earnings were to continue to be available to finance the new industries.

African countries quickly moved beyond this set of parameters in their taxation of agricultural exports. The financial requirements of the new industries generated higher and higher levels of agricultural taxation and a corresponding tendency to starve the agricultural sector of vital capital inputs for infrastructure, storage, and research. As agricultural output declined, governments frequently compounded the error. Rather than curtail expenditures on urban industries and reallocate their resources to the restoration of agriculture, governments often sought to make up for falling export earnings by increasing the level of agricultural taxation.

Since the failure of import substitution in Africa can be explained on the basis of departures from a theoretical model, it would be tempting to consider whether the model would be workable if it were tested in its pure form. This question is so hypothetical that its consideration here would be theoretically unproductive and possibly damaging, for it might only encourage the assumption that once mistakes and abuses were corrected, an improved version of ISI would be sustainable. The overriding issue for the new African political economy is not whether a version of ISI faithful to the theory could be attained but the validity of the basic assumptions about trade that first gave rise to a protected and statist industrial sector; namely, trade pessimism and entrepreneurship pessimism.

The Critique of Trade Pessimism

The dominant political reality of Sub-Saharan Africa in the 1980s has been rapid reform of the postindependence policy framework and the near universality of trade liberalization and the implementation of market-based approaches to development. In a majority of African societies, governments are actively dismantling the old framework and replacing it with liberal, market-based approaches to growth that feature a high degree of openness to international trade. According to the World Bank, thirty-one out of forty-five independent countries in this region adopted policy reform efforts during the 1980s, with nineteen of these characterized as "strong."[29] Even this list was not complete, as a number of countries that had initiated policy reform were too early in the process for an evaluation to be made. There seemed little doubt that the old ISI / statist approach had, at long last, reached the end of its tenure.

Many factors have contributed to the massive effort to restructure Africa's economic systems. An inventory of the sources of change would begin with the fact that the economic devastation produced by the old policies had finally become so painfully apparent that it could no longer be concealed beneath the rhetoric of socialism or distorted statistics intended to suggest improvements in social justice. In addition, the economic ruin produced by the ISI / statist policies was so extreme even in comparison to other developing areas that the blame for Africa's devastation could no longer be plausibly assigned to exogenous factors such as the international trading system or negative external shocks.

Still another impetus to change was generational change, the gradual disappearance of the postindependence generation of political leaders, with such longtime proponents of state control as Julius Nyerere, Kenneth Kaunda, and Léopold Senghor, for example, finally removed from positions of authority. International pressures have also been at work. With the end of the cold war, the ability of African governments to exploit geopolitical leverage to extract financial assistance has been dramatically lessened, and diminishing aid flows have both exposed underlying economic weaknesses and stimulated domestic pressures for reform. Perhaps the most powerful impetus to change, of course, has been the relentless and powerful pressure of the international lending institutions such as the World Bank and International Monetary Fund (IMF). Their ability to withhold or confer financial aid based on a government's acceptance and implementation of prescribed policy changes, combined with their ability to persuade the majority of bilateral donors to insist upon economic reforms as a condition of their own development assistance, is so important that it sometimes appears to leave African governments with very little independent policy choice.

All of these factors help greatly to illuminate the reasons why so many African governments have been prepared to accept the necessity of transforming their postindependence policy frameworks. But factors that explain the readiness to accept change are only partially suggestive in explaining the direction this change has assumed. A major question remains. Why has policy reform taken the form of economic liberalization?

There is nothing inevitable about this trend. In some African countries political leaders have been prepared to accept civil war and political devastation rather than policy changes that might lessen their grasp or the state's grasp (the two are often the same) on economic resources. In others, political leaders continue to cling to old beliefs about the impoverishing effects of trade and the need for state-sponsored industrialization as a means of overcoming this problem. These leaders generally would prefer reforms that preserve the essentials of an ISI approach while, perhaps, bringing the implementation of this strategy closer to its theoretical model.

The politically painful process of dismantling Africa's import-substituting industrial systems and the restrictive trade practices that have been put in place to support them—a process generally termed structural adjustment—is impossible to explain through the pressure group–urban bias approach. For while this theory provides an adequate explanation of political persistence, it is not useful in explaining political change. But just as it had the greatest difficulty in explaining why policy first originated, it also has insurmountable difficulty in explaining change, especially rapid change of economic policy.

The pervasiveness of economic liberalization, then, calls for an explanatory factor above and beyond those that illuminate the international and domestic pressures for change. The new political economy finds this factor in the intellectual realm. The explanation for liberalization is identical to the explanation of why African governments first adopted an ISI approach, the inspirational and empowering effect of ideas. The continentwide trend toward liberalization has been prompted largely by the force of a new set of intellectual convictions about the economic sources of development.

During the 1970s the economics profession underwent a sea change. The trade pessimism of the development economists came under severe criticism from orthodox economists who believed in a positive correlation between trade and economic growth.[30] By the end of the decade, an intellectual revolution had taken place. The case against trade pessimism and the strategy of import substitution to which it gave rise had been made so forcefully that the consensus of the profession had shifted. Development economics had all but ceased to exist, at least insofar as this term connoted the need for a separate subdiscipline based on the premise that the world's developing countries were governed by different economic principles than its developed ones.[31]

The list of those to whom this revolution is intellectually indebted is extensive, but a small number of scholars stand out as having particular importance: Bela Balassa, Jagdish Bhagwati, Anne O. Krueger, Deepak Lal, and Michael Michaely. The intellectual influence that these economists have had would be difficult to overstate. They can be credited with having shifted the climate of opinion in development studies and with constructing the theoretical foundations of the new political economy.[32] In so doing, they set the intellectual stage for Berg and Bates.

Within this group Anne O. Krueger stands out as uniquely important. In the mid-1970s she and Bhagwati, working under the sponsorship of the National Bureau of Economic Research (NBER), organized and coedited a series of studies of the relationship between trade and economic growth. This series, which included both case studies and more general theoretical volumes, was completed in 1978 with the publication of Krueger's synthesizing monograph, *Liberalization Attempts and Consequences.* The Krueger-Bhagwati series constitutes an intellectual landmark. It not only presented a powerful critique of import substitution but set forth a commensurately powerful case for the classic doctrine of comparative advantage and openness to trade.

The Case for Free Trade

To understand Krueger's ideas, it is best to begin with her response to Chenery, contained principally in an article entitled "Comparative Advantage and Development Policy." Acknowledging the force of Chenery's argument—"his essay stood for well over a decade as the definitive statement of the profession's understanding of the trade-policy and growth relationship"—and the fact that his position is not easily susceptible of theoretical critique—"theoretically . . . there is no way to resolve the argument"—Krueger suggested that the principal rebuttal of the protectionist position lies in the economic facts.[33]

Three fact patterns show decisively that openness to trade produces higher rates of sustained economic growth than ISI and protectionism.

1. Countries that practice trade openness and emphasize exports enjoy higher rates of economic growth than countries that do not.

2. Countries that shift from a protectionist position to openness to trade enjoy an acceleration in their rates of economic growth when they do so.

3. The new higher rates of economic growth associated with trade openness are sustained over longer periods of time than can be explained by a simple onetime shift in the allocation of economic resources. This strongly suggests that deeper, systemic considerations have come into play.

The empirical evidence for these propositions is overwhelming. It demonstrates convincingly that while the development economists were elaborating an approach to growth based on protectionism, the economic realities of the developing world were providing the basis for a contrary truth.

Krueger believes that the challenge to political economy, now that the empirical relationship between openness to trade and economic growth has been established, is to ascertain the theoretical reasons why the protectionist position was so badly mistaken. Since the bulk of Krueger's highly prolific career has been devoted principally to this challenge, it would be impossible here to do more than provide a threadbare sketch of a few of her key arguments.

Krueger's analysis divided the theoretical case for free trade into three broad categories; technological considerations, economic considerations, and considerations of political economy.

Technological Considerations

By technological considerations, Krueger principally referred to a set of constraints that derive from the small size of the market available to import-substituting firms. Since these produce for domestic consumption, their potential markets are inherently smaller than those of firms that have an international orientation. As a result, their irreducible base costs per unit of production, or "indivisibilities," are higher than those of firms that can sustain longer production runs.

Krueger also demonstrated that the larger market available to export-oriented firms permits a more rapid growth of value added for the same amount of growth of fixed and human capital. The relevant concept here is the incremental capital/output ratio (ICOR). The goal of economic growth is to have a low and declining ICOR; i.e., to have each unit of capital generate a larger and larger amount of economic output. The evidence shows unambiguously that export-oriented countries attain this goal far more readily than those that orient their production toward a relatively small domestic market.

The reason for this is that the element of competition inherent in production for the international marketplace makes it essential for manufacturing firms to use their productive resources as efficiently as possible; that is, to use the least expensive mix of productive inputs to attain a given value of output. In African countries capital tends to be scarce and therefore expensive relative to the abundant supply of unskilled and therefore low-cost labor. If international competition had been allowed to influence the continent's factor intensities, it would have generally promoted the development of industries that are highly intensive in their use of unskilled labor and constrained the development of those that are more capital-intensive.

Import substitution has led Africa in exactly the opposite direction. The tendency toward currency overvaluation that is inherent in the ISI approach as a means of subsidizing capital costs encourages capital-intensiveness. Even the most casual observers of the continent have observed frequently that its industries appear to be capital-intensive even while there are vast reserves of unemployed and underemployed laborers flocking to its cities.

Economic Considerations

Comparable factors are at work, for Krueger, in the purely economic realm. Given the small size of domestic markets in Africa, the market for any given commodity will be dominated either by a single firm that satisfies the entire market or by a few firms that are small in size. In the former case the factor of productive efficiency brought about by competition will be lost. In the latter, any possibility of economies of scale will be lost. These observations have a direct bearing on the claim that import-substituting industries eventually might be able to compete in the international marketplace. The opposite is the case. Because there is no incentive for the efficient use of resources, and practically no possibility that efficient economies of scale can be attained, import-substituting firms probably would require greater and greater levels of protection to insulate them from international competition.

Considerations of Political Economy

Krueger is rare among orthodox economists in her remarkable sensitivity to the impact of political considerations on economic outcomes. That sensitivity is basic to the concept that many would regard as her most enduring contribution to the study of development; namely, the idea of the rent-seeking society.[34] The basic idea is disarmingly simple. When a society imposes a limitation on trade, as in the form of quantitative restrictions on imports, it is creating an artificial scarcity. The opportunity to ameliorate that scarcity, as in the form of an import license, is a valuable commodity. Those who control this commodity—i.e., the bureaucrats with an authority to dispense licenses—are no less likely to market them at a favorable price than those who possess other scarce commodities. They will find a ready demand for licenses among those who can market the goods whose importation it allows for further profit.

Political scientists have commonly used the term *rent seeking* as if it were merely an economic euphemism for corruption, the act of bribery involved in obtaining an import license from the official in charge of dispensing it. While an act of corruption is indeed involved, this usage does not fully reflect the economic ramifications of the process, the tendency to retard and distort the economic growth of a society.[35]

The key then is to understand how rent seeking imposes real economic costs on the society where it arises. Krueger pointed out that there would always be certain kinds of economic costs involved with a licensing system, even if the licenses were dispensed in a strictly rigorous manner. Business entrepreneurs would need to spend their own time and energy to pursue licenses and create staff positions simply to fill out the necessary paperwork. In addition, a fairly large bureaucracy would need to be created to issue licenses and monitor their use. To the extent that a licensing system necessitates the construction of unproductive and otherwise unnecessary bureaucracies in both the industrial and state sectors, a certain amount of welfare loss would be unavoidable.

But the economic and developmental loss is greater than this and derives from the fact that in a rent-seeking society vast resources are often spent on the competition for licenses and the governmental positions that dispense them. A few simple examples may help illustrate this point. Certain forms of bribery do involve a net welfare loss, as when a firm must add the (nonworking) relatives of a bureaucrat to its payroll. Sometimes funds that might be invested in productive activity are diverted elsewhere, as when a family allocates its savings to educate a child for a government position simply because that position has a rent-seeking potential. Those finances would be unavailable to finance improvements in its farm or other business enterprise. Sometimes import licenses for intermediate goods (e.g., transportation equipment) are conferred in proportion to a firm's productive capacity, thus encouraging the development of productive capacity for which there is no market.

In extreme cases an entire factory or even industry might be created, under the guise of import substitution, simply because its existence became the basis to obtain import licenses. All of these forms of activity, generally subsumed under the term *rent seeking,* involve major economic losses to the society.

Abuse of office is by no means confined to developing countries, but controlled trade regimes with quantitative import restrictions have been more common in these societies than in the more industrial countries of the world, and especially in Africa. And such trade regimes provide exceptionally fertile ground for rent-seeking practices. Krueger herself believes that absent rent seeking, technological and economic considerations alone would provide an adequate explanation for the dismal economic performance of controlled trade regimes. But from the standpoint of the new political economy, the order of causal priority can be reversed. Remove the technological and economic factors, and the ubiquitous tendency toward rent seeking, by itself, explains why import substitution has failed so badly.

In sum, the concept of rent seeking provides a compelling argument against those who favor a statist approach to development and the burdensome bureaucratic apparatus this requires. It further is not only the best explanation but possibly the only one for the disheartening gap between the theory and practice of import substitution in Africa and elsewhere. Otherwise inexplicable in purely economic terms, this gap is as close as the new political economy has come to identifying the causal epicenter of Africa's economic decline. The seeming universality of the gap between the theory of import substitution and its actual implementation also constitutes as conclusive an answer as is presently possible to the hypothetical question of whether a pure, undeformed version of import substitution might be possible. Statist systems that combine the structural opportunity for corruption with an economic incentive to practice it inevitably are likely to experience poorer economic performance than those that do not.

A Note on Entrepreneurship

Recall here that Africa's adoption of a statist approach to import substitution was based on two intellectual ideas. The first, articulated by Chenery, was concern about market failure. The second, articulated by Ward, was a belief that the lack of entrepreneurship required an activist state. Krueger's analysis provides a reason to set aside concerns about market failure: the economic consequences of government failure, arising from a *dirigiste* approach to trade and industrial development, are even greater.

But what of Africa's alleged lack of entrepreneurship? Suppose that the economic reforms currently under way actually do succeed in creating a free-market environment. Is there an entrepreneurial class sufficiently robust to take advantage of this environment and, through its investment and trading activities, launch an economic revolution? Though this question apparently involves an empirical matter, its best answer is in fact highly theoretical, for the response to entrepreneurship pessimism is ultimately based on a consideration of the ways in which societies encourage or discourage individuals from assuming entrepreneurial roles.

The principal response to the entrepreneurship pessimism articulated by Barbara Ward is contained in an article by William J. Baumol entitled "Entrepreneurship: Productive, Unproductive, and Destructive." Summarizing his argument, Baumol stated: "While the total supply of entrepreneurs varies among societies, the productive contribution of the society's entrepreneurial activities varies much more because of their allocation between productive activities such as innovation and largely unproductive activities such as rent-seeking or organized crime. This allocation is heavily influenced by the relative payoffs society offers."[36] Every society then, has a certain stock of entrepreneurship. The central question is whether the incentive structure of an economy provides rewards for activities that promote economic growth or activities that retard it.

The force of Baumol's argument is to suggest once again that much of the widely accepted developmental analysis of the African continent has reversed the order of cause and effect. A statist approach to development is not necessitated by the fact that the supply of entrepreneurship is low. The supply of productive entrepreneurship is low because statist economic systems impose penalties on those with entrepreneurial talent and confer the greatest rewards on those who can take advantage of the economic opportunities inherent in a rent-seeking system. Richard Sandbrook, one of the most astute critics of the new political economy, concurs in the view that valuable entrepreneurial skills have been lost because of an inappropriate system of incentives. "Ambitious individuals seek to make their fortunes through parasitic manipulation of the government's regulatory and spending powers rather than through productive activity. Risk-taking, market-oriented entrepreneurial activities are seldom the quickest and easiest road to wealth."[37] Entrepreneurship in Africa is not in scarce supply. The problem is that Africa's economic systems have provided no incentives—indeed, have erected significant barriers—for those who would accumulate capital and invest it in productive enterprise.

The analytic and policy implications are unmistakably clear. The adequacy or inadequacy of Africa's supply of entrepreneurship cannot possibly be determined until the structure of its economic system is fundamentally altered. Until the greatest economic rewards go to those who engage in productive economic activity, rather than the illicit marketing of goods that government policy has made artificially scarce, it would be premature to judge whether African entrepreneurship is adequate to a developmental challenge.

Conclusion: The Role of the State

The most common misunderstanding of the new political economy is that it is implacably antistatist and views economic development largely as a matter of "shrinking the state." This misconception derives from the fact that orthodox political economists such as Berg and Bates have been

harshly critical of the role that African governments played in the postindependence period. But it would be incorrect to conclude from this viewpoint
that the new political economy envisions a minimal role for government in
the development process.[38] The issue is not whether there is a vital role for
government but, rather, what roles governments can and must play well
and what roles they cannot. The new political economy calls for government to reduce its role dramatically in certain areas but at the same time to
increase the scope of its activities dramatically in others.

At the very least the role of government begins with the creation of a
politically stable and economically secure environment. Given political conditions in many parts of Africa, this is no mean task. But no meaningful
economic activity is possible where people have occasion to fear loss of life
or property due to war, ethnic strife, or the predatory activities of governmental agents. Above and beyond the creation of civil order, the role of
governments includes the definition and impartial enforcement of property
rights. The central importance of legally secured property rights as a basis
of economic growth has been recognized by a generation of the leading
scholars of the new political economy, including Armen Alchain, Harold
Demsetz, and Douglass North.[39]

It would be foolhardy here to attempt to treat this enormous and highly
complex literature. But from the standpoint of development policy, one
basic fact stands out. Entrepreneurship is utterly unlikely to play a constructive role in an environment where business people fear loss of capital
or physical assets or the profits they have made by engaging in productive
enterprise. The securing of property rights in Africa must begin with a
recognition that the animus against social inequality that has driven so
much of African development policy including its statist approach to industrial enterprise has been premised on a blanket notion of the illegitimacy of
private wealth. There has been a wholesale failure to differentiate between
legitimate profit making, as when venture capital is placed at risk in the
process of production, and the wealth that occurs in illicit ways, from rent
seeking, bribery, and corruption.

The effective securing of property rights begins with legal reforms that
carefully differentiate between these two sources of wealth and that legiti-
mize the former. It also includes regulation and monitoring of the banking
system so that both individuals and institutions can save safely, with full
confidence that their savings are being prudently managed and invested.

Contrary to much academic imagery, the new political economy acknowledges that markets fail and that governments have a vital and indispensable role to play in providing social goods that the market mechanism is unlikely to supply in amounts that are adequate for economic growth. The government's essential role includes the provision of physical infrastructure, not only an adequate road, railroad, and harbor system but telecommunications and educational facilities. Public investment in education, sometimes infelicitously termed human capital, is considered especially important because of its direct relationship to economic growth. Markets also fail in environmental matters, and governments have a role to play not only in safeguarding the physical environment but in improving and repairing it where damage has been done. No less an avowedly antigovernmental institution than the World Bank has offered a fairly extensive list of essential governmental functions: "An abbreviated list of indispensable interventions would include the maintenance of law and order, the provision of public goods, investments in human capital, the construction and repair of physical infrastructure and the protection of the environment."[40] In these areas and others where market failures can be identified, a governmental role is the absolute precondition for economic vitality.

That being said, the present academic debate over the appropriate role for government has moved far beyond the World Bank's somewhat narrow conception that government intervention is justified only in those vitally important areas where market failure is likely. Scholars of the newly industrializing countries (NICs) of East Asia, for example, are engaged in an intense dialogue about whether, to what degree, and precisely how a more proactive pattern of state intervention may have contributed to the economic success of countries such as Japan, Korea, Taiwan, and Singapore.[41] Although it would be wholly premature to characterize the conclusions of this debate, there are increasingly powerful reasons to believe that the formula that produces sustained economic growth is far more complex and elusive than is conveyed by the bank's simple notion that governments should leave markets alone and confine their role to the correction of market failure.

The fact is that the governments of the East Asian NICs participate actively in the management of their economies in a whole variety of ways. In certain of the NICs, for example, governments act as bankers to designated industries, providing low-interest loans to firms or conglomerates that have or are likely to have successful records as exporters. In doing so, these governments have exhibited a viewpoint strongly reminiscent of

Hollis Chenery's, showing little confidence that market forces alone would direct adequate long-term capital investment toward industries whose potential to capture important international markets lay at some indeterminate point in the future. Some, but not all, of the NIC governments have also contravened the dictates of free trade by providing considerable protection of their domestic markets so that high rates of profit from domestic sales could be used to sustain fierce and sometimes only minimally profitable international competition. In addition, these governments occasionally have offered direct subsidies to industries and companies that are internationally active, disciplining these subsidies according to the degree of international success.[42]

There is great difficulty in isolating the relevance of the Asian experience for contemporary Africa. Not only do the patterns of governmental intervention and support vary so considerably from one Asian country to the next that no single formula for success is discernible, but Africa appears to present a set of political problems wholly different from those experienced by the Asian NICs. These problems can be broadly lumped under the category of institutional weakness. If the governments of the East Asian NICs have any single common denominator, it is that they are sufficiently strong to have been able to avoid becoming the captives of the industries their policies are intended to promote. They have been able to empower economically skilled technocracies that have retained the ability to withdraw domestic subsidies, protections, and special privileges from firms that do not compete effectively in the international marketplace.

The lesson of Africa's past is that African governments have not exhibited this institutional capability. As Africa's experience with import substitution demonstrates, its governments instead have tended to become the captives of inefficient and unprofitable industries and have consistently come under the influence of the powerful coalitions of workers and managers who benefit from them. Far from empowering professional technocrats, Africa's political leaders have tended to view economic resources as a means of maintaining power and control.

Against this background, there thus could be the greatest economic danger in interpreting the East Asian experience as a basis for expanding the economic role of government. The new African political economy continues to have its greatest intellectual relevance as an analysis of the degree to which government failures in the past devastated the economic basis of a continent. Its ideas stand as an enduring object lesson of the folly of repeating those mistakes.

Notes

1. James S. Coleman and C. R. D. Halisi, "American Political Science and Tropical Africa: Universalism vs. Relativism," *African Studies Review* 26, nos. 3/4 (Sept./Dec. 1983): 25–62.

2. World Bank, *Accelerated Development in Sub-Saharan Africa: An Agenda for Action* (Washington, D.C., 1981), and Robert Bates, *Markets and States in Tropical Africa: The Political Basis of Agricultural Policies* (Berkeley and Los Angeles: Univ. of California Press, 1981).

3. See, for example, U.S. Department of Agriculture, Economic Research Service, *Food Problems and Prospects in Sub-Saharan Africa: The Decade of the 1980's* (Washington, D.C., 1981).

4. For an excellent contemporary discussion of this crisis, see John Ravenhill, "Reversing Africa's Economic Decline," *World Policy Journal* 7, no. 4 (1990): 703–32.

5. The terminology is sometimes confusing. A currency is "overvalued" if the exchange rate is too low; that is, too few units of local currency exchanged for $1 (U.S.) or some other hard currency.

6. Economists use the term *moral hazard* to refer to a situation in which overspending is encouraged because the (marginal) cost to an individual of an action is less than the (marginal) cost to society. For a full definition, see David W. Pearce, ed., *The MIT Dictionary of Modern Economics* (Cambridge: MIT Press, 1989), p. 287.

7. Bates, *Markets and States*, p. 3.

8. For an outstanding treatment, see David B. Abernethy, "Bureaucratic Growth and Economic Stagnation in Sub-Saharan Africa," chap. 9 in *Africa's Development Challenges and the World Bank: Hard Questions, Costly Choices*, ed. Stephen K. Commins (Boulder, Colo.: Lynne Rienner, 1988), pp. 179–214.

9. I am indebted to Professor J. Clark Leith, Department of Economics, University of Western Ontario, for this idea embodied in his term "resource glue."

10. Michael Lipton, *Why Poor People Stay Poor: Urban Bias in World Development* (Cambridge: Harvard Univ. Press, 1976).

11. Ibid., pp. 61–62.

12. Merilee Grindle, *The New Political Economy: Positive Economics and Negative Politics*, Harvard Institute for International Development, Development Discussion Paper no. 311, Aug. 1989, p. 38.

13. See Elliot Berg and Jeffrey Butler, "Trade Unions," in *Political Parties and National Integration in Tropical Africa*, ed. James S. Coleman and Carl Rosberg (Berkeley and Los Angeles: Univ. of California Press, 1964), and Michael F. Lofchie and Carl G. Rosberg, Jr., "The Political Status of African Trade Unions," in *The Role of Labor in African Nation-Building*, ed. Willard A. Beling (New York and Washington, D.C.: Praeger, 1968).

14. The author is indebted to the anonymous University Press of Virginia reader of this manuscript for these observations.

15. See, for example, William H. Friedland, *Cooperation, Conflict, and Conscription: TANU-TFL Relations, 1955–1964*, New York State School of Industrial and Labor Relations, Cornell University, Reprint Series, no. 222 (Ithaca, N.Y., 1967); St. Clair Drake and Leslie

Alexander Lacy, "Government versus the Unions: The Sekondi-Takoradi Strike, 1961," in *Politics in Africa: 7 Cases*, ed. Gwendolen M. Carter (New York: Harcourt, Brace & World, 1966); Jon Kraus, "Strikes and Labour Power in Ghana," in *Development and Change* 10, no. 2 (April 1979): pp. 259–86.

16. I am deeply indebted for the observations that follow to Professors J. Clark Leith of the Department of Economics, University of Western Ontario, and Professor Deepak Lal, Department of Economics, UCLA, and especially to the latter's book *The Poverty of Development Economics* (Cambridge: Harvard Univ. Press, 1985).

17. For a fuller explication of the ways in which development economics departed from the orthodox tradition, see Albert O. Hirschman, *Essays in Trespassing: Economics to Politics and Beyond* (Cambridge: Cambridge Univ. Press, 1981), chap. 1, "The Rise and Decline of Development Economics."

18. Hans W. Singer and Javed A. Ansari, *Rich and Poor Countries* (London: George Allen & Unwin, 1975), p. 65.

19. Hollis Chenery, "Comparative Advantage and Development Policy," in *Structural Change and Development* (New York and London: Oxford Univ. Press for the World Bank, 1979), p. 275.

20. W. Arthur Lewis, *Some Aspects of Economic Development* (Accra-Tema: Ghana Publishing Corporation, 1969), p. 8. Lewis was an influential adviser to the government of Ghana, and this book originated as a series of lectures at the University of Ghana.

21. One of Lewis's most famous and widely cited essays is titled "Economic Development with Unlimited Supplies of Labour." This essay, first published in 1954, is reprinted in A. N. Agarwala and S. P. Singh, eds., *The Economics of Underdevelopment* (London: Oxford Univ. Press, 1958).

22. Barbara Ward, *The Rich Nations and the Poor Nations* (New York: Norton, 1962), p. 99.

23. For this section of the chapter, I am deeply indebted to Professor J. Clark Leith, Department of Economics, University of Western Ontario.

24. United Nations, Economic Commission for Africa, *African Alternative Framework to Structural Adjustment Programmes for Socio-Economic Recovery and Transformation* (AAF-SAP) (E / ECA / CM.15.6 Rev. 3).

25. For a succinct defense of the theory of import substitution, see Henry Bruton, "Import Substitution," chap. 30 in *Handbook of Development Economics*, vol. 2, ed. Hollis Chenery and T. N. Srinivasan (Amsterdam: North Holland, 1989).

26. By far the best case study of protectionism in Africa is J. Clark Leith, *Ghana* (New York: National Bureau of Economic Research, 1974). This extremely important book deserves far greater attention than it has received among scholars of African development. Though it is devoted only to Ghana, Leith's general observations pertain to a host of other African societies including Tanzania and Zambia. Much of the descriptive material in this section is drawn from the Leith study.

27. Leith, *Ghana*, p. 77.

28. One example may illustrate the seriousness and intractability of this problem. Kenya has long been considered one of Africa's few examples of sound economic management. But as recently as 1990/91, parastatal deficits accounted for approx-

imately 20 percent of the government's budget deficit and a loss of more than 1 percent of GDP (*Financial Times* (London), Jan. 8, 1992).

29. The World Bank and the UNDP, *Africa's Adjustment and Growth in the 1980's* (Washington, D.C., 1989), Annex, p. 32.

30. An excellent discussion can be found in P. F. Leeson, "Development Economics and the Study of Development," chap. 1 in P. F. Leeson and M. M. Minogue, *Perspectives on Development* (Manchester and New York: Manchester Univ. Press, 1988).

31. See, for example, Dudley Seers, "The Birth, Life, and Death of Development Economics," *Development and Change* 10, no. 4 (Oct. 1979): 707–19.

32. It would only be fair to add that this revolution has not been universally acclaimed. For a dissenting voice sympathetic to development economics, see John Toye, *Dilemmas of Development* (Oxford and New York: Basil Blackwell, 1987).

33. See Anne O. Krueger, *Perspectives on Trade and Development* (Chicago: Univ. of Chicago Press, 1990), chap. 3, "Comparative Advantage and Development Policy," p. 50.

34. Anne O. Krueger, "The Political Economy of the Rent-Seeking Society," *American Economic Review* 64, no. 3 (June 1974): 291–303.

35. If our definition of *rent seeking* were limited to simple acts of bribery, the net welfare of society might not be greatly affected. One person, the bribe taker, would be slightly better off; another, the bribe giver, would be slightly worse off. Net social income would remain unchanged.

36. William J. Baumol, "Entrepreneurship: Productive, Unproductive, and Destructive," *Journal of Political Economy* 98, no. 5, pt. 1 (1990): 893.

37. Richard Sandbrook, "Taming the African Leviathan," *World Policy Journal* 7, no. 4 (Fall 1990): 677.

38. Bates's book on Kenya is an attempt to identify the critical role of political institutions in development. See Robert H. Bates, *Beyond the Miracle of the Market: The Political Economy of Agrarian Development in Kenya* (New York: Cambridge Univ. Press, 1989).

39. The classic contributions include Armen A. Alchian, "Some Economics of Property Rights," *Il Politico* 30, no. 4 (1965): 816–29; Harold Demsetz, "Toward a Theory of Property Rights," *American Economic Review* 57, no. 2 (1967): 347–59; Douglass C. North, *Structure and Change in Economic History* (New York & London: Norton, 1981). More recent contributions include Thrainn Eggertsson, *Economic Behavior and Institutions* (Cambridge and New York: Cambridge Univ. Press, 1990), and Yoram Barzel, *Economic Analysis of Property Rights* (Cambridge and New York: Cambridge Univ. Press, 1989).

40. *World Development Report*, 1991, p. 131. For an earlier detailing of the bank's view of the role of the state, see World Bank, *World Development Report 1987* (New York and Oxford: Oxford Univ. Press, 1987), chap. 4.

41. For an outstanding survey of this debate, see Robert Wade, "East Asia's Economic Success: Conflicting Perspectives, Partial Insights, Shaky Evidence," *World Politics* 44 (Jan. 1992): 270–320.

42. For an excellent case study, see Alice Amsden, *Asia's Next Giant: South Korea and Late Industrialization* (Oxford and New York: Oxford Univ. Press, 1989).

6

STATE, CHOICE, AND CONTEXT
COMPARATIVE REFLECTIONS ON
REFORM AND INTRACTABILITY

THOMAS M. CALLAGHY

Introduction: Confronting Intractability

AFTER THIRTY YEARS of independence, a "new realism" may be emerging about Africa—one much less optimistic about the possibility of rapid socioeconomic and political transformation than earlier views. In 1991, for example, the World Bank pointed out that "the 1980s saw a sharp divergence in economic performance across developing regions."[1] A continuum, representing an enormous chasm, runs from East Asia, down through Latin America, Eastern Europe, the Middle East, and South Asia to Africa. The disparities between these regions preceded the 1980s, but they were seriously aggravated by this "lost decade." The average annual aggregate real GNP per capita in developing countries increased 2.5 percent between 1965 and 1989. In East Asia it grew 5.2 percent a year, while in Africa it increased only 0.4 percent a year. Thus, some regions have performed better than others, and some countries in each region have outperformed others in the same area. Within the overall trend for Africa, there is some diversity, but its significance remains unclear.

While the World Bank expects these cross-regional disparities to grow, its assessments have often been overly optimistic. This is especially true for the weakest of the regions—Africa. In its 1991 *World Development Report,* the World Bank for the first time candidly admitted that many of its past projections, even the low-case ones, were overly optimistic. The bank forthrightly declared that it had been "generally too hopeful about growth in the 1980s." Except for East Asia, the high cases were too favorable, with the low cases being "much closer to the mark." For Latin America, however, "even the low-case projections were too optimistic." For Africa, both the high and low cases "were revised downward" over time to a "fairly significant" degree as a result of "sharp economic deterioration."[2]

The bank is now carefully hedging its assessments for Africa. In 1991, for example, it saw "the first tentative signs of economic recovery" but expected a "fragile" recovery, with many economies remaining in "precarious" conditions. But for the countries that it saw as reforming, it was much more optimistic. They were "expected to grow relatively fast in the 1990s and to show significant improvement in performance over the 1980s." The "ifs" are quite substantial, however: "Such sustained growth could be achieved if these countries maintain steady progress in implementing structural reforms, if their terms of trade do not deteriorate significantly, and if gross disbursements of official development assistance increase by about 4 percent a year in real terms. Much depends on the supply response induced by these conditions. So far, supply has responded hesitantly because of inadequate infrastructure and little confidence in the permanence of the reforms."[3]

The World Bank's assessment for Africa's nonreformers is more likely to hold for the continent as a whole, precisely because reform is so very difficult: "These economies can expect significant deterioration in coming years. . . . They have become estranged from the world economy, and their isolation is expected to grow in the coming decade unless their domestic political and economic policy situations turn around significantly and international efforts to support growth in these economies are renewed." Unfortunately, "the composition of Africa's sources of external finance reinforces the composition of its production, exports, and debt in limiting Africa's opportunities in the medium term."[4]

Some Africans also have a sense of this "new realism." In the late 1980s, for example, Chinua Achebe, the eminent Nigerian writer, lamented about the intractability of African reality: "Nkrumah once said 'Seek ye first the political kingdom and everything else will be added unto you.' And it seemed so plausible then. It was only 30 years ago, and look! We sought the 'political kingdom' and nothing has been added unto us; a lot has been taken away." Upon becoming the president of Zambia in late 1991, Frederick Chiluba discovered Zambia's terrible reality. A year later he noted that "something is terribly wrong with our continent. How else can we explain to ourselves the misery and destruction that has taken place and continues to take place in Africa? . . . Africa's lag vis-à-vis the rest of the world is astronomical. . . . The continent is now so marginalized that our share in world trade is a shameful 0.7%. The combined gross domestic product (GDP) of Sub-Saharan Africa, including South Africa, is far below that of the Netherlands." Michael Chege, a leading African scholar and fellow contributor to this volume, has noted that "only with the emergence of African states that foster individual freedoms and market economies with complementary public sectors will the continent receive the attention it deserves. African societies might then graduate from being passive recipients of charity to full actors in global politics."[5]

The limited efficacy of IMF / World Bank–sponsored neoorthodox versions of structural adjustment in Africa reflects this intractability. In this sense Africa seems to be "lost between state and market."[6] Its countries do not have the type of states and markets they need to sustain such reform efforts. Successful reform in Africa seems to require a quite special, and rare, conjuncture of factors and conditions, such as have existed in Ghana since 1983.[7] It has become clear that it is not just a question of reordering policies but, rather, one of constructing a whole new context. In the 1980s the new orthodoxy dominant among major First World actors viewed the state as a key obstacle to development, whereas for structuralists, who long stressed powerful historically rooted constraints, the key obstacles were to be found in internal and external socioeconomic structures. For Africa it seems that both sides may be correct. In addition, these policy and structural obstacles inhibit both import-substitution industrialization and export-oriented economic activity, public and private. Unfortunately, nobody seemed to have a good theory of reform, of either the state or the larger socioeconomic context. In the early 1980s the strategy was to get the state out of the economy; by the late 1980s external actors were emphasizing contextual factors, including political liberalization or "democratization" which was now claimed to be a necessary and positively reinforcing correlate.[8]

In the early 1980s the international financial institutions believed that altering the economic policy framework would bring relatively rapid improvement. They were wrong. As a result, they now talk quietly among themselves about Africa's "intractability," while cheerleading those seriously attempting it in order to combat an increasing prevalent "Afro-pessimism." Does this mean that there is a better counterfactual strategy, one more suited to African realities, out there somewhere just waiting to be discovered? The answer is a qualified no, itself a striking reflection of the degree to which Africa is hemmed in and of the fact that everybody's expectations have been unduly high given the nature and complexity of African conditions.

As a result of this "intractability" in the face of policy change, the IMF and the World Bank have developed an increasingly long laundry list of relevant variables, ranging from defending the fragile ecology to protecting property rights via good governance. In Africa the fund and the bank have been learning by doing and often experimenting without buffering much of the negative consequences of their efforts. This laundry list is most evident in the World Bank's 1989 long-term perspective study, *Sub-Saharan Africa: From Crisis to Sustainable Growth.*[9] Most of these variables are not easily susceptible to the effects of policy change. External actors have discovered that many things are necessary but not sufficient—correct policies that "get the prices right," investment, aid, voluntary lending, debt relief, political will and stability, decent levels of state capacity, and institutional and attitude change, for example. In a sense, this expanding laundry list is a wish list not generically unlike the one contained in the Organization of African Unity's (OAU) Lagos Plan of Action, which the fund and the bank criticized so strongly.

Consequently, the projected time frame for reform has moved, from three to ten to twenty years. But the international financial institutions do not really know how to operate in such a lengthened time frame, nor are they really equipped to do so. Learning lessons and being able to apply them are different things. The IMF and the World Bank, and all other major actors, lack the detailed knowledge and data, analytical frameworks, institutional capacity, and resources to implement the new lessons, especially since the larger contextual variables are both diffuse and daunting. The inability of the international financial institutions (IFIs) to come up with a clear and operational definition of *governance* is but one vivid example. In addition, the laundry list is now so long and broad that it is difficult to decide which items to work on first, how to go about it, and how to allocate scarce resources.

Approaches to structural adjustment in Africa that center on choice and policy imply that if policy is changed, proper incentives will be created that will lead to significant economic growth and change. This view has proved to have quite limited utility, however. As a result, by the late 1980s a shift had begun toward more institutionalist forms of analysis that stress the intermediary role and semiautonomous nature of organizational structures in both the economic and political realms. For example, in a section on "Institutional Reform and Sub-Saharan Africa" in its 1989 *Adjustment Lending* report, the World Bank noted: "The supply response to adjustment lending in low-income countries, especially in SSA [Sub-Saharan Africa] has been slow because of the legacy of deep-seated structural problems. Inadequate infrastructure, poorly developed markets, rudimentary industrial sectors, and severe institutional and managerial weaknesses in the public and private sectors have proved unexpectedly serious as constraints to better performance—especially in the poorer countries of SSA. Greater recognition thus needs to be given to the time and attention needed for structural changes, especially institutional reforms and their effects." Such views are beginning to influence neoclassical economic theory, especially via the "new institutional economics" represented by the work of Oliver Williamson and the efforts of Douglass North to merge theory with economic history.[10]

To many in the policy community, Africa has increasingly come to be viewed as a very difficult case. Analysts and policymakers alike have begun to realize that "markets can operate effectively only if underpinned by appropriate institutions." How do such institutions develop, and where do they come from? Interesting work is now under way in this "new institutionalist" vein. Will this get us further along analytically, or do we need to take into account yet another level of analysis, one that would complement rather than substitute for choice-theoretic and new institutionalist perspectives? Do we need to move "the study of developmental politics out of the realm of macrosociology and into the realm of political economy . . . by stressing the microeconomics of institutions and their impact upon political incentives" as a way of providing "the microfoundations for the macrothemes dominating the statist literature"?[11] Or is a more balanced view in order, one which does not reject the importance of macrosociological and historical perspectives? Robert Bates, a leading practitioner of political economy, has called for such a synthesis: "In the early years of political economy, 'rational choicers' posed as revolutionaries, attacking their sociologically minded brethren. Now it may be time to promote the synthesis and re-integration of these traditions. Because they work in cultures possessing distinctive beliefs, values, and institutions, those studying the developing areas may be best placed to take this important step."[12] In his recent theoretical work, Douglass North has begun to do this by stretching his institutionalist perspective toward macrosociological concerns with ideologies, ideas, informal norms, and culture; the results so far have been quite mixed, however.[13]

In my view, we need an analytic attack that takes simultaneous advantage of choice-theoretic, new institutionalist, and macrosociological and historical perspectives. Some of the latter, especially those grounded in Weber, are in many senses an "older institutionalism," as they focus on the logics of institutional development and change as seen in and resulting from concrete struggles between and among states and social groups over time. They constitute a historically grounded view of institutions which goes beyond the "contractarianism" of much of the "new institutionalism."[14] Such a broader perspective has some sobering lessons about voluntarist approaches to institutional development and change, so common to the IMF and the World Bank, which stress the ability of actors to achieve their goals, and about economic and political development more generally. It emphasizes that change is slow, uneven, and the result of concrete political and socioeconomic struggles, and above all that there are complex relationships among "institutional sets" in different arenas of societies. By considering whether Africa really is a special case in terms of the political economy of structural adjustment, and of economic and political development more generally, I attempt in this chapter to illustrate the benefits of trying "to promote the synthesis and re-integration" of the choice-theoretic, new institutionalist, and macrosociological and historical traditions.

We first examine the relationship between choice, institutions, and context in the transformation of East Asia's economic "miracles." Korea serves as an example of the achievements of the major East Asian newly industrializing countries. It is selected because it has the most similarities to the African situation. This East Asian developmental experience is then briefly contrasted with that of key Latin American NICs to highlight further the importance of institutional and contextual factors. In order to assess the relevance of these experiences to African attempts to transform their states from predatory to developmental ones, the case of Nigeria under the military regime of General Ibrahim Babangida (1985–) is scrutinized. Nigeria's efforts at economic and political reform are the closest parallels in Africa to East Asia's apparently quick economic transformation. We then examine Africa's postcolonial macrosociological and historical context, especially the nature of the state as it interacts with deeply rooted cultural patterns of authority, social logics, and incipient forms of class formation to produce specific types of capitalism and relations with external actors, resulting in a quite intractable contemporary reality. Finally, the conclusion evaluates the prospects for positive change in Africa and what external actors can do to facilitate it by more effectively mixing and balancing choice, institutionalist, and contextual perspectives.

THOMAS M. CALLAGHY

Choice, Institutions, and Context: The Political Economy of Transformation in Korea

Much of the recent discussion of economic development success stories such as Korea and Taiwan gives the impression that if proper economic policy and institutional choices are made, countries can improve their performance dramatically and quickly. Occasionally such arguments are extended to political policy and institutions as well. Korea in particular has been used as an example of a typical "predatory" state which rapidly transformed itself into a "developmental capitalist" one via export-oriented industrialization.[15] Is it possible that, like Korea, a few African states might be able to adapt similar policy and institutional arrangements and achieve similarly quick and dramatic results? In 1950 Korea had a per capita income of $146 (in 1974 U.S. dollars), while the figures for Nigeria and Kenya were $150 and $129 respectively.[16]

Both Frederic Deyo and Stephan Haggard have pointed to three primary elements in the transformation of East Asian states. For Deyo they are central to what he called "a strategic capacity model of development": "state coalitional autonomy, institutional consolidation, and the temporal sequence and nature of political and economic linkages to core societies." Haggard pointed to the state's political autonomy from key social groups, centralized and insulated technocratic economic policy-making and implementation, and the role of international political and economic conditions, especially market forces and the geopolitical interests of major states. To this third factor I add a larger set of contextual variables—the overall level of development of state, social, and economic capacities. These contextual variables operate at a primarily macrosociological and historical level. In this respect Haggard appropriately cautioned about the applicability of the East Asian experience to other areas: "A number of historical contingencies, including extensive American interest and assistance and peculiar social and political structures, provided crucial background conditions for reform. Policy is unquestionably an important input to development. Overemphasizing it, however, can lull us into an unwarranted optimism by suggesting that economic development can be accelerated 'if only' the correct policies are put in place. Historical experience suggests the size of that 'if.' Positive theories of public policy and historical analysis of particular cases—in short, investigations of the policy *process*—are needed to supplement the wide literature on the consequences of policy reform."[17]

Korea's transformation has deep roots in the Japanese occupation of the peninsula from 1910 to 1945, one much more intense than the colonial experience in Africa. Building on earlier traditions, the Japanese erected a centralized colonial state around a strong bureaucracy and coercive police and military apparatus. They implanted a state-directed model of development pursuing mercantilist regional policies. Although Korea was at first primarily an exporter of agricultural products, particularly sugar and rice, considerable industrial and infrastructural development was initiated. Much of the industrial plant was in the north, creating an entrepreneurial-managerial class, much of which eventually fled to the south after partition.

The postwar Syngman Rhee regime was typical of many Third World countries. Although formally democratic, it was in fact a personalized and corrupt authoritarian regime built around rent-seeking patronage networks linked to the dominant party. It pursued import-substitution policies based on an overvalued exchange rate and political control of foreign exchange and imports. Rents kept the army, the bureaucrats, and the emerging business class loyal. The regime had a dualistic economic policy-making structure in which small groups of technocrats were constantly swamped by the dominant political rather than economic logics. Despite pressure from the United States to reform—including an early form of conditionality—the government saw no incentive to do so, at least not until growth rates slowed dramatically at the end of the 1950s and a decline in American assistance became apparent.

The Rhee government went through the motions of administrative and technocratic institutional reform in large part as a defensive response to American pressure. Technocratic development enclaves within the government were created, tightly linked to foreign advisers. These enclaves produced very little positive change; however, they were to become the foundation for later changes. Modest attempts at economic stabilization also had little impact on the corrupt political system. Business groups were tied to the government via rent-seeking activity within the ISI political economy. Despite its misgivings, the American government provided vast support for the government before, during, and after the Korean War (1950–53); the primary concerns were United States security and geopolitical interests in the region. The United States not only helped to put down peasant revolts and to control the emergence of leftist groups, but it also imposed an important land reform. The war greatly militarized Korean life and increased the size and professionalism of the army. There was little in this government, however, to suggest imminent economic success and transformation.

Opposition to the Rhee government increased as the 1950s came to an end. After major unrest and a student revolt in 1960, Rhee was forced to resign and go into exile. The Second Republic of Chang Myon aimed to eliminate corruption and engage in serious economic reform, but it was overwhelmed by the new, more open political context, the effects of attempted economic stabilization, and the efforts of key groups to control and exploit the crony state. Under Park Chung Hee, the military stepped into the gap in May 1961, justifying its move as necessary to end corruption and achieve real economic development.

The new reformist military leadership under Park was not heavily tied to established political or social elites, and it set out to eradicate the old crony networks and the predatory state during the early 1960s. Pivotal to this effort were the centralization of political power, autonomy from societal group pressure, and centralized and insulated economic decision making by technocrats. The military believed economic development was in its long-term political and security interests, but radical junior officers had different ideas about how to achieve it than had the senior officers.

The military leadership moved haltingly toward a new export-oriented development strategy due to the early exhaustion of import substitution, the need for revenue, the necessity to live up to promises of economic development, and dependence on United States aid and advice. Despite the powerful influence of the American government, however, the new strategy was not liberal. Rather it was heavily mercantilist, with a precarious balance or tension resulting from the interplay of this strategy with market-based neoclassical factors such as domestic and international competition, what Robert Gilpin had called "benign mercantilism."[18] The strategy had its roots in the period of colonial occupation by the Japanese, the model of authoritarian and statist capitalist development of the 1930s in Japan itself, the incipient economic institutional reforms of the Rhee era, and the powerful pressures, assistance, leverage, and advice of the United States government (and later the World Bank). It was also based, however, on the eventual American acquiescence in the heavily statist thrust of the new strategy.

Although the military promised a return to civilian rule by May 1963, it moved quickly to limit severely political pluralism and participation, temporarily banning more than four thousand politicians. It also purged the bureaucracy and the military, using as its main instrument the newly created Korean Central Intelligence Agency. Park tried to back away from the pledge of democratic rule, but under strong United States pressure he relented. The result was the strongly presidential structure of the Third Republic, which was in turn further consolidated with the Yusin Constitution of 1972. As Chalmers Johnson has noted, "South Korea is ostensibly a democratic country but actually a militarily dominated single-party regime—close in form, if not in ideology, to Japan of the 1930s and 1940s."[19] It was a hard authoritarian state with capitalist economics of a very mercantilist cast, a highly militarized, national security state forever using the threat of renewed Communist aggression from the north as a legitimating and justificatory injunction. Central to the Korean transformation was the basic continuity and enforced stability of this sort of government over the course of several formal changes of regime, a process which lasted well into the 1980s.

Major social groups were kept at bay via coercion and institutional control—especially peasants, students, and above all labor. This is not to say there was not important societal opposition. There was, and it was constant but tightly contained. Even the rapidly developing private business sector was closely controlled while being supported and nurtured by the government. Restructured state-business relations were crucial to the new export-oriented development strategy. After initial attacks on business groups for their corruption and unproductive rent-seeking behavior, the government entered into a tacit alliance with business, which it firmly controlled yet with which it intensively interacted via credit, subsidies, exchange of information, entry into foreign markets, and macro and micro policy incentives and constraints. Peter Evans has called this "embedded autonomy."[20]

To manage this new structure of benign mercantilism, an institutional revolution of economic centralization was carried out that allowed a large role for insulated technocratic endeavor and external advice while still being closely tied to the very top of the presidential political structure. At the heart of this new institutional structure were the Economic Planning Board (many of whose technocrats had been educated overseas) and extensive external economic advice, primarily from the United States and the World Bank. These changes built on the halting but ineffective reform efforts that the Rhee government had undertaken to pacify the American government. The new economic institutions reshaped the existing bureaucracy, thereby increasing its status and power and eliminating it as a major source of opposition to economic reform.

It is important to note that corruption and rent seeking were never fully eliminated and were often the substance of opposition charges. They were, however, significantly reduced. The state was no longer the predator of the Rhee era; it was becoming a developmental state, if a quite harsh one. Crash export-oriented industrialization was now the top priority, but it was controlled tightly by the benign mercantilism of the newly centralized authoritarian state. It was not a laissez-faire neoclassical economic strategy. The United States acquiesced to it, largely for geopolitical reasons.

Thus this new strategy emerged incrementally from the tension-filled triangular relationship between the military, the technocrats, and the United States. Each side learned from the other, although not evenly or completely. The United States was a crucial patron. It was key to internal security and regional stability, to advice and pressure, resources, training, markets, and ultimately to acquiescence to mercantilism. Advice and pressure had not worked with the Rhee government because it had not seen the political logic or economic necessity of the proposed changes. Because of the Korean government's need for revenue, the United States was able to push the Park regime to normalize relations with Japan and participate in the Vietnam War. However, none of this could have been accomplished unless the larger contextual framework had also been conducive—i.e., basic societal and cultural integration, a tradition of centralized and relatively effective bureaucratic capacity, the basic foundations of a viable and vibrant private sector, prior land reform, and high levels of educational achievement. Timing, in terms of the condition and openness of the world economy, also played a major role.

Essential to this East Asian model of economic development are the use of and benefits from what is usually called dependence. Deyo pointed to "the external underwriting of strong, developmentalist states . . . the importance of external geopolitical factors in fostering the domestic political and institutional capacity to manage external economic relationships . . . the positive effects of external political ties for subsequent capacity to manage developmental processes on behalf of strategic goals. . . . Foreign markets, capital, and technology . . . have played an important role in East Asian development. In addition, it is clear that external political linkages have been important for the formulation of development strategy, political structure, and external finance."[21] In other words, the larger macrohistorical and sociological context is vital for the success of choice-theoretic and institutionalist strategies of transformation. It is important to keep all three perspectives in mind. Bruce Cumings's argument that the developmental success of Korea (and Taiwan) is historically and regionally specific is worth citing:

State, Choice, and Context

Crucial to the emergence of strong, developmentalist states in Taiwan and South Korea was the Japanese colonial emphasis on economic growth directed by a centralized state, neomercantilist regional development policies, and authoritarian political regimes that precluded the emergence of populist challenge to colonial rule. Under Japanese rule, extensive industrial and infrastructural investment provided a base for subsequent industrial growth. The postwar American hegemony fostered developmentalist, authoritarian, anticommunist states in a newly revived, Japan-centered, capitalist regional economy; organized labor and opposition groups were repressed. Like prewar colonialism, this postwar tutelary control encouraged industrial and development policies to foster economic stability in a geopolitically important region. And as in Japan, industrial policy was implemented through close state-industry linkages.[22]

For the United States this meant acquiescing in institutional and policy forms of mercantilism far beyond what it would either permit reformist elites in other regions, such as Africa, to carry out or allow the IMF and World Bank to support.

East Asia in Comparative Perspective

In order to complement the use of the East Asian cases for analyzing the situation in Africa, we need to delineate briefly the key differences between East Asian and Latin American NICs. These differences relate to the nature of external capital, the degree of autonomy from social groups, the sequence of development, and the level of state capacity. Korean and other East Asian NICs relied much less heavily than Latin American countries on direct foreign investment, and what they used was much less continuous over time and thus not as deeply rooted politically and economically. Korea had much more direct external aid, given the geopolitical context of the United States asserting a new regional hegemony rather than maintaining one. Korea also relied on borrowing more heavily and sooner in the developmental sequence, while allowing much less full foreign ownership.

For a number of reasons, the East Asian states manifest a greater autonomy from societal groups than is the norm in Latin America. As Peter Evans noted, contrary to United States experience in Latin America, "the geopolitical context of American aid [in East Asia], combined with the absence of previous ties to traditional elites, meant that the political leverage afforded by aid was not used on behalf of traditional rural elites but on behalf of a thorough land reform in both countries [Korea and Taiwan]."[23]

This point could also apply to business groups, thereby explaining United States acquiescence in intense mercantilism. Imperial Japan did not leave behind a coherent, politically powerful local bourgeoisie or remnants of its own, but it left conditions and a model which could foster the growth of a coherent bourgeoisie. It was to be one tightly controlled by the state, however. Business clearly does not dominate the "triple alliance" in East Asia. The newly militarized and centralized states worked with a more conducive colonial legacy and a pervasive security threat, and they dominated business before and during the rise of export-oriented industrial structures. This, in turn, permitted a more nuanced approach to external capital.

Again, external geopolitical and economic interests are the keys. Evans starkly sketched the differences between East Asia and Latin America, at least for the 1960s and 1970s: "In Latin America geopolitical influences might be summarized as U.S. attempts to protect the economic status quo without doing grave violence to reality. In East Asia such a summary would be ludicrous. There U.S. hegemony is again a central feature of the geopolitical environment, but the way in which the United States has defined its postwar interests had different consequences for the development strategies of the East Asian NICs. In East Asia, U.S. geopolitical concerns stimulated attacks on vested economic interests . . . and support for economically interventionist states."[24] The developmental sequence is thus different in East Asia and Latin America. As Deyo pointed out, "The externally fostered emergence of strong exclusionary states before extensive industrialization or linkage to foreign capital permitted East Asian governments to impose preemptive controls over both emergent social classes and external capital. . . . This sequence clearly differentiates the Asian NICs from their counterparts in Latin America, where less effective bureaucratic authoritarian controls were instituted after the emergence of powerful labor unions, the growth of an entrenched bourgeoisie, and extensive penetration by foreign capital."[25]

Lastly, there is also on average a difference in state capacity. As Deyo noted, "Both the relative autonomy of the state apparatus and the effectiveness of state intervention [in East Asia] are well beyond what can be observed in Latin America."[26] The new institutional economics stresses the constraints on economic production generated by organizational structures, but it unnecessarily downplays the positive role that the state can play in economic transformation. As the Korean case demonstrated, they can clearly create opportunities as well as obstacles. Type, timing, and context are the keys. In time, however, opportunities can turn into constraints.

Korea in the 1980s faced precisely this dilemma as the need to liberalize both economically and politically became increasingly obvious from domestic evidence and via external "advice." Economically Korea was losing the balanced tension between state and market that is so central to benign mercantilism. The state was increasingly becoming hostage to its business clients. Attempted political liberalization also alters the political logic that made state autonomy from societal pressure possible. By the late 1980s, with diminished insulation, more participatory politics, and the continuity of strong opposition forces, the political logic had shifted. It has become harder to maintain technocratic control of spending and of the economy more generally. Thus the political logic in which new or old institutions are embedded is crucial.[27] We now turn to see how these various factors play out in the case of Nigeria.

Nigeria: Toward a Capitalist Developmental State?

Nigeria under General Ibrahim Babangida is as close to a capitalist developmental state as Africa is likely to get, but its chances of succeeding are not high.[28] Its similarities to and differences from Korea and the other East Asian and Latin American NICs operate at all of the principal levels of our analysis: policy choice, institutional structure, and macrosociological and historical context, especially colonial legacy, geopolitical context, and developmental sequence.

The colonial legacy was much less intense for Nigeria than for Korea in all these areas: centralized state formation based on earlier traditions; bureaucratic and coercive structures; industrial and infrastructural development, including an environment for the development of a new entrepreneurial-managerial class; restructuring of the social context; and the provision of a developmental model. Nigeria is a loosely integrated, artificial "container state," not a well-integrated sociopolitical unit with a long history of basic cultural unity and centralized rule.

On the other hand, strong similarities exist regarding the immediate postcolonial regime. The Nigerian one was predatory, personalized, formally democratic, massively corrupt via systematic rent seeking and patronage, and based on a weak import-substitution political economy. A centralizing and reformist military elite replaced this regime in 1966. It did so again in 1985 after a second failed attempt at democracy, but the military had been in power from 1966 to 1979 with little to show for its reform and development efforts. While more coherent and professionalized than most

African militaries (largely due to a bloody civil war), the Nigerian military does not come even close to Korean levels of coercive or organizational capabilities or discipline. Society is much less militarized, and there is no pervasive security threat. The military considers reform and economic development in its long-term political interest, but as in Korea, there are serious disagreements within the military about the best way to pursue these goals. Factionalism within the military is always a concern.

In the late 1980s and the early 1990s, the Nigerian military maintained autonomy from major social pressures, but it was fragile, and the control structures were neither as institutionalized as in Korea nor as backed up by coercive capabilities. Technocratic enclaves were created that were protected, but they were not as extensive, centralized, or professionalized. General Babangida made good progress in centralizing them, but overall bureaucratic capabilities remained considerably lower. Under IMF and World Bank auspices, the regime attempted basic stabilization and structural adjustment measures, but the results were modest and precarious. The class basis for the development of a bourgeoisie is larger than in most other African states but far from the foundations in Korea in the early 1960s. In addition, the reform thrust of the IMF and the World Bank attacks rather than allows a benign mercantilist strategy to operate, although these two external institutions may be learning about what is possible and desirable.

The geopolitical context for Nigeria is very different from that for Korea. There is no hegemonic power with a particular interest in Nigeria or Africa more generally, especially one with vital security and economic interests at stake. As a result, there is no equivalent to the continuous United States provision in Korea of protection, military development, vast resources, leverage, advice, training, open markets, capital, and technology. Most importantly, there is no big-power acquiescence in a benign mercantilist form of development, nor a willingness to lean on the IMF and the World Bank to allow such a strategy. The increasing influence of the Japanese in the fund and the bank may begin to change this, but these two institutions are not likely to play as effective a role in Nigeria as they and the United States did in Korea. Given past mistakes and current debt levels, oil revenue is not a panacea for Nigeria either, and there is very little interest in commercial lending or direct foreign investment. Moreover, it is not a particularly auspicious time for a major export drive to enter the world economy, although there is a large potential internal market, maybe even a regional one. Current world debt difficulties and the limited efforts to alleviate them do not bode well for structural transformation.

Development sequencing is vastly different in Nigeria than in Korea. The Babangida regime promised a return to multiparty democracy by January 1993. It thus did not proceed sequentially to tackle the rent-seeking, prebendal polity and its ISI political economy; serious political, security, and economic centralization; an export-oriented development strategy based on a controlled but rapidly developing bourgeoisie and benign mercantilism; and, finally, economic and political liberalization. Instead, it tackled all of them simultaneously. As 1993 neared, older political and economic logics came roaring back to life both inside and outside the military, undermining many of the changes made by Babangida. External actors distanced themselves, and the economic reform effort essentially died before the political transition was complete. In November 1992, in a desperate attempt to salvage the reform effort, Babangida postponed the political transition until late August 1993. This move is not likely to work, and Nigeria will have achieved political liberalization but killed economic reform in the process.

Finally, the larger macrosociological and historical context is strikingly different for Nigeria. Evans has pointed to the comparatively much more bureaucratic environment of the larger Latin American NICs (such as Brazil and Mexico)—that is, to a substantial difference in the types of operative economic statism and overall levels of development. The differences with East Asia would be even more striking. Comparing Brazil with Nigeria, he noted that

> to call Nigeria the 'Brazil of Africa' underlines the differences between the two continents as much as it does the similarities between the two countries. In an African context the structure of the Nigerian economy may appear relatively advanced; in a Latin American context it would appear anachronistic. From the role of the state to the position of the multinationals, the structure of the Nigerian elite is in many ways more suggestive of the period of classic dependent development in Brazil and Mexico. In both Brazil and Mexico the central state apparatus has succeeded in imposing its authority on regional elites. In Nigeria this process is just beginning. The degree of regional integration that characterizes contemporary Nigeria resembles that of Mexico in the days before the PRI or Brazil during the old republic.[29]

Ultimately then, as Haggard and Chung-in Moon noted, "The South Korean case suggests likely prerequisites for such policy reform that are not likely to be found widely in the developing world." Evans made a similar point: "Extracting structural relations from the context of one region and using them to make predictions—or, more dangerously, policies—in the

other would be a bad mistake. . . . Careful analyses of concrete historical situations must precede any expectations about results from policy."[30]
These points are especially relevant to Africa.

Both choice-theoretic and institutional perspectives on structural adjustment and economic development are important, but the larger context
must also be kept in mind. Goran Hyden is correct that there are "no
shortcuts to progress."[31] Capitalist developmental states are not likely to
pop up out of the ground in Africa anytime soon, in part because the
IMF / World Bank "structural adjustment" efforts aim to take Africa "back
to the future," that is to the primary-product export economy inherited at
independence, and make it work right this time.[32] This outcome is to be
achieved by realigning policy choice and institutional structures—all in the
context of an antimercantilist bias. Thus it is actually a readjustment to an
earlier pattern, not structural adjustment along the lines of the East Asian
and Latin American NICs. Africa's primary dilemma may be that this "readjustment" may be all that is possible given the larger macrosociological and
historical context. Distressingly, however, the prospects for success even in
this readjustment are not high for many African countries. Given their
macrosociological and historical context, they may indeed be "lost between
state and market." It is to this larger, and apparently quite intractable,
context that we now turn.

Africa's Macrosociological and Historical Context

To a great extent the literature of both international relations and neoclassical economics have assumed the existence and viability of the state; they
have taken it as a given. To a lesser extent the literature of comparative
politics has done the same. Africa belies the validity of such assumptions,
however. The state in Africa is indeed problematic, and the efforts of external actors to restructure it, as part of their attempt to cope with Africa's
severe economic crisis, have posed a state problematic which preoccupies
policymakers and analysts alike.

Most of Sub-Saharan Africa is now suffering from dual crises of the state
and the economy. The state is seen as being in decline, characterized vari-
ously as "overdeveloped," "underdeveloped," and "soft." Evidence abounds
of diminishing control, repression and extraction, resilience of traditional
authority patterns that mix in complex ways with new processes, corrupt
and inefficient administration, enormous waste, poor policy performance,
debt and infrastructure crises, curtailment of capacities, endemic political

instability, and societal resistance and withdrawal. On the economic side, with declining or negative growth rates and stagnant or falling per capita income figures, balance of payments and debt service problems became more severe in the 1980s, requiring IMF and World Bank programs with their attendant conditionality packages and consequences. Many commodity prices dropped while most import prices remained high. In many countries agricultural production fell while aid levels stagnated. Health and nutrition levels declined while informal or *magendo* economies become more important as states weakened and formal markets declined. "Socialist" states performed poorly and "capitalist" ones not significantly better. Hopes for economic growth and development have shriveled on all sides.

These two crises of state and economy are clearly linked. Africa's economic crisis is as much political as economic. Recent discontent with existing conceptualizations of the African state and an accompanying preoccupation with the "decline of the state" have much to do with the way the state has been studied. Recent notions of the overdeveloped, underdeveloped, or soft state, as well as "uncaptured" populations and "exit options," are a reaction to the shattered illusions of a postcolonial voluntarist view of the state held by many analysts and actors alike. This view had various modernization, democratic, neocolonial, socialist, and revolutionary versions. There was an assumption of malleability of both state and society, of linear success and increasing strength that has been belied increasingly by reality. Underlying the new discussions is often a tone of surprise and bewilderment.

Why this intractability? We have the contrasting views of dependency theory and of neoclassical economic development theory. One stresses externally based obstacles, the other internally based ones. The IMF and the World Bank, on the one hand, and the Organization of African Unity and the Economic Commission for Africa, on the other, have their own perspectives and proposed remedies. Both dependency theory and neoclassical development theory, however, have suspect counterfactual arguments. Dependency theory assumes that if the external constraints of the world capitalist economy and the international state system disappeared, either capitalism would somehow develop "normally" in Africa and in a balanced, humane manner, or socialism could be accomplished easily. Neoclassical development theory assumes that if all policy distortions disappeared, the laws of comparative advantage and free-market economics would allow capitalism to blossom. Both are only partially true.

This current dismal politicoeconomic conjuncture in Africa raises some large questions. How capitalist is Africa now? Is the state a hindering or facilitating factor, or both? What role does culture play? African states are certainly soft, yet they are also quite authoritarian. They are what one might call lame Leviathans. If African states are not modern bureaucratic states, they clearly are not modern capitalist ones either. The calculability nexus is weak; state arbitrariness, instability, corruption, and inefficiency are high. The personalization or patrimonialization of power and authority structures, political and nonpolitical, is pervasive. Entrepreneurs, both domestic and foreign, do not control all the means of production, especially in the rural areas, as important restrictions on the commodification of these factors remain. Liquidity preferences remain high, and investment patterns lean heavily toward speculation and the short term. Technologies remain rudimentary, and new ones are not easily transferable. Markets are not well developed as economic, political, and social impediments continue to exist, and in many cases formal markets are actually shrinking while informal economies are growing to fill the gap. Noncapitalist modes of production remain important while only partial incorporation into the world economy is the norm. National financial, banking, and monetary systems are unsophisticated, and transportation and communications infrastructure, already weak, is disintegrating in many areas of the continent.

If states are not well developed, if there is little modern capitalism or socialism in Africa, and if most of the factors that facilitate their development remain weak or nonexistent, how likely is Africa to acquire strong and effective states or become significantly developed anytime soon? I think the answer is "not likely." Certainly international trade alone will not develop Africa or further underdevelop it for that matter. Internal obstacles to development in Africa are as important as those imposed by the world capitalist economy and international state system—if not more so. And the political and social obstacles are as important as the economic ones—if not more so. If the record of socialism in Africa is weak and modern capitalism does not exist, what does? The answer is syncretic economies with very mixed modes of production, noncapitalist social logics, heavily patrimonialized administrative states with their own political logics, statist economic policies, and a form of patrimonial capitalism.

Africa clearly remains only partially capitalist, despite the impact of roughly eighty years of direct colonial domination and twenty-five years of neocolonial influence. The colonial powers, try as they did, were unable to ensure that production was orderly and predictable throughout Africa, and they were only partially effective at incorporating the continent into the

world economy. Precolonial forms of production and economically relevant cultural patterns were not fully eliminated or even seriously weakened. In fact, in some parts of the continent market forces have actually
weakened in the postcolonial period. In the rural areas and small towns,
Africans often engage in straddling—that is, maintaining one foot in the
"national" market economy and the other in the informal and subsistence
economies. Others have gone further by exercising their exit option—with-
drawing almost completely from the formal economy and its links to the
predatory national state. Urban populations also attempt to straddle the
formal and informal economies as much as they can.

The search for internal and external sovereignty, authority, and unity
remains very incomplete in most African countries and has been increasingly tested in the early 1990s. For African ruling groups of all ideological
and policy persuasions, the need for greater authority over their societies
and territories is a primary concern. Efforts at state formation and the
processes of class formation are two of the most salient characteristics of
the contemporary African condition. Authoritarian forms of rule resulted
not from high levels of power and legitimacy but from the tenuousness
of authority. The quest for sovereignty takes place within the context of
poorly organized states with limited power resources which attempt to rule
societies that are heterogeneous internally and dependent externally. This
general condition has continuously frustrated efforts to formulate grand,
all-encompassing typologies of rule that productively differentiate between
African states.

The modal African state, whether authoritarian or democratic, is an
organization of domination controlled with varying degrees of efficacy by a
ruling group or class that competes for power and sovereignty with other
political, economic, and social groups, both internally and externally. It is
only partly autonomous, as it seeks to cope with constraints and uncertainty and to manage its dependence internally and externally. The rulers
thus struggle for unity and power simultaneously on two fronts. To increase state power is to reinforce their own power and to further their
interests. Internally the state must concern itself with ethnic, regional,
religious, linguistic, and other particularisms, as well as strongly rooted
universalistic religions (specifically Islam and Christianity), pluralist groups,
and emerging class structures. Externally the state combats major legacies
of the colonial state—essential linkages to the world capitalist system; the
pervasive influence of a wide variety of international organizations, particularly the IMF and the World Bank; and the competing states and ide-

ologies of the international state system. Yet the international system is also heterogeneous and divided; states, corporations, organizations, and classes pursue their own interests. This allows African states some relative autonomy. The degree of autonomy, both internal and external, must be empirically investigated in each case and over time, not dogmatically denied or proclaimed. The external and internal fronts of the battle interact in complex, shifting, but persistent ways as the two sides of the same fragile coin for these poorly developed states.

The characteristics of the modal African state are not likely to be altered very much by the varying processes of political liberalization sweeping Africa in the early 1990s. The previous experiences of Ghana and Nigeria, or of nineteenth-century Latin America, with returns to democratic rule do not lead to optimism, despite the current rhetoric of the major industrial democracies, the IMF, and the World Bank about the need for, and positively reinforcing character of, simultaneous economic and political liberalization. Thus far in Africa the patrimonial administrative state remains basically untouched by the pursuit of various political visions, especially those of development and democracy.[33]

The inherited colonial state has been patrimonialized and "debureaucratized" in the postcolonial era. Bureaucratic norms and principles have not persisted but rather have disappeared slowly. Some observers have stressed the "decay" or "decline" of the state in Africa, as a result of which the more impersonal institutions of the once-potent colonial state now lie in ruins. This "crisis of the state" is characterized by the emasculation of the probity, competence, and credibility of inherited state structures, such that corruption has become a defining characteristic.[34] In fact, two conceptually distinct but interrelated processes are at work: (1) the progressive personalization and functional contraction of the inherited colonial state structures, and (2) the normal cycles of fluctuating political control and extraction characteristic of the early stages of state formation. These processes have been accelerated by the economic and fiscal crises of African states since the mid-1970s. A strong functional, if not formal, contraction—not to say atrophy—of the structures established by the colonial state has taken place. Many of them barely operate at all, and in this sense the new postcolonial state produces only a few more services. Finally, African states are often in deep financial difficulty as well—even on the brink of bankruptcy. Regular sources of revenue are not adequate or are poorly organized, extensive borrowing and debt are common, corruption is rampant, and scarce resources are squandered by ruling groups. Thus, for the first thirty years of independence, the authority of the African state has often appeared both hard and soft at the same time, a sort of authoritarian bragging which drowns in an often mocking passivity.

An increasing number of observers agree that in Africa the weakness of class formation may be as essential to stress as its importance. Both aspects are true. Many also would agree that over thirty years most African countries have developed a dominant—but weakly so—ruling or political class and that it has had a class project of self-aggrandizement. The state in Africa, directly or indirectly, has definitely been the major avenue of upward mobility and accumulation. The new ruling group was created out of the state structures that it came to control after independence, and, contrary to the "normal" Marxist pattern, it has used the state to build an economic base for itself, rather than using a preexisting economic base rooted in the dominant mode of production to take over the state and use it to defend its economic interests. It has used the state to extract resources from other social groups, and it has then used these resources to reinforce the state and its control of the state.

Because of the nature of the African ruling class, it is inappropriate to call it a national bourgeoisie or state bourgeoisie, as is commonly done. Historically a bourgeoisie denotes a productive class, and the African ruling class is not productive. Any assumption that there is a dominant class in power in most African countries capable of ensuring the reproduction of capitalism must be seriously questioned. At the same time, class consciousness outside the ruling class is increasingly important. Significant class organization is lacking, however, resulting in weak and inchoate class politics.

The importance of the relationship between class and clientelism needs to be stressed. Patron-client politics can be both a class and a nonclass phenomenon. It can help to consolidate the position of ruling groups by establishing and reinforcing intraclass linkages. This type of politics also takes place between members of the ruling class and other emerging classes. In the process it helps to mitigate some of the negative consequences for the ruling group of the increasing class consciousness of many social groups. It is important to keep in mind that there are also external patrons and clients. As Frederick Cooper has noted, "The point is not that the existence of advanced capitalist countries and powerful corporations makes domestic accumulation impossible—the alternative paths are crucial, for example, in Brazil . . .—but that it presents choices to a ruling class which allow it to accumulate much wealth and some capital without a direct assault on the autonomy of the cultivators. . . . African kings . . .—like their modern-day counterparts—found that external relationships can be easier to develop than internal control and that those relations can bring in wealth even if they provide little basis for continued growth or security."[35]

Under the formal political structure of African regimes, a unifying perceptual and operational cultural idiom has emerged which is deeply embedded in society as well as in the state—that of patrimonialism and patron-client relations. Behaviorally this common idiom relates to processes by which allied actors obtain or lose, open up or close off, or become increasingly or decreasingly conscious of access to life and mobility chances.

In the turmoil of early and middle 1960s, the patrimonial idiom emerged quickly in the insecurity and strife of the major structural change brought on by independence. Competing local, regional, and national forms of patrimonialism—"traditional" and "modern"—struggled with each other in the context of very high uncertainty and anxiety. Patron-client linkages, simply the most handy and convenient type of organization, became a major structural form of political and economic struggle. They helped to consolidate and structure the new regimes and the political ruling classes emerging out of them, while at the same time diffusing popular discontent. Patron-client ties served class and particularistic, state and societal, political and economic interests. The patron-client idiom was thus both contextual and protean.

These processes highlight the contradictions of culture. While the fluidity and contextuality of cultural phenomena are central, potent patrimonial idioms with deep roots in the past remain very powerful. They mix and clash with the imposed cosmologies of colonial rule, Christianity, and capitalism. At the same time, both cultural fluidity and rootedness are strongly affected by the nature of the extant political structure. Africa is a cultural world of both simultaneousness and syncretism.[36]

This cultural matrix is well rooted at all levels of the social hierarchy, even with those who have very little chance of social improvement. As Jan Vansina has noted, the rapidly expanding members of the urban poor "share the belief that somehow they can perhaps make it and in any case that there are in nature, patrons and clients, powerful ones and weaker ones." This patrimonial matrix is both condemned and expected. What Richard Joseph said about Nigeria holds equally well for most of the rest of Africa: "Those who achieve public positions will find themselves violently assailed for their abuse of office while being simultaneously prevailed upon to procure some benefits for their artificially expanded networks of sectional supporters."[37]

State, Choice, and Context

The centrality of all these political and cultural forms reinforces many of the nondevelopmental aspects of both the economy and the state, rather than fostering their redefinition. They also generate very particular forms of capitalism and relations with external actors.

Patrimonial Capitalism: The Dominance of Political and Informal Economic Logics

The most common result of the macrosociological and historical syndrome of political, cultural, and social characteristics discussed above has been a weak and unproductive form of political capitalism—the juncture between patrimonial administrative states and certain types of mostly commercial capitalism. As such, it is a form of political capitalism very different from that of the East Asian and Latin American NICs. Max Weber called such a political economy "patrimonial capitalism," and he pointed out that it is usually not conducive to the development of either bureaucratic states or modern capitalism:

> The important openings for profit are in the hands of the ruler and his administrative staff . . . [so] capitalism is thereby either directly obstructed . . . or is diverted into political capitalism. . . . As a rule, the negative aspect of this arbitrariness, is dominant because—and this is the major point—the patrimonial state lacks the political and procedural predictability, indispensable for capitalist development, which is provided by the rational rules of modern bureaucratic administration. Instead we find unpredictability and inconsistency on the part of the court and local officials, and variously benevolence and disfavor on the part of the ruler and his servants. It is quite possible that a private individual, by skillfully taking advantage of the given circumstances and of personal relations, obtains a privileged position which offers him nearly unlimited acquisitive opportunities. But a capitalist economic system is obviously handicapped by these factors, for the individual variants of capitalism have a differential sensitivity toward such unpredictable factors. Wholesale trade can tolerate them most easily, relatively speaking, and adapt itself to all changing conditions . . . and the formation of trade capital is feasible under almost all conditions of domination, especially under patrimonialism. It is different with industrial capitalism. . . . It must be able to count on the continuity, trustworthiness and objectivity of the legal order, and on the rational, predictable functioning of legal and administrative agencies. Otherwise those guarantees of predictability are absent that are indispensable for the large industrial enterprise. They are especially weak in patrimonial states.[38]

Weber stressed that under patrimonialism the enormous "opening for bribery and corruption would be the least serious effect if it remained a constant quantity, because then it would become calculable in practice. But it tends to be a matter which is settled from case to case with every individual official and thus highly variable."[39] This affects both the indirect role of the state in the development of modern capitalism and its direct role via regulation and the parastatal sector. Pumping large amounts of money into such a political economy clearly cannot be expected to make much of a positive difference. Nigeria readily leaps to mind. Unless other major changes are made first, the solution to Africa's development crisis will not be found in pouring significantly more resources into the continent.

Weber stressed that "in the interest of his domination, the patrimonial ruler must oppose . . . the economic independence of the bourgeoisie." This did not mean that the ruler succeeded, as the result emerged "everywhere according to the outcome of the resultant historical struggles."[40] In other words, different countries followed different paths as the result of concrete conflicts between actors, the outcomes of which could not be fully predicted. There is thus nothing mechanistic or deterministic about Weber's views on state and class formation or the development of capitalism. The same holds for Africa today. The paths that different countries take are determined by the presence and balance of opportunities and struggles among rulers, emerging classes, status groups, organizations, and particularistic forces, both internally and externally. As Cooper pointed out, "Africa itself is heading in different directions."[41] The different trajectories of Ghana and Somalia in the 1980s and early 1990s constitutes one vivid example.

This African form of patrimonial capitalism has been reinforced by a powerful socioeconomic and cultural logic important in much of continent today. Precolonial patterns were only partially modified by colonial domination, such that property rights were politicized rather than privatized in many parts of Africa, and strategies of accumulation were directed toward building up power over resources rather than increasing productivity. Commercialization often occurred within a framework of conflicting legal and political principles and practices, so people sought to strengthen their access to markets and purchasing power by fostering relations of loyalty and dependence. As a result, how economic resources were used became less important than how they were acquired. This social logic results in a pattern of economic development in which the growth of transactions tends to outpace the growth of production, small-scale enterprises proliferate, and labor productivity remains low. Such a logic increases uncertainty, inhibits long-term productive investment, and is not particularly favorable to the development of effectively entrepreneurial states or robust private sectors.[42]

Clear evidence now exists of the increasing scale of long-standing informal economy or magendo phenomena in Africa. Much of this economic activity is composed of various forms of commercial capitalism that attempt to operate outside both the formal market and the state, often crossing or ignoring national boundaries. Less evidence exists of productive activity based on significant new long-term investment. The bulk of the informal economy is still oriented toward survival and coping with a deteriorating socioeconomic, ecological, and political situation.

Signs exist that some informal economy activity could begin to redefine certain types of patron-client relationships away from the political logic of the state toward a social logic of accumulation and production outside the state.[43] But is this magendo activity important enough to indicate a significant move anytime soon away from the political and social logics discussed above toward more productive economic ones? No, it is not—at least not for quite some time for most countries. It is still far from clear that the calculation nexus of the informal economy will allow it to expand and transform itself into more sophisticated and long-lasting forms of capitalism or to produce social groups that will seek to influence or take control of the state and transform it.

Whatever one thinks about the role of foreign capital in Africa, it is important to point out that the barriers and obstacles discussed here affect foreign capital as well. As a result, an involuntary marginalization of much of the continent is under way within the world economy.[44] Because foreign capital has considerable power to select the type of state with which it cooperates, it is very doubtful that Africa will play a significant role in current shifts in the patterns of production in the international division of labor. For most Western businessmen Africa has become a voracious sinkhole which swallows their money with little or no return.

From this point of view, the laments of international organizations and development economists about the intractable underdevelopment of Africa are not just conspiratorial attempts to conceal the pillage of Africa but rather reflections of the fact that Africa is an underexploited continent. Africa's current dismal situation is not predominantly the result either of its dependent position in the world economy or of its relationship to dominant countries in the international state system. Clearly what happens to Africa will be the combined result of the type of economic policies chosen and the effects of world market forces, the international state system, internal socioeconomic structures, and the state. If—and there is no certainty— Africa eventually develops some systematic form of modern capitalism, it will have to tackle many of the elements and processes with which other regions have struggled.

While the private sector can do more than it is now allowed to do, modest expectations for both state and market are in order. Africa needs both stronger, more effective markets and states. In reference to the more developed Latin American states, two astute observers have noted that "the more social relations . . . approach contractual market exchange and bureaucratic organization, the greater is the likelihood of effective state intervention, since market exchange and bureaucratic organization are major institutional forms that encourage instrumental behavior and protect it by institutional differentiation and insulation. . . . The increasing penetration of civil society by market exchange and bureaucratic organization provides a partial explanation for the greatly increased, if not unlimited, transformative capacity the modern state displays in contrast to patrimonial rule in agrarian societies."[45] The adjustments desired by external actors and some African officials are enormous, much more than anywhere else. As noted in the introduction, it is not just a question of reordering policies but rather of constructing a whole new context so that Africa will no longer be lost between state and market. After roughly thirty years of independence, most of Africa is not effectively socialist, or capitalist, or even statist. Socialist and statist efforts have come to very little, and current economic and political liberalization efforts may not have a major positive impact. The central task for Africa now, therefore, is how to cope with the no-man's-land between state and market and between internal and external actors.

Conclusion: From Malignant and Benign Mercantilism to Embedded Liberalism?

As the historical record of early modern Europe and nineteenth-century Latin America suggests, pessimism and optimism, and thus assessments of intractability, depend on where one stands—France in the 1780s, Brazil in the 1880s, or Ghana in 1980s. Whether Africa is considered a special case also depends on where one stands analytically. One can be relatively pessimistic about Africa's prospects in the short and medium term but guardedly optimistic about the long-term prospects. It is necessary to beware, however, of what I call the "fault of analytic hurry"—the desire to rush things along whatever the path, to see things as real before they actually are, to read substantive weight into social processes, institutions, and actors that do not possess it. This has been one of the major problems with the analysis of class factors in Africa for some time. It could apply just as easily to bureaucratization, the significance of informal economies, the spread of the market, the viability of the private sector, or the prospects for effective structural adjustment or political liberalization. Analysts cannot rush or control social processes. Change is usually slow, incremental, uneven, often contradictory from a given analytic point of view, and dependent on the outcome of unpredictable socioeconomic and political struggles.

This is not to say that striking change is completely out of the question. Since early 1983 the regime of Jerry Rawlings in Ghana has engaged in sustained and, by African standards, quite remarkable efforts at structural adjustment. The success resulted from a rare conjuncture of factors, including luck, but that it occurred at all reminds us to heed the caution of Stephan Haggard and Robert Kaufman: "If economists often tend toward voluntarism, in which political constraints are explained by lack of 'will,' political scientists can be overly deterministic."[46] It is not likely, however, that there will be many Ghanas over the next several decades. It is not even clear that the Ghanaian success is sustainable, despite the triumph of Rawlings in democratic elections in late 1992. Ghana's experience does indicate, however, that African countries can go in different directions. A few countries may do modestly well while much of the rest of the continent sinks ever deeper into decline. African reality may well be deeply intractable because of the often negative synergy between policy, institutional, and macrosociological constraints, but it is not fully immune to sustained creative effort under the right conditions. What can be done to help foster facilitating conditions? This concluding section investigates ways in which external actors can assist Africans to confront their difficult problems more effectively.

There is a need for a balanced tension between state and market, not only for the economic logic of change but also for its political logic. Most Western states have pursued a balanced tension between economic and political logics in practice, if not in rhetoric, since at least the end of World War II. The dominant political economy of these industrial countries points to the importance of the political link between state and market. Such a link is as important for the efforts of Third World countries to engage in effective economic reform and development as it has been for the prosperity, stability, and transformation of Western industrial states over the last forty years.

Contrary to popular assumption and official rhetoric, orthodox liberalism has not been the dominant form of political economy in the West. Instead, it has been "embedded liberalism," a compromise which involves the use of state power in the interests of both domestic social stability and international economic adjustment.[47] At the international level market forces have been permitted to move, if haltingly, toward comparative advantage and adjustment, but even here interventionist policies have been important. State power has been employed to restructure the economy and buffer the disruptive domestic social consequences of liberal economics at the international level as trade, finance, production, and technology have evolved. As a result, international economic liberalism and domestic political stability and prosperity via state intervention coexist in a strained and uneasy balance, mediated by politics.

The compromises of such a political economy are sometimes viewed as liberalism with lots of cheating. But the "cheating" is in fact an inherent and defining characteristic of the system. In other words, international economic liberalism exists, but it is compromised by being embedded in the political and economic realities of domestic state-society relations. International economic efficiency is not sacrificed to domestic political stability, or vice versa; a modus vivendi is established through embedded liberalism by uniting the entanglements of domestic and international politics and economics. Embedded liberalism is a form of mercantilism, but a relatively mild one. It is distinguished from benign mercantilism by the fact that market forces play a more dominant role. Japan and Korea, for example, are cases of benign mercantilism, not embedded liberalism, despite Japan's formally democratic political structure.

The compromise of embedded liberalism has not been fully extended to the Third World by Western countries.[48] Certainly many Third World states, and nearly all African ones, need to move from malignant or unproductive mercantilism toward benign mercantilism or embedded liberalism. Whether they will do so is another story. Largely for geopolitical and domestic reasons, the United States is trying to push Japan, Korea, and Taiwan from benign mercantilism to a form of embedded liberalism, although it will not be the neoclassical liberalism preached by the IMF and the World Bank. Most other Third World countries are expected to conform to the IMF and World Bank's vision of neoclassical structural adjustment and economic development. This is very difficult for even the strongest and most effectively developmental states. Chile and Mexico, for example, are countries with relatively high levels of technocratic and bureaucratic capabilities and substantial political insulation—but quite different political structures—that have attempted to implement orthodox economic adjustment programs. Despite their capabilities and insulation, they have had to engage in important political and economic buffering and continued state interventionism.[49]

A major dilemma thus confronts structural adjustment and economic development in the Third World generally, but especially in Africa: they cannot take place without an important role for the state, without some form of benign mercantilism or embedded liberalism that is sensitive to issues of policy choice, institutional structure and capability, and macro-sociological context. The East Asian and Latin American cases discussed here provide strong evidence for such a view. Along with the IMF and the World Bank, the major industrial countries still insist that African and other Third World countries move as far as possible toward a liberal neoclassical political economy which they do not practice themselves. For geopolitical reasons the United States acquiesced in an important state role in East Asia and, despite recent liberalization pressures, still does so. The Western industrial democracies may be forced to do the same for other areas of the Third World for both geopolitical and economic reasons linked to the health of the world economy and the international financial system. Africa desperately needs such patience and acquiescence.

Clearly the IMF and World Bank and many policy and academic analysts need to rethink their views on the role of the state. As Tony Killick has so aptly put it, the neoorthodox move away from the state has become "a reaction too far."[50] "Getting the state out" is not likely to be particularly efficacious, much less feasible. Making proper policy choices is necessary but not sufficient. There is some tentative evidence that the international financial institutions have started to rethink their position, at least at the conceptual level. In its reports on Africa in the late 1980s, the World Bank began tacitly to admit more of a role for the state in economic transformation. With the 1991 *World Development Report*, however, the shift became more explicit.

Referring to "the remarkable achievements of the East Asian economies, or with the earlier achievements of Japan," the report asks, "Why, in these economies, were interventions in the markets such as infant-industry protection and credit subsidies associated with success, not failure?" Its answer, in short, is that these "market-friendly" state interventions were "carried out competently, pragmatically, and flexibly," were terminated if they failed or outlasted their usefulness, did not distort relative prices "unduly," and were export oriented, "moderate" rather than all-encompassing, undertaken reluctantly and openly, and constantly disciplined by international and domestic markets. In sum, according to the bank, these "market-friendly" forms of state intervention "refute the case for thoroughgoing dirigisme as convincingly as they refute the case for laissez-faire."[51] Effective outward-oriented transformation thus quite clearly can be achieved without following all the liberal economic mantras of the IMF and the World Bank. While the capabilities of African countries are weak at the moment, they need to work in this direction, however slowly and carefully. Japan, now the second largest shareholder in the World Bank, is working aggressively to strengthen such an evolution of views.[52]

In fact, this new emerging view of the World Bank still significantly underestimates the type and degree of state intervention in cases such as Korea, as well as the importance of larger macrosociological and historical factors. It does, however, represent an important shift toward a more balanced tension between state and market, one which has long been evident in the practice, if not the rhetoric, of northern industrial democracies. It is not a view fully shared so far by the IMF or many Western governments, however. It is also not a view shared by many longtime critics of the World Bank, those seeking a "new political economy of development" which continues to stress the state over the market. This is indicated by the title of a recent representative book attacking Western "neo-liberalism": *States or Markets? Neo-Liberalism and the Development Policy Debate.*[53] A more balanced viewpoint would require *States and Markets*.

While all sides still need to seek a properly balanced tension between state and market and between policy, institutional, and macrosociological factors, admitting the need for it is an important first step. It does, nevertheless, open up a large Pandora's box, one which Western actors have wanted to keep closed. Once you concede a serious, nonliberal role for the state, you then must decide on specific types and instances of state intervention. This is an enormously difficult thing to accomplish and clearly constitutes the current policy frontier. The elegant parsimony of the neoclassical vision has been replaced by messy ambiguity and relativity generated by a belated recognition of the importance of institutional and larger macrosociological factors. Such an admission does not, however, imply that the state capabilities necessary to engage successfully in such intervention will exist when and where they are needed.

State, Choice, and Context

Reforming existing state and private institutions or creating new ones will help to make choice-centered approaches to reform more effective, but it is difficult to do and sustain over time. The larger context in which such efforts take place is crucial. In rethinking the role of the state and the possibilities for reform in Africa, one needs to use and integrate choice-theoretic, new institutionalist, and macrosociological and historical perspectives. Sensitivity to the institutional and contextual dilemmas of policy choice faced by African leaders must be kept clearly in mind. In discussing the choices confronting the Rawlings government in Ghana, Kwesi Botchwey, longtime minister for finance and economic planning, vividly illustrated these dilemmas: "We were faced with two options, which we debated very fiercely before we finally chose this path. I know because I participated very actively in these debates. Two choices: We had to maneuver our way around the naiveties of leftism, which has a sort of disdain for any talk of financial discipline, which seeks refuge in some vague concept of structuralism in which everything doable is possible. . . . Moreover, [we had to find a way between] this naivete and the crudities and rigidities and dogma of monetarism, which behaves as if once you set the monetary incentives everybody will do the right thing and the market will be perfect."[54]

External actors have begun to understand such dilemmas and the intractability they produce. A "new realism" does appear to be emerging, but it remains very incomplete. Oddly enough, just as this new realism has begun to take hold, a "new illusion" has also appeared—the belief by the now "triumphant" industrial democracies that successful economic liberalization requires simultaneous political liberalization. These powerful states are now preaching a brilliant vision of global transformation via the magic of the market and the ballot box. Democratization has replaced anticommunism as the international rallying cry. It is not at all clear, however, that these two forms of liberalization are positively reinforcing. The track record of both the Third World and now of the former Second World is not reassuring. If the positive link does not, in fact, exist, this new vision, or rather illusion, may seriously weaken the hard-won lessons of the new realism.[55]

Notes

1. World Bank, *Global Economic Prospects and the Developing Countries* (Washington, D.C., May 1991), p. 6.

2. World Bank, *World Development Report 1991: The Challenge of Development* (New York: Oxford Univ. Press, 1991), pp. 28–29.

3. World Bank, *Global Economic Prospects*, pp. 6, 58.

4. Ibid., pp. 58, 4.

5. Interview with Chinua Achebe in Anne Belsover, *African Events*, Nov. 1987, p. 77; Frederick Chiluba, quoted in " 'No One Else Will Solve Our Problems,' Chiluba Tells OAU," *Africa News* 36, no. 7 (Aug. 3–16, 1992): 6; Michael Chege, "Remembering Africa," *Foreign Affairs* 71, no. 1 (1992): 146.

6. See Thomas M. Callaghy, "Lost between State and Market: The Politics of Economic Adjustment in Ghana, Zambia, and Nigeria," in *Economic Crisis and Policy Choice: The Politics of Adjustment in the Third World,* ed. Joan Nelson (Princeton, N.J.: Princeton Univ. Press, 1990), pp. 257–319. On the reform efforts, see Thomas M. Callaghy, "The Political Economy of African Debt: The Case of Zaire," in *Africa in Economic Crisis,* ed. John Ravenhill (New York: Columbia Univ. Press, 1986), pp. 307–46; Callaghy, "Africa and the World Economy: Caught between a Rock and a Hard Place," in *Africa in World Politics,* ed. John Harbeson and Donald Rothchild (Boulder, Colo.: Westview Press, 1991), pp. 39–68; Thomas M. Callaghy and John Ravenhill, eds., *Hemmed In: Responses to Africa's Economic Decline* (New York: Columbia Univ. Press, 1993).

7. On Ghana, see Callaghy, "Lost between State and Market"; Donald Rothchild, ed., *Ghana: The Political Economy of Reform* (Boulder, Colo.: Lynne Rienner, 1991); Jeffrey Herbst, *The Politics of Reform in Ghana, 1982–1991* (Berkeley: Univ. of California Press, 1993).

8. For dissenting views on this topic, see Thomas M. Callaghy, "Political Passions and Economic Interests: Economic Reform and Political Structure in Africa," in Callaghy and Ravenhill, *Hemmed In;* "Civil Society, Democracy, and Economic Change in Africa: A Dissenting Opinion," in *Civil Society and the State in Africa,* ed. Naomi Chazan, John W. Harbeson, and Donald Rothchild (Boulder, Colo.: Lynne Rienner, 1993); and "Vision and Politics in the Transformation of the Global Political Economy: Lessons from the Second and Third Worlds," in *Global Transformation and the Third World,* ed. Robert O. Slater, Barry M. Schutz, and Steven R. Dorr (Boulder, Colo.: Lynne Rienner, 1993).

9. World Bank, *Sub-Saharan Africa: From Crisis to Sustainable Growth* (Washington, D.C., 1989).

10. World Bank, *Adjustment Lending* (Washington, D.C., 1989), p. 3. On the new institutional economics, see Oliver E. Williamson, *The Economic Institutions of Capitalism* (New York: Free Press, 1985), and Thrainn Eggertsson, *Economic Behavior and Institutions* (Cambridge: Cambridge Univ. Press, 1990). See also Douglas C. North and Robert P. Thomas, *The Rise of the Western World: A New Economic History* (Cambridge: Cambridge Univ. Press, 1973), and Douglass North, *Structure and Change in Economic History* (New York: Norton, 1981).

11. Robert H. Bates, *Beyond the Miracle of the Market: The Political Economy of Agrarian Development in Kenya* (Cambridge: Cambridge Univ. Press, 1989), pp. 4, 6.

12. Robert H. Bates, "Macro-Political Economy in the Field of Development," Duke University Program in International Political Economy, Working Paper no. 40, June

1988, p. 56. Bates has made major contributions to both micro- and macropolitical economy.

13. See Douglass C. North, *Institutions, Institutional Change, and Economic Performance* (Cambridge: Cambridge Univ. Press, 1990).

14. Robert H. Bates, "Contra Contractarianism: Some Reflections on the New Institutionalism," *Politics and Society* 16, nos. 2/3 (1988): 387–401. See also Randall Collins, *Weberian Sociological Theory* (Cambridge: Cambridge Univ. Press, 1986); Peter B. Evans, Dietrich Rueschemeyer, and Theda Skocpol, eds., *Bringing the State Back In* (Cambridge: Cambridge Univ. Press, 1985); and Thomas M. Callaghy, "The State and the Development of Capitalism in Africa," in *Precarious Balance: State and Society in Africa*, ed. Donald Rothchild and Naomi Chazan (Boulder, Colo.: Westview, 1988), pp. 67–99.

15. See Chalmers Johnson, "Political Institutions and Economic Performance," in *The Political Economy of the New Asian Industrialism*, ed. Frederic C. Deyo (Ithaca, N.Y.: Cornell Univ. Press, 1987), pp. 136–64. This section draws on Stephan Haggard, Byung-kook Kim, and Chung-in Moon, "The Transition to Export-Led Growth in Korea: 1954–1966," Working Paper, Center for Research on Politics and Social Organization, Harvard University, n.d.; Haggard, "The Politics of Industrialization in Korea and Taiwan," paper prepared for a conference on "Explaining the Success of Industrialization in East Asia," School of Pacific Studies, Australian National University, Sept. 9–12, 1985; Haggard and Moon, "The South Korean State in the International Economy," in *The Antinomies of Interdependence*, ed. John Gerard Ruggie (New York: Columbia Univ. Press, 1983), pp. 131–89; Haggard and Moon, "Institutions and Economic Policy: Theory and a Korean Case Study," n.d.; Haggard, *Pathways from the Periphery: The Politics of Growth in the Newly Industrializing Countries* (Ithaca, N.Y.: Cornell Univ. Press, 1990); Alice Amsden, *Asia's Next Giant: South Korea and Late Industrialization* (New York: Oxford Univ. Press, 1989); Gary Gereffi and Donald L. Wyman, eds., *Manufacturing Miracles: Paths of Industrialization in Latin America and East Asia* (Princeton, N.J.: Princeton Univ. Press, 1990); and Robert Wade, *Governing the Market: Economic Theory and the Role of Government in East Asian Industrialization* (Princeton, N.J.: Princeton Univ. Press, 1990), and "East Asia's Economic Success: Conflicting Perspectives, Partial Insights, Shaky Evidence," *World Politics* 44, no. 2 (Jan. 1992): 270–320.

16. Johnson, "Political Institutions," p. 5.

17. Frederic C. Deyo, "Introduction," in Deyo, *New Asian Industrialization*, p. 20; Haggard, "Politics of Industrialization," p. 30. See also Bruce Cumings, "The Origins and Development of the Northeast Asian Political Economy," in Deyo, *New Asian Industrialism*, p. 81.

18. Robert Gilpin, *The Political Economy of International Relations* (Princeton, N.J.: Princeton Univ. Press, 1987), pp. 32, 404–5.

19. Johnson, "Political Institutions," pp. 144, 138; Haggard and Moon, "South Korean State," p. 158.

20. Peter B. Evans, "The State as Problem and Solution: Predation, Embedded Autonomy, and Structural Change," in *The Politics of Adjustment: International Constraints, Distributive Conflicts, and the State*, ed. Stephan Haggard and Robert R. Kaufman (Princeton, N.J.: Princeton Univ. Press, 1992), pp. 139–81.

21. Deyo, "Coalitions, Institutions, and Linkage Sequencing," in Deyo, *New Asian Industrialism*, p. 239.

22. Cumings, "Origins and Development," p. 81. See also Deyo, "Introduction," p. 18.

23. Peter B. Evans, "Class, State, and Dependence in East Asia," in Deyo, *New Asian Industrialism*, p. 210.

24. Ibid., p. 222.

25. Deyo, "Coalitions," p. 240.

26. Ibid., p. 221.

27. See Haggard and Moon, "Institutions and Economic Policy"; Callaghy, "Political Passions" and "Vision and Politics."

28. This section is based on Callaghy, "Lost between State and Market"; interviews in New York, Washington, and London; and 1987 and 1991 trips I made to Nigeria. See also Thomas M. Callaghy, "Democracy and the Political Economy of Restraint in Nigeria," paper for the conference on "Economy, Society and Democracy," Washington, D.C., May 1992; Jeffrey Herbst and Adebayo Olukoshi, "Nigeria," paper prepared for the World Bank project on "The Political Economy of Structural Adjustment in New Democracies," 1992.

29. Peter B. Evans, *Dependent Development* (Princeton, N.J.: Princeton Univ. Press), 1979, p. 309.

30. Haggard and Moon, "South Korean State," p. 141; Evans, "Class, State," p. 223.

31. Goran Hyden, *No Shortcuts to Progress* (Berkeley: Univ. of California Press, 1983).

32. On the "back to the future strategy," see Thomas M. Callaghy and John Ravenhill, "How Hemmed In? Lessons and Prospects of Africa's Responses to Decline," in Callaghy and Ravenhill, *Hemmed In*.

33. See Thomas M. Callaghy, "Politics and Vision in Africa: The Interplay of Domination, Equality and Liberty," in *Political Domination in Africa: Reflections on the Limits of Power*, ed. Patrick Chabal (Cambridge: Cambridge Univ. Press, 1986), pp. 30–51; "Political Passions and Economic Interests"; "Vision and Politics."

34. For this view, see Crawford Young, "Patterns of Social Conflict: State, Class, and Ethnicity," *Daedalus* 111, no. 2 (Spring 1982): 94.

35. Frederick Cooper, "Africa and the World Economy," *African Studies Review* 24, nos. 2/3 (June/September 1981): 45, 51–52.

36. See Thomas M. Callaghy, *Culture and Politics in Zaire* (Ann Arbor: Center for Political Studies, Univ. of Michigan, 1988); Michael G. Schatzberg, "Power, Language, and Legitimacy in Africa," paper for the conference on "Identity, Rationality, and the Post-Colonial Subject," Columbia University, New York, Feb. 28, 1991; and Michael G. Schatzberg, "Power, Legitimacy, and 'Democratization' in Africa," paper presented at the Woodrow Wilson International Center for Scholars, Washington, D.C., June 17, 1991; these two papers are part of a larger project entitled "Contested Terrain: Political Thought, Language, and Legitimacy."

37. Jan Vansina, "Historical Overview: Zaire," National Council of Churches of Christ, 1983, p. 8; Richard Joseph, "Class, State, and Prebendal Politics in Nigeria," in *State and Class in Africa*, ed. Nelson Kasfir (London: Frank Cass, 1984), p. 33.

38. Max Weber, *Economy and Society* (Berkeley: Univ. of California Press, 1978),

pp. 238, 1094–95. See also Randall Collins, "Weber's Last Theory of Capitalism: A Systematization," *American Sociological Review* 45 (Dec. 1980): 925–42.

39. Weber, *Economy and Society*, p. 238.

40. Ibid., p. 1107.

41. Cooper, "Africa," p. 49.

42. See Sara Berry, *Fathers Work for Their Sons: Accumulation, Mobility, and Class Formation in an Extended Yoruba Community* (Berkeley: Univ. of California Press, 1985), and "Coping with Confusion: African Farmers' Responses to Economic Instability in the 1970s and 1980s," in Callaghy and Ravenhill, *Hemmed In*.

43. See Janet MacGaffey, *Entrepreneurs and Parasites: The Struggle for Indigenous Capitalism in Zaire* (Cambridge: Cambridge Univ. Press, 1987).

44. On Africa's simultaneously increasing marginalization and dependence, see Callaghy, "Africa and the World Economy."

45. Dietrich Rueschemeyer and Peter B. Evans, "The State and Economic Transformation: Toward an Analysis of the Conditions Underlying Effective Intervention," in Evans, Rueschemeyer, and Skocpol, *Bringing the State Back In*, p. 71.

46. Stephan Haggard and Robert Kaufman, "The Politics of Stabilization and Structural Adjustment," in *Developing Country Debt and Economic Performance*, ed. Jeffrey D. Sachs (Chicago: Univ. of Chicago Press, 1989), p. 248.

47. The term and concept are John Ruggie's; see "International Regimes, Transactions, and Change: Embedded Liberalism in the Postwar Economic Order," *International Organization* 36, no. 2 (Spring 1982): 398–99, 404, 413.

48. See John Ruggie, "Political Structure and Change in the International Economic Order," in Ruggie, *Antinomies*, pp. 423–87.

49. See Thomas M. Callaghy, "Toward State Capability and Embedded Liberalism in the Third World: Lessons for Adjustment," in *Fragile Coalitions: The Politics of Economic Adjustment*, ed. Joan Nelson (Washington, D.C.: Overseas Development Council, 1989), pp. 115–38; Nelson, *Economic Crisis and Policy Choice*.

50. Tony Killick, *A Reaction Too Far: Contemporary Thinking about the Economic Role of the State* (Boulder, Colo.: Westview Press, 1990).

51. World Bank, *World Development Report 1991*, p. 5, see also pp. 39–40.

52. See Susumu Awanohara, "More Ways to Skin a Cat," *Far Eastern Economic Review*, June 18, 1992, pp. 60–61; Michael Hirsh, "Another Road to Riches in Asia," *San Francisco Examiner*, Nov. 29, 1992, pp. E1, E5–6.

53. Christopher Colclough and James Manor, eds., *States of Markets? Neo-Liberalism and the Development Policy Debate* (New York: Oxford Univ. Press, 1991).

54. Quoted in "Ghana: High Stakes Gamble," *Africa News* 31, no. 2 (Jan. 23, 1989): 10.

55. See Callaghy, "Political Passions," and "Vision and Politics."

7

LEARNING FROM THE KENYA DEBATE

COLIN LEYS

WHAT WAS THE "Kenya debate" about? Ultimately, it was about whether capitalistic development is possible at the "periphery" of the world capitalist system, or, more accurately (since in the real world nothing is excluded absolutely), "whether or not there are theoretical reasons for thinking that the ex-colonies cannot 'adopt the bourgeois mode of production' and develop their productive forces within it" (in the words of the paper which originally provoked the debate).[1] In the late 1970s English-speaking students of African development, influenced by the rather categorical versions of dependency theory popularized by development theorists such as André Gunder Frank and Samir Amin, were largely convinced that Africa could not develop under capitalism. Consequently, questioning this, in relation to Kenya, provoked a general debate focused on an African country which had been more intensively researched than most.

The aim of this chapter is to look back at the debate in the light of what has happened since—both in development thinking and in Kenya. It begins with a very brief summary of the debate: readers who are familiar with it may well prefer to start at the following section.

The "Kenya Debate"

Dependency theory, which had informed my previous work on Kenya, suggested that there were three seemingly insuperable obstacles to the development of Kenya under capitalism: (1) the structures of the colonial economy, which appeared unconducive to the efficient use of national resources but which were taken over largely intact by the incoming independent regime, (2) the monopoly power of foreign capital, on which the small African business class seemed heavily dependent, and (3) the state, which seemed increasingly preoccupied with the use of economic resources

Learning from the Kenya Debate

(access to credit, import licenses, profitable franchises, etc.) to buttress the political power (and the personal fortunes) of the president and his closest associates.[2]

But by 1978 I came to think that the question of the further development of Kenya under capitalism should be regarded as open, not foreclosed, for two main reasons: first, Michael Cowen had shown that before colonial rule there had been a capital-accumulating class among the Kikuyu of Central Province and that this class, after many vicissitudes under colonialism, had emerged as a core element in the class that had come to dominate Kenyan politics since independence; second, it was evident that this class had succeeded in occupying one sector after another of the modern Kenyan economy during the postindependence years of 1964–76 to the point where they were in 1977 even beginning to enter the manufacturing sector, and that while they were doing all this, not only was there no catastrophic drop in output (as had happened under Amin in Uganda, for example), but the average annual real growth rate was 6 percent. It was also clear that their access to state power had been an important instrument of their advance; through legislation and administrative action they had been able largely to take over large-scale capitalist agriculture and to become established in trade, tourism, urban and coastal real estate, small-scale building, import-export trade, and so on. There was also evidence of growing social integration among the members of this class, and there were signs of the emergence of a consciousness of their class position and interests—the beginnings of an awareness of the requirements (legal, international, etc.) for the consolidation and defense of these interests—including an emerging critique of the arbitrary and rapacious behavior that had been indulged in by leading members of the Kenyatta regime.

Looking back at Marx's analysis of why capitalism first became established when and where it did (i.e., in the seventeenth century and in Britain, as opposed to, say, the Netherlands), I noted that he had explained it (in *Das Kapital* 1:pt. 8) in terms of a combination of factors that happened to occur then and there, and not at some other time or place; and I argued that when looked at in this way, Kenya might likewise be seen as exceptionally equipped (by African standards) with the combination of factors (in particular, its exceptionally strong indigenous accumulating class) needed to overcome the contemporary constraints to capitalist development to which dependency theory pointed.

The debate was joined when two experts on industrialization in Kenya, Raphael Kaplinsky and Steven Langdon, argued that this was so improbable as to be virtually impossible. Kaplinsky took the view that any peripheral country that does not have either a large internal market or the good fortune to be able to profit from a particular and perhaps unique phase in the global development of capitalism (like the NICs) faces absolute limits to capitalistic accumulation, whether or not it has a domestic class of accumulators with precolonial roots: "The in-built contradictions of economies of this type [i.e., other than those with large internal markets like India or Brazil] make it difficult to foresee that such a pattern of accumulation—with or without foreign capital—can proceed in a viable form."[3] Langdon's position was similar, in that he considered that "the Kenyan bourgeoisie's alliance with foreign capital . . . means that the indigenous bourgeoisie *cannot* carry forward a broad transformation of social relations . . . because it is dependent on foreign capital" whose technology choices constituted, in his eyes, an insuperable barrier to such a transformation. He differed from Kaplinsky in explicitly not ruling out the possibility of a capitalist transformation of Kenya ("this is not to say that [a broad capitalist transformation of social relations] is . . . impossible in Kenya"), but he could imagine it occurring only if for some as-yet-unforeseen reason this suited the needs of foreign capital.[4] The domestic capitalist class, in his view, was dependent on foreign capital and, by virtue of that dependency, incapable of bringing about such a transformation.[5]

Why Return to the Kenya Debate?

In general such debates are not resolved but tend to peter out in mutual fatigue and indifference, while the central issues that seemed to be so importantly at stake cease to compel attention and are replaced by new preoccupations. Noting this in his 1985 review of the debate, Gavin Kitching suggested that in this instance it was because all the contending participants were unclear (or if clear, uncomfortable) about the political implications of their respective theoretical positions. Being unwilling to confront these explicitly, they (we, that is) expended energy on disputing the significance of the factual evidence on Kenya's postindependence development, the nature of the manufacturing fraction of the indigenous bourgeoisie, the role of the state, and so on, rather than acknowledge that what the debate really brought into focus was the very different and problematic alternative political commitments and strategies that we were implicitly endorsing.

According to Kitching, those on the Cowen-Leys-Swainson side of the debate really believed that a capitalist development was the best hope currently available for countries like Kenya. Kaplinsky and Langdon, for their part, would have liked such development to be possible (Langdon, in fact, explicitly speculated on the possibility that its necessarily limited life might be prolonged by a strategy of income redistribution—enlarging internal markets for manufactures—introduced by a populist coalition of enlightened state technocrats and what Latin American analysts like to call the "popular sectors"); but they actually believed it to be impossible, although they did not spell out the political implications of their pessimism. Kitching himself looked for the construction of "a sophisticated socialist movement . . . among the working classes of Africa as they slowly expand through time." He considered that this would "take a long time and that a prolonged period of struggle against a developing capitalism is one of the prerequisites of its creation. To that extent I am 'happy' to see continued capitalist development in black Africa (though this may or may not occur)."[6]

None of these political stances would, of course, have been very acceptable to progressive Kenyans, and it was an unstated (and perhaps unacknowledged) awareness of this, Kitching thought, that led to the debate being abandoned by all the original participants, who on the whole liked to think of themselves as progressive too.

Whether or not Kitching's diagnosis of the reasons for the inconclusive outcome of the debate was correct, the impulse behind his intervention was sound: the failure to resolve such debates means that the confusions involved are likely to recur, after some time, in new forms. While we must accept that in social life problems recur constantly and that this will often be little affected by the extent to which social scientists succeed in identifying and understanding them, this is not an excuse for social scientists not at least trying to reach agreement about what the problems are and how they should be understood. In this case, where we are dealing with issues that have very practical current political implications—the development strategies of governments and aid donors, the political strategies of political and social movements—the obligation to try to draw up the accounts of the debate is surely real.

For in its widest sense, the debate was a confrontation between competing paradigms or metatheories about what is happening in the ex-colonial world and our reasons for studying it. In particular, it was an encounter between the dependency approach to development, and that approach's implicit political commitments, and the approach of "orthodox" or "classical" Marxism, and its implicit commitments. And since, as Dudley Seers and others have pointed out, classical Marxism has much in common with classical political economy, from which modernization theory is also derived, the Kenya debate can be read as a text in which, to varying degrees, all the principal attitudes, assumptions, and commitments current in development studies today are manifested and tested.[7]

This chapter does not try to offer a full reading of the Kenya debate considered in this way. It aims simply to consider the theoretical context in which the debate occurred and offers some conclusions about the relation between the dependency and classical Marxist approaches that the passage of time suggests are reasonable. Then it returns to the debate in the light of what happened in Kenya in the 1980s, indicating some empirical questions which, with hindsight, it might have been more useful to ask.

The Theoretical Context

As between dependency theory and "classical" Marxism, and perhaps "modernization" theory too, there is at least general agreement that the ex-colonies (or "underdeveloped," "Third World," or "periphery" countries) exist in a world in which there is a world market, and increasingly a world system of industrial production, dominated by the economies and state power of the advanced capitalist countries.[8] Roughly, dependency theorists tend to think that it is not possible for the ex-colonies to overcome their poverty and technical backwardness by trading in this world market or by adopting the mode of production of the advanced countries, based on private property in the means of production, because the prior dominance of the advanced countries in both the market and the global division of labor means that it will never bring them the desired benefits. Classical Marxists, on the other hand, tend to think that (1) the geographical spread of capitalist production relations has been going on since at least the sixteenth century and has been accelerating since the end of formal empires, and (2) the "law of value" (in the commonsense meaning of competition in world markets from goods produced ever more cheaply through the constantly rising productivity of labor that is the distinctive consequence of capitalistic production) gradually forces all countries to adopt this mode of production, on pain of being pauperized if they don't. As Marx put it, cheap manufactures eventually "batter down all Chinese walls" that hitherto protected the precapitalist periphery.

The extreme positions of the two approaches are represented by the early writings of Frank, on the one hand, and by Bill Warren's posthumous book, *Imperialism: Pioneer of Capitalism.*[9] Frank originally said that capitalist growth was impossible for the periphery so long as it was linked to the metropoles and advocated a revolution capable of leading an autonomous growth strategy based on cutting those links of dependency. Warren at least implied that capitalist growth was inevitable, apparently everywhere.

In practice few people today hold these extreme positions. Dependency theorists like Fernando Enrique Cardoso, noting that Brazil was undergoing rapid growth and a rapid transformation of precapitalist social relations in the 1960s, argued that dependency relations only make the course of such "dependent accumulation" more difficult and its long-term results more problematic, less certain to be beneficial in the way the modernization school assumed. Classical Marxists like Geoffrey Kay or John Sender and Sheila Smith, on the other hand, while arguing that the spread of capitalist market and production relations is more or less universal, do not maintain that it necessarily results everywhere in sustained economic growth, let alone eventual "high mass-consumption society" (in Walt Rostow's famous phrase).[10]

At first sight, then, the differences between the two approaches would seem to have become relatively narrow. Why should dependentistas not agree that the spread of capitalism is indeed more or less universal, and the classical Marxists not agree that dependency theory points out many of the ways in which, under contemporary conditions, the results of this process are unlikely to bring to at least very many underdeveloped countries the sort of benefits that people have in mind when they talk about "development"?

There are no doubt many reasons why such a convergence has not occurred, from intellectual inertia to political and personal factors of all sorts. But at the level of academic exchange, one can see that there are some latent assumptions that still divide the two schools. Dependentistas tend to minimize the significance of cases such as Brazil or India (large internal markets) or the smaller NICs (exceptional international conjuncture in the 1960s and 1970s) and to go on thinking that for virtually all the remaining underdeveloped countries, growth under capitalism, let alone any beneficial kind of development, really is impossible. (This was clearly the view of Kaplinsky and Langdon in the Kenya debate.) On the other hand, classical Marxists tend to believe that although the process of transition to capitalism at the periphery will not be pleasant (i.e., it will be uneven, full of crises and contradictions, and will cause widespread human suffering, just as it did in Europe), it nevertheless will eventually occur, and it will replace the "idiocy of rural life" with industrialization, without which development is meaningless.

Classical Marxists point out that the dependentistas seem to assume the possibility of an alternative historical path of development which the periphery might follow—free from the irrationality, unevenness, and suffering involved in capitalist development—whereas no such path is shown to be possible even in theory, let alone in current reality. Like Mrs. Thatcher in 1980, the classical Marxists declare that for the time being "there is no alternative" to capitalist development. Yet dependentistas might point out with equal justice that the classical Marxists seem to assume that this development will occur in such a way that whatever its costs, it can be relied on eventually to industrialize the whole periphery.[11] But just as capitalism developed unevenly in today's industrial economies, marginalizing and pauperizing whole regions while concentrating production and wealth in others, so on a world scale whole countries and even regions seem likely to become chronically, and for all practical purposes permanently, marginal, with the added problem that their labor power is not even required elsewhere but on the contrary is excluded by increasingly rigorous controls over migration, while rates of population growth undreamed of when today's industrial countries were developing are pushing them rapidly toward terminal Malthusian crises.[12]

Thus both sides make implausible assumptions, and neither has a tenable political position—at least for most of Sub-Saharan Africa. Dependentistas tend to assume an alternative historical path which is not plausibly shown to exist even in theory, let alone one which existing organized social forces appear capable of implementing. Classical Marxists and modernizers, on the other hand, tend to assume a future outcome which is very hard to imagine for many countries, and which in any case seems to postpone practical action on behalf of the "popular sectors" far into that improbable future.

Of the two, the dependentistas' implausible assumptions are the less incapacitating, and no doubt this is one of the reasons why the dependency perspective is (as Björn Beckman pointed out) still broadly dominant among progressive thinkers and activists in Africa and among the so-called development community in the advanced capitalist countries, including academic students of development.[13] Dependency theory focuses on the "bad side" of the capitalist development that is occurring in the periphery, and it identifies the chief beneficiaries of the process (foreign capital, local compradors) as agents of the ills it brings. It rarely confronts the practical question of what social forces will support the alternative development strategy that it implies is available, and how their apparently conflicting interests will be reconciled within it.[14] So it gives the appearance of being compatible with the populist-nationalist sentiments of most of those who contest the prevailing direction of development inside the periphery countries.

But this does not make the dependency position intellectually or politically acceptable. Evidently both sides need to abandon their untenable assumptions and converge around a program of inquiry in which both the long-term economic implications of what is happening in any given country and the corresponding implications for political action and alternative development strategies are seen as much more open. It would also be healthy for the political and strategic issues to be discussed explicitly, not least by the "aid community," who have great influence in the countries concerned while not sharing their fate. The shared assumption should be that the periphery countries are indeed being forced to "adopt the bourgeois mode of production," and the shared question should be: With what consequences for each one? From the dependency perspective we can draw a set of questions about the contradictions involved, which tend to restrict the speed of the adoption process, determine its specific forms (cf. "dependent accumulation"), and define its potential costs and benefits for various segments of the population. From classical Marxism we get a focus on the forces (economic, political, and cultural) that tend to sustain the process and, in particular, the new social forces created by it, whose struggles will be, if not decisive, at least very important in deciding how, and with what consequences, the contradictions are resolved.

But neither approach warrants any determinism. The questions resulting from combining them should be looked upon as genuinely open. Many of today's industrialized countries once exhibited many of the characteristics that are seen as dooming today's peripheral economies to perpetual stagnation.[15] The internal contradictions in any given individual country today may seem more acute, and the external environment of late twentieth-century global capitalism, dominated by multinational corporations (MNCs), regulated by the IMF, and policed by the United States, may seem more hostile, than was the case one or two hundred years ago for any of today's industrial countries. It is also true that not every country can be a pole of capital accumulation. But the fact is that we cannot know in advance how the contradictions will develop or be dealt with in any given case, or how the social forces at work inside and outside a country will develop and interact—least of all in the post–USSR, post–Warsaw Pact age. There are certainly more ways in which contradictions will be resolved, and more possibilities of social evolution within the complexities of the evolving world market, the world system of production, and the world political order, than have yet been seen or even imagined. It is impoverishing, as well as dogmatic, to suppose that we can have in general a "correct" political line in relation to the peripheral countries.

Rather, the time has come to acknowledge that only the analysis of the social forces at work in each individual country and their political and organizational capacities can permit intelligent political choices to be made or alternative development strategies to be evolved. In some cases it may make sense to adopt a "proletarian" stance, looking to the political potential of the organized working class as a force for social and economic advance; in others, this may make no sense. At any rate, a discussion of the sense it makes ought to be as much part of the agenda of development research as the study of any other aspect of social change.

The Relevant Facts

What sort of facts are relevant to the issues raised in the Kenya debate? What principally strikes one, in the light of such reflections, is that in the Kenya debate attention was focused on the wrong factual issues. Critics have argued that the empirical evidence adduced was often ambivalent, capable of being read as supporting either position: a question of whether the bottle was seen as half empty or half full.[16] There is undoubtedly some force in this criticism, but the more serious defect was that the debate focused on the wrong sort of things.

Specifically, Kaplinsky and Langdon focused on five main issues: (1) the capability of the Kenyan capitalist class, and specifically the extent to which it was displacing foreign capital; (2) whether the Kenyan state was under its control, or at any rate responsive to its wishes, vis-à-vis foreign capital; (3) whether capitalist production relations had spread since independence; (4) whether the growth that had occurred was "successful" or "viable"; and (5) whether such growth was likely in the future.

These issues reflected their understanding of what had to be denied if the dependency interpretation of Kenya was to be upheld, and some of the confusions involved have been sufficiently pointed out by Björn Beckman and Gavin Kitching. The last two of the five issues addressed by Kaplinsky and Langdon are self-evidently unrewarding since growth that seems unsuccessful from a dependency viewpoint obviously can seem significant and potent from an opposite viewpoint. The question of how far capitalist relations of production actually had spread was more interesting but was equally liable to degenerate into a mere contraposition of two incompatible but equally plausible ways of reading the same evidence.[17] But it is the issue of the capacity of the domestic bourgeoisie and the closely related issue of the role of the state that best illustrate the way abandoning the false opposition of dependency theory and classical Marxism allows us to go beyond the inconclusive results of the Kenya debate.

Kaplinsky and Langdon read the new antidependency stress on the growth of an internal capitalist class as reflecting the view that the existence of such a class was almost a sufficient condition for capitalist growth. Hence, to defend the dependency position, they had to show that it was not efficient or strong, not independent of foreign capital (let alone in the process of displacing it), and in any case no "better" than foreign capital in terms of its use of local inputs, levels of protection, efficiency, etc. In the same way they assumed that the state must be shown not to be an "instrument" of this class.

By now it is easy to see that the existence of an internal capitalist class, even a relatively nationalist and efficient one, is not a sufficient condition for capitalist growth; in some circumstances perhaps it might not even be a necessary condition. Similarly with the state: whether or not it is in general more responsive to the domestic capitalist class than to foreign capital is a priori not conclusive for the prospects for capitalist development either. The whole question was wrongly posed in these terms. What needed to be asked was what were the chief issues affecting the prospects for capitalist growth, and what dynamic forces were at work that would most likely determine how these issues would be resolved.

Nonetheless it seems perverse to suppose that the prospects for capitalist development are not affected in any way by the size and nature of the domestic capitalist class; there was a rational kernel in the emphasis laid on it in my 1978 article, even if the reasons were unclear. First, foreign manufacturing capital, organized in MNCs, is not interested in undertaking or organizing the production of most of its needed inputs, let alone local production in every country where it is established. To establish the linkages that are necessary to the deepening and extension of capitalist production, an internal capitalist class is usually necessary, and the fact that by 1977

Kenyan capitalists had taken over substantial parts of some of the most important sectors of the Kenyan economy without reducing the overall rate of growth suggested that they had the capacity to make these linkages.

Second, a politically powerful domestic class of capital with an orientation to production is likely to be necessary to secure the political (as opposed to the economic) conditions for the expansion of capitalist production. Otherwise the state is unlikely to sustain the policies needed to resolve the multiple contradictions involved in the process of expanding capitalist relations of production and sustaining capital accumulation in face of opposition from other classes and interests. The evidence that suggested such a class might be forming in Kenya, with a productivist culture stemming from the precolonial history of the Kikuyu, was the second reason for the emphasis on it in my 1978 article. In retrospect, it seems to me that the second of these reasons was the more important. It now seems to me less important that the domestic bourgeoisie should be efficient—technically, financially, or otherwise—as capitalists, as individual accumulators, than that they should be competent politically, as a class: that they should, as a class, recognize the requirements of capital accumulation for capital as a whole and be able to see to it that these requirements are met. This is the issue that should have been the main empirical focus of the Kenya debate.

This is not to say that the question of the technical competence of the domestic capitalist class is unimportant. A comparison of the fate of retail trade after its Africanization in Kenya, with the results of the same experience in Uganda or Tanzania, might be instructive in this respect. There is also a significant connection between this question and that of the class's political competence, in that the African bourgeoisie in Kenya has chosen to accept the continued presence of most of the Kenyan-born Asian capitalists, whose technical competence has been a major factor in maintaining efficiency and output during the period of African entry into the accumulation process.[18] But this very point reinforces the prior importance of the domestic class's political role, since technical competence is—within limits, to be sure—something that can be acquired by various means, provided the need for it is recognized. What cannot be imported or purchased are the cohesion, organization, leadership, and political skills needed to secure the hegemony of the accumulating and above all the productive class, so that state policy serves the needs of capitalist production.

If this is accepted, the interesting empirical questions to ask about Kenyan development in the years since independence are different from the ones that occupied most of the space in the Kenya debate. Much of the macroeconomic evidence remains as capable as ever of conflicting interpretations. Thus real GDP rose at an average rate of 4.1 percent a year from 1980 to 1989, keeping pace with population growth; this was barely two-thirds of the average rate for the first fifteen years of independence but still contrasted very favorably with the rest of Sub-Saharan Africa, which as a whole grew at an average annual rate of only 2.1 percent over the same period. On the other hand, the structure of the economy did not change during the 1980s, agricultural productivity stagnated, the balance-of-payments gap grew, foreign exchange reserves fell dramatically, and the external debt burden rose from 50 percent of GNP in 1980 to 72 percent in 1989 (though this too still compared favorably with the 1989 average of 97 percent for Sub-Saharan Africa as a whole). There were thus serious failures, as well as achievements. The question that most needs to be asked is: How far has the class that has the greatest interest in surmounting and resolving the problems confronting capitalist development in Kenya identified these problems or shown itself able to tackle them?

Capitalist Development in Kenya

A good starting point is the analyses made on behalf of British investors by papers like the *Financial Times* or organizations like the Economist Intelligence Unit. In the mid-1980s British capital had some £1 billion invested in Kenya (far ahead of any other country; United States companies, the next largest foreign group, had some £325 million).[19] This literature immediately establishes two things. First, there is a broadly shared understanding of the main problems facing capitalist development in Kenya. Second, the "aid community" functions, from the point of view of foreign capital, very much as a sort of state apparatus of international or global capital, supplementing the technical capacities of the peripheral state and reflecting the concerns of the "international" (i.e., British, United States, German, etc.) corporate bourgeoisie. This is obvious enough in the case of the institutions designed for this purpose, such as the World Bank, the IMF, the International Development Agency (IDA), the OECD, and the European Community; but bilateral aid to Kenya is also coordinated internationally, via a "consultative group" of bilateral donors meeting in Europe with Kenyan representatives under the sponsorship of the bank. The role of Kenyan capitalists and the Kenyan state may be important, but by now they are operating as part of a wider and very powerful system for managing capital accumulation on a world scale. The way the Kenyan state (the Kenyan "authorities" in aid community parlance) grapples with the contradictions of Kenyan development is strongly influenced by the general consensus of global capital about what is necessary for capitalist development in Kenya.[20]

This consensus is not necessarily wise, nor is it always complete. For example, in 1982–85 the World Bank was criticized within the aid community for a dogmatic concern with liberalization measures (e.g., in relation to maize marketing) not based on real considerations of efficiency.[21] Peter Coughlin has similarly shown that uncritical, dogmatic pressures from the IMF and the World Bank for import liberalization in the mid-1980s, supposedly in the interest of forcing manufacturers to become efficient and switch to export markets, failed to respect the time it takes to establish and deepen efficient manufacturing sectors or to recognize the extent to which their inefficiencies were due to factors beyond the manufacturers' control. In general, he argued persuasively, the bank and the IMF failed to recognize the extent to which import substitution in Kenya, far from being exhausted, "had just begun" and would remain an essential counterpart to export-based industrialization for a long time to come.[22]

However, in general one can see that the aid community, with the leverage of structural adjustment loans conditionality, has played a central and largely consistent role, politically as well as technically, in identifying and attempting to resolve the contradictions of capitalist development in Kenya since the 1970s. Martin Godfrey, after surveying the successive policy conditions imposed by the aid community down to 1985, concluded that "a negative interest rate, overvalued currency, 'high' wage economy, has been transformed into a positive real interest rate, market exchange rate, low wage economy, in which agricultural producers continue to be offered attractive price incentives. . . . it clearly reveals the influence of the IMF and the Bank."[23] What did this community see as the major problem then confronting further development in Kenya?

The "fundamental" or "underlying" problem was seen as population growth, which was believed to be the highest in the world at 4.1 percent.[24] There will be an additional work force of several millions by the year 2000, most of whom cannot expect to be employed for wages and who will increasingly lack access to land. Without very costly irrigation, only some 20 percent of the country is arable. In addition, land is still the most reliable source of capital accumulation by the Kenyan African bourgeoisie, as well as a source of security, social status, and political influence. Consequently land reform, which in theory could provide most of the new work force with a livelihood for at least some time to come, reducing the risk of political instability and expanding the domestic market for manufactures, is not discussed. Diana Hunt, in particular, has argued that "a radical redistribution of land in both the large and small farm sectors, with a 3-hectare ceiling on existing farms in the high potential areas (larger in the low potential areas) might . . . generate some 3.1 million new farms and some 1.55 million man-years of employment. . . . There can be no doubt that land reform presents the *single most effective means* available of expanding productive employment in agriculture within this period [i.e., to the year 2000]." But "so far the landed elite among those who hold power in the Moi regime have successfully prevented any moves in this direction. This problem cannot change unless a majority of those landowners come to see personal as well as social advantage in such measures. For them to do this would mean that they must elect to forgo the main and most secure outlet for capital accumulation that has until now been available to them."[25]

This puts increased pressure on the state to clear the way for more rapid industrialization. The easy phase of import-substitution industrialization, if not ISI in general, is considered to be over, so that the strategy has shifted to making manufacturing efficient enough to sell in export markets. The central idea here is that Kenya must emulate the NICs and compete in world markets, at least in those most geographically accessible. There are many doubts whether this is practicable, even if the government can stand the strain of enforcing the very unpopular further structural adjustment measures that the aid community sees as necessary for the purpose. As Godfrey frankly expressed it: "Is the growing pressure of labour on land, combined with the recession and the IMF / World Bank stabilization and structural adjustment programme, transforming Kenya into a land of cheap labour, expensive capital and competitively priced currency, thus poised to become an exporter of labour-intensive manufactured goods? Kenyan wages have still some way to fall before they are as low as those in some South and South East Asian labour surplus economies."[26]

But the need to expand manufacturing's share of GNP, mainly via an expansion of manufactured exports, is seen as inescapable (with accompanying measures to try to keep agricultural output rising as fast as population and to expand earnings from tourism). What then are seen as the main requirements for and obstacles to this?

Here the answer tends to vary with the standpoint of the commentator. While IMF experts stress macroeconomic, fiscal, and monetary policies, bilateral aid negotiators stress administrative competence, and industrial economists stress technical competence on the part of the state apparatus.[27]

But what they all agree on is that there is a conflict between Kenyan capital that was "entrenched" in the early postindependence years, especially in commerce (by Kenyanization policies and by ISI itself), and the needs of the manufacturing sector now.[28] In particular, people with political influence illegally import goods that undercut the market of a vulnerable local manufacturer; while other manufacturers, who have monopolies, use their political influence to resist measures intended to liberalize imports and make them more efficient.[29] The senior staff of large, inefficient parastatals (who include some large independent accumulators, especially through landownership) resist their privatization or the introduction of more competition. Politicians resist fiscal discipline in order to channel resources to their constituencies or into the pockets of themselves and their backers. For example, one of the main contributors to the budget deficit of 1986, which totally broke the government's commitments to the bank and the IMF, was £33 million spent on the All Africa Games, of which the auditor said £14 million were lost through inefficiency and corruption.[30]

In good years international capital is apt to feel sympathetic toward the Kenya government's political dilemmas, and especially its sensitivity to public opposition to measures that cut real incomes or aggravate inequalities, and it has been known even to smile indulgently at populist extravagances such as Moi's £10 million bill in 1988 to celebrate ten years of his own rule. But at other times it expresses its anxiety in stern language: "The question remains whether the country's leaders have the political will to push through the necessary reforms while Kenya has the resources to undertake them [i.e., the population-land crisis has not yet come to a head], or whether they will be swayed by short-term gains."[31]

On the whole, the aid community has got what it wanted in Kenya, and the other side of the coin is that for its part, it has also been willing to help stave off political threats to further capital accumulation by providing enough external finance to allow the economy to go on expanding. The consultative group has consistently met most of the Kenya government's requests, making it one of the largest per capita recipients of external capital flows in Sub-Saharan Africa and one of the first debtor countries to benefit from the debt cancellations following the 1988 OECD summit in Toronto ($435 million of debt was canceled by West Germany, about $200 million by France, $178 million by the United States, $150 million by the United Kingdom, $109 million by Canada, $20 million by the Netherlands, and about $10 million by Belgium—even though Kenya did not fall in the category of most indebted countries that the Toronto initiative was intended to help).

And, on the other side of the coin again, the Moi government's consistently pro-Western foreign policy was an obvious counterpart to this.

The main contradiction of capitalist development, then, as the aid community sees it, is as follows: As the population grows, there is a growing risk of catastrophic increases in deprivation, leading to political instability and the disappearance of the conditions for a rate of capitalist growth capable of outpacing the growth of needs. The option of land reform, which would buy time and widen the domestic market for manufactures, is blocked by the interests of the large landowners who are essential to the capitalist development strategy. The resulting necessity to rely all the more heavily on manufacturing exports confronts numerous secondary contradictions. It means overcoming the entrenched interests of various powerful segments of the domestic capitalist class, and it means imposing further cuts in the real incomes of wage earners. But failure to move in this direction carries the risk that capital accumulation will falter. This is already a threat. Through the 1980s private foreign investment stagnated (a significant number of foreign firms actually withdrew—25 out of 140 United States companies, in fact), and there was a great deal of covert flight by domestic capital, to the point where the aid community expressed concern that Kenyans' transfers of funds abroad were significantly offsetting the very substantial inflows of aid. In 1987 the IMF estimated that $1.2 billion was held by Kenyans in nonbank accounts overseas; the Kenyan government responded by prosecuting a few Asian businessmen for exchange violations.[32]

It is clear that the government's reluctance to impose further costs on the rest of society for the sake of manufacturing—whether further reductions in real wages and cuts in services for the poor or the denial of profitable import licenses and the like to its wealthy backers—was not unconnected with the fact that Africans (as opposed to Kenyan Asians) were still virtually unrepresented in manufacturing. Coughlin's conclusion, based on research into several sectors of manufacturing in the mid-1980s, is hard to dispute:

> Kenyan manufacturing industry is almost exclusively owned by MNC's, Kenyan Asians, or government parastatals; Africans own very few medium or large-sized manufacturing firms. This has seriously impeded any identification of interests between local industrialists and the political circles. As a result, the government's economic policies and bureaucratic decisions are frequently detrimental to the nation's long-term industrialization. Just occasionally do politicians oppose and defeat colleagues who arrange lucrative but improper deals with importers. . . . Only after more Africans own and manage man-

ufacturing enterprises and ensure that their economic interests are well represented politically will policy become better harmonised with the needs of
industry.[33]

But on the other hand, it was also important to retain and reassure the
Kenyan Asians, whose capital and managerial and technical skills were such
an important reason for the relative efficiency of the nonagricultural sectors
of the Kenyan economy. When in 1986 President Moi called for more
indigenization, there was no sign that it was because he had grasped the
strategic importance of identifying African capital with manufacturing. It
seemed rather to pander to racial resentment, and it aggravated Asian
insecurity.[34]

This general contradiction—i.e., between the needs of capitalist development and the political conditions for it, including the entrenched interests
of the Kenyan capitalist class—appears to be inherent in the process of
capitalist development itself, at least in the late twentieth century and in a
country such as Kenya. There are, however, other aspects of Kenyan policy
in the 1980s which are less easily accounted for. Two in particular stand out:
Kenya's relations with its neighbors, Uganda and Tanzania, and the use of
political power to acquire assets or to punish and impoverish critics, often at
the cost of considerable economic losses.

With regard to the first, the collapse of the East African Community in
1977 cut Kenya's manufactured exports to Tanzania from over K£20 million
in 1975 to a mere K£1,800 in 1978.[35] The reopening of the border between
the two countries in 1983 led to a strong recovery of exports to Tanzania by
1985, but meantime the losses had been costly, and the cause is generally
seen as having been mainly ideological—i.e., dislike of Nyerere's "African
socialism" coupled with an unrealistic expectation that Tanzania would
agree to remain in a common market in which Kenya ran a large and
permanent trade surplus with both its neighbors. A similar lack of sensitivity seems to have marked Kenya's relations with Uganda following the
accession to power of Museveni's National Resistance Movement in 1986,
with the harassment of Ugandans in Kenya and periodic semiblockades of
Uganda's imports through Mombasa, pushing Uganda to search seriously
for an alternative route through Tanzania. In both cases a dysfunctional
political animus, compounded by national chauvinism, seems to have governed policy-making, rather than a concern for the good trading relations
that would maximize the prospects for Kenyan manufactured exports over
the long run.[36]

With regard to the use of political power to acquire assets or punish critics, this is for obvious reasons less fully documented, even when it is well known, although some famous cases do get reported. In a well-publicized case in 1989, the main maize-milling company, Unga, stopped production for several weeks because it was prevented from getting essential supplies in the course of a struggle to force its African owners to cede a share of control to others closer to the president. Many similar cases, often ending in bankruptcies and unemployment, could be cited.[37]

What these practices show is that the "predatory capitalism" that marked the 1960s and early 1970s under Kenyatta was strongly renewed under Moi as the Kalenjin notables sought to enrich themselves by means similar to those used by the Kikuyu notables under Kenyatta. Whether or not there had been a growing desire among the Kikuyu capitalist class to transcend this kind of behavior, with the chronic insecurity it generated, in the final years of the Kenyatta regime, its resumption by Moi gave it a new lease on life. It set back the development of a more productivist bourgeois culture. For example, far from upgrading the skills and autonomy of the judiciary (a matter of increasing concern to leading Kenyan capitalists in the mid-1970s), in 1988 a constitutional amendment removed the security of tenure of High Court and Appeal judges and made them liable to dismissal by the president acting alone. Moreover, these changes came "at a time when some members of Kenya's judiciary [had] voiced fear about increasing political influence over legal decisions."[38] What is more, the new "predatory capitalism" was pursued at the expense of Kikuyu capitalists, more than of non-Africans, as had been the case in the 1960s and 1970s, aggravating ethnic divisions between Kenyan capitalists.

This draws attention to what is perhaps the most fundamental weakness of the Kenyan African capitalist class, looked at from the angle adopted here. The evidence indicates clearly that it was far from having "formed itself into a class," far from having organized itself around a shared project for the transition to sustainable capitalist development in Kenya. On the contrary, it remained deeply permeated and divided by ethnic consciousness, still strongly reliant on political influence (rather than market competitiveness) for its profits and security, still rather ignorant of and unsympathetic to the needs of modern industry, hardly any of which it owned. It tolerated the non-African Kenyan capitalists but was not inclined to make any sacrifices for their interests. The productivist values of the precolonial Kikuyu accumulators brought to light by Cowen may have been important, but they had been diluted, to say the least, and somewhat overlaid by other values and practices since colonial times. Rather than develop political institutions capable of organizing its collective class interests and attaching other classes to itself through political leadership, it continued to rely on Bonapartism, ceding political power to a single individual in return for having all other possible centers of power subordinated to him.[39] And the Bonaparte in question was no strategist of capitalist development.

As a result, at the end of the 1980s no prospect of a solution to the fundamental or underlying problem of capitalist development in Kenya was in sight or even being discussed, and many of the secondary contradictions discussed above remained equally unresolved. What Godfrey had written in 1985 could have been repeated almost word for word in 1990: "In general, the prospect is of scraping through quite successfully for another five years even though the fundamental problem facing the economy [the rising labor/land ratio] remains largely unaddressed."[40]

Yet relative to other African countries, Kenyan development remained buoyant, and the 1980s business literature on Kenya reflected this ambivalence, commenting on the "context of relative optimism," on the "good" prospects for manufacturers, noting some of the surprisingly large advances that have been achieved in particular areas (e.g., a 25 percent growth of manufactured exports in 1988), and judging that social inequalities will not lead to political instability in the medium run, and so on. Partly this reflects the relatively short-run perspective of much international capital. It also partly reflected a general conviction that Kenya would not be "allowed," in the immediately foreseeable future, to go into a destabilizing economic crisis, given its importance for the strategic interests of the United States. (This belief was supported by the facts. So long as the Moi regime's repression of all opposition seemed compatible with further accumulation, little criticism of it was voiced by the aid community states, in spite of the official post-Helsinki emphasis on human rights in Communist regimes. But once Moi's repression began to get out of hand, with the murder of his foreign minister (who was suspected of being about to disclose the extensive corruption of many of his colleagues), the disaffection of the intellectual and professional middle class, and growing popular demonstrations calling for democracy, the aid community applied firm pressure on Moi to make concessions, culminating in the abrupt decision in late 1991 to accept multi-party elections for early 1992.[41]

The literature also, I suspect, reflects a general assumption that other things being equal there is a dynamic tendency in the capitalist system for problems to be overcome—in one way or another. But the literature's concern with political stability registers the fact that the political threat to continued accumulation is permanent and unpredictable. It has been well said that in economics, one is never looking over the edge of the abyss: the market always levels the future off to a gradual slope. No such benign mechanism is at work in politics. The "impending crisis" of which Hunt wrote, the "underlying problem" of the aid community in relation to Kenya, is one where the social tensions caused by deepening landlessness and unemployment can be contained, in the longer run, only by diverting resources indispensable for sustaining growth.

Nonetheless the outcome is not predetermined, and meantime what needs to be done is to study the social forces that are being brought into being by capitalism in Kenya—and not least the Kenyan capitalist class, whose conflicts and collaborations will determine how the problem is eventually articulated, in what forms it presents itself, what responses are offered, and what they imply for the accumulation process. The Kenyan bourgeoisie, seen through the unsentimental eyes of international capital, does not appear in a particularly flattering light; but it does not appear uniformly incompetent either, or as incapable of learning, and it does not have to shoulder the task of resolving the contradictions of capital accumulation in Kenya unaided—it has interested and willing foreign collaborators. It is not written in stone that capital will not find solutions to the problems that confront it in Kenya—at whatever cost to those who do not own any.

Notes

1. Colin Leys, "Capital Accumulation, Class Formation, and Dependency: The Significance of the Kenyan Case," *Socialist Register 1978* (London), p. 241.

2. Colin Leys, *Underdevelopment in Kenya: The Political Economy of Neo-Colonialism, 1964–1971* (Berkeley and Los Angeles: Univ. of California Press, 1974).

3. Raphael Kaplinsky, "Capitalist Accumulation in the Periphery: The Kenyan Case Re-examined," *Review of African Political Economy* 17 (Jan.–April 1980): 103–4.

4. Steven Langdon, "Industry and Capitalism in Kenya: Contributions to a Debate," in *The African Bourgeoisie: Capitalist Development in Nigeria, Kenya, and the Ivory Coast*, ed. Paul M. Lubeck (Boulder, Colo.: Lynne Rienner, 1987), p. 346. Langdon's paper was originally presented at a conference in 1980 and was commented on together with Kaplinsky's by Gavin Kitching in his "Politics, Method, and Evidence in the 'Kenya Debate,'" in *Contradictions of Accumulation in Africa: Studies in Economy and State*, ed. H. Bernstein and B. Campbell [Beverly Hills, Calif.: Sage Publications, 1985], pp. 115–52.

5. There were several other contributors to the debate, notably Nicola Swainson,

"The Rise of a National Bourgeoisie in Kenya," *Review of African Political Economy* 8 (1977): 39–55, and *Foreign Corporations and Economic Growth in Kenya* (London: Heinemann, 1980); J. S. Henley, "Capitalist Accumulation in Kenya: Straw Men Rule OK?" *Review of African Political Economy* 17 (Jan.–April 1980): 105–8; and Colin Leys, "Kenya: What Does 'Dependency' Explain?" ibid., pp. 108–13. All of these contributors broadly took the line reflected in my 1978 paper. Björn Beckman, in "Imperialism and Capitalist Transformation: Critique of a Kenyan Debate," ibid., 19 (Sept.–Dec. 1980): 48–62, took a line closer to the one I now hold; see also his "Imperialism and the 'National Bourgeoisie,'" ibid. 22 (1981): 5–19. Kitching, "Politics, Method, and Evidence," adopted a position close to that of Warren (discussed below).

6. Kitching, "Politics, Method, and Evidence," pp. 147–48.

7. Dudley Seers, "The Congruence of Marxism and Other Neo-classical Doctrines," discussion paper, Institute of Development Studies, University of Sussex, Aug. 1978; Alain Lipietz, "Marx or Rostow?" *New Left Review* 132 (March–April 1982): 48–58. I do not agree with the polemical thrust, or with all of the analysis, of Lipietz's critique, but the general point—that the political implications of a modernization and an orthodox Marxist interpretation of development in the Third World may be hard to distinguish in practice—is valid. See also Manfred Bienefeld, "Dependency Theory and the Political Economy of Africa's Crisis," *Review of African Political Economy* 43 (1988): 68–87, esp. 84–85.

8. The label "dependency theory" is used here to cover all the variants of this approach, from the nineteenth-century Latin American historiography relied on by André Gunder Frank in his *Capitalism and Underdevelopment in Latin America* (New York: Monthly Review Press, 1967) and the very general theory advanced in that book, to the much more tentative theoretical perspectives offered by Henrique Cardoso and Enzo Faletto in *Dependency and Development in Latin America* (Berkeley: Univ. of California Press, 1979), and all the many middle-level theoretical efforts and monographs belonging to this school of thought. The label "classical Marxism" is used to cover the point of view of writers like Geoffrey Kay (in *Development and Underdevelopment: A Marxist Analysis* [London: Macmillan, 1975] and Michael P. Cowen and Bill Warren, who see themselves as developing rather than revising the analysis of capitalism proposed by Marx in *Das Kapital* and Lenin in *The Development of Capitalism in Russia*.

9. Cf. Frank, *Capitalism and Underdevelopment in Latin America* and "The Development of Underdevelopment," in his *Latin America: Underdevelopment or Revolution* (New York: Monthly Review Press, 1969); Bill Warren, *Imperialism: Pioneer of Capitalism* (London: New Left Books, 1980).

10. Cardoso and Faletto, *Dependency and Development in Latin America;* Kay, *Development and Underdevelopment;* John Sender and Sheila Smith, *The Development of Capitalism in Africa* (London: Methuen, 1986).

11. This point is developed in relation to the debate about development in the Atlantic Provinces of Canada in Colin Leys, "Populism, Socialism, and the Struggle of Primary Producers," in *Restructuring and Resistance in Atlantic Canada,* ed. Bryant Fairley, Colin Leys and James Sacouman (Toronto: Garamond, 1990).

12. The potential of the AIDS epidemic to anticipate such crises in several African

economies has, it seems, still to be registered theoretically in the wider debate about African development.

13. Beckman, "Imperialism and Capitalist Transformation," p. 60.

14. For an interesting exception, see Björn Beckman, "Peasants and Democratic Struggles in Nigeria," paper presented to the AKUT conference on Labor and Democracy, Uppsala, Sept. 1986. The difficulties that Beckman bravely confronted in this paper are highly significant.

15. Cf. Gavin Kitching, "The Role of a National Bourgeoisie in the Current Phase of Capitalist Development: Some Reflections," in Lubeck, *The African Bourgeoisie*, pp. 27–55.

16. See Beckman, "Imperialism and Capitalist Transformation," pp. 53–54 and Kitching, "Politics, Method, and Evidence," pp. 127–31. See also Martin Godfrey, "Kenya: African Capitalism or Simple Dependency?" in *The Struggle for Development: National Strategies in an International Context*, ed. Manfred Bienefeld and Martin Godfrey (London: Wiley, 1982), pp. 265–91, esp. pp. 272–74.

17. Kitching took Langdon to task for using wage employment as a proportion of total employment as an indicator of the spread of capitalist production relations, arguing that the "development of commodity production under capitalism" need not involve the "universalization of the capital / wage labor relationship, but was registered in a long-term increase in commodity output and labour productivity, and so on" ("Politics, Method, and Evidence," p. 124). While this is true, I think Langdon was also justified in pointing out that if wage labor remains constant, at a small proportion of total labor, it raises a question about the viability of capitalist development—about the ability of capital to make total labor more productive and to accumulate surplus value from it, which is the necessary basis of capitalist growth. On the other hand, it is clear that the scale of nonenumerated wage labor is now of the same order as enumerated wage labor, and since by definition its precise size is unknown, it is not possible to say whether trends in wage employment in Kenya show that capitalist production relations are "spreading" or not. The figures used by Langdon to illustrate his point were for enumerated wage labor only (Langdon, "Industry and Capitalism," pp. 352–53).

18. The significance of this aspect of Kenyan development has been the subject of some important research by David Himbara. Himbara has argued that the Kenyan "Asians" have actually been wholly, not partly, responsible for the domestic element in successful accumulation in Kenya: see David Himbara, *The Role of the Entrepreneurial Class in Kenya* (Boulder, Colo.: Lynne Rienner, forthcoming).

19. *Africa Research Bulletin,* June 30, 1986.

20. Incidentally, it is hard to imagine that anyone reading this literature could suppose that international capital has an interest in keeping Kenya "underdeveloped," so that its weight in the Kenyan economy made successful capitalist development there less likely, as the dependency literature used to suggest.

21. Martin Godfrey, *Kenya to 1990*, Economist Intelligence Unit Special Report no. 1052 (London: The Economist, 1986), pp. 23–24.

22. Peter Coughlin, "Toward a New Industrialisation Strategy in Kenya?" discussion paper, Industrial Research Project, Univ. of Nairobi, 1987, p. 2. Economic liberals would,

no doubt, argue that even if the source of inefficiencies lies beyond the control of the manufacturers, they remain inefficient nonetheless and should cease production in the interest of the whole economy. Fortunately the heyday of this credo seems to be passing and a more realistic view, concerned with the building of long-term productive capacities, seems to be coming back into vogue.

23. Godfrey, *Kenya to 1990*, p. 18.

24. Interestingly, no mention ever seemed to be made of the probable impact of AIDS on the bank's projection of 35 million Kenyans by the year 2000, or 80 million by 2035. In Uganda rates of HIV infection of 15 percent have been found in surveys of rural areas, with much higher rates in towns. Informed opinion holds that similar rates will be found in Kenya after a lag of several years.

25. Diana Hunt, *The Impending Crisis in Kenya: The Case for Land Reform* (Aldershot: Gower, 1984), p. 288. Hunt's assumptions can of course be challenged, but no other equally large-scale means of absorbing surplus labor has yet been proposed.

26. Godfrey, *Kenya to 1990*, p. 79. Kenyan wages were reduced in real terms by about 20 percent between 1981 and 1985.

27. Coughlin, "New Industrialisation Strategy," p. 9 and passim.

28. For a pioneering study of the significance of "entrenchment" in Africa, see Gunilla Andrae and Björn Beckman, *The Wheat Trap* (London: Zed Press, 1985).

29. Cf., e.g., *Africa Research Bulletin*, Nov. 30, 1987.

30. Ibid., Nov. 15, 1988.

31. Ibid., (citing the *Times* and the *Financial Times*), Nov. 30, 1988.

32. Ibid., Oct. 31, Nov. 30, 1987. Coughlin, "New Industrialisation Strategy," gave various examples of the way funds are transferred abroad, in spite of measures adopted in the 1960s and 1970s to prevent this.

33. Coughlin, "New Industrialisation Strategy," p. 16.

34. "The talk of 'Kenyanisation' has now turned to 'indigenisation.' . . . Kenyans interpret the word 'indigenisation' as excluding local whites and Asians. Yet the 70,000-strong Asian community, already jittery about the remote possibility of a coup d'etat, dominates important sectors of the Kenyan economy" (*Africa Research Bulletin* Jan. 31, 1987).

35. *National Development Plan, 1989 to 1993* (Nairobi: Government Printer, 1989), p. 7.

36. Ugandans believed that the 1987–88 holdup of Ugandan imports was a means by which some powerful Kenyans who had invested in trucks to transport Ugandan coffee exports sought to thwart the Uganda government's policy of diverting these exports back to the much cheaper railway (*Africa Research Bulletin*, Jan. 31, 1988).

37. One case that symbolizes them all occurred in Kisii in the mid-1980s. Two women's groups had obtained power-driven grain mills through the assistance of foreign NGOs. One group had been helped to secure this assistance by a former MP and critic of the regime, George Anyona. At the ceremony to inaugurate the installation of the mill, the police came, broke up the concrete foundation, and removed the mill to the Kisii police station to make it clear that such benefits were not to be had except through patrons approved by the regime.

38. *African Research Bulletin*, Sept. 15, 1988.

39. See Peter Anyang' Nyong'o, "State and Society in Kenya: The Disintegration of the Nationalist Coalitions and the Rise of Presidential Authoritarianism, 1963–1978," *African Affairs* 88 (1989): 229–51.

40. Godfrey, *Kenya to 1990*, p. 90.

41. Donor pressure was first concerted at the consultative group meeting in December 1990 and reached its peak in August–September 1991, when both Norway and Denmark had halted their aid programs and others were threatening to (*Africa Research Bulletin*, Nov.–Dec. 1990 and Sept.–Oct. 1991). The British government naturally (in view of British capital's special place in Kenya) dragged its feet and continued publicly to support the Moi regime's monopoly of power as late as September 1991.

PART III

RULERSHIP, LEADERSHIP, AND DEVELOPMENT

8

SWAPPING DEVELOPMENT STRATEGIES: KENYA AND TANZANIA AFTER THEIR FOUNDING PRESIDENTS

MICHAEL CHEGE

A S AFRICAN COUNTRIES make the difficult transition from state-run econ-omies and political authoritarianism to democracy and market-driven development, it is important to recall that popular discontent with the existing situation often arose from very contradictory origins, depending on the country. At the development policy level, for example, a thriving economy in one country may have generated animated agitation for re-distribution of gains from growth, while in a different setting a stagnating economic system may have provoked renewed agitation in favor of growth-oriented policies that are under attack elsewhere. Because policy reforms in such cases would be at cross-purpose, it is necessary for scholars to specify the reasons underlying given outbursts of citizens' demands and to evaluate their empirical validity critically if they are to make useful contribution to the new debate on democracy in Africa. In that intellectual process lessons drawn from comparative case studies have much to offer.

This chapter attempts to draw some lessons in development practice and epistemology from the experience of two East African states—Kenya and Tanzania—that adopted contrary economic and ideological paths not long after crossing the threshold of political independence in the 1960s. Using the political and economic programs of the incumbent regimes as a bench-mark, this essay attempts to delineate the social interests and political arguments underpinning the recent policy changes in production and dis-tribution that have departed substantially from the development founda-tions laid down by their two founding presidents. It argues that in both countries the current political fault line on the production-distribution nexus may have unwittingly but quite fortuitously produced the most realistic cleavages yet for initiating competitive multiparty politics. Such a political system in turn may be harnessed to provide some long-term answers to the universally tortured question of the most congenial economic policies toward sustained growth with social equity—an issue which is as central to the development debate in Kenya and Tanzania today as it was in the 1960s.

Under their founding presidents Kenya and Tanzania, respectively, became the controversial exemplars of Third World developmental capitalism and socialism in East Africa. After a violent anticolonial struggle, Kenya under Jomo Kenyatta (1963–78) essentially pursued market-based economic policies that placed a premium on individual incentives. The government permitted state intervention in the economy principally to facilitate African entry in the business sector and to provide infrastructure to complement private enterprise. These domestic policies were interwoven into external initiatives to expand Kenya's role in international commodity trade, to promote tourism, and to attract private, direct foreign investment. Economic growth and development were conceived as prerequisites for redistribution of incomes. In the words of the government's economic blueprint, *African Socialism and Its Application to Planning in Kenya:* "The most important [policy] is to provide a firm basis for rapid economic growth. Other immediate problems such as Africanization of the economy, education, unemployment and welfare services and provincial policies must be handled in ways that will not jeopardize growth. . . . Growth then is the first concern of planning in Kenya."[1]

In contrast Julius Nyerere, Tanzania's first president (1962–85), whose anticolonial struggle against the British was anything but violent, took a different direction in intent, if not—as his left-wing critics maintain—in concrete action. After five years of independence, Nyerere lost faith in development institutions inherited from colonialism. He considered dependence on external-funded development programs as a snare intended to maintain the country's integration in the orbit of Western markets and inevitably, he reasoned, pro-Western foreign policies. In February 1967, therefore, Tanzania's ruling party at the time, the Tanganyika African National Union (TANU), adopted the Arusha Declaration on Socialism and Self-Reliance, marking a clear retreat from previous aid-driven policies. "How can we depend on foreign governments and companies for a major part of our development without giving those governments, and companies a great part of our freedom to act as we please?" inquired the declaration, adding that people, not money, were the motor force of social transformation.[2] Development in this case primarily meant initiating communal village settlements using local materials and simple technology. Government support to meet basic human needs, notably food, education, health, water, and transport, would then be provided. The Arusha Declaration had no industrial program to speak of, and it was decidedly antiurban. In the true physiocratic tradition, Nyerere expressed the fear that towns would fleece the countryside since peasant production was the sole genuine source of marketable surpluses and hence national wealth.[3]

Although Tanzania was already achieving some of its highest real annual GDP growth rates ever (over 5 percent in the decade after independence in 1961), the Arusha Declaration abominated creeping economic inequalities among Africans in Tanzania and mapped out a nonviolent, non-Marxist road to agrarian socialism under an austere, self-denying political leadership, best exemplified by Nyerere himself. In so many words, equitable income distribution, particularly in favor of the peasantry, took priority over economic growth within the inherited economic structures, the opposite of Kenya. This neat contrast, however, should not hide the fact that the fundamental conflict, in theory at least, was about the means to achieve related ultimate objectives. While the Kenyatta government believed growth was a means to income redistribution, Tanzania saw egalitarian ethics and complementary organizations as a prerequisite for raising savings and productivity. The contrasting starting points of these policies invited immediate comparison.

Such comparison arose from the social scientist's desire to ascertain the consequences of contrary development policies in roughly equivalent national circumstances. Although not quite identical, Kenya and Tanzania had a lot in common: British colonialism, predominantly agricultural economies, cross-border cultural ties, and an inherited common market.[4] This academic interest in turn received sustenance from the sharp intellect, originality, and morally persuasive tone that informed Nyerere's argument.

Thus "Tanzaphilia" was born—a largely uncritical intellectual fascination with the novel development experiment in Tanzania in contradistinction with Kenya's conservatism.[5] It drew a vast number of well-intentioned activists, donors, and professionals who flocked into Tanzania to give a helping hand to a unique effort which had reversed the normal order of Third World development priorities by placing the welfare of the rural poor at the top of its political agenda. By the 1970s Tanzania was the leading recipient of official development aid per capita in Sub-Saharan Africa. And Kenya—depending which yardstick of economic values one espoused—was either a classic Third World dependency economy at the mercy of Western multinationals and their local accomplices or an example of vibrant indigenous capitalist development which dependency adherents and neo-Marxists had argued was both unachievable and undesirable.[6]

The complete development balance sheet in either country is more complicated than that. Kenya achieved impressive real GDP growth rates averaging 5.7 percent between 1967 and 1984[7] and undertook considerable diversification, especially in agricultural production. The economy also received considerable stimulus from import-substitution industrialization in the decade following independence. The motor force of growth in the earlier years, however, was increased smallholder production of tea and coffee. Ecological conditions restrict the cultivation of these crops primarily to the central Kenya highlands, a factor which proved to be of greater political significance in the Moi years than any of the economic planners in the 1960s had imagined. Because incomes and assets outside smallholder farms in Kenya were distributed highly inequitably, success in growth spurred a cascade of academic, donor, and local advocates of more egalitarian development policies.[8] Their demands included regional equality, greater economic space for the informal sector, land redistribution, and small-scale labor-intensive industries with strong backward linkages to agriculture. This is the economy that Kenyatta bequeathed Moi in 1978—a high growth system facing mounting pressure for redistribution in favor of disadvantaged classes and rural regions.

Meanwhile, in Tanzania economic development took an entirely different course. By the calculations of Benno Ndulu, a leading Tanzanian economist, the economy began to slacken in the early 1970s, resulting in a decline of 0.2 percent in real per capita GDP growth rate between 1976 and 1984.[9] High inflation, decaying infrastructure, shortages of basic consumer goods, and declining production characterized the economy that Ali Hassan Mwinyi took over from Julius Nyerere in 1985. His immediate task, therefore, was to put the economy on a productive footing once again without openly renouncing its entrenched redistributive ethic. While Moi's problem was to address the issue of redistribution—particularly across ethnic lines—without jeopardizing the economy's productive base, Mwinyi's top priority was to spur productivity while avoiding new and politically untenable income inequalities. Under their second generation of leaders, the two states thus began the search for the optimal sequence between growth and income distribution, starting from opposite ends.

In a remarkable article on this subject, Richard Sklar has appealed for new "synthesizing ideas" in African development that would harness the productivity aspects of capitalism to the redistributive imperatives of socialism.[10] In Sklar's view contemporary African economic experience testifies to difficulties in pursuing both objectives simultaneously. But the rest of this chapter argues that recent observation of economic policy in Kenya and Tanzania provides some evidence that addressing these issues sequentially may be one way out of that dilemma, particularly if the helter-skelter methods that both countries have adopted so far could be replaced by more rational and democratic policies.

Shifting Involvements in Production and Distribution: A Concept

Some lucky countries—Taiwan, for instance—have undergone rapid industrial transformation combined with a comparatively high degree of national income distribution.[11] Most of the industrialized capitalist countries, the ex-Communist countries of Eastern Europe, and the Third World may not be so fortunate in resolving the dilemma of accelerating production and avoiding income inequality. For Kenya and Tanzania, at any rate, current realities are such that the incumbent governments have inherited transposed choices in that difficult sequence and have made a virtue out of necessity. To analyze the most salient features observable in either country, some theoretical guidance may be helpful.

According to Albert O. Hirschman, modern societies appear to oscillate between moments of private interests—raising personal incomes, attending to career development and individual welfare—and exuberant phases of intense public action.[12] The latter evidently arise from disappointments with the outcome of the former. Prolonged pursuit invites "contradictions" in the Marxist sense, which manifest themselves in sizable outbursts of public action in the interests of the welfare of the larger community and in the desire to introduce more social concern into individual human endeavor. Over time, however, public action begins to yield diminishing individual returns due to underestimation of the long-term personal sacrifice entailed by large-scale social change. Such disappointment may be exacerbated by the pervasiveness of the so-called free-rider problem: the existence of beneficiaries who do not fully shoulder the costs. This sets the stage for a sobering return to greater attention to individual business and personal and family welfare.

A recent example of this sequence is the boisterous, often egalitarian social movements of the 1960s in the West and the relatively tranquil individual-growth-oriented 1980s. But the notion applies with equal force to the outbreaks of hopes and national pride generated by the Eastern European revolutions of 1989, which has gradually yielded to personal disappointment as individuals are exposed to the tender mercies of the new markets, an institution whose benevolence they no doubt overestimated. Because it is so much ahead of its erstwhile compatriots, Poland is an excellent example, but the same could be said of the former East Germany, Hungary, and Czechoslovakia.[13]

Transferred to the development dilemmas of East Africa, this concept raises the prospects of explaining the transition from preoccupation with personal incentives and production-oriented development strategies to collective-redistributive ones, and vice versa. The success in economic growth in Kenya invited political agitation and rationalization for equitable income distribution, while in Tanzania the search for market-based growth was spurred by the economic ruins wrought by the Ujamaa version of socialism and its tight reins on individual accumulation.

To understand the limits of this sequence in either direction, however, there are critical intervening variables which cannot be overlooked and which therefore call for elaboration. The first one concerns the extent to which vested interests beholden to the old order threaten the incumbent innovating regime, the capacity of the old guard to slam the brakes of reform. Theirs is essentially a conservative case resting on the fear that precious, tested, national values might be thrown out with the reformist bathwater. The second one is centered on the extent to which economic programs adopted in the transition—from production to distribution or vice versa—are consistent with instrumental (or formal) rationality in the Weberian sense; that is, the degree to which the cause-effect relationships assumed by the new policies are validated by incrementally accumulating empirical evidence.[14] Under this scheme of reasoning, rational policy choice calls for the abandonment of programs whose success is denied by incoming factual data and their replacement by more effective alternatives. And should successive policy initiatives prove incapable of approximating the overall substantive goal, it, too, is eliminated and replaced by a different one which is more logically and technically tenable; by a "substantively rational" one, in Weber's terms. The demise of Leninist systems in Eastern Europe is a recent example of this.

At the moment a combination of vested interests and a series of substantively irrational decisions threaten to produce prolonged economic stagnation, even violence, in both Kenya and Tanzania. The reforms undertaken in both countries so far show little promise because they are hostage to irrational policies and powerful conservative interests. The rest of this chapter is devoted to demonstrating the interplay of ideas and social factors underlying this tragic eventuality.

Daniel Arap Moi and the Road to Ethnic Egalitarianism

Kenya is an ethnically pluralistic society, even though its major ethnic identities—as elsewhere in Sub-Saharan Africa—date no further back than the colonial period.[15] Popular discontent with the pattern of growth in the Kenyatta years was reflected in the resentment of the political and economic domination of national affairs by the Kikuyu, who are centrally located in the geography, economics, and history of the country. Their proportional overrepresentation in the cabinet, government institutions, the new business opportunities opened to Africans after independence, and education was called into evidence to substantiate the case for equitable ethnic representation.[16] Three as-yet-unexplained political assassinations— of Pio Gama Pinto in 1965, Tom Mboya in 1969, and J. M. Kariuki in 1975— reduced the Kenyatta government's political assets and also narrowed its regional and class base. The conspicuous consumption that accompanied the coffee boom of 1975–77 fortified the anti-Kikuyu sentiments, coffee being grown predominantly in central Kenya.

At bottom, this accusation was anchored on a conspiracy theory: throughout the Kenyatta era, it was repeatedly argued, the predominantly Kikuyu elite in policy-making positions had systematically contrived to corral power and economic resources for their ethnic community. Under this reasoning, achievement on merit and the historically uneven regional response to opportunities in the marketplace counted for little. The theory also assumed zero-sum distributional principles: whatever progress the advanced group made was equivalent to the losses incurred by those who fell behind.[17] Markets and their results in particular were suspect and often were depicted as camouflage for depriving the weaker communities and individuals of their "just" share. Contrary to Adam Smith's socially beneficent "invisible hand" in the competitive marketplace, there were therefore no mutually beneficial economic transactions in this post-Kenyatta economics, be it in trade, investment, or agriculture, only amoral, strong-arm "grabbing" by the better-off.[18]

True, a section of the Kikuyu bourgeoisie in Kenyatta's era had grossly abused state power and were corrupt and avaricious. From 1978 onwards, however, this group was held responsible for most Kikuyu economic advance, regardless of how historically legitimate that advance might have been. Its rapacious ways provided a convenient scapegoat for the failure of others and was used to justify many spurious policies in the name of compensating ethnic communities that had lost out under Kenyatta.

Although it was hardly evident at the time, Moi's presidency depended most solidly on Kenya's outlying areas—the coast, parts of the Rift Valley, Western Province, and a substantial (and numerically superior) Luo constituency, which was deliberately cut off from commensurate access to power following Tom Mboya's assassination in July 1969 and the virtual political banishment of Oginga Odinga thereafter.[19] But as of 1978 this coalition could even count on the outer limits of Kikuyuland (Nyeri and Muranga), thus isolating Kenyatta's Kiambu home district. This by any measure is the majority of Kenya. Had a presidential election been held in 1978, as some of Moi's opponents had suggested, he might have won it with a landslide.

Neither is popular disenchantment with new wealth, such as that which underlined the 1978 pro-Moi coalition, a historical or cultural novelty. As Hirschman has written: "I have come across much evidence that, in the West, each time economic progress has enlarged the availability of consumer goods for some strata of society, strong feelings of disappointment in, or of hostility toward, the new material wealth have come to the fore. Along with appreciation, infatuation and even addiction, affluence seems to produce its own backlash."[20]

And indeed, for all the bitterness against the Kikuyu elite's economic head start, there was considerable fascination with its possessions and lifestyle among its bitterest opponents. It speaks to this ambivalence that within a matter of weeks in 1991 one prominent government leader was quoted as warning the Maasai against selling land to "marauding wealthy buyers," often Kikuyus, while another public official was exhorting Luhya women in Western Kenya "to form corporate land-purchasing firms like the Lari, Gatundu and Juja groups in Central Province."[21] Thus, despite the rhetorical disparagement of grabbing, fairness at the outset of Moi's rule in fact was perceived in terms of ethnic redistribution of what the Kikuyus had accumulated most of: top government positions, managerial posts in the parastatals, wide access to Western education, business opportunities, cash crops, eminence in nationalist history, and above all political power.

Besides personal political outrage at the poor social status of the mainly pastoralist communities that came to be called "neglected tribes," Moi was particularly incensed by the sad fate of the ordinary or small man in the hands of the African nouveaux riches of the previous era. Oppositions to Moi's populist approach, especially by Kenyatta's well-heeled government elite, therefore was depicted as moral depravity, selfishness, and the lack of compassion for the poor. The similarity between this political outlook and the vicious scorn that Nyerere poured on the new African bureaucratic and commercial petite bourgeoisie in 1967 ought to be immediately clear. The Kenya version, however, lacked the intellectual finesse of its Tanzanian counterpart, and it was carefully targeted to one ethnic group rather than a single class; but anybody who misses the logic informing the political and economic strategies of the Moi regime in its cradle is bound to go astray in understanding the characteristics and behavior that became evident in its mature phase.

As Gavin Kitching has reminded us, the issue of distribution is central to modern populism, which conceives it essentially in ethical and moral terms.[22] Notwithstanding its intense emotional appeal, such populist reasoning often takes on the characteristics of faith and becomes hermetically sealed against contrary evidence and rational disputation once it assumes power. Acceding to the forces of reason and facts in the manner specified by Weber is not populism's strongest suit.

In the midst of the ethnic egalitarian euphoria that swept Kenya in the late 1970s, no one reckoned with the Kikuyu dominance among the landless, urban shanty dwellers and unemployed that accompanied the burgeoning capitalist development in central Kenya. And just as Tanzania erected a national program of agrarian socialism on the historically and factually untenable premise that "traditional" African societies were "communalist" until corrupted by an individualistic colonial capitalism, Kenya's policies on ethnic egalitarianism were based on evidence that is either highly contentious at best or outrightly contrived at worst.

Consider the colonial period for a start. Robert L. Tignor has written one of the best yet least-read books on the differentiated impact of colonialism in central Kenya—the crucible of colonial politics and economics—down to the 1930s.[23] In dispassionate analysis imbedded in meticulous detail, Tignor documented the striking advances made by the Kikuyu in comparison with their neighbors in adopting Western education, deepening the local impact of colonial rule, and making innovations in new cash crops, trade, nationalist political consciousness, labor migration, and the dissolution of traditional barriers to economic progress. He also recounts the high social costs in land alienation, forced labor, and squatting that constituted the flip side of these developments. In the subsequent decades the evolution of community-financed independent schools in Central Province and the expansion of such business opportunities as the colonial government permitted Africans have been recounted as essential ingredients of the brewing nationalist movement in Kenya in the 1940s.[24]

After the Mau Mau rebellion erupted from the constitutional confines of African nationalism in 1952, the colonial government soon acceded to the age-old nationalist demand to permit Africans in Central Province to grow coffee, tea, pyrethrum, and other high-value crops. Under the leadership of the deputy director of agriculture in 1955, R. J. Swynnerton, individual land tenure in Central Kenya became a condition of the new cash-crop agronomic system, which pushed Kikuyu country economically further ahead of the rest of the country. Coffee earnings in particular widened the gap between Central Province smallholders and African farmers in the rest of Kenya.[25]

From the standpoint of British colonialism, it was necessary to create a Kikuyu yeomanry as a buffer against the land-short Mau Mau rebels, so the Swynnerton plan reasoned. The program was one of counterinsurgency policy rather than distribution of imperial economic largesse. Indeed, there is evidence that most investment in new Kikuyu smallholder coffee and tea was raised internally and was combined with plenty of household labor.[26] Yet one president and one generation later, the Swynnerton plan and its results were divined as part of the colonial favors the British colonial authorities bestowed to the Kikuyu by spokesman of the then "neglected" communities.[27] New wealth, following Hirschman, evidently provokes not just resentment and the urge to catch up but also a tendency to distort unsavory facts. In such circumstances, passion overleaps rational economic analysis.

In the late 1980s it became Kenya government policy to extend production of the robusta coffee variety (suitable to the poorer, lower-altitude districts) to areas where coffee had not been seriously cultivated before, namely, the coast, Nyanza, parts of the Rift Valley, and Western Province, in the name of promoting economic equality. Previous to that, arabica smallholder coffee was confined to the central Kenya highlands and, to a lesser extent, Kisii, Bungoma, and Kitale. Yet by the late 1980s international robusta coffee prices were at their lowest since the Great Depression, following a glut in world markets and the collapse of the International Coffee Agreement in 1989. This policy also contravened Kenya's quota allocation under the International Coffee Agreement, which the country actively supported.

At the same time the clout and autonomy enjoyed by large-scale (mostly Kikuyu) coffee growers and the cooperative sector were systematically whittled down. In 1989 the Kenya Coffee Growers Association—the organ of the coffee plantation sector—was summarily banned by presidential order. This was an agrarian-interest organization of the sort Michael Lofchie has claimed underpinned productive agricultural policies in postindependence Kenya.[28] Such groups were clearly in their twilight by 1990. Agricultural cooperative unions in districts like Kiambu were already being run by the government ostensibly to avoid "mismanagement and corruption," as was the apex of the coffee industry, the Kenya Planters Cooperative Union (KPCU), in order to eliminate the influence of the "corrupt," propertied coffee growers who had come onto the scene in the 1950s and dominated the industry after independence. Growing state intervention in agriculture and the individual interests of the coffee planters were on a collision course. The coffee farmers protested the costs of a new layer of rent-seeking bureaucrats and the increasing delays in payment that came with it. The banned growers association was vocal in pointing out that rising domestic, politically inspired costs, combined with falling international prices, would seal the industry's doom. But factual calculations like these as a rule do not enter into ethical ethnic-parity strategies of the kind then in vogue in Kenya, any more than they did in Tanzania's 1976 disastrous dissolution of cooperatives (in Kilimanjaro, Arusha, Bukoba, and Rungwe) in the interests of regional economic uniformity and the subsequent takeover of their functions by government agencies.[29]

The struggle for uniform agricultural development abetted by open political succor subsequently took an unprecedented offensive in Kenya's farming history. In 1988 smallholder tea growers west of the Rift Valley (Kisii, Kericho, Kakamega, and Nandi) demanded equal payment per kilogram of green tea as received by their counterparts east of the Rift Valley (that is, in central Kenya), whose tea leaves, by dint of superior quality, were bringing three or four times what the west Rift variety earned at international auctions.[30] This led to a shake-up in the Kenya Tea Development Authority (KTDA)—a model of smallholder agricultural enterprise by World Bank standards—whose management was reshuffled to reflect Kenya's ethnic proportions rather than competence.[31] The assault on quality and productivity criteria by values of equality across regions in the tea industry had commenced in earnest, and the forces of production-based incentives were on the defensive, as the next phase of developments in that industry demonstrated.

Combined with the first output from the Nyayo Tea Zones Development Authority—a new government institution charged with extending tea production into hitherto forested, state-owned areas—the already congested KTDA factories failed to cope with unprecedented tonnage of green tea delivered by smallholder producers in many areas. (The year 1989 was a wet one favorable to tea production.) In the process KTDA management must have got their priorities wrong, at least according to tea farmers in Murang'a (Central Province) who went on a violent rampage against KTDA property and personnel in November 1989 and organized a boycott in 1992. The farmers protested reduced payments and congestion in factories that led to deterioration in tea quality. A widespread and growing boycott of tea delivery in the region was lifted only after the government had promised a commission of inquiry to assuage the grievances of smallholder tea farmers. Like its counterpart beverage, coffee, the future of tea production was going through turbulence as the state sought a workable transition to an ethnically equitable redistribution formula of Kenya's smallholder tea proceeds.

Unfortunately for this egalitarian agricultural policy, the international coffee market—even for Kenya's quality arabica—could not have been less propitious. Average coffee prices fell by 23 percent in 1989 alone. The ethnic deck shuffling of the industry's management, coupled with delays in payment to farmers and rising food prices, prompted neglect or outright uprooting of coffee trees. Adverse international factors had now joined such defective policies to send the coffee sector on a tailspin. Total Kenya coffee production, which averaged 120,000 metric tons between 1985 and 1988, fell to 84,000 metric tons in 1991. Tourism superseded coffee and tea as the nation's top foreign exchange earner.

Linkages between tourism and the growth of African business enterprise in Kenya, however, had always been tenuous. The sequence of African capital accumulation in the postcolonial period has been traced predominantly from agriculture into trade, transport, and real estate. By the late 1970s local capital gradually was making inroads into manufacturing.[32] At the time prospects of an African bourgeoisie in production and all its probable consequences became the centerpiece of the Kenya development debate. With the benefit of hindsight, it is now clear that not only did that debate ruffle more intellectual feathers than it deserved to, but—most significantly—the socioeconomic trajectory it assumed was far from the tragic reality, which soon caught up with the indigenous capitalist class of the 1970s, reducing it to a crippled shadow of its former self in barely one decade. The debate went astray primarily because it failed to reckon with political permutations writ large in the Kikuyu predominance in the data that all the academic debaters handled.

A Kikuyu edge over other African communities in business predated independence. In Nakuru, for instance, M. Tamarkin found striking evidence of this before, during, and after the Mau Mau rebellion.[33] and it was also true of Nairobi and other major central Kenya towns. State intervention in support of African business in the Kenyatta era gave this business class an extra spurt and definitely widened the economic distance between them and their other ethnic compatriots. Yet as in agriculture, it is important to give due weight to the role of owner-raised capital in the historical emergence of this group instead of depicting it as yet another instant ethnic creation of the Kenyatta era. After 1978 the ground swell of discontent from communities lagging in business provoked an official backlash which manifested itself in piecemeal, sometimes discreet and sometimes open, emasculation of the would-be indigenous industrial bourgeoisie. The threat to this class did not arise from an overdomineering international capital as Raphael Kaplinsky had feared[34] or from an antagonistic laboring class whose whereabouts in the anticipated (but ill-analyzed) political dispensation concerned Gavin Kitching.[35]

In the early 1980s the business and industries going under for one reason or another read like a rundown of the leading indigenous firms analyzed in the 1970s by Nicola Swainson and Raphael Kaplinsky.[36] The last of the leading African directors in Kaplinsky's 1977 list of top local businessmen who had a foothold in government, Maina Wanjigi, was dismissed from the cabinet and suspended from the ruling Kenya African National Union (KANU) party in June 1990 for protesting the demolition of an informal-sector settlement in central Nairobi. Among the companies of which he was a director, the most significant, East African Bag and Cordage, had succumbed to irregular, cheap jute bag imports from Bangladesh. Charles Rubia and Kenneth Matiba, also prominent businessmen in the 1970s, fell out with the regime for their outspokenness against corruption and autocracy. Both campaigned for political accountability, multiparty politics, and democratic governance in Kenya for most of early 1990 and that July were detained without trial for a year. It is significant that their arrest (and that of Raila Odinga) came soon after an openly publicized meeting between them and the veteran nationalist Oginga Odinga, who was by then a businessman and industrialist.

The adumbration of the Moi government's policy toward indigenization of business came in dribs and drabs, and without much fanfare, but its long-term import was unmistakable for all that. There had to be "fair" ethnic distribution in business even at the risk of postponing some productive enterprises. A series of Kikuyu-owned banks and financial institutions went under in the mid-1980s. A Kikuyu-owned paper mill planned for Thika with a K Sh 950 million (US $60 million) loan from the World Bank's International Finance Corporation (IFC) was officially halted in 1985. Three years later its parent firm—Madhupaper International—was sold to well-connected local interests. The sale was a veritable coup de grace after Madhupaper owners had run through a gauntlet of receiverships and court cases arising from financial problems with state-owned banks.[37] Putting the policy in clear relief, a *Weekly Review* pointed out that "ethnic consider-ations . . . militated against a smooth privatization of parastatals in Kenya. Though the government agreed to the principle of privatization a whole decade ago, no parastatal has been privatized to this day. The reason being that the only people with the wealth to buy up the parastatals are Kenya Asians and the people of Central Province (i.e. Kikuyus)."[38]

The newly industrializing countries of Thailand, Indonesia, and Malay-sia, though invariably sensitive to ethnic representation in business, never-theless gave considerable economic latitude to ethnic minority Chinese to forge ahead using their external business and kinship connections to good national economic effect in which all groups gained. In contrast, Kenya was pioneering in a business and industrial strategy of ethnically apportioned quotas in a stagnating business sector. And no law or commercial conven-tion could withstand the might of the incoming, erstwhile "neglected" business class as it acquired unparalleled fortunes in the nation's history.[39]

Outside the business sector, and without much publicity, the ethnic quota allocation system was introduced in secondary school admissions and in postsecondary educational institutions. As in socialist Tanzania, where preferential secondary school admissions had penalized the more advantaged Chagga and the Haya, this policy favored the smaller ethnic groups at the expense of the more educationally advanced and larger Luo and Kikuyu communities. At the university level, however, the fourfold expansion in admissions, the new universities, and the abolition of the al-legedly Kikuyu-dominated advanced-level secondary forms V and VI were expected to suffice for the equalizing task. Ethnic proportions in the public bureaucracy, parastatals, and other government-supported institutions be-came an established but hushed criterion in appointments and promotion, as ethnic patronage played havoc with merit in public service employment.

Swapping Development Strategies

A system in which the state is committed to achieving a degree of intercommunal balance in resource distribution in both public and private sectors calls for a strong, centralized decision-making process. Peter Anyang' Nyong'o has traced the early origins of presidential authoritarianism in Kenya, while Cherry Gertzel, Yash P. Ghai, and J. P. W. B. McAuslan have observed the progressive concentration of executive power at the expense of the legislature and judiciary under Jomo Kenyatta.[40] Under Moi, Kenya fell under a highly interventionist presidential rule which made the earlier period liberal in comparison. This new structure of governance in Kenya, however, is quite congruent with the system of political values and development policies discussed above. Once it was decided that government is primarily an instrument for replacing a debauched and unjust system with a fair and morally grounded one, the immediate priority was reduced to one dimension: devising the rapid means of attaining a compassionate and humane society—fulfilling the needs of the "little" people or communities. Any dissent to the logic underlying the goals or the intellectual validity of the means was deemed as spiritual corruption at best or delaying conspiratorial tactics at worst.

Action-oriented government of this kind results in compulsive zeal to achieve multiple goals simultaneously and to cut administrative corners with unusual rapidity. "We must run while others walk," Nyerere is reported to have said.[41] "Kenya is on the run," Moi constantly reminds his countrymen. To hasten project implementation Moi—like Nyerere at one stage—undertakes manual work personally, and he has initiated and supervised in person the construction of new schools, roads, hospitals, and anti–soil erosion projects.

In 1983 the government introduced a new system of education comprising eight years of primary school, four of secondary school, and four of university first degrees—the 8-4-4 system. It ushered in an intensive, brand-new education-for-production syllabus purportedly to produce self-employable school graduates in handicrafts and informal-sector enterprises. The declared intention of the new system was to replace the supposedly elitist education system inherited at independence with a vocation-based one. Under Ujamaa, Tanzania of course had plenty of experience with this.[42] When the first secondary school results under the new curriculum were announced, they were so disappointing that the Kenya National Union of Teachers blamed them on hasty implementation by the Ministry of Education and consequent lack of equipment and books. The union was immediately chastised by the government for that judgment. Excellent roads traversed low-traffic, low-productivity areas presumably to stimulate development. The Kenya Railways, on political orders, introduced a shuttle for the transport of short-distance intercity commuters literally overnight and lost money in the process. Such examples became commonplace across many of Kenya's economic sectors.

It would be surprising if this policy-making model were free of internal contradictions and abandoned ambitions, rather like the eccentric succession of "operations"—Vijijini (villages) in 1973, Kilimo cha Kufa na Kupona (agriculture for life) in 1972, Dodoma (new capital) in 1971, Maduka (termination of individual shops) in 1976—that characterized TANU's rule in Tanzania during the 1970s. Naturally, therefore, some immediate turnabouts like the repeal of fees in government hospitals in August 1990 were made. Likewise the decision to split KTDA into two organizations, one for each side of the Rift Valley, was abandoned. But just as often policies that derogated from instrumental rationality and failed were blamed on saboteurs or hiccups caused by unnationalistic management, the overall normative objective being treated repeatedly as sacrosanct and therefore not negotiable.

This is what made it urgently imperative for the government to work for a "cohesive" national community whose bonds of patriotic fraternity would dissolve all internal conflicts: a sharing and caring family within national boundaries united in undivided loyalty to one supreme leader. Once again the communitarian values of some ethnographically unspecified African "traditional" society were invoked. Western values and high performance standards were denigrated as moral perversion. And hence the need to revitalize the KANU party from its lethargic days of the 1970s and turn it into an active all-embracing national union, not unlike TANU under Nyerere. In the late 1980s, therefore, Kenya's leading women's national organization, Maendeleo ya Wanawake (Women for Progress), became a party organ, while the only national trade union confederation, the Central Organization for Trade Unions was also formally affiliated to KANU. An active, highly educated staff to manage the party head office was appointed. The KANU Youth Wing assumed unprecedented prominence in implementing critical party and local branch policies. Academics and journalists were hired to conduct party propaganda. This monolithic, steamrolling political machinery on the run to an all-pervading new spiritual order could not be detained by individual political dissent or debate.

The government's wrath against advocates of multiparty politics in 1990 and 1991, and other forms of political criticism prior to that, is only understandable against such a backdrop. Its philosophical stand was rooted in ethical justification for regional equality as a means of creating national unity. And this was antithetical to the canons of market-friendly political democracy that were in vogue the 1990s worldwide. Democrats like Rubia, Matiba, and Odinga, the government argued, sought to introduce political pluralism and enhanced accountability as a smoke screen for naked political ambition. Free-market forces and the rule of law were spurned because they would undermine policies of ethnic preference, so central to the regime's strategy. Most well-meaning and democratic government critics were therefore depicted as renegades from African traditions, carriers of polluted foreign ideas, and puppets of external masters.[43]

By 1990 the regime's approach had reached its limits. Having maligned, intimidated, and silenced legitimate political dissent, the government had painted itself into a corner. In February 1990 the minister of foreign affairs, Robert Ouko, died in circumstances that suggested political assassination, provoking antigovernment rioting. The state's behavior in the interim had invited a deluge of critics—clergy, lawyers, journalists, and intellectuals—who were galvanized by commitment to individual rights, the rule of law, political toleration, and accountable governance. Over time, the government had sidelined many popular national leaders who took an independent line (like Martin Shikuku, the late J. M. Seroney, and Masinde Murilo) and made common cause with the younger professionals. This local, critical, and increasingly popular leadership was reinforced by human rights activists in the West, the mass democratic movements in the rest of Africa, the collapse of Communist regimes in Eastern Europe, and the return of democracy in the foreign policy agenda of Western states, particularly the United States Congress. Hence the widespread antigovernment demonstrations and riots in Nairobi and central Kenya in July 1990 following the arrests of Rubia and Matiba.

The events immediately preceding the riots, such as the violent defiance of the Nairobi Muoroto slum dwellers, the public display of Kenyatta portraits in *matatu* or public taxis, and the popularity of antigovernment music cassettes showed how deep down to ordinary people the impact of political resentment was. The multiethnic crowds that turned up at the funeral and memorial of the outspoken Anglican bishop Alexander Kipsang Muge, himself a Kalenjin like Moi, in August 1990 showed how widespread in the country discontent with the regime had become. The politics of ethnic redistribution with autocracy had run out of steam and lost credibility. Just as Moi's group might have won elections in 1978, they might equally well have lost an electoral contest in 1991 by a wide margin if these signs were any-thing to go by. And hence the Moi regime's steadfast resistance to the intro-duction of competitive multiparty politics. When Oginga Odinga launched the abortive National Democratic party (NDP) in February 1991, he chose the platform of individual freedom, economic reconstruction, restoration of high performance standards in government, and incentives to the private sector.[44] South Korea and Mauritius were mentioned with admiration. This theme was repeated in the manifestos of the three major opposition par-ties—Forum for Restoration of Democracy (FORD)-Kenya, FORD-Asili, and the Democratic party—which were registered in early 1992 following widespread internal unrest and external donor pressure. But for the change in time and circumstances, this logic might have been Tom Mboya's KANU defending the production-first policies of the government in the 1960s.

The pendulum had swung away from the 1978-style populism. But to a government based on faith rather than fact, this reality could never be conceded. Instead the Moi government began consolidating its base in the former Kenya African Democratic Union (KADU) areas and, as in the 1960s, raising the specter of Kikuyu domination. This was followed by massacres and eviction of Kikuyu immigrants in the Rift Valley. The December 1992 multiparty general election was conducted against a background of official exhortation of marginal ethnic groups to physically resist the opposition in order to hang onto the gains made since 1978. Leadership divisions among the new anti-Moi parties gave this strategy a decisive advantage. Using a combination of intimidation, election rigging, gerrymandering, and unfair rules, the Moi government was returned to power in January 1993 with only 36 percent of the popular vote. The stage was thus set for a prolonged and perhaps violent struggle between the distribution-oriented KADU (now KANU) versus the coalition of new opposition that supported production and efficiency.

In the era of new global liberalism, the Kenya government was paying dearly for its intransigence as a major holdout against the tide of multiparty politics and toleration that has swept Africa since 1990. A diplomatic row with Norway led to the termination of a K Sh 1 billion ($40 million) aid program in mid-1991, while Denmark froze its $27 million aid package to Kenya to protest large-scale embezzlement and Kenya's deteriorating hu-man rights record. In November 1991 the country's leading donors froze $100 million in program aid, pending improvements in its human rights record and economic management.

All this bodes ill for an economy in Kenya's condition. Falling foreign aid receipts aggravated an already precarious foreign exchange situation and cut into the government's development budget, 67 percent of which was financed by external grants (and the remaining 33 percent mostly by external loans) in the 1991 fiscal year. Internal liquidity and economic growth suffered from local financing of a rising government deficit amounting to 6.4 percent of the GDP in 1990, which had been primarily caused by political payoffs and pay raises to security branches of the public service. All this manifested itself into two concrete realities: declining standards (or unavailability) of government services and deterioration of the already creaky economic infrastructure.[45] Kenya's robust private sector provided alternatives—in education, health, private household security, etc.—but only up to a point, and at a price which excluded the poor and the marginal, in whose name the new vision of equality had been inaugurated.

By 1990 the motor of growth in smallholder agriculture had run its course. The political climate was unlikely to allow external grants and loans to take agriculture's place. Despite heroic attempts to liberalize international trade and establish duty-free "export-processing zones," British, American, and other Western capital was divesting from Kenya.[46] And although the country had a high (20 percent) domestic investment rate, new capital was channeled increasingly into construction and nontradables rather than manufacturing or agriculture. Tourism, the leading foreign exchange source, was extremely vulnerable to political unrest and adverse international publicity.

With a constant per capita GDP growth rate officially estimated at −0.9 percent between 1980 and 1987, Kenya was economically stagnating.[47] Combined with escalating self-induced ethnic animosity and mounting resistance to political liberalization, such an economic slowdown provided the lethal ingredients that had rent many African states asunder. Alternatively, the factors could make for the perpetual economic sclerosis and political authoritarianism that have become bywords for Zaire; it all depends on how sensible and constructive the alternatives to the current crisis are likely to be.

Ali Hassan Mwinyi and Market-Driven Policies to Increased Productivity

While comparisons between governance in Kenya and Zaire in the 1980s were made frequently,[48] any attempt to compare economic conditions in Tanzania of the 1980s with those in Zaire invited opprobrium and scorn from the authorities in Dar es Salaam. Such anger is not without cause. The pervasive deterioration of public infrastructure, shortage of basic necessities, rising and generalized poverty, massive inflation, parallel marketing, and corruption that made the Tanzania economy resemble Zaire so much had arisen from an entirely different set of national policies and aspirations. For unlike in Zaire, the road to economic disaster in Tanzania had been paved with the best of intentions: the goal there was a conflict-free commonwealth of peasant villages working communally with their leaders, a long way from exploitation, big cities, and impersonal industrial modernism.

In 1967 the Tanzanian public welcomed these sentiments and Ujamaa in rallies and demonstrations that were conveniently forgotten in the hardship period of the 1980s. The dimensions of Tanzania's economic setback are not disputed even in its own ruling circles where, as in Eastern Europe, past "mistakes" are admitted. The gravity of those "mistakes" has recently been presented in graphic terms by Michael Lofchie.[49] In 1967, 50 percent of the plantations producing sisal fiber, the country's leading foreign exchange earner, were nationalized, and production fell from an average 200,000 tons in the 1960s to 40,000 tons in 1984, with most of the latter coming from the few remaining private estates. Coffee and tea production stagnated, while the cotton yield fell by 40 percent between 1967 and 1986. Food and cereal production appears to have increased, but not enough to deter food imports. Capacity utilization in industry, afflicted by inefficient management and shortage of parts and inputs after the commodities boom of the mid-1970s, dropped from 52 percent in 1976 to 25 percent in 1985. The domestic inflation rate officially rose from 12 percent in 1970 to 44 percent in 1984. This disaster occurred in a country which all this time received the highest official development assistance per capita in the region, peaking at $35 in 1981 and maintaining that position at $41 in 1988.

The explanation for this appalling economic record is the subject of continuing controversy. Issa Shivji and other socialist intellectuals consider that the reversal of working-class control over industrial management established in 1971 under the austere Mwongozo or leadership code—and best exemplified by the Mount Carmel incident—dealt a fatal blow to the prospects of proletarian power in Tanzania; its future was subsequently compromised by a "bureaucratic bourgeoisie" in league with Western imperialists.[50] From her no less socialist perspective, Suzanne Mueller, however, dissents from that perspective, arguing that socialism never had a chance in Tanzania, primarily because of the squeeze that Ujamaa imposed on individual household production in agriculture at the outset and the rein-troduction of colonial-type, coerced agricultural labor instead of market-driven proletarianization in the countryside. In her view these policies preemptied expanded private farm production and growth in national agri-cultural turnover.[51] Some of Mueller's arguments have received partial backing from an extended survey of agricultural production and inequali-ties in Tanzania from a neoclassical economics perspective.[52] Although this study discounted the rise of inequalities—particularly across regions—it nevertheless reported that individual farm production suffered from the demands of communal labor and, more significantly, from lack of adequate farm implements and inputs.

In contrast to those arguments, Goran Hyden maintained that when confronted by a self-willed, independent peasantry, the state in Tanzania lacked the administrative capacity and resolve to transform peasant produc-tion into either a modern capitalist or a socialist agrarian system. Under Ujamaa the Tanzania state had failed to "capture" peasant production for the purpose of primitive socialist accumulation, while private capital was even less successful in expropriating the peasantry, which, following Marx, was the genesis of original capitalist industrial accumulation.[53] Hyden's was essentially a case for thoroughgoing internal social transformation of the peasantry into some other class—best exemplified in the English enclosures movement and the Soviet agrarian collectivization of the 1930s. Uncaptured peasant production and, in Hyden's words, the "economy of affection" embellished or infused into it stood in the way of this breakthrough. But there could be no shortcuts to the inexorable peasant-free progress to a modern industrial society.[54]

The World Bank and the IMF for their part were less ambitious. As quintessential true believers in neoclassical economics they argued that all Tanzania needed to do was to eliminate price distortions within and across economic sectors and lower inflation in order to restore private incentives and thus resurrect growth and productivity. Hence the insistence on de-valuation to reflect the going exchange rates of the Tanzanian shilling in convertible currency, higher prices to farmers, reduction of the government budget deficit and internal bank borrowing to avoid crowding out private investors, divestiture of loss-making parastatals, and elimination of price controls and restrictions on domestic and international trade.

To the Nyerere government in the early 1980s—caught in the vise of an economic slump and the need for external borrowing—this sounded like sheer political blackmail; a formula for the reversal to market-based private production rejected at Arusha in 1967 and a cut in public-funded social services—education and health—which were the very pride of Ujamaa. The government and intellectuals sympathetic to it shifted the blame primarily to external causes: adverse terms of international trade leading to a fall in agricultural inputs, the oil price shocks of 1973 and 1979, the collapse of the East African Community in 1977, and the 500 million Tanzanian shillings spent on the war to oust Idi Amin from Uganda in 1979.

Yet as recent studies have revealed, Tanzania suffered less from external economic shocks—declining terms of trade, higher interest payments on external debt, loss in external demand, etc.—than its neighbors Kenya and Malawi, which nevertheless fared much better than Tanzania in agricultural and industrial growth.[55] This line of analysis therefore pointed out domestic policy inadequacies as the real culprit behind Tanzania's poor economic performance.

In fairly quick order historical events and the reaction of Tanzanians to the economic predicament they had been led to were to demonstrate how farfetched some of these theories were, and how close to home the solution really was. For accumulating evidence now demonstrates that faced with mounting disappointments arising primarily from declining productivity under the collectivist Ujamaa—shortages, inflation, and collapsing public services—most Tanzanians turned to the surreptitious and officially maligned "parallel markets" to satisfy their individual subsistence needs and to raise personal incomes. Among other reasons, Hirschman has written, "increasing economic difficulties that compel concentration on finding a job, keeping it and making ends meet" lead citizens to become wholly absorbed in the pursuit of private affairs.[56] This phenomenon explains a great deal of the popular economic behavior in Tanzania after the mid-1970s and the frustration of the government in maintaining control over pervasive individual participation in the parallel markets.

Actually the term *parallel market* in economic circumstances like those prevailing in Tanzania in early 1980s is a misnomer. It assumes a working market at official prices. But when state-owned shops display empty shelves, government clinics lack medicine, state-owned transport is permanently unavailable, and foreign currency is rationed by political order, the so-called parallel market is the only market, often the sole reliable source of goods and services, albeit at prices the government, like the European medieval "moralists," considers "exploitative" and "unjust."[57] For a while the Tanzania government insisted on the archaic moral economics that the high prices prevailing in this market were not the product of manifest supply shortages but the handiwork of crafty "economic saboteurs" intent on economic self-aggrandizement contrary to what Ujamaa and its canons of sharing within African familyhood stood for. But in the end, by 1986, the market and its individualism had triumphed over the state. In fact, Tanzanian public institutions had caved in to private gain as bureaucratic positions were used—in Weberian "prebendal" fashion—to trade supposedly free government services for individual gain, and as corruption crept into the inner sanctums of power.

By 1990 the Mwinyi government had given full rein to private enterprise, something the Nyerere government always tolerated but treated with great equivocation and suspicion.[58] And in February 1991 the National Executive Committee of Tanzania's ruling party, Chama Cha Mapinduzi (CCM)— TANU's successor as the single party in 1977—allowed party members to rent houses, draw several salaries, and own shares in public or private companies. These decisions in effect dispensed with the Arusha Declaration's exhortation of leaders to refrain from engagement in capitalist (or feudal) enterprises, and they effectively nullified the 1971 Mwongozo leadership code that required party leaders to divest any personal interests they had in business, industry, or real estate. It was, however, politically imprudent to state the realities in these stark terms. The CCM conservative guard, often backed by statements from Nyerere, insisted that Tanzania was irrevocably socialist. President Mwinyi was thus reduced to defending this belated concession to private enterprise as a necessary step in "consolidating socialism and self-reliance."[59]

It was not the first time East Africans had been treated to a defense of private enterprise in the name of socialism. Kenya's Sessional Paper No. 10 on African Socialism of 1965 made a case for raising productivity grounded in individual incentives by appealing to the nebulous doctrine of African socialism. And as in Kenyatta's Kenya, blatant accumulation of wealth and growing opposition to it by 1991 had become part of Tanzania's economic and political scene. The country thus had come full circle from the egalitarian enthusiasm generated after Arusha in 1967. But to understand the succession of political and economic events that led Tanzania to the turnabout in legitimizing private enterprise in early 1991, it is necessary to backtrack to the economic scenario that was produced by Ujamaa.

As macroeconomic measurements, the statistics of the development debacle that the country suffered in the 1970s and 1980s cannot adequately describe the full dimensions of individual suffering at the micro level. Yet one must look there for the origins of the multiple personal economic calculations that added up to falling total production and sparked the mass exodus toward individual participation in unofficial markets, first and foremost as a matter of personal survival and later as a means of capital accumulation.

At individual level the average 1.7 percent annual decline in per capita income between 1980 and 1987 manifested itself concretely in high inflation, shortage of basic necessities, lining up for rations of scarce consumer products including food, and finally total disappearance of basic household goods from state retail outlets. "In 1984" one peasant in Shinyanga said, "I once had to travel 150 kilometers to look for a bar of soap."[60] Others in that region made do with precolonial herb-based substitutes for soap, and the very poor returned to bark cloth in place of the cotton fabrics they had worn for years. Between 1973 and 1986 shortages of essential foodstuff in Dar es Salaam were so severe that many individuals could hardly afford the basic needs—clothing, food, health services—whose mass provision Ujamaa had made its paramount objective. According to a sympathetic Western donor, "The outward signs of economic deterioration seem everywhere evident. . . . Long lines form early in Dar es Salaam outside a medium-sized bakery for white bread. There is shortage of almost all consumer staples: flour, cooking oil, sugar, kerosene, charcoal and clothing. . . . The Government's policies do not seem able to secure a minimum level of food for the urban population. As for the rural population, there is virtually nothing to buy."[61] In 1990 the then minister of state in charge of economic planning, Professor Kighoma Malima, admitted that monthly wages in Tanzania could hardly meet family needs for a week.[62] But in Tanzania, as elsewhere, necessity became the mother of invention; in this case individual initiative overcame official barriers to augmenting personal incomes in order to guarantee basic subsistence.

In agriculture producers reacted in a positively rational manner if one presupposes the existence of a market despite heroic state efforts to eliminate or distort it in the interests of socialist doctrines. In one of the earliest attempts to analyze the relationship between state-dictated prices and household agricultural production in Tanzania, Frank Ellis found a general pricing bias against farm products but emphasized that export producers had suffered greater real income losses than food-crop farmers.[63] This alone would be enough ground to explain a shift in peasant production in favor of food products. But recent data on actual operations of the so-called parallel market provide an even more compelling case for that trend.

In a recent study T. L. Maliyamkono and M. S. D. Bagachwa have demonstrated that between 1982 and 1988 market prices for cereal staples were consistently higher than official ones.[64] In the early eighties they rose above fixed government prices by a factor of four. Grain therefore found its way into unofficial market channels despite opposition by, and sometimes collusion with, state officials. These nonofficial channels included local village markets and regional markets based on hinterland supplies infiltrated to major cities and towns like Dar es Salaam, Lindi, Dodoma, Tanga, Kigoma, Mwanza, and Bukoba. The networks covered the entire country. A sample of 385 rural households covering eight administrative regions revealed that most of their income was derived from sales in unofficial markets.[65] There were also considerable cross-border food exports drawn by higher prices to Kenya, Burundi, and Uganda. In addition, ill-advised uniform panterritorial pricing of agricultural goods provided open incentives for middlemen to purchase farm produce in areas with low transport costs at above official prices for sale in high-priced urban or external markets. At the same time such a pricing policy subsidized production in areas with high transport costs like Iringa, Mbeya, and Ruvuma, adding to the losses of the state-owned National Milling Corporation. Between 1971 and 1987 Maliyamkono and Bagachwa calculated that unofficial-economy food markets accounted for the largest share of the grain market.[66] Depending on the year, this proportion was as high as 94 percent for maize (1982–83) and 93 percent for rice (1986–87), averaging around 80 percent for cereals in the decade.

As individual income maximizers, therefore, agricultural producers had surpassed the government's National Milling Corporation as the primary suppliers of grain and probably other food products (like millet and legumes) to the nation. Far from being self-sufficient, autonomous producers who were marginal to the market, as Goran Hyden had argued, the peasant had not exercised an "exit option" from exploitative statist policies. The Tanzanian primary producers had on the contrary integrated themselves solidly into a market of their own choice.[67] The statistics of agricultural produce delivery through unofficial channels demonstrated the strength of market forces in supplanting the state, not a producer retreat into autonomous subsistence. The data are the mark of a vibrant domestic and regional agricultural market rather than the triumph of affectionate peasant bonds based on household subsistence production. These markets also provided open testimony of the incapacity of the Tanzanian state to impose a successful price-control regime in agricultural production and marketing.

This phenomenon is replicated in the field of trade in goods and services.

Shortages of industrial inputs and raw materials and mismanagement in state firms led to a capacity utilization in manufacturing running at 25 percent in 1985. Declining imports after 1974 became another contributing factor to the falling supply of consumer goods. And as in agriculture, panterritorial official pricing of the 3,000 commodities in 1978—again premised on the dubious interests of equality—provided an open invitation for middlemen, sometimes in collusion with state sources, to purchase in bulk in Dar es Salaam for disposal to outlying areas at a profit, for the fact was that given the poor state of transportation, no trader, nor the government, could supply the countryside at official prices without sustaining losses. Second-economy prices ranged between 100 and 400 percent over official ones, even though the officially harassed market sources were no more reliable than state-dependent retail outlets.[68] So pervasive were illegal enterprises in the service sector that unofficial financial dealers in Dar es Salaam were depriving the state commercial banking monopoly of business because by one account "they were considered easier and more efficient to deal with."[69] By mid-1991 it was estimated that 35 percent of Tanzania's money supply was circulating outside the official banking system, primarily in the hands of illegal moneylenders. The liquidity required for transactions in the parallel markets was so high that borrowers were paying a 120 percent interest for loans in the illegal banks, as opposed to the official 30 percent in the cash-starved state bank.

In international trade rapacious businessmen took to illegal harvesting of the nation's natural assets and the exporting of nature's products for want of domestic industrial and agricultural goods. In the ten years between 1979 and 1989, 697,548 kilograms of raw ivory were exported from Tanzania, reducing its elephant herd from 203,900 in 1981 to 61,000 in 1989.[70] Gold, precious stones, wood carvings, hides and skins, and cattle on the hoof were habitually smuggled into neighboring countries—principally Kenya—in return for hard (or Kenyan) currency or consumer goods. There were occasional court cases involving seizure of illegal exports, but these constituted probably no more than the tip of the iceberg.[71] As in agriculture, the service sector and consumer goods market—whatever moral value one attached to it—had triumphed over regulated controls by the state.

In a last-ditch effort to nail down "economic saboteurs" the Nyerere government closed all the international borders in April 1983, and under the direct leadership of the late prime minister Edward Sokoine, the army and police began a systematic nationwide crackdown on "hoarders" and "smugglers." It uncovered large fractions of the unofficial market, but for all its efforts it netted no major businessmen or public officials. On the contrary, the scare given the secondary market diminished overall supplies further and aggravated the shortages. But the Nyerere government ignored factual analysis and was single-minded in pursuing controls. In the following year the Central Bank of Tanzania building in Dar es Salaam was burned in as-yet-unexplained circumstances. A plot against the government involving some military officers had been uncovered in January 1983. The government appeared to be having second thoughts.

Between 1984 and 1985 it adopted some hesitant steps toward economic liberalization: a modest (5 percent) devaluation of the shilling, the reduction of government ministries from twenty-two to fifteen, and a managerial reshuffle in unprofitable state enterprises. As Benno Ndulu has remarked, the reforms were too weak to trigger an economic turnaround, principally because they avoided pricing issues and counted too heavily on massive external resource inflows that did not materialize.[72] In 1985 Julius Nyerere resigned from the presidency. However feebly, the concession to a liberal, market-driven solution to Tanzania's economic crisis had been made. The World Bank and IMF were standing by with their well-known brand of economic assistance.

In June 1986 the first Consultative Group meeting of Tanzania's leading donors in nine years took place in Paris, under the World Bank's chairmanship and with President Ali Hassan Mwinyi's full support. This was followed by the adoption of the current economic recovery program with its market-based production priorities, which have been achieved at the expense of increasing income inequalities and the virtual collapse of the government-provided social services—especially health and education—introduced in the 1960s. And so the Tanzania shilling was devalued by 95 percent in the succeeding seven years. The list of price-controlled goods under the National Price Commission went down from 3,000 in 1978 to a mere 12 in 1988. The external trade liberalization program was ahead of that of Kenya, allowing exporters to retain part of their earnings in convertible currency. State control of cereal staples came to an end. But there was still plenty of ground to cover. None of the 350 government firms had been privatized. The old CCM Ujamaa guard valued them too much as Tanzania's socialist patrimony and strongly resisted any change. The budget deficit showed no signs of falling, principally because the state would not lay off its surplus bureaucrats or let go loss-making public corporations. Yet, albeit at exorbitant prices, consumer goods were finally available in the shops, and this made a difference in ordinary lives.

Registering a positive GDP growth rate per capita for the first time in 1987 (1.1 percent) followed by another 1.3 percent in 1988, Tanzania's economy appeared to be on the mend. Tanzania certainly outperformed Kenya in constant agricultural growth rates up to the 1990s even though it began at an abysmally low level. Inflation was brought down from 44 percent in 1984 to 23 percent in 1989. Producer cooperatives and local authorities were allowed to function once again. The country became self-sufficient in food production.

But this was a mixed blessing. As Weber remarked, a full-fledged market economy requires not just free pricing but also a sedentary—as opposed to a free-lance—industrial class, set up with the aim of making profits on a sustained, long-term basis, using impersonal managerial calculations in the process.[73] To back this up, the system called for a neutral and efficient public bureaucracy guided by legal-rational norms. Tanzania had neither of these yet. Economic growth was taking place without the development of social and economic infrastructures, both of which had steadily gone into ruin for want of adequate maintenance over the years. The greatest constraint in the agricultural sector, for instance, was poor road conditions, which made it impossible to deliver farm produce to markets and towns. The World Bank was funding reconstruction of 90 percent of the national road network, which was judged unusable in 1991.[74]

Investment in human resources also suffered. Given the commitment to reduce the public budget deficit, the economic recovery program had made deep cuts in health and education. Health facilities lacked basic medicines, and schools were understaffed and underequipped.[75] The primary school enrollment rate fell from 98 percent in 1981 to 76 percent in 1988. The University of Dar es Salaam, once a showcase in East Africa, suffered financial cuts in real terms, resulting in deterioration of the physical plant and a staff exodus.

Most significantly, the Mwinyi government was afflicted with what is now reckoned to be the Achilles' heel of African development—an unreliable and unaccountable administrative machinery to implement its development programs. As a knowledgeable correspondent remarked, "Today Tanzania can have their huge public service. One thing it certainly does not do is work."[76] Having sustained an estimated 85 percent decline in real wages in the past decade, public servants resorted widely to business sidelines dependent on patronage from their positions or practiced outright corruption. Between 1985 and 1990 some $130 million was lost in credit to cooperatives. Some of it went to fictitious farmers who delivered *mazao hewa* (air or nonexistent products). The incompetent city administration in Dar es Salaam was the subject of popular outrage and the butt of rude jokes. By June 1991, for instance, residential neighborhoods like Tandika and Temeke had been without water for at least six months. Industries along Pugu Road and the airport suffered routine water shortages. Government ministries carried payrolls full of ghost workers. President Mwinyi personally fired the head of Customs and Sales Tax Department in May 1990 because of the loss of state revenue to collusion between tax dodgers and government staff. The gravity of the situation facing President Mwinyi is best symbolized by the forced retirement of the director of the anticorruption squad, Zakaria Maftah, in April 1990. A cabinet reshuffle the previous month in which three ministers were dropped—but absolved of any wrongdoing—changed little. Soaring crime and police incapacity to counteract it forced neighborhood associations and the CCM party cells to organize Sungu Sungu, militia night patrols, to combat household and business burglaries in the towns and cities.

There were reflections of the social conditions in next-door Kenya in some of this, but state institutions in Kenya had never been so dilapidated. There were also dashes of Kenya's economic history of the 1960s and 1970s in the conspicuous consumption of newfound wealth and the negative popular reaction to it. Nyerere is said to have been outraged by the sudden surge in expensive personal cars negotiating Dar es Salaam's potholed roads once import and exchange controls were relaxed. An enterprising indigenous Tanzanian manufacturer won the DHL Corporation's "Businessman of the Year" award for the African region in 1989.[77] In October 1990 another local businessman bought a portrait of Pope John Paul II at a million Tanzanian shillings ($5,000) during a fund-raising dinner in honor of the pontiff, in a country where just less than $10 a month is the minimum wage. These individuals, and many others like them, would have fitted in the character mold of Kenya's indigenous African bourgeoisie in the second half of the Kenyatta regime. And their emergence as a distinct class drew similar pejorative and populist remarks to those observed earlier in Kenya.

In November 1990 the Reverend Charles Mtikila of the Full Salvation Church accused Tanzania's ruling party of being dictatorial and of turning Tanzania into "a man eat man society;" the ultimate weapon in the Nyerere government's arsenal of denigration, which had been used exclusively to describe capitalist Kenya in the 1970s.[78] And as if inspired by Proudhon's populist remark that all property is theft, Mwinyi's new minister for home affairs, Augustine Mrema, unleashed yet another solo but highly popular campaign, against "hoarders," "overchargers," the "corrupt," and "smugglers." Like the Sokoine 1983 effort, Mrema's initiative ignored the structural conditions that produced bureaucratic corruption: price distortions in a segmented market whose internal communications were disjointed, real negative interest rates that deflected savings from official banks, and widespread rent-seeking behavior prompted by the incomplete nature of economic reforms.[79]

The new wealth resulting from liberal productionist policies and the popular hostility it provoked explain the ambiguous political proclamations of the Mwinyi government: it encouraged private enterprise but denied having swerved from the goals of socialism and the Arusha Declaration. Yet once again the popular reaction to new prosperity combined the contradictory characteristics of resentment and admiration. The economic behavior of most Tanzanians by the early 1990s combined a resentment of the nouveaux riches and an unmistakable rising interest in raising individual and family income.

All this was a far cry from the political tracts of the party apparatchiks and scholars extolling the virtues of the communalist peasants and workers whose well-being had been sacrificed to international capital by the petite bourgeoisie in government. In the Maliyamkono-Bagachwa survey, 54 percent of the workers interviewed—a proportion slightly higher than that of traders—supplemented their incomes by engaging in secondary economic activities.[80] A vast proportion of the urban labor force (92 percent), according to the same authors, supported economic liberalization not because it opened doors to instant prosperity but because the previous alternative was infinitely worse.

Ulanguzi, a comprehensive Swahili term covering activities that generate personal income by any means forbidden by the Arusha Declaration or the state, became popularized in its practical nationwide application.[81] Civil servants and university lecturers ran taxis and farmed chicken and dairy cattle in once-fashionable suburbs or near the city. Between Ujamaa in 1967 and economic liberalization in the 1980s, secondary economic activities in fact altered the Tanzanian household division of labor fundamentally. In a survey of urban-based women in Dar es Salaam in 1988, Aili Mari Tripp found that 66 percent of her respondents were self-employed, in comparison with only 4 percent in a similar sample in 1972.[82] This was a change in response to economic hardships of the 1980s. While such women were engaged primarily in selling cooked food at the lower end of the income range, their professional and semiprofessional counterparts had advanced into "shipping and receiving companies, secretarial services, private schools, textile factories, bakeries, flour mills and dry-cleaning."[83] Michael Cowen's and Kabiru Kinyanjui's Kenyan notion of "straddling" in individual accumulation between paid employment and private investment had finally arrived in Tanzania, via discontent with the local version of socialism.[84] At whatever end of the income scale they happened to be, self-employed women earned more in profits than they would have been paid in formal jobs.

The Swahili word coined to cover these transclass and ubiquitous business activities is *miradi*, often literally translated as "projects," but meaning projects under personal control and ownership. A more faithful rendering of its senses therefore would be "individual enterprise." No word could summarize any better the political and economic transition that Tanzanian society had undergone from the euphoric days of the Arusha Declaration and its glittering communal promises, through disappointment with it, to the retreat into personal initiative. In 1992 the CCM government also acquiesced to the registration of opposition parties that gave this individualistic economic trend some concrete political expression.

Political Symmetry of the Production-Distribution Sequence

The transition culminating in the triumph of individual enterprise in Tanzania and that which has produced a popular backlash against ethnic-ascriptive distribution policies in Kenya shared a common constraint: their onward progress was severely handicapped by the incapacity of incumbent states to respond to new social demands in a democratic and economically rational manner. In Tanzania the social pains of half measures in economic reform and the absence of infrastructure and a legal-rational administrative machinery to complement private enterprise produced early reform fatigue and widespread political cynicism. As Julius Nyerere proclaimed in June 1990, the ruling party was not popular, and it held to power only because of the one-party constitutional provision. Despite growing international protest, the government in Kenya showed little remorse in its unrelenting persecution of the advocates of liberal democracy, the rule of law, and nondiscriminatory policies in private enterprise, even after the donors cut off aid in November 1991.

By 1990 the political ferment in both countries produced open demands for the legalization of new political parties pledged to reversing the current governing policies. To the extent that the political fault line between the ruling parties and their opponents lay—in part at least—along the production-distribution divide, that division may provide the new secular political parties of Africa with a long sought ideological legitimacy. For while one side would stress the need for social equity, its rivals would emphasize individual responsibility and the productivity policies that are necessary to keep the system running. Such a party system in turn may institutionalize sequential emphasis on growth and redistribution, thus offering these countries a chance of successive, incremental policy adjustment to conflicting social demands—the best, if not the perfect, solution that modern industrial democracies have managed to offer so far.[85]

The analysis of the pro-Moi political coalition after 1978 noted that some of the political ideas and social groups on which it was founded harked back to the defunct KADU party of the 1960s. In time, these policies blossomed into the rhetorical reverence of premodern rural values, preference programs for "neglected" ethnic groups, and by 1991 open calls by prominent government supporters for the reintroduction of the quasi-federalist *majimbo* or constitution—the linchpin of KADU's platform before independence.[86] The similarity of the vanquished 1992 opposition coalition and its political platform to the KANU of mid-1960s make it seem that throughout the years there have been only two political menus offered to the Kenyan electorate: the quintessential KADU now led by Moi and the KANU of the fragmented 1992 opposition, characterized respectively by the distributionist and the growth perspectives in their most general terms. The most realistic response to the current political and economic crisis in Kenya, therefore, would be to recognize these two durable tendencies in Kenya's political history and devise an equitable two-party system based on them. The country could then count on the social stability that might be gained from sequential emphasis on production and distribution over time.[87]

In Tanzania, likewise, current opposition politics also contain a flavor of history repeating itself. The leading advocate of political pluralism is Chief Abdallah Fundikira, once Tanzania's justice minister, who resigned from the government in 1963 in protest against the proposal to introduce one-party rule. As a Kenyatta-government nominee, he subsequently served as the chairman of the defunct East African Airways in Nairobi. Among the leading lights in the National Committee for Constitutional Reform, which he leads, are many ruling-party castaways or people who never believed in Ujamaa in the first place. As one of them, C. Stanley Kamana, executive editor of the new opposition periodical, *Family Mirror,* remarked, "The problem with Tanzania is that it has always tried to practice socialism with people who secretly believed in capitalism."[88] The battle between the fifteen new opposition parties and the old socialist guard in the ruling party is all but joined. In the context of contemporary international political realities, the most prudent constitutional alternative for Tanzania would be to give full leeway for the liberal, market-oriented political opposition to coalesce into a solid alternative to its egalitarian policies. In the fullness of time, the opposition's democratic capitalism would produce its own variety of popular disappointment and probably pave the way for the return of community values and egalitarian economics.

Conclusion

This chapter opened with remarks on the need to explore the intellectual framework underlying the shifting interests between production and distribution in Kenya and Tanzania. So far the discussion has concentrated on demonstrating that even though the two countries have not crossed paths moving in opposite directions, their incumbent leaders have espoused development strategies and political rhetoric that the national founding fathers, Kenyatta and Nyerere, might have considered political heterodoxy, only suitable to the state next door. The gradual rejection of the economic and political heritage was explained in terms of the disenchantment with growth associated with marked inequalities between ethnic groups in Kenya and the backlash generated by economic hardships primarily caused by failure in Ujamaa's egalitarian policies in Tanzania. I also have tried to document that over time Moi's populist program has generated considerable internal opposition partly inspired by the norms of productive resource allocation, the rule of law, and nondiscriminatory achievement (as opposed to ethnic-based ascriptive) criteria in recruitment, which have been on the defensive for a decade of his rule. In Tanzania, meanwhile, opposition to inequalities and newly acquired wealth was gathering momentum. Fortuitously, as this essay has sought to demonstrate, the policy differences between the incumbent governments and new forces of opposition might form the foundation for rebuilding competitive multiparty political systems in which power would alternate between distribution-centered and individualistic, production-oriented political parties. It is now time to summarize the respective roles of objective social analysis and the danger posed by vested antireform interests in generating or blocking policies that respond positively to the alternating social impulses between production and distribution.

Like all social inquiry, development studies as controversial as those published on East Africa over the last three decades have been animated by personal values whether or not these were spelled out by the scholars concerned. There has been passionate commitment to political ideologies, as well as maligning or adulation of individual leaders. There is nothing pernicious, and a good deal that is commendable, in this; choice of subjects of scientific inquiry is largely a matter of individual values. However, once past that stage, it is sheer professional negligence to be cavalier with factual data—to the extent that these are known—particularly when they contradict personally valued political beliefs. Kenyans and Tanzanians have paid dearly for policies and myths that should have been thrown overboard by more rigorous and objective analysis but were kept alive by intellectual propaganda and political canvassing among thinkers.

Thus although one cannot gainsay the values of "fair" or "just" income distribution that informed the Moi and Nyerere governments in very different ways, it is professionally indefensible to ignore the fact that justice and fairness in distribution must be measured against individual, group, or class contribution to production. Injustice is committed when individuals or groups obtain proportionately less than their contribution to the production of the proceeds, even though, as Barrington Moore has reminded us, the notions of what constitutes contribution and reward are themselves subject to constant public negotiation.[89] Popularly accepted norms of social justice therefore often may tolerate substantial degrees of material inequality. For however morally objectionable they might be, mere statistical differences in wealth, in and of themselves, cannot prove individual or social injustice until causal relationship between individual contribution to production and apportionment in the distribution thereof is established. Yet casual and impressionistic observations of social and economic differences are precisely the base on which the redistributive policies in the two countries were constructed. And even this mattered less than the moral commitment to the egalitarian ideals and immediate political action to assuage those who supposedly had been wronged by uncaring domestic and international market forces and impersonal, Western-imposed administrative and legal policies.

It may be considered heretical to say so, but the eclectic blend of traditional rural, anticapitalist, egalitarian values that the Moi government espoused, while not entirely identical to Nyerere's refined Ujamaa, actually sprang from the same populist intellectual pedigree. As is well known by now, the development of modern capitalism has been met everywhere by waves of moral resentment and the clarion call for a return to the often romanticized "pure" and simple peasant or "folk" values of the past. Barrington Moore spoke of this moralizing, anticapitalist, antiforeign, and anti-intellectual belief system as "Catonism," having traced it back to the reign of Cato the Elder (234–149 B.C.).[90]

In both its left- and right-wing varieties, Catonism assigns the moral high ground to the peasants, who are portrayed as the real custodians of pristine national values. Deference to ordinary rural people is a canon of the Moi regime. It was central to Ujamaa, and it is a recurring theme in radical Kenyan creative writing like that of Ngugi wa Thiongo. That Moi's brand of populism took such a repressive turn owes more to the poorly reasoned and corrupting zeal that characterized its implementation than to any substantive generic difference from the other manifestations of populism.

On the economic plane Catonism finds succor in physiocratic notions of peasants as the sole producers of economic surplus, which subsequently is appropriated by other "parasitic" classes, often in collusion with foreigners. For solutions, it dotes on wholesale spiritual regeneration and abhors mass industrial urbanism, which is seen as spiritually corrupting and dehumanizing. Realistic social analysis is abjured as detached and elitist, and a premium is placed on action with a "human touch." It stressed equitable distribution of income and underestimates the inevitable costs in its production. In concrete terms it is clearly discernible in such modern movements as African socialism, the Russian Narodniki, Gandhism, and the new Islamic fundamentalist politics. Elements of these ideas can be found in varying combination in the socialist Tanzania of the 1960s and the capitalist Kenya of the 1980s.

In either case uncritical intellectual inputs helped to fan the political flames, rather than illuminate social realities. Thus the influential 1972 International Labor Organization (ILO) report on Kenya disparaged creeping rural inequalities on the basis of highly sketchy evidence and contained recommendations on education-with-production, ethnic quotas in resource allocation, the splitting of large farms, district-based planning to promote regional (ethnic) economic equality, and promotion of the indigenous informal sector.[91] In time these ideas became the standard for criticism of the Kenyatta government and, in turn, government policies in the 1980s. Scant reference was made to previous colonial data on the problems of manual and vocational education or subsequent research—particularly Michael

Cowen's work—that debunked the prognoses of rural income inequalities as commercial agriculture took root and also demonstrated the interdependence between informal-sector prosperity and a growing (and multinational) industrial sector.[92] In Tanzania flattering academic evaluations of Ujamaa unsupported by objective factual analyses were commonplace until the food and agricultural crisis of 1973–74. A particularly well-informed source, for example, stated that "the transition to socialism in Tanzania could be said to be nearly accomplished" in 1977.[93] The soapless peasants of Shinyanga and shirtless laborers in Dar es Salaam might have disagreed. By the same token the shanty dwellers of Nairobi—struck by economic recession and violently evicted from their homes and businesses in 1990 and 1991 for pro-opposition sympathies—have real cause to doubt the creed of brotherly love among small-scale business people that informed the Moi government policy on the informal sector. By eschewing a calculating, secular, and rationalist outlook, Catonism in both Kenya and Tanzania hurt most those it claimed to support—the poor and the marginalized, for it promised what objective reality denied it the capacity to deliver.

The transition out of Catonism in Tanzania in fact came with Nyerere's candid admission that from a production point of view, Ujamaa had failed its own test and his eventual decision to retire from politics. In assessing the limits of how far the Mwinyi government can go, however, one cannot ignore the vested interests of old CCM *nomenklatura*, who feared that the equality they had striven for and the perks they had earned in doing so would be put in jeopardy by thoroughgoing market reforms and state divestment from the parastatals. Nyerere himself often stated that socialism had an assured place in Tanzania, whatever reforms others desired. All this forced Mwinyi to tread most carefully in the first five years of his presidency. After the October 1990 elections, Mwinyi constituted a cabinet of his choice, but against this political background he could not abandon his political heritage entirely.

The even less tolerant Moi government in Kenya argued that any transition to the pluralistic politics and rule of law advocated by its opposition would jeopardize gains made in redistribution, rather like Mwinyi's old party-line conservative critics. Only this time, the benefits in jeopardy were those of the small "tribes," and hence the revival of the 1960s KADU-style demands for a quasi-federal majimbo to secure these gains and the bizarre predictions of ethnic conflagration if political pluralism were adopted. As in the 1960s the specter of Kikuyu (or Kikuyu-Luo) domination was raised again in Kenya to bring smaller groups into line, with varying success. The degree of change that democratic forces in Kenya could make, therefore, was constrained by the ability of reformers to lay the ghost of ethnic domination and win over the confidence of communities that felt privileged and protected under Moi.

In 1992 the Kenya government was smarting under political pressure for keeping the forces of individual capitalist enterprise and personal liberties—both raring to go—on a tight leash in the name of ethnic economic and political equality. In Tanzania the state appeared to have lost anchor and any control it previously had over a surging mass of individual enterprises that were pulling it hither and thither and getting away with a lot in defiance of the emaciated governmental structures. The priority of production at last had been conceded. On the stage of East African politics, the polar-opposite development models of Kenya and Tanzania were still in place. To some extent, they appear to have swapped scripts, if not roles. But in their new parts, they had demonstrated neither convincing effectiveness nor a full mastery of the art of transition.

Notes

1. Republic of Kenya, *African Socialism and Its Application to Planning in Kenya* (Nairobi: Government Printer, 1965), p. 18.

2. "The Arusha Declaration," in J. K. Nyerere, *Freedom and Socialism* (Nairobi: Oxford Univ. Press, 1968), p. 241.

3. Ibid., pp. 242–43. The eighteenth-century school of French economists, the Physiocrats, believed agriculture was the exclusive source of value. See Ronald Meek, *The Economics of Physiocracy* (Cambridge: Harvard Univ. Press, 1963).

4. Joel D. Barkan and John J. Okumu, eds., *Politics and Public Policy in Kenya and Tanzania* (New York: Praeger, 1979), is an outstanding example. See also Ahmed Mohiddin, *African Socialism in Two Countries* (London: Croom Helm, 1981).

5. Ali A. Mazrui coined this term in "Tanzaphilia," *Transition* 6, no. 31 (1967): 20–26.

6. The genesis and subsequent developments of the Kenya debate on African capitalism are dealt with by Colin Leys in chap. 7 above.

7. Uma Lele, "Sources of Growth in East African Agriculture," *World Bank Economic Review* 3, no. 1 (1989): 121. This translates to per capita growth rates of 1.8 percent given the country's annual 3.9 percent population increase. Observing the economies of Eastern and Central Africa over these years, Lele pointed out that Kenya had the strongest macroeconomic indicators overall.

8. The alarm was sounded by the 1972 ILO-UNDP Mission on Unemployment to Kenya, whose volume *Employment, Incomes, and Equality in Kenya* (Geneva: ILO, 1972) had effects beyond Kenya's borders. Indirectly it led to the concepts of "growth-with-redistribution" in development studies of the 1970s and "basic needs" in the 1980s. This

evolution is analyzed by Tony Killick in "Trends in Development Economics and Their Relevance to Africa," *Journal of Modern African Studies* 18, no. 3 (1980): 367–86. Politically, protest against growing income inequalities and the increasing presence of foreign capital was led by the opposition Kenya Peoples Union party and, after its ban in 1969, by outspoken parliamentarians like J. M. Kariuki, who was assassinated in 1975.

9. Benno Ndulu, *Tanzania: Stabilization and Adjustment Policies and Programs* (Helsinki: WIDER Publications, 1987), p. 1.

10. Richard Sklar, "Beyond Capitalism and Socialism in Africa," *Journal of Modern African Studies* 26, no. 1 (1988): 1–21.

11. T. H. Lee and Kuo-Shu Liang, "Taiwan," in *Development Strategies in Semi-Industrialized Economies,* ed. Bale Balassa et al. (Baltimore: Johns Hopkins Univ. Press, 1982), pp. 310–50, attributes this equality to equitable land reform in the 1950s.

12. Albert O. Hirschman, *Shifting Involvements: Public Interest and Private Action* (Princeton, N.J.: Princeton Univ. Press, 1982).

13. "A year and a half after launching an extraordinary scheme to propel their country from communism to capitalism, few Poles are in the mood to trumpet the virtues of their program. Industrial production and real wages have slumped dramatically . . . and the former heroes of Solidarity are beginning to hear boos" (*Newsweek* [International Edition], Sept. 23, 1991, p. 9). The *Economist,* Sept. 14, 1991, p. 15, describes the swing in German national mood from "euphoria" in 1989 to the current "gloom."

14. Hans Gerth and C. Wright Mills, *From Max Weber: Essays in Sociology* (New York: Oxford Univ. Press, 1958), pp. 293–94.

15. The deluge of literature on development, class politics, and African capitalism in Kenya has crowded out a competent treatment of the origins and course of ethnic politics in Kenya since Marc Howard Ross's book, *Grassroots in an African City: Political Behavior in Nairobi* (Cambridge: MIT Press, 1979), but for some fine remarks, consult Aidan Southall, "The Illusion of Tribe," *Journal of Asian and African Studies* 5, nos. 1/2 (1970): 33–35. Colin Leys, *Underdevelopment in Kenya: The Political Economy of Neo-Colonialism, 1964–1971* (Berkeley: Univ. of California Press, 1974), pp. 198–206, also makes extremely enlightened remarks on the issue.

16. See, for instance, Vincent B. Khapoya, "Kenya under Moi: Continuity or Change?" *Africa Today* 27 (May 1978): 17–32.

17. This parallels the dependency hypothesis is that the gains in trade and investment made by the industrialized North amount to the losses suffered in the process by the underdeveloped South—a favorite thesis of Nyerere, which he also applied in explaining rural-urban inequalities in Tanzania. Unlike the Physiocrats and in contradiction with this notion, Adam Smith warned that "we must not . . . imagine that the gain of the town is the loss of the countryside. The gains are mutual and reciprocal" (Adam Smith, *The Wealth of Nations* [New York: Modern Library, 1937], p. 356).

18. Within populist historiography the notion that stealing is the organizing formula in the capitalist market goes back at least to the French syndicalist and pamphleteer Pierre-Joseph Proudhon (1809–1865) who proclaimed that "all property is theft." It has survived in different guises as reactionary rhetoric against the social jolt that capitalist development inflicts on all premodern societies. While from the right the incoming

Moi regime denounced "grabbing" under Kenyatta, the left-wing novelist Ngugi wa Thiongo—a leading critic of Kenyatta's (and Moi's) policies—wrote that " 'Theft is holy' . . . sums up the new creed of the neo-colonial bourgeoisies," in his *Decolonizing the Mind* (London: James Currey, 1987), p. 3.

19. Subtract the Luo from this political sum and what remains is the ethnic bedrock of the Kenya African Democratic Union (KADU) of the 1960–64 ex-colonial period, of which Moi was national chairman. KADU sought to protect the weaker ethnic groups from supposedly imminent Luo-Kikuyu domination after independence. See George Bennett and Carl Rosberg, *The Kenyatta Election: Kenya, 1960–1961* (Nairobi: Oxford Univ. Press, 1961), pp. 37–45.

20. Hirschman, *Shifting Involvements*, p. 46. Apart from the Kenyan examples cited here, there is supporting evidence from other African contexts. Writing on the Kanuri community's reaction to the more educated and entrepreneurial Ibo in northern Nigeria, Ronald Cohen remarked: "The Kanuri are ambivalent about the Ibo. In general, Ibo are disliked, mistrusted and even despised. . . . Yet the Kanuri grudgingly admire the Ibo for their Western education, salaried jobs and high living standards" (Cohen, "Social Stratification in Bornu," in *Social Stratification in Africa,* ed. Arthur Tuden and Leonard Plotnicov [New York: Free Press, 1970], p. 243).

21. See the *Nairobi Times,* Aug. 19, 1991, for the speech by the assistant minister in the Office of the President, John Keen, on protecting "minority communities," especially the pastoralist Maasai, in the land market. A speech by Andrew Ligale, permanent secretary for transport and communications, delivered in Vihiga, Western Province, appeared in the same newspaper on July 3, 1991.

22. Gavin Kitching, *Development and Underdevelopment in Historical Perspective* (London: Methuen, 1982), p. 16.

23. Robert L. Tignor, *The Colonial Transformation of Kenya: The Kamba, Kikuyu, and Maasai from 1900 to 1939* (Princeton, N.J.: Princeton Univ. Press, 1976).

24. Carl G. Rosberg and John Nottingham, *The Myth of "Mau Mau": Nationalism in Kenya* (New York: Praeger, 1966), pp. 25–31, 134–35. See also Tignor, *The Colonial Transformation,* pp. 269–72; Gavin Kitching, *Class and Economic Change in Kenya: The Making of an African Petite Bourgeoisie, 1905–1970* (New Haven: Yale Univ. Press, 1980), pp. 159–87; M. P. Cowen, "Wattle Production in Central Province," Department of Economics, Univ. of Nairobi, 1975.

25. Judith Heyer, "The Origins of Regional Inequalities in Smallholder Agriculture in Kenya," *Eastern African Journal of Rural Development* 8, nos. 1/2 (1975): 142–81. It must be remarked that Kisii and Meru districts had been growing coffee since 1932. By its first few years of production, Central Province had caught up in quality and yields per acre, and it eventually surpassed both.

26. L. H. Brown, *Agricultural Change in Kenya, 1945–1960* (Stanford, Calif.: Food Research Institute, 1968) p. 56ff.; J. C. de Wilde, *Experience with Agricultural Development in Topical Africa* (Baltimore: Johns Hopkins Univ. Press, 1967), pp. 198–207.

27. See, for instance, *Weekly Review,* Dec. 14, 1990, p. 20, for the oblique but common remarks on how "the dominant ethnic group . . . conspired with the settlers" to take over agriculture and business.

28. Michael Lofchie, *The Policy Factor: Agricultural Performance in Kenya and Tanzania* (Boulder, Colo.: Lynne Rienner, 1989), pp. 186–92.

29. For a forceful and well-informed account, see Sam Magimbi, "Co-operatives in Agricultural Development," in *Capitalism, Socialism and the Development Crisis in Tanzania*, ed. Norman O'Neil and Kemal Mustapha (Aldershot, U.K.: Avebury Press, 1990), pp. 81–100.

30. See the plea for "uniform prices" by the Nandi District KANU chairman in the *Standard*, Nov. 29, 1988. The minister for agriculture, Elijah Mwangale, described the demands for equal payments by political leaders west of the Rift Valley as "explosive" and reiterated that "the only reason for the price differential was the quality from East (of the Rift) was better" (*Daily Nation*, Nov. 12, 1988). This did not cut much ice with his critics.

31. A positive evaluation of KTDA's role in smallholder rural development and public sector enterprise is to be found in Geoffrey Lamb and Linda Muller, *Control, Accountability, and Incentives in a Successful Development Institution: The Kenya Tea Development Authority* (Washington, D.C.: World Bank, 1982).

32. Colin Leys, "Accumulation, Class Formation, and Dependency: Kenya," in *Industry and Accumulation in Africa*, ed. Martin Fransman (London: Heinemann, 1982), pp. 177–84.

33. M. Tamarkin, "Tribal Associations, Tribal Solidarity, and Tribal Chauvinism in a Kenya Town," *Journal of African History* 14, no. 2 (1973): 268–71. "In 1956," he wrote, "a survey of African traders in Bondeni and Burma market showed that forty-eight traders were Kikuyu, compared to twelve Luo, ten Arabs and a few others" (p. 269). See also Colin Leys, *Underdevelopment in Kenya*, pp. 202–3, for some extremely perceptive remarks and data on this issue. Tabitha Kanogo, *Squatters and the Roots of Mau Mau* (Nairobi: Heinemann, 1987), p. 109, provides interesting evidence of Kikuyu domination of food trade in a town as far away from central Kenya as Nyaribari, Kisii, in the 1940s.

34. Raphael Kaplinsky, "Capitalist Accumulation in the Periphery: Kenya," in Fransman, *Industry and Accumulation*, pp. 193–221.

35. Gavin Kitching, "Politics, Method, and Evidence in the Kenya Debate," in *Contradictions of Accumulation in Africa*, ed. Henry Bernstein and Bonnie Campbell (Beverley Hills, Calif.: Sage Publications, 1985), pp. 147–48.

36. Nicola Swainson, *The Development of Corporate Capitalism in Kenya, 1918–1977* (Berkeley: Univ. of California Press, 1980), pp. 182–211; Kaplinsky, "Capitalist Accumulation," pp. 202–8.

37. See *Weekly Review*, March 31, 1989, pp. 10–16, for details.

38. Ibid., Jan. 25, 1991, p. 34.

39. See, for instance, the details on business corruption in the *New York Times*, Oct. 21, 1991, p. A4. A new generation of Kenyan Asian entrepreneurs emerged from business alliances with the previously underrepresented groups in commercial ventures involving spectacular takeovers, primarily of branches of local multinationals and some local firms. See *Industrial Review* (Nairobi), Sept. 1989, for a portrait of industrialist Ketan Somaia.

40. Peter Anyang' Nyong'o, "The Disintegration of Nationalist Coalitions and the

Rise of Presidential Authoritarianism in Kenya," *African Affairs* 88, no. 351 (1989): 229–51; Cherry Gertzel, *The Politics of Independent Kenya, 1963–68* (Nairobi: East African Publishing House, 1970), pp. 150–73; Y. P. Ghai and J. P. W. B. McAuslan, *Public Law and Political Change in Kenya* (Nairobi: Oxford Univ. Press, 1970), pp. 220–58.

41. William Edgett Smith actually made this slogan the title of Nyerere's biography, *We Must Run While Others Walk* (New York: Random House, 1971).

42. For a brief evaluation of the futility of these efforts, see Kenneth King, "Secondary Education in Tanzania," in *Tanzania after Nyerere*, ed. Michael Hodd (London: Frances Pinter, 1988), pp. 121–32. For the importance attached to "practical" education for Africans by successive British colonial governments, see Marjorie Mbilinyi's work, especially "Education for Rural Life or Education for Self-Transformation," East African Social Sciences Research Conference, Dar es Salaam, 1973.

43. Which ironically is how Kenya's ideological left-wing depicts the Moi and Kenyatta "neocolonial" governments, for reasons which (as when given in Tanzania of the 1960s) differ from those of the Moi government more in rhetorical style than substance.

44. See *Nairobi Law Monthly*, no. 30 (Feb. 1991): 27–39, for the NDP manifesto.

45. In the second half of the 1990 / 91 fiscal year, government ministries reduced their expenditure by 15 percent to meet stringent revenue conditions, with a corresponding decline in efficacy.

46. Paul Bennell, "British Industrial Investments in Sub-Saharan Africa: Corporate Response to the Economic Crisis of the 1980s," *Development Policy Review* 8, no. 2 (1990): 155–77, indicates that out of a total of 57 British companies with industrial investment in Kenya, 10 withdrew from equity involvement between 1979 and 1989. According to another source, by 1989 "most of the 100 or so U.S. companies in Kenya had sold or withdrawn their subsidiaries" (*Wall Street Journal*, Aug. 17, 1989). And by February 1991 only 2 of 14 Japanese companies established in Kenya shortly after independence were left "due to adverse government policies," according to the Nairobi *Sunday Times*, Feb. 24, 1991.

To the Kenyan leftist ideologues this presumably calls for celebration, Western "monopoly capital" and its local agents having been consistently depicted by them as the source of all of Kenya's political problems. It is ironic that their most cherished hopes are being achieved by their nemesis, the incumbent government in Kenya.

47. World Bank, *Sub-Saharan Africa: From Crisis to Sustainable Growth* (Washington, D.C., 1989), p. 221. Per capita growth rate was 4.7 percent in 1965–73 and 1.3 percent between 1973 and 1980. The high population growth rate (4 percent) explains little of this variation since, as a constant, it cut across all the years in question. Obviously a falling population growth rate will raise personal incomes, and given the fact the GDP was still growing overall (3.8 percent on average between 1980 and 1987), falling per capita incomes may hide the fact that some sections of the population were doing extremely well in comparison with the majority.

48. See Blaine Harden, *Africa: Dispatches from a Fragile Continent* (Boston: Houghton Mifflin, 1990), pp. 248–70.

49. Lofchie, *The Policy Factor*, pp. 75–142.

50. Issa Shivji, *Class Struggles in Tanzania* (London: Heinemann, 1975), and more

recently "Workers in Struggle," in *Capitalism, Socialism, and the Development Crisis*, ed. O'Neil and Mustafa pp. 177–206. At Mount Carmel a local rubber factory was expropriated by its seventy-seven-person labor force in June 1973 who then fired management, all in the name of Nyerere and Mwongozo, which demanded respect and deference to workers by management. The government cracked down on this and other similar syndicalist activities and brought back the unions under state control (see Andrew Coulson, *Tanzania: Political Economy* (London: Oxford Univ. Press, 1980, pp. 284–98). The theme depicting the alliance between international capital, the bureaucratic bourgeoisie, traders, and "kulaks" as the scourge of socialism in Tanzania recurs in leftist explanations of Tanzania's economic regression and is fairly extensive. For a recent review, see Rukhasan Siddiqui, "Socialism and the Ujamaa Ideology," in O'Neil and Mustafa, *Capitalism, Socialism, and the Development Crisis*, pp. 30–34.

51. Suzanne Mueller, "Retarded Capitalism in Tanzania," *The Socialist Register*, 1980, pp. 203–26. See also her "Barriers to Further Development of Capitalism in Tanzania: The Case of Tobacco," *Capital and Class*, no. 15 (1981): 23–54.

52. Paul Collier, Samir Radwan, and Samuel Wangwe, *Labor and Poverty in Rural Tanzania* (New York: Oxford Univ. Press, 1990), pp. 81–106, 115–22, 127–36.

53. Goran Hyden, *Beyond Ujamaa in Tanzania: Underdevelopment and an Uncaptured Peasantry* (Berkeley: Univ. of California Press, 1980).

54. Goran Hyden, *No Shortcuts to Progress: African Development Management in Perspective* (Berkeley: Univ. of California Press, 1983), pp. 191–213.

55. Uma Lele and L. Richard Myers, *Growth and Structural Change in East Africa* (Washington, D.C.: World Bank, 1989), pp. 17–18.

56. Hirschmann, *Shifting Interests*, p. 4.

57. R. H. Tawney, *Religion and the Rise of Capitalism* (Hammondsworth: Penguin Books, 1938), pp. 48–53, argued that the intellectual leap from the medieval concept of morally sanctified "just prices . . . fixed by common authorities . . . or by common estimation" to the recognition of the role of "economic expediency" is the most fundamental characteristic of modern economic thought. There is a close intellectual affinity between the Nyerere government's moral abhorrence of the "unjust" prices of "overcharging" traders and "grabbing" in markets as understood in post-Kenyatta's Kenya.

58. Jeannette Hartman, "The Rise of Private Capital," in O'Neil and Mustafa, *Capitalism, Socialism, and the Development Crisis*, pp. 233–49, argues that the hostility to private capital under Nyerere is overestimated and that Mwinyi inherited a system with a capitalist class raring to go.

59. *Daily Nation*, Feb. 28, 1991.

60. *Africa Events*, Dec. 1990, p. 22.

61. Cited in J. L. Maliyamkono and M. S. D. Bagachwa, *The Second Economy in Tanzania* (London: James Currey, 1990), pp. ix–x.

62. *Africa South*, Dec. 1990, p. 43.

63. Frank Ellis, "Agricultural Price Policy in Tanzania," *World Development* 10, no. 4 (1982): 263–83. See also Lofchie, *The Policy Factor*, pp. 136–42.

64. Maliyamkono and Bagachwa, *The Second Economy*, pp. 78, 152.

65. Ibid., p. 128.

66. Ibid., p. 151.

67. Hyden, *Beyond Ujamaa in Tanzania*, pp. 12–28, and *No Shortcuts to Progress*, p. 71 for details on the "exit option."

68. Maliyamkono and Bagachwa, *The Second Economy*, p. 89.

69. *African Business*, Nov. 1990, p. 43.

70. *Financial Gazette* (Harare), March 1, 1991.

71. For instance, in January 1991 police confiscated $180,000 worth of illegal ivory at the NOTCO shipyard in Dar es Salaam, allegedly bound for South Korea. In June of the same year, authorities intercepted $500,000 in gold and hard currency at Dar es Salaam airport (*African Events*, Aug. 1991, pp. 40–41).

72. Ndulu, *Tanzania*, pp. 26–36.

73. Garth and Mills, *From Max Weber*, pp. 67–68, 49.

74. *Standard*, Aug. 13, 1991.

75. Ernest Harsch, "Tanzania: Difficult Road to Reform," *Africa Recovery* 4, no. 2 (1990): 13–14.

76. *Standard*, Jan. 3, 1992.

77. *African Business*, May 1990.

78. Cited in *New African*, Dec. 1990.

79. For instance, despite the massive devaluations, the Tanzanian shilling was still overvalued by about 50 percent (*Africa Analysis*, Jan. 11, 1991), thus refueling the informal currency market and the inevitable favoritism and political pressures on foreign currency allocation at the Central Bank.

80. Maliyamkono and Bagachwa, *The Second Economy*, pp. 125–26.

81. As did new Swahili phrases like *bei ya mruko* (unofficial price), *mazao hewa* (air or nonexistent product), *chai* (bribe), *vidudu* (contraband), vigogo (racketeers), and many others. The fact that these terms were so widely understood testified to their frequent and widespread usage in "parallel" economic transactions.

82. Aili Mari Tripp, "Women and the Changing Urban Household Economy in Tanzania," *Journal of Modern African Studies* 27, no. 4 (1989): 608.

83. Ibid., pp. 610–12. One of her respondents expressed her tongue-in-cheek thanks to Nyerere for "putting Tanzanians through so much hardship . . . [that] . . . today, most women are in business and no longer dependent on men" (p. 614), in yet another demonstration of popular disappointment yielding to individual enterprise in its latest gender-based expression.

84. See Michael Cowen and Kabiru Kinyanjui, "Some Problems of Capital and Class in Kenya," Institute for Development Studies, Nairobi, Occasional Paper no. 20, 1977.

85. Thus just as the Thatcherite policies in Britain edged out the Labour party's unions-driven welfarism-with-no-growth in 1979, the Swedish electorate in 1991 opted for an individualist, market-oriented government after years of social democracy with its "cradle-to-grave" state care. Likewise, once the fascination with growth through market economies in Eastern Europe has run its course, the voices of "social justice" and resentment of the excesses of capitalism will set in, thus giving opposition to current reformers a solid political platform. There is ample evidence of this on the horizon already. See the *Economist*, Sept. 21, 1991.

86. See *Weekly Review,* Aug. 23, 1991, and Sept. 20, 1991.

87. To argue, as the Kenyan government won't do, that competitive party politics would lock the small ethnic groups permanently out of power is contradicted by the plurality of support Moi himself commanded in 1978.

88. Quoted in *Washington Post,* Sept. 26, 1990.

89. Barrington Moore, Jr., *Injustice: The Social Basis of Obedience and Revolt* (London: Macmillan, 1978), pp. 43–44.

90. Barrington Moore, Jr., *The Social Origins of Dictatorship and Democracy* (Boston: Beacon Press, 1966), pp. 491–96.

91. ILO, *Unemployment, Incomes, and Equality,* pp. 73–81, 241–52, 300–303, 318–23.

92. Some of this material is reviewed in Gavin Kitching, "Politics, Method, and Evidence."

93. R. H. Green, *Towards Socialism and Self-Reliance: Tanzania's Striving for Sustained Transition Projected* (Uppsala: Scandinavian Institute of African Studies, 1977), p. 24.

9

THE POLITICAL ECONOMY OF
AFRICAN PERSONAL RULE

ROBERT H. JACKSON AND CARL G. ROSBERG

Poor peasant, poor king; poor king, poor kingdom.—François Quesnay

Only governments can raise or lower the level of nations.—Voltaire

African Political Economy

IN A TIMELY 1967 article, James Coleman called for an end to the division between political science and economics and their reunion in development studies of African countries.[1] He argued that economic policies reflect political decisions: countries are concrete wholes, and disciplines that focus on the economy or on the state by themselves are fostering abstractions that have no counterparts in reality. Coleman's essay can be read as expressing the interdisciplinary approach to development studies, a path he encouraged as director of the Institute for Development Studies at the University of Nairobi (1967–71). There was a revival of political economy in the 1970s, although mostly of a neo-Marxian kind, in which political scientists and sociologists, but few economists, participated.[2] However, liberal political economy became prominent in the 1980s, particularly in international development circles such as the IMF and the World Bank.[3]

Coleman asked us to examine the economic consequences of political decisions. Here we attempt to do just that. Our focus is a historical branch of political economy which was prominent in many European countries before the industrial revolution and dominated economic thinking before Adam Smith: mercantilism, or the political economy of the princely state. Today mercantilistic ideas are forgotten (except by historians), and most political economists probably think this is a good thing. As long as the system of governance that such ideas presuppose is dead, forgetfulness incurs no cost. In the developed world it is dead. In the Third World and particularly Sub-Saharan Africa, however, personal governance—although admittedly not strictly speaking the princely state—still holds sway in many countries. Mercantilism, as one writer recently put it, is "nearer . . . to present-day Third World conditions" than its successors, and its literature "provides many fertile analogies for the study of modern underdevelopment."[4] Our aim is to select one or two leading ideas from dynastic political economy and apply them to postcolonial African states.[5] We believe these ideas shed light on important facets of these states that would remain obscure if considered only from the vantage points of neo-Marxian or neoclassical political economy. We argue that the political economy of the princely state helps us to understand the widely noted patrimonial characteristics of African states—such as nepotism, patronage, and corruption— and their implications for the development of what are almost everywhere still overwhelmingly agrarian economies. Before focusing on Africa, let us briefly elaborate on this point.

The Princely State

"The political conception of the princely state is the interest of the ruler."[6] This disarmingly simple statement of Ludwig von Mises, originally written in 1919, sums up an idea which dominated West European political economy from the Renaissance to the French Revolution and was prominent in Central and Eastern Europe until the end of World War I. In this lengthy period the state was the expression not of the people or even the bourgeoisie but merely of a ruling dynasty and its confederates and hangers-on. Here also were doctrines that Adam Smith and the classical liberal economists condemned and Karl Marx parodied in his biting critique of Louis Bonaparte, a prince sharing more than a few similarities with certain Third World and African rulers who have enriched themselves and their political associates at the expense of a disorganized peasantry.[7]

In order to grasp Mises's idea, we should abandon the main assumptions that have preoccupied most leading political economists since Adam Smith—i.e., that economic theory and practice are about peoples or at least classes, rather than rulers; that their object is to enlarge the wealth (and welfare) of nations or extensive groups, and not only ruling elites; that free exchange has broken through the feudal restrictions and monopolies that characterized the premodern world; that the socioeconomic interests, expectations, or demands of large groups shape economic and political relationships. In other words, political economy has come to be understood today in both its liberal and socialist variants as an inquiry into transactions and forces involving and affecting large populations both within and between nations.[8]

By contrast, the political economy of the dynastic state focuses on a far more restricted subject. Lands and people are nothing more than objects of princely ownership and demands: the "property" of the ruler. When territories are acquired, their populations are acquired at the same time; consequently in the European dynastic state, rulers and ruled often come from entirely different national groups. This was strikingly evident in Central Europe, where the Hapsburgs ruled not only Germans but also Bohemians, Moravians, Slovaks, Poles, Hungarians, Slovenians, and Croatians (among others), and in the southern Balkans, where the Ottomans controlled Slav, Albanian, Greek, Macedonian, Romanian, and other peasantries. The interest of the ruler, the dynasty, and the empire (which amounted to the same thing) was the overriding object of political economy, which was a body of instrumental knowledge at the service of autocrats. This extractive and fixed zero-sum view of wealth resulted in governments treating their subject populations as suppliers of income (and sometimes manpower) who existed to sustain the power, wealth, and privileges of the ruling elite.

A fundamental characteristic of European dynasticism was the lack of distinction between the state and the ruler, as expressed in the famous claim of Louis XIV: "L'état, c'est moi." Here is the hallmark and hubris of absolutism, which dominated European statecraft for almost three centuries and was, according to Mises, "still alive at the three European imperial courts [Vienna, Berlin, and St. Petersburg] until the . . . upheavals [of World War I]."[9] Thus the wealth of a country and its inhabitants was dynastic and not individual, communal, or national. The extensive domains of the Hapsburgs and Hohenzollerns and the much farther flung territories of the Romanovs (which by the eighteenth century stretched from the Baltic to the Pacific) were ultimately the property not of the peoples who lived in them but of the ruling dynasty that held them as its sovereign estates.

Since these lands were largely, if not indeed overwhelmingly, agricultural, the political economy of dynasticism often therefore came down to that of agricultural estate management. "Princes regard countries no differently from the way an estate owner regards his forests, meadows, and fields. They sell them, they exchange them . . . and each time rule over the inhabitants is transferred also."[10] While the nobility and gentry also had their landed estates, in the Continental absolutist state these lands were held on sufferance from the crown and were not independent of it. The ethics of estate management, both for the ruler and the landlords, was to pass the estate on to one's successor at least in the same condition as one received it and if possible in a more developed state. Rulers and landlords enjoyed an institutional insurance policy which in ordinary circumstances guaranteed their tenure until they died, at which time it would be passed on to their dynastic successors, usually their children. In these circumstances it was possible to invest in the long term with the confidence that the fruits of such investment would be enjoyed if not by the current lord and his family and immediate circle, then at least by their children.

The point and dynamic of dynastic economic statecraft was fundamentally political, however. "The princely state strives restlessly for expansion of its territory. . . . The more land and the more subjects, the more revenues and the more soldiers. . . . Smaller states are always in danger of being swallowed by larger ones."[11] Political economy came to have a prominent place in the instrumental knowledge of statecraft that was built up; all of it aimed at enabling the dynasty to expand or at least survive, permitting the current trustees of the royal patrimony to pass it on to their successors if not enlarged, at least not diminished from what it had been when they inherited it. Of course failures as well as successes were registered, as could be expected in a system which was ultimately competitive and combative. There was no insurance against a ruler (or advisers) who refused or failed to master the arts of statecraft. Nor was there insurance against unfortunate geopolitical location. Many of the smaller and weaker states of Europe, and even some of the larger and stronger ones, failed to meet the test of a competitive system and temporarily or permanently disappeared as a result of either conquest or voluntary incorporation into other political units. Poland was partitioned and divided between Russia, Prussia, and Austria in 1795 and ceased to exist as a sovereign entity until 1916. From this example it is clear that the failure of one state was simultaneously the success of others in a zero-sum international political game focused largely if not exclusively on the possession of territory, the principal source of wealth and power.[12]

The age of absolutism was strongly marked by the demotion and even dissolution of various autonomous communities and bodies that were the legacy of feudalism, such as landed nobility, clergy, towns, universities, and guilds. It was the achievement of the absolutist states to rise above feudal particularisms and establish the unquestioned authority of the crown throughout their jurisdictions: "The absolute ruler not only regards every other community between his subjects as dangerous, so that he tries to dissolve all traditional comradely relations between them that do not derive their origin from state laws enacted by him and is hostile to every new formation of community . . . [but also] in seeking to tear apart all class ties to make subjects out of nobles, the bourgeoisie, and peasants, the prince atomizes the social body and thereby creates the precondition for the rise of a new political sentiment."[13] The dynastic state also was characterized by its uses of various royal privileges, grants, licenses, and other dispensations issued to individuals or groups to enhance its authority and control over important sectors of the society and economy.[14]

Probably the greatest success story of European absolutism was France in the seventeenth century, when Jean Colbert (1619–1683) served as chief adviser to Louis XIV. Colbert was the leading architect of a unified and powerful French monarchy in which the estates were subordinated successfully and permanently to the crown. His economic policy was that of protection and regimentation (as one historian puts it); these contained the seeds of later economic nationalism, but in Colbert's time they aimed solely at enhancing the power and wealth of the monarchy.[15] The absolutist French state presided over not only the destruction of feudalism but also the creation of a nation which for seventeenth-century Europe was unprecedented in its size; the dynasty came to depend upon its twenty million subjects for whatever success it enjoyed both militarily and economically.[16] In the end, however, it was destroyed by its own creation.

The French experience is not a trustworthy guide to the fate of European dynasticism, however. In Central and Eastern Europe the dynastic states never obliterated feudal society as thoroughly as did France. Indeed, they were in no position to do so since they were multinational empires, and nationalism would have ripped the state apart rather than unified it. They succeeded only in subordinating the diverse ethnolinguistic peasantries while accommodating the rise of middle-class groups of businessmen, intellectuals, and artists who opposed the excesses and abuses of absolutism. Opposition was evident in the revolutions of 1830 and 1848, which shook the confidence of the absolute monarchs and their advisers although they failed to overthrow them.[17] The Hapsburg monarchy is the clearest example of the failure of Central European dynasticism: throughout the nineteenth century it tried to reduce or contain rising social pressures from new urban groups and classes, some of whom were simultaneously the intellectual voices of various subordinated nationalities, such as the Hungarians,

Czechs, or Croats. It is perhaps only a slight exaggeration to say that the political self-consciousness of these nationalities was largely the work of their urban intelligentsias, who were themselves created by the empires and who increasingly elected to write and propagandize in their native languages rather than German. Their voices could not be silenced forever.

Throughout most of the nineteenth century the Ottoman Empire had been "the sick man of Europe." By the twentieth century this could also be said of the Hapsburg and Romanov dynasties. They all confronted the rising internal pressures outlined above. In the end it required war to make their debilities clear, to destroy the absolutist states, and to bring about the international enfranchisement (based on self-determination) of their numerous subordinated nationalities. The League of Nations legitimated and legalized the partition of these empires and the liberation of their nationalities, thereby fundamentally altering the political map of Central and Eastern Europe.

In the remainder of this chapter we argue that the European partition and colonization of the African continent in the late nineteenth century was an act which created political systems that in some important respects reflected the dynastic states of Eastern Europe. The European empires in Africa looked rather like the Austro-Hungarian or Russian or Turkish empires except that these colonial territories were overseas. African lands and populations added to the economic assets of the imperial states. Cheap labor was available for the development of cash-crop agriculture and mines, whose products could be exported and sold at a profit on world markets or at a guaranteed price in the metropole. The colonies were small annexes to the metropolitan economy: at a minimum they were expected to provide a tax base for colonial government, making it unnecessary to draw on the imperial treasury (a move which would have been unpopular), and to provide opportunities for profitable investment and trade.[18]

The postcolonial states inherited this system of political economy from their colonial predecessors, but the new African rulers soon proceeded in most cases personally to appropriate the inherited government powers and assets in a manner not unlike the dynastic rulers of the East European past. However, there was one fundamental difference between the dynastic states of Europe and the personal regimes of Africa: the latter lacked any institutional mechanism for the transfer of power and wealth from one ruler to the next. The effect of this was to discourage long-term investment and economic management of a mercantilist kind and to encourage corruption and consumption—in some countries even to the point where the national treasury was in danger of being exhausted. Thus, instead of providing a mechanism of economic growth and development, African personal regimes actually became an instrument of economic contraction and deterioration. Whereas one can speak of a political economy of the European princely state, one is inclined to speak of a political dyseconomy of the African personal regime.

The Colonial State

Although African economic development never lived up to the dreams of some imperialists and capitalists and more than a few lost rather than made money, Africa was incorporated into the imperial economies and the world economy. The colonial territories specialized in the export of various primary commodities: the Gold Coast (Ghana) in cocoa, Senegal in peanuts, Guinea in bananas, Sudan in cotton, Nigeria in peanuts, cocoa, and palm oil, Uganda in cotton and coffee, Zanzibar in cloves, the Congo (Zaire) and Northern Rhodesia (Zambia) in copper, Mozambique in cotton, Kenya in coffee and tea, Tanganyika (Tanzania) in sisal, Angola in coffee, Southern Rhodesia (Zimbabwe) in tobacco and sugar—to name a few. While most colonies carved out a niche for such exports, economic development was rarely large. The cocoa economy of the Gold Coast produced substantial increases in per capita income during colonial times, making the colony the richest British holding in Sub-Saharan Africa. However, the Gold Coast was only a minor appendage to the British Empire. Moreover, the African continent as a whole was of limited importance to the world economy.[19] This economic insignificance continued after independence and remains today: in 1970 Africa's share of world commerce was only 2.4 percent; by the mid-1980s it had fallen to 1.7 percent.[20]

The European acquisition of populated African territory went against the democratic principles of social mobilization and political citizenship that by the late nineteenth century were transforming and in many cases already had transformed European countries into national states. Colonialism was a throwback to the era of dynastic states in its approach to the acquisition and holding of territory. Possession was based on either unequal treaties with African rulers or, if they resisted, conquest. African international frontiers were arbitrary. Most colonies were composed of many culturally diverse populations, and nearly all empires consisted of geographically separated territories. Intraimperial boundaries were sometimes redefined, with the result that colonial jurisdictions could be created, enlarged, reduced, or extinguished—without consultation with the indigenous peoples. Upper Volta (Burkina Faso) appeared, disappeared, and reappeared on the map of French West Africa. Germany acquired approximately 100,000 square miles of territory from France to be added to Kamerun (Cameroon) for recognizing France's protectorate over Morocco in 1911. Five thousand square kilometers was transferred from Tanganyika to Rwanda-Urundi in 1923. The frontier between Uganda and Kenya was moved westward, and as a result Kenya expanded considerably.[21] Imperial powers did not consider that Africans had legitimate political interests in such questions. They were objects or at most subjects of colonial policy, which was determined and in many places even executed without their involvement. Paternalism was the rule.

In the typical interwar colonial governments we see few signs of prototype modern states. Rather, we see very small authoritarian governments that in manpower, finances, facilities, equipment, and materiel were more like local administrations than anything else. The European layer of domination was remarkably thin throughout Sub-Saharan Africa during the entire colonial era.[22] Colonies resembled the postfeudal and preindustrial states of Europe, also small-scale operations by twentieth-century standards. In addition, their simple and usually agrarian economies were more like those of old Europe, except that they were geared to exports. Even the most elaborate colonial government in tropical Africa—the Belgian administration in the Congo, which ruled a huge territory of more than 900,000 square miles and at independence in 1960 a population of fifteen million— was not a big operation, although it was the closest any African colony came to being an instance of etatism.[23] In our terms the Congo was reminiscent of the more successful dynastic states of old Europe, and its administration bore more than slight resemblance to Colbert's France.[24]

It was not until after World War II that changes introduced by colonial powers began to transform society. All colonial powers of course had pursued policies that either directly or indirectly, deliberately or inadvertently, had resulted in social changes: they had introduced literacy and often education; they had printed and circulated money; they had mobilized labor and provoked migration; they had fostered the construction of harbors, railways, and roads; they had promoted investment in cash crops or mines; they had built towns some of which grew into cities. In short, they had fostered the conditions for novel occupations: cash-crop farmers, landless agricultural laborers (in settler societies such as Kenya and Southern Rhodesia), miners, servants, clerks, businessmen, teachers, and in a few cases

lawyers and doctors (among others). Increasing numbers of people traveled, took up residence, and sometimes began to live permanently away
from their traditional rural communities.[25] A major contribution of James
Coleman to African studies was his comprehensive documentation and
analysis of this process of social mobilization in colonial Nigeria.[26]

After the war the British—and later and more reluctantly the French, and
the Belgians—embarked on constitutional changes to accommodate within
new political frameworks not only these novel societal roles and groups,
which were minorities, but also the large majority of rural Africans who
were less affected by social change. Such constitutional engineering was
most evident in British Africa, where it was a necessary preliminary to
decolonization and the transfer of power. It was introduced in French and
Belgian territories far more abruptly and belatedly in the late 1950s. In
Portuguese Africa it was never tried. Instead the imperial power defied
world opinion and resisted African demands for independence. As a result,
by the 1960s armed national liberation movements came into existence in
Guinea-Bissau, Angola, and Mozambique; they had international moral
and material support, the latter from Communist powers. They eventually
succeeded in securing a transfer of power in 1974–75 following a military
coup in Portugal in April 1974. In Southern Rhodesia (Zimbabwe) the
presence of a constitutionally and economically privileged white settler
community complicated and interrupted the British effort at constitutional
decolonization and led to a civil war between the illegal white regime of Ian
Smith and African liberation movements armed and supported by foreign
sources; the war was not resolved until 1979–80.[27] Namibia's independence
from South Africa under United Nations auspices in 1990 brought to an end
a long and bitter struggle of African liberation.

These social and political developments rarely resulted in the creation of
what might reasonably and accurately be termed civil societies and nation-
states.[28] Coleman thought of such developments in terms of nationalism.
But they seldom if ever were the equivalent of the rise of subject peoples
and the overthrow of dynasticism in Europe. Africans did indeed rebel
against colonialism, their rebellion hastened the transfer of power, and
the colonial powers returned home. However, a civically competent and
constitutionally enfranchised population upon whom the sovereignty of
the state rested did not emerge—at least not in most countries or for any
significant period. No self-aware national citizenry was created. Nor were
autonomous economic groups, based on property and particularly land
ownership, encouraged. Counterweights to themselves were precisely

what most new African rulers feared most, and they usually set about promptly after independence to reduce or eliminate them.

The coming of independence led to the widespread establishment of political and military monopolies and to restrictions on the autonomy of embryonic civil and political associations. Few African rulers would tolerate such associations, which might serve as bases for political opponents. Opposition parties were usually outlawed, and their leaders either co-opted into the monopoly or denied the opportunity to participate in politics legally. While constitutions described the formal arrangements of governance, the real authority usually resided in the person of the new African rulers, many of whom adopted the trappings of presidential monarchs. Whether there would be stability and peace or not often depended almost entirely on the will and skill of such individuals. Palace politics was an exclusive affair of the elite from which the general population was excluded.[29] In effect, something resembling European dynastic regimes came into being in twentieth-century Africa.

The Personally Appropriated State

The ex-colonial government administration became the central pillar of virtually every new state in Sub-Saharan Africa, but it was not employed in the same manner as it had been under European command. Previously it had operated in the normal bureaucratic way as an instrument of policy: colonial government was the principal means by which European imperial powers ruled their African territories and subjects. Its essential executive, administrative, professional, and technical personnel were Europeans who had been carefully selected for their posts and were expected to make a career of them. They were imperial proconsuls in elitist administrations who formed their own social circles isolated from surrounding African social influences; in most countries very few Africans were ever admitted to the ruling class before independence. There was more than a hint of Plato's guardian class in colonial administration.[30]

After independence most small ex-colonial state apparatuses sooner or later were transformed into far larger patrimonial-type administrations in which staff were less agents of state policy (civil servants) than proprietors, distributors, and even major consumers of the authority and resources of the government. Government administration came to be viewed as a source of power, prestige, and enrichment for those who were clever or fortunate enough to control and staff it. Its operations were affected by norms of personalism, familism, and ethnic favoritism. Although this transformation from instrumental to proprietary administration varied from one country to the next, it was evident in most, and sometimes significantly so.[31]

The emergence of personally appropriated government can be attributed to related factors, which of course are more evident in some countries than in others and which we can identify only in passing. First, decolonization was understood by many Africans as an opportunity not merely to take control of their own political destiny but also to acquire and enjoy a Western standard of living. An example was the widespread expectation that African officials must have the same salaries and perquisites as their European predecessors, even though their country was no longer connected with a European imperial state where high standards existed and could be sustained without difficulty. There was little perception that state salaries, perquisites, and emoluments should be adjusted downward in recognition of the poverty of the newly independent country. This cargo-cult mentality was by no means confined to elites but was widely disseminated among the politically aware population.[32]

Second, such unrealistic political expectations led eventually to enormous costs as civil service and public sector employment got out of control. According to the World Bank, Africa has levels of "public employment" substantially higher than Asia or even Latin America.[33] This happened, in part, because at the same time the state was being indigenized, it also took on—under the influence of statist and socialist doctrines—additional responsibilities, such as planning, managing, and executing the development process, often through new parastatal organizations. In other words, at the very time that the capability and reliability of the state apparatus was decreasing owing to unusually rapid and wholesale Africanization, it was in many countries being greatly enlarged. Zambia, for example, despite an extreme shortage of university-trained personnel, expanded its bureaucracy some sixfold in the first decade of independence, during which time the process of Zambianization was completed.[34] Ghana's bureaucracy increased eightfold between 1972 and 1980, while Tanzania's tripled in the same period. During a five-year oil boom in the early 1980s, Cameroon doubled its number of civil servants. Many other examples could also be given.[35] Consequently, salaries and perquisites consume a generally very high proportion of government budgets.

Third, the domestic social environment encouraged, if indeed it did not insist upon, the appropriation of state offices and the redirection of government opportunities and resources into the service of personal, familial, and ethnic interests. Unlike their European predecessors, African officials were not sheltered from the surrounding society. They were intimately connected to it by ties of kinship and clan and ethnic affiliation and therefore were exposed (as their European predecessors never had been) to its expectations and demands.[36] Consequently, nepotism, patronage, clientage, and corruption became far more distinguishing features of most African states than of their colonial predecessors. Among the most important societal conditions for this Africanization of the state were political cultures that conceived of government offices and resources in terms of possession and consumption; multiethnic societies whose groupings wanted at least their equitable share of the governmental cake, if they could not have it all; politicians who recognized that granting or denying access to government offices and resources was a crucial modus operandi for expanding and retaining power, and, of course, the absence of, or at most the scarcity of, alternative sources of power, status, and wealth.[37]

Fourth, the political institutions, legal norms, and administrative regulations that defined the uses and abuses of political power and almost always were inherited from colonial regimes proved to be largely and in some cases entirely without legitimacy or force when confronted by the above-mentioned social dynamics. They were abstract, remote, impersonal, and therefore unreal: phantoms that nobody could see, hear, touch, taste. In Western countries even at the best of times it is difficult to justify government policies by reference to impersonal public or social interests that are remote from the ordinary citizen. But at least in these countries there is a developed sense of citizenship, and governments are accountable to mass electorates that regularly install and remove them over the heads of vested interests. In most African countries a sense of citizenship or government accountability is either nonexistent or embryonic, and political life is propelled by a strong awareness of the concrete, the here and now, the personal and familial, and therefore the palpable and the real.[38]

Fifth, many African countries experienced serious political instability and civil strife (as indicated, for example, by military coups and internal wars) that had the effect of sharply reducing political time horizons so that rulers (and their confederates) focused their attention on consuming state resources and transferring abroad for safekeeping what could not be spent locally. Where there is a major producer of foreign earnings—such as mining corporations or agricultural marketing boards—and governments are weak, corrupt, or undisciplined, the export sector is often targeted for political exploitation. It is of course impossible to determine the amount of public funds that have been misappropriated. The World Bank conservatively estimates that "hundreds of millions of dollars have been siphoned off to private bank accounts outside of Africa."[39] In Zaire it is reported that President Mobutu Sese Seko alone by 1984 had accumulated personal wealth of $5 billion.[40] Western bankers, when pressed about their unwillingness to get involved in African debt forgiveness, have implied that a substantial proportion of their previous loans to African countries had ended up in the West in the private accounts and holdings of African political elites without ever being invested in Africa.[41] This short-term personal incentive to diminish the wealth of the nation in regimes of African personal rule may be contrasted with the institutional incentive of dynastic regimes to invest in the future wealth and welfare of the dynastic state.

Finally, unlike most states elsewhere in the world today and in the past—including the dynastic states of old Europe—African countries became members of a benign and even benevolent international community which treated them as protectorates. African sovereignty was guaranteed by the United Nations, and rival power blocs of the cold war upheld it because each bloc was competing for the public approbation of the Third World. In the usual argument the cold war led to threats and acts of foreign intervention in African states—as in Ethiopia and Angola.[42] However, we believe these are exceptional cases and that the major effect of the East-West conflict was the creation of a space for the emergence and survival of marginal states. Such a guarantee appears to have had several consequences. African personal regimes did not have to worry about foreign intervention, invasion, or occupation. Nor did they have to be concerned with developing military, administrative, fiscal, and economic capabilities to deter intervention or confront it should it happen. In brief, they were freed from what has been an important international motivation historically to engage in state building and economic development.[43] They were actually supported by the West, particularly the United States, for geopolitical reasons related to the East-West conflict.[44] Thus, they were not under the same external compulsions to engage in developmental activities, and whether they did or not was therefore determined more by their own choices and the domestic situation in which they found themselves. In most cases the choice was to use the scarce resources of what were always impoverished countries for their own benefit.

To sum up, many if indeed not most African rulers discouraged rather than encouraged self-discipline, rationality, cost-consciousness, future-orientation, and similar behavior that makes for development in the longer term. Most became infected by nepotism, patronage, corruption, and tribalism. Such governments usually could not be relied upon to promote development, except incidentally as an unintended by-product of their self-indulgence. Indeed they existed for purposes that might be summed up as enhancing the life-styles of the political elites who controlled them. Politics came down to a struggle for the spoils of the state. We believe that these pathological characteristics—which by the late 1960s had already been documented by one very perceptive observer—have important implications for African political economy.[45]

The Political Dyseconomy of Personal Rule

Africa's rulers have confronted many difficult choices since independence but among the most difficult has been that between tolerating (and perhaps even indulging) the politics of spoils and trying to restrain or at least deflect it for the sake of national wealth and public welfare. We consider here a few instances of each tendency.

Where African leaders have tolerated and even invited nepotism, clientelism, and corruption within the state apparatus—often fostering what can only be called a corrupted state—we usually witness economic difficulty and decline, what might be termed a political dyseconomy. The elite are a heavy drain on what are usually not very strong economies in the first place, and they weaken and debilitate them further. In highly unstable regimes where personal rulers enter and exit through revolving doors, with many attempting to appropriate as much as they can in the shortest time possible, this is usually a predictable consequence. However, even where personal rulers are survivors and hang on to power for lengthy periods, the same debilitating process can be perpetuated, and decline can be equated to the prolongation of the regime. Among some of the countries where this has happened are Mobutu Sese Seko's Zaire, Kenneth Kaunda's Zambia, and Siaka Stevens's Sierra Leone.

Zaire is the classic case of the corrupted state in Africa and home to *le mal zairois,* the Zaire disease.[46] The state has been bound to the compulsive desire of President Mobutu to survive politically. This preoccupation comes before everything else. Zaire is potentially a rich country, certainly by African standards, with a sizable population of about thirty-five million, ample productive land, and abundant natural resources. Yet a hallmark of the country in the past fifteen years or more has been a decline in its resource-based economy, partly as a result of falling world copper prices. In 1987 with a GNP per capita of $150, Zaire was the third poorest country in Africa.[47] There have been few state-supported efforts to develop agriculture to counteract this decline. Zairois absolutism has completely lost sight of the public good. Instead of attempting to promote the wealth and welfare of the population, the government ignores the people. Ordinary people sustain themselves by subsistence farming or by eking out a living in the vast informal sector of self-help production and exchange that constitutes the real economy of the country and ironically serves to balance the dys-economy of the formal sector.

Mobutu has maintained power for a quarter century by mastering the skills of political survival: co-opting elites into the government, offering and withholding state privileges, using favors as a means of making individuals dependent on him, and resorting to threats and coercion if all else fails. What is "the state" in Zaire? If not simply Mobutu, then certainly the system of patronage, corruption, and coercion centered upon him. The copper industry has been the declining treasure trove of Mobutu's corrupted state; Mobutu survives politically and enriches himself economically primarily by taking a percentage off the top of copper export sales. In the past Mobutu also has cultivated ties with developed countries—particularly the United States, which has been prepared for the sake of its own foreign policy interests to regard him as an ally and provide him with aid to prevent the collapse or overthrow of his regime. The World Bank and the IMF have likewise supported Mobutu, but they have been frustrated in obliging his government to conform to their fiscal and monetary disciplines. With the ending of the cold war this is changing. Zaire's ruler has been deprived of uncritical foreign support; this is a serious deprivation as his hold on power weakens, and rivals are willing to exploit it. He has found the United States and other powers insisting on political reforms, such as democratization, if he wishes to enjoy continued United States assistance. He may find international financial institutions unwilling to make the concessions they have in the past if he can no longer count on the support of the United States. By 1992 he was finally obliged by internal riots and the rebellion of elements of his own army at least to share power with elements of the opposition.[48] This predicament is not confined to Mobutu but is complicating the lives of all despots who in the past have survived at least in part by exploiting the East-West conflict for their own ends.

Zambia bears many similarities to Zaire.[49] Here, too, the copper-exporting industry is in decline, not only from falling world prices but also from a gradual exhaustion of deposits. It has been exploited politically to support a bloated establishment of some 90,000 among whom patronage and corruption have been extensive. Zambians themselves have described the bureaucracy as "ineffective and inefficient," more concerned with filling out forms than meeting national objectives. In December 1987 the chairman of the Zambian Public Accounts Committee, discussing mismanagement of foreign aid, noted that "in most cases there is no accountability, resulting in a lot of money being either misapplied or misappropriated."[50] As in Zaire, external loans feed the system. But the external dependency of Zambia on a single export commodity is greater than that of Zaire and exceptional even for Africa. Zambia is the one-industry country par excellence. Furthermore, with declining copper prices this has translated into heavy dependency on the IMF and World Bank for loans. Traditional agriculture—food production—has been neglected. This was true even at the time of independence in 1964, but food dependency has more than doubled since then, along with urbanization; today almost half the population lives in cities and towns.

Kenneth Kaunda ruled the country for a quarter century, during which the economy has been highly politicized. Besides the large cohort of government employees, organized mine workers and urban residents generally have been the main beneficiaries of government-subsidized prices for food and other commodities. This has required the depression of prices paid to farmers for their food crops. Furthermore, the agricultural sector has been deprived of the incentives and resources to grow (e.g., fertilizers, roads, markets). In effect, peasant farmers have been exploited to support urban residents, and the agricultural economy has been undermined. Unlike in Zaire, where Mobutu's predation promoted dyseconomy, in Zambia it was Kaunda's lack of political strength and will to resist the self-indulgence of the key groups upon whom his regime depended for survival that promoted dyseconomy. He catered to them and in the course of doing so bankrupted his country. Zambia became by African standards a very heavily indebted country, with a total external debt in 1988 of about $6,500 million; per capita debt is the second highest in Sub-Saharan Africa, behind only the Ivory Coast. Unlike the Ivorian case, however, virtually all Zambian debt is from public sources: few significant private bankers or investors have been willing to lend money to Zambia. For them there is not an economy worthy of the name in which to invest. Foreign governments and international organizations, such as the IMF and World Bank, have really been providing welfare funds more than business credits. In short, to survive,

Kaunda took the politically easy course, which has unfortunately required the depletion of the economy. He blamed his problems on circumstances beyond his control, such as low world prices for Zambia's copper and high interest rates on Zambia's loans, which no doubt have been constraints on his freedom of action. But instead of taking the best course in the circumstances, he surrendered to those constraints, becoming, in effect, their prisoner.

During the 1970s Kaunda projected an image of the great African liberator, struggling first against Portuguese colonialism, then against Ian Smith's racist government of Rhodesia, and finally against apartheid South Africa. For a long time it worked, and his Western creditors ignored his economic mismanagement. But in the early 1980s he was obliged by the IMF—which is after all a bank and not a charity—to make structural reforms that involved abandoning subsidized food prices and devaluing the currency to real values—i.e., those determined by exchange rates and not by government fiat. Urban riots and strikes at the end of 1986 and beginning of 1987 influenced him to terminate the IMF restructuring program in May 1987. However, desperate for new loans to feed the political appetites of its supporters, Kaunda's regime returned to the IMF program in 1989. In 1990 Kaunda promised to abolish the one-party state and institute multiparty democracy in 1991; in the elections he was defeated by Frederick Chiluba, a trade unionist and leader of the Movement for a Multiparty Democracy.[51] Whatever the shape of the new order, Zambian agriculture will have to be transformed and integrated into the country's economy. Prudent rulership has long demanded this policy, which would have been necessary in a one-industry country even if the copper industry had not suffered a decline.

Toward the end of colonial times and for about ten years after independence in 1961, Sierra Leone was a comparatively prosperous country.[52] During this period the small West African state achieved an average annual economic growth rate of over 7 percent, one of the highest in black Africa, derived mainly from mining exports (diamonds, gold, iron, and bauxite). Agriculture was also important. Sierra Leone consequently has substantial economic resources, which, if properly managed, could benefit its population. However, during the personal rule of President Siaka Stevens (1968–85), a measure of political stability based on the distribution of spoils was purchased at the price of economic decline, which became precipitous in the mid-1970s and continued until Stevens voluntarily gave up power in 1985. There was a negative rate of growth between 1980 and 1987. Although the country suffered from the economic shocks of the 1970s and early

1980s—rising oil bills, reduced prices for raw material exports, higher inflation, increased interest rates on foreign borrowing—decline was not inevitable. According to a recent analysis, "In his memoirs . . . Stevens admitted
candidly that he had attached more importance to politics than to economics."[53] Like Kaunda, Stevens indulged rather than resisted a political
culture which "encourages or tolerates maladministration, bureaucratic
incompetence, and corruption," all of which have resulted in a parasitic
state feeding on a debilitated economy.[54] A thriving black market in diamonds, a major export earner, rewarded many officials who were in a
position to suppress it and simultaneously deprived the state of foreign
earnings and the public benefits that could have accrued from them. Although Sierra Leone's political culture invited such conduct, Stevens had
some choice about accepting it.

Although leaders in general are confined by circumstances—which may
sometimes be very restrictive—it is difficult to imagine a situation where
they do not have some latitude in decision making. To believe otherwise is
to subscribe to a determinism which not only eliminates political choice
but also denies government the possibility of turning difficult situations
around. There was some evidence of at least the start of a positive change in
Sierra Leone. In 1985 Stevens was followed by his chosen successor, Major
General Joseph Saidu Momoh, who proclaimed a new order and embarked
on an economic reform program of structural adjustment encouraged and
supported by the IMF and World Bank. He initially spoke out forcefully
against personal abuses of public office and dismissed corrupt ministers.
However, years of decay precipitated and sustained by the self-indulgence
of the elite were not going to be ended overnight. Even with assistance
from international bodies and ample mineral resources, it would take years
to turn the declining economy of Sierra Leone around. By the time of
the April 1992 coup by young "unco-opted" officers that Major General
Momoh's presidency was supposed to safeguard against, little if any economic progress had been achieved. Rather, corruption and decay characterized the regime, and Sierra Leone found itself at the bottom of the
United Nations Human Development Index. The "skilled political leadership" that David Luke and Stephen Riley recognized in 1989 as essential to
bring about some economic growth and progress failed to come forth "to
insulate the fragile basis and management of the economy from the kinds
of pressures that are inherent in the neo-patrimonial character of the regime."[55] The new military regime of Captain Valentine Strasser has a for-

midable task ahead in fostering political, social, and economic reform to this badly governed country.[56]

In most African countries there have been expectations and pressures which if not resisted would lead to a corrupted state and a declining economy, and in many they have been indulged by the political leaders with those results. However, in some countries such conditions have not been totally accepted by those who rule. In Kenya, Côte d'Ivoire, and Malawi the political economy for most of the time since independence has registered growth and even development, rather than stagnation or decline. We believe that the conduct of the rulers is an important element of the explanation.

The key to the positive relation between personal rule and economic development in Kenya was President Jomo Kenyatta (and his advisers), who saw his future interest in developing the modern administrative service and agricultural system inherited from the colonial period.[57] Colonial Kenya was noteworthy for its highly developed agricultural economy, which had to sustain settlers from Europe at a European standard of living, and its bureaucracy, which supported and serviced this economy. Kenyatta's government recognized that this colonial inheritance, particularly the cash-crop agricultural export system, was crucial to national development and therefore had to be preserved and promoted, not exploited or corrupted. Kenyatta built up the administrative state as a development institution and isolated it as far as possible from patronage politics. The role of agricultural experts in policy-making continued and expanded. Productive European-occupied land was transferred to Africans by means of a system of freehold tenure. Kenya's African smallholders became independent cash-crop producers and were allowed to earn near world prices for their coffee and tea. Furthermore, productive landholding by African elites in the agricultural system was not only permitted but encouraged, and their holdings were a source of both status and substantial income. They consequently asserted and secured a measure of independence from the state that is unusual for contemporary Africa and gives indications of an emergent civil society. In short, many Kenyans, smallholder peasants and large-holder gentry alike, acquired a stake in the inherited agricultural system and an interest in its effective servicing by a reliable and technically competent government administration.

Many studies explain Kenya's economic success by noting the rational interest in the agricultural sector. There undoubtedly have been strong constituencies supporting agricultural development.[58] But there were (there always are) other interests as well. Kenya is as exposed as any African country to the debilitating consequences associated with the personally appropriated state. Although the political culture of nepotism, patronage, and corruption was present in Kenya, it was not allowed to threaten modern administrative and agricultural institutions. Only in the years immediately preceding Kenyatta's death in 1978 had the political culture begun to interfere with these institutions. Kenyatta understood the crucial importance of the colonial legacy for Kenya's economic future, and he was not deflected by alternative ideologies, such as socialism (which encourages statism). He listened to practical agricultural experts, who knew very well what the agricultural system required of the government.[59] Finally and perhaps most important, he exercised effective control over the political process and resisted political demands to corrupt the state apparatus.

Kenya's success may not last, however. President Daniel arap Moi—who constitutionally succeeded Kenyatta in 1978—has been attempting to govern with less reliance upon Kenyatta's Kikuyu followers and more support from many parts of the country which are outside the most productive sectors of the agricultural export economy. He seems prepared to take certain risks with the economy if it is necessary to remain in power. He has attempted to redistribute wealth from the more productive beneficiaries of the Kenyatta regime to his own less productive supporters, who probably feel that they are entitled to such benefits now that they are in power. Indeed, many of Moi's ethnic supporters—who are Kalenjin—occupy major positions of power and authority in the state.[60] Moi's efforts to hang on to power have unleashed dyseconomies, and Kenya could become just another stagnating or declining African country. While a change of ruler and regime gave new hope to Zambia, in Kenya the change from Kenyatta to Moi has led to the opposite effect.

What may be occurring in Kenya, however, is not merely a shift of the state's patronage as some individuals and groups rise in the ruler's favor and others fall. It may also be the transformation of society, from one based primarily on parochial groups to another encompassing broader interests and ideals—i.e., a rudimentary civil society. New groups and classes are emerging, especially among the better educated who might be prepared to demand laws and policies that address their nonparochial concerns. Demands have been registered for civil and political rights, including political participation based on free elections involving more than one party. In an effort to hang on to power, Moi—the patronage politician par excellence—

responded in the predictably authoritarian way by clamping down. He has failed to silence the opposition, and the conflict persists, preparing the way for political change with the encouragement of Western powers since 1990. Under pressure from international donors, Moi accepted in December 1991 multipartism.[61] The first multiparty election in twenty-six years occurred in December 1992, with Moi retaining the presidency but with only a bare plurality or about 36 percent of the vote among a divided opposition.

Félix Houphouët-Boigny, for thirty-two years the president of Côte d'Ivoire, has held to the view that politics must be subordinated to economics.[62] He made it clear at independence in 1960 that economic growth and development were the unquestioned goal of his government: production came before participation and distribution. It was not until the 1980s that he began to relent by permitting competitive elections for legislative seats within the framework of his single ruling party. He encouraged foreign (particularly French) investment and invited high-level manpower from France to serve as both economic advisers and policymakers. Houphouët-Boigny played Louis XIV and his French technocrats Colbert in a statist economy which differed from mercantilism mainly in seeking substantial foreign investment. The state encouraged cash-crop agriculture in coffee and cocoa by small-scale peasant producers, who created an economic surplus which was heavily taxed and reinvested by the state. Although the government taxed this productive peasantry, it took care to maintain higher prices than neighboring Ghana, also a major producer of cocoa; this was sufficient to sustain production and deter the peasants from smuggling their product abroad. During the 1970s Côte d'Ivoire displaced Ghana as the world's leading cocoa producer and surpassed Nigeria in palm oil production while also becoming the largest coffee producer in Africa. The country sustained an average annual economic growth rate of about 7 percent, an achievement referred to as "the Ivorian miracle." In the same period highly politicized Ghana, with virtually identical resources, suffered an equally stunning economic decline under a succession of unstable civilian and military regimes.

Ivorian neomercantilism ran into difficulties in the 1980s as a result of declining world commodity prices combined with heavy foreign borrowing. By 1989 the debt had accumulated to some $14 billion, second in aggregate only to Nigeria's but in per capita terms the highest in Sub-Saharan Africa. Economic growth was only slightly more than 2 percent during the 1980s. (Several African economies were by then registering negative rates.) By the mid-1980s problems of servicing the debt had led to restructuring agreements with the IMF. This placed downward pressures on government (and related) salaries and upward pressures on prices, provoking serious political dissatisfaction. In the spring of 1990 riots broke out in Abidjan, the capital, and Houphouët-Boigny (then aged about eighty-five) announced that there would be political changes, particularly the establishment of a multiparty system with greater accountability. In late autumn 1990 Houphouët-Boigny was reelected in a multiparty national election. Consequently, although Côte d'Ivoire had for two decades escaped the worst debilities of patrimonial government (there always was a certain incidence of corruption), by 1990 it was no longer able to avoid simultaneous external pressures for greater self-discipline and internal demands for increased political participation.

Malawi was also a neomercantilist agricultural success story, at least until the 1980s.[63] Dr. Ngwazi Kamuzu Banda, president for life, has been the sole ruler of the country since independence in 1964. The holding company he owns is the largest single shareholder in two commercial banks; he also own agricultural estates. Even the ruler, therefore, is a major mercantilistic, as are other members of the ruling elite, who have been encouraged by Banda to become mercantilists themselves.

Malawi has an overwhelmingly agrarian economy, divided between small-scale peasant producers and large estates. Development policy has deliberately favored the latter at the expense of the former. The main export cash crops are tobacco, sugar, and tea. Peasant producers have been prohibited from growing the most valuable tobacco, which fetches higher prices on world markets. Between 1964 and 1984 the output of tobacco produced on estates increased by 15 percent annually. Wages of estate workers—who by 1980 were half the work force of the country—were kept deliberately low to generate funds for reinvestment. In an effort to secure the supply of labor, the government prevented Malawians from traveling to other countries (including South Africa) to find work at higher wages.[64] For most of the 1970s about two-thirds of the profits of the state marketing boards, to which peasants were forced to sell their crops, were reinvested in the estates. Another 22 percent was invested in commerce and industry.[65] This policy has resulted in one of the highest average annual growth rates of GNP in Sub-Saharan Africa since the end of colonialism: almost 6 percent between 1965 and 1973, about 5 percent for the rest of the 1970s, and just under 3 percent for most of the 1980s (when many other African economies were not growing at all or were shrinking).[66]

The Malawian policy deliberately withheld the surplus created by peasant producers and farm workers and transferred it to large estates and private companies, some of them owned by the president and other members of the ruling elite. In short, producers were regarded and treated, in the classical mercantilistic manner, as merely instruments of production. Banda and other members of the ruling elite were direct beneficiaries of the policy. Moreover, the controls placed by the state on ordinary Malawians have been severe, and the accumulated human costs in exploitation and repression, according to human rights organizations, have been very high.[67] In 1989 the United States and other Western countries became openly critical of the climate of political repression in Malawi.[68]

Between 1979 and 1981 problems arose: exports and export prices declined while imports continued to rise, resulting in increased borrowing and heavier debt. Borrowing for prestige projects added considerably to the problem. While IMF and World Bank policies and programs of structural adjustment assisted in restoring the modern estate economy, the dire poverty of the peasantry persisted and probably got worse as a result of population growth. To overcome this problem and to attain overall growth in the economy, reforms were prescribed by the World Bank and international donors. At the end of the 1980s the focus was on how to increase peasant welfare without undermining the modern agricultural sector.[69] By 1992 Western donors were denying economic aid to Malawi because of its continued human rights violations, and open opposition to Banda's regime, which had not been seen for almost three decades, was occurring.[70]

These examples suggest that where governments recognize that the agricultural system is the main (if not the sole) source of economic development and that agriculture must therefore be supported rather than exploited, we see an economic policy consistent with Quesnay's maxim, "Poor peasant, poor king; poor king, poor kingdom." Such a policy places economic production (and producers) before political distribution (and consumers). Above all, it controls or contains the patronage system and prevents the rush for political spoils from undermining the productive sectors of the economy. A weak or irresponsible leader who must indulge the spoils system to create or maintain political support cannot be expected to follow this policy. It requires a leader with sufficient authority and will to resist the political pressures, but not to the point of imposing his own will regardless of human costs—as in Banda's Malawi. The ruler of a successful economy must be enlightened—that is, not only must he understand the economic as well as the political consequences of his actions, but he must also possess what Max Weber called the "ethics of responsibility."[71] He must have both the right ideas and the determination to act on them, as well as the strength of character to take responsibility for the consequences of his actions and to change his policies if they fall too heavily on some. If he has the authority and the will but not the right ideas, economic disaster rather than development could result—as happened in Nyerere's Tanzania. If he lacks responsibility, suffering may be the outcome.

International Political Economy

It is evident that political decisions have economic consequences, as Coleman argued. In Africa the choices that favored appropriation of an expanded state apparatus by elites have been pursued at a very heavy cost to the welfare of the majority of rural Africans. We have suggested that these have been political choices (at least in significant part) rather than political necessities. That there were choices is evident from the reactions of Western suppliers of aid: they have lost confidence in Africa's regimes and increasingly expect to have a say in how their contributions are allocated. African governments are being subjected to scrutiny and criticism from Western governments, which previously had accepted the thesis that the difficulties of these governments were not of their own making but rather were determined by Africa's disadvantaged position in the global economy.

What was striking about Sub-Saharan Africa in the 1980s was its almost singular position as a global region of political dyseconomy—decay rather than development. In 1987 the population of the region was estimated at 450 million; the gross domestic product was some $135 billion, which—the World Bank points out—was the same as that of Belgium, a country of only 10 million people.[72] During the 1980s World Bank reports were increasingly concerned about one element in the African "crisis": the role of government.[73] In his foreword to the 1989 report, World Bank president Barber Conable stated: "A root cause of weak economic performance in the past has been the failure of public institutions. Private sector initiative and market mechanisms are important, but they must go hand-in-hand with good governance—a public service that is efficient, a judicial system that is reliable, and an administration that is accountable to its public. And a better balance is needed between the government and the governed."[74] That was the plainest statement by a leading international development organization that Africa's economic adversities can be attributed in significant part to a root political cause within Africa: bad governance.

This negative appraisal of African governments deserves a comment which can serve as our conclusion. If Conable's remarks are representative of the thinking of Western governments—and we think they are—African rulers in the future will have more difficulty in avoiding responsibility for the adverse economic conditions of their countries. The appraisal also suggests that Western-financed international development organizations will be establishing guidelines for good governance and productive political economy and expecting African rulers to conform to them. African attempts to place the blame for failure elsewhere will be met with greater skepticism. This view probably reflects the extent to which the ethical assumptions of liberalism, which place responsibility on sovereign individuals and sovereign governments, are displacing those of socialism. Liberal doctrine, which gained ground in the West in the 1980s under the influence of resurgent market economics, received a powerful stimulus by events in Eastern Europe, which witnessed the fall of personal and party dictatorships.

International involvement in African political economy has been evident for some time in the various "structural adjustment" programs of the IMF (supported by the OECD). On pain of being denied future credit, African governments are required to subject their fiscal and monetary policies to severe macroeconomic discipline, aimed primarily at liberating the African farmer and eliminating the unearned privileges and subsidies of the urban classes and governmental elites. By 1990 some thirty African countries had signed restructuring agreements with the IMF. Restructuring aims mainly at enlarging markets and fostering private entrepreneurship while reducing both government intrusiveness in the economy and government size. The latter is accomplished by privatizing or eliminating unproductive parastatals, most of which not only fail to make a profit but also are a serious drain on the productive sectors of the economy, particularly agriculture. The World Bank seems to be indicating that the very institutions and operations of government henceforth will be subject to scrutiny, presumably with the aim of encouraging (or possibly even inducing) reforms. If this is so, it suggests an emerging international relationship between African governments and representatives of the IMF, the World Bank, and the OECD countries which has the earmarks of trusteeship, at least of an informal kind.

It also suggests that African governments must become more publicly accountable domestically, so that not only ethics but also mechanisms of responsible government will be put in place that can prevent the dyseconomies and abuses of power often associated with personal rule. If the experience of other continents is indicative, it is not sufficient to rely on the will, intelligence, and responsibility of rulers. Other means of disciplining and legitimating state power are also necessary. Some international donors seem disposed to link economic aid with domestic political reforms. And ordinary Africans in many countries are demanding pluralist democracy. Africans are aware of the dramatic events that brought down personal and party dictatorships in Eastern Europe, and they want the same. Across the continent demands for political pluralism have been registered, and in several cases they are not only challenging political monopolies but actually provoking constitutional reform.

Notes

1. James S. Coleman, "The Resurrection of Political Economy," *Mawazo* 1, no. 1 (June 1967): 31–40.

2. See, among many others, Colin Leys, *Underdevelopment in Kenya: The Political Economy of Neo-Colonialism, 1964–1971* (Berkeley and Los Angeles: Univ. of California Press, 1974); P. C. W. Gutkind and I. Wallerstein, eds., *The Political Economy of Contemporary Africa* (Beverly Hills, Calif., and London: Sage Publications, 1976); Samir Amin, *Neo-Colonialism in West Africa* (Harmondsworth: Penguin Books, 1973); Giovanni Arrighi and John S. Saul, *Essays on the Political Economy of Africa* (New York: Monthly Review Press, 1973), Clarke Ake, *A Political Economy of Africa* (Harlow: Longmans, 1981).

3. The clearest example remains the work of P. T. Bauer. See his *Equality, the Third World, and Economic Delusion* (Cambridge: Harvard Univ. Press, 1981), and *Reality and Rhetoric* (Cambridge: Harvard Univ. Press, 1984). See also Elliot J. Berg, "The World Bank Strategy," in *Africa in Economic Crisis*, ed. John Ravenhill (New York: Columbia Univ. Press, 1986), pp. 44–59; and World Bank, *Accelerated Development in Sub-Saharan Africa* (Washington, D.C., 1981), of which Berg was the main author.

4. Keith Hart, *The Political Economy of West African Agriculture* (Cambridge: Cambridge Univ. Press, 1982), pp. 14–15.

5. Robert H. Jackson and Carl G. Rosberg, *Personal Rule in Black Africa: Prince, Autocrat, Prophet, Tyrant* (Berkeley, Los Angeles, and London: Univ. of California Press, 1982).

6. Ludwig von Mises, *Nation, State, and Economy*, tr. L. B. Yeager (New York and London: New York Univ. Press, 1983), p. 31.

7. Karl Marx, *The Eighteenth Brumaire of Louis Bonaparte* (New York: International Publishers, 1963).

8. See chaps. 5 and 7 above.

9. Mises, *Nation, State, and Economy*, p. 31.

10. Ibid., p. 32.

11. Ibid., p. 37.

12. Charles Tilley, "Reflections on the History of European State-Making," in *The Formation of National States in Western Europe,* ed. Tilley, (Princeton, N.J.: Princeton Univ. Press, 1975), pp. 3–83; E. J. Jones, *The European Miracle: Environments, Economies, Geopolitics in the History of Europe and Asia* (Cambridge: Cambridge Univ. Press, 1981), chaps. 6 and 7; Bertrand Badie and Pierre Birnbaum, *The Sociology of the State,* tr. Arthur Goldhammer (Chicago and London: Univ. of Chicago Press, 1983), pp. 67–92.

13. Mises, *Nation, State, and Economy,* p. 33.

14. See J. J. Spengler, "Mercantilistic and Physiocratic Growth Theory," in *Theories of Economic Growth,* ed. B. F. Hoselitz, (New York: Free Press, 1960), pp. 45–46.

15. Sir George Clark, *The Seventeenth Century* (London: Oxford Univ. Press, 1960), pp. 69–70.

16. See Pierre Goubert, *Louis XIV and Twenty Million Frenchmen,* tr. Anne Carter (New York: Vintage Books, 1972).

17. See Geoffrey Bruun, *Nineteenth Century European Civilization* (New York: Oxford Univ. Press, 1960), chap. 3. See also Mises, *Nation, State, and Economy,* pp. 120–21.

18. L. H. Gann and Peter Duignan, eds., *The History and Politics of Colonialism, 1870–1914,* vol. 1, *Colonialism in Africa, 1870–1960* (London and New York: Cambridge Univ. Press, 1969).

19. Lord Hailey, *An African Survey: Revised 1956* (London: Oxford Univ. Press, 1957), pp. 816–70, 1484–1534. See also Melville J. Herskovits and Mitchell Harwitz, eds., *Economic Transition in Africa* (London: Routledge and Kegan Paul, 1964); Andrus M. Kamarck, *The Economies of African Development* (New York and London: Praeger, 1967); A. G. Hopkins, *An Economic History of West Africa* (New York: Columbia Univ. Press, 1973).

20. World Bank, *Sub-Saharan Africa: From Crisis to Sustainable Growth* (Washington, D.C., 1989), p. 19.

21. Saadia Touval, *The Boundary Politics of Independent Africa* (Cambridge: Harvard Univ. Press, 1972), pp. 4–17; Hedley Bull, "European States and African Political Communities," in *The Expansion of International Society,* ed. Hedley Bull and Alan Watson (Oxford: Clarendon Press, 1985), pp. 99–114.

22. A. H. M. Kirk-Greene, "The Thin White Line: The Size of the British Colonial Service in Africa," *African Affairs* 79, no. 314 (Jan. 1980): 25–44.

23. Crawford Young portrays the Congo government as a "behemoth" consisting of "10,000 Belgian civil servants in the administration, magistrature, and army," but this is impressive only by the standards of most other colonial governments in Africa, which operated on a far smaller scale. See Crawford Young, *Politics in the Congo: Decolonization and Independence* (Princeton, N.J.: Princeton Univ. Press, 1965), p. 11.

24. Compare the analysis of Thomas M. Callaghy, *The State-Society Struggle: Zaire in Comparative Perspective* (New York: Columbia Univ. Press, 1984), pp. 111–37.

25. For a pioneering study on social change by a distinguished anthropologist, see Melville J. Herskovits, *The Human Factor in Changing Africa* (New York: Knopf, 1962).

26. James S. Coleman, *Nigeria: Background to Nationalism* (Berkeley and Los Angeles: Univ. of California Press, 1958). See also Thomas Hodgkin, *Nationalism in Colonial Africa* (London: Frederick Muller, 1956); James S. Coleman and Carl G. Rosberg, eds., *Political*

Parties and National Integration in Tropical Africa (Berkeley and Los Angeles: Univ. of California Press, 1964); David E. Apter, *The Gold Coast in Transition* (Princeton, N.J.: Princeton Univ. Press, 1955); Ruth Schachter Morgenthau, *Political Parties in French-Speaking West Africa* (Oxford: Clarendon Press, 1964); Michael F. Lofchie, *Zanzibar: Background to Revolution* (Princeton, N.J.: Princeton Univ. Press, 1965); Henry Bienen, *Tanzania: Party Transformation and Economic Development* (Princeton, N.J.: Princeton Univ. Press, 1970); Carl G. Rosberg and John Nottingham, *The Myth of "Mau Mau": Nationalism in Kenya* (New York: Praeger, 1966); Robert I. Rotberg, *The Rise of Nationalism in Central Africa: The Making of Malawi and Zambia, 1873–1964* (Cambridge: Harvard Univ. Press, 1965); William J. Foltz, *From French West Africa to the Mali Federation* (New Haven and London: Yale Univ. Press, 1965); Brian Weinstein, *Gabon: Nation-Building on the Ogooué* (Cambridge: MIT Press, 1986); Aristide R. Zolberg, *One-Party Government in the Ivory Coast* (Princeton, N.J.: Princeton Univ. Press, 1969); Martin Kilson, *Political Change in a West African State: A Study of the Modernization Process in Sierra Leone* (Cambridge: Harvard Univ. Press, 1966); Victor T. E. Le Vine, *The Cameroon Federal Republic* (Ithaca, N.Y., and London: Cornell Univ. Press, 1963); Richard Sklar, *Nigeria Political Parties: Power in an Emergent African Nation* (Princeton, N.J.: Princeton Univ. Press, 1963); René Lemarchand, *Rwanda and Burundi* (New York and London: Praeger, 1970).

27. Michael Clough, ed., *Changing Realities in Southern Africa* (Berkeley, Calif.: Institute of International Studies, 1982); Michael Crowder, ed., *The Cambridge History of Africa*, vol. 8, *From c. 1940 to c. 1975* (Cambridge: Cambridge Univ. Press, 1984); John A. Marcum, *The Angolan Revolution: Exile Politics and Guerrilla War, 1962–1972*, vol. 2 (Cambridge and London: MIT Press, 1978). See also Prosser Gifford and WM. Roger Louis, eds., *The Transfer of Power in Africa: Decolonization, 1940–1960* (New Haven: Yale Univ. Press, 1982), and *Decolonization and African Independence: The Transfer of Power, 1960–1980* (New Haven and London: Yale Univ. Press, 1988).

28. For a review of conceptual meaning and issues of "civil society" in Africa, see Peter M. Lewis, "Political Transition and the Dilemma of Civil Society in Africa," *Journal of International Affairs* 46, no. 1 (Summer 1992): 31–54; Dwayne Woods, "Civil Society in Europe and Africa: Limiting State Power through a Public Sphere," *African Studies Review* 35, no. 2 (Sept. 1992): 77–100.

29. Jackson and Rosberg, *Personal Rule in Black Africa;* Martin Kilson, "Authoritarian and Single-Party Tendencies in African Politics," *World Politics* 15, no. 2 (Jan. 1963): 262–94; Bereket H. Selassie, *The Executive in African Governments* (London: Heinemann, 1974); Aristide R. Zolberg, *Creating Political Order: The Party-States of West Africa* (Chicago: Rand McNally, 1966); Ruth Berins Collier, *Regimes in Tropical Africa: Changing Forms of Supremacy, 1945–1975* (Berkeley, Los Angeles, and London: Univ. of California Press, 1982). See also Samuel Decalo, *Coups and Army Rule in Africa: Studies in Military Style* (New Haven and London: Yale Univ. Press, 1976); Mustaphe Benchenane, *Les régimes militaires africains* (Paris: Publisud, 1994); Isaac James Monroe, ed., *The Performance of Soldiers and Governors: African Politics and the African Military* (Washington, D.C.: Univ. Press of America, 1980); Claude E. Welch, Jr., *Soldier and State in Africa: A Comparative of Military Invention and Political Change* (Evanston, Ill.: Northwestern Univ. Press, 1970).

30. L. H. Gann and Peter Duignan, eds., *The History and Politics of Colonialism, 1870–1914*, vol. 2, *Colonialism in Africa, 1870–1960* (London and New York: Cambridge Univ. Press, 1970).

31. Robert H. Jackson and Carl G. Rosberg, "Personal Rule: Theory and Practice in Africa," *Comparative Politics*, no. 4 (July 1984): 421–42; Thomas M. Callaghy, "The State as Lame Leviathan: The Patrimonial Administrative State in Africa," in *The African State in Transition*, ed. Zaki Ergas (London: Macmillan, 1987), pp. 87–116; Christopher Clapham, *Third World Politics: An Introduction* (Madison: Univ. of Wisconsin Press, 1985), pp. 39–89; Richard Sandbrook with Judith Barker, *The Politics of Africa's Economic Stagnation* (Cambridge: Cambridge Univ. Press, 1985); Larry Diamond, *Class, Ethnicity, and Democracy in Nigeria: The Failure of the First Republic* (Syracuse, N.Y.: Syracuse Univ. Press, 1988); J. Gus Liebenow, *Liberia: The Evolution of Privilege* (Ithaca, N.Y.: Cornell Univ. Press, 1969), pp. 131–47; Goran Hyden, *No Shortcuts to Progress: African Development Management in Perspective* (Berkeley and Los Angeles: Univ. of California Press, 1983), pp. 33–83; J. G. Williams, *Patrimonialism and Political Change in the Congo* (Stanford, Calif.: Stanford Univ. Press, 1972); J. F. Médard, "The Underdeveloped State in Africa: Political Clientelism and Neopatrimonialism," in *Private Patronage and Public Power: Political Clientelism in the Modern State*, ed. Christopher Clapham (London: Pinter, 1982), pp. 97–111.

32. David Abernethy, "Bureaucratic Growth and Economic Decline in Sub-Saharan Africa," in *Africa's Development Challenges and the World Bank*, ed. Stephen K. Commins (Boulder, Colo., and London: Lynne Rienner, 1988), pp. 178–209.

33. World Bank, *Sustainable Growth*, p. 56.

34. Ravi Gulhati, *Impasse in Zambia: The Economics and Politics of Reform* (Washington, D.C.: World Bank, 1989), p. 29.

35. See, particularly, John A. A. Ayoade, "States with Citizens," in *The Precarious Balance: State and Society in Africa*, ed. Donald Rothchild and Naomi Chazan (Boulder, Colo., and London: Westview Press, 1988), pp. 107–8; James Brooke, "Cameroon Battles against Bureaucracy," *New York Times*, Sept. 7, 1987. See also Clement Cottingham, *Contemporary African Bureaucracy: Political Elites, Bureaucratic Recruitment, and Administrative Performance* (Morristown, N.J.: General Learning Press, 1974).

36. Robert M. Price, *Society and Bureaucracy in Contemporary Ghana* (Berkeley and Los Angeles: Univ. of California Press, 1975). See also Richard A. Joseph, "Class, State, and Prebendal Polities in Nigeria," in *State and Class in Africa*, ed. Nelson Kasfir (Totowa, N.J., and London: Frank Cass, 1984), pp. 21–38; and Larry Diamond, "Class Formation in the Swollen African State," *Journal of Modern African Studies* 25, no. 4 (1987): 567–96.

37. Victor T. LeVine, *Political Corruption: The Ghana Case* (Stanford, Calif.: Hoover Institution Press, 1975); Ken C. Kotecha, with Robert W. Adams, *The Corruption of Power: African Politics* (Washington, D.C.: Univ. Press of America, 1981); Gideon S. Ware, *Leadership and Underdevelopment in Africa* (Nairobi: Gideon Ware, 1981); Nelson Kasfir, "State, *Magendo*, and Class Formation in Uganda," in Kasfir, *State and Class in Africa*, pp. 90–101; Larry Diamond, "Political Corruption: Nigeria's Perennial Struggle," *Journal of Democracy* 2, no. 4 (Fall 1991): 73–85.

38. Robert H. Jackson and Carl G. Rosberg, "Democracy in Tropical Africa: Democracy versus Autocracy in African Politics," *Journal of International Affairs* 38, no. 2 (Winter 1985): 293–305; Larry Diamond, Juan J. Linz, and Seymour Martin Lipset, *Democracy in Developing Countries: Africa*, vol. 2 (Boulder, Colo.: Lynne Rienner, 1988).

39. World Bank, *Sustainable Growth*, p. 61.

40. Crawford Young and Thomas Turner, *The Rise and Decline of the Zairian State* (Madison: Univ. of Wisconsin Press, 1985), p. 440.

41. It is interest that "Kevin Chang and Robert Kumby of New York University estimated that African individuals hold about $40,000 million of assets in industrial countries" (*Africa Confidential* 32, no. 2 [Oct. 25, 1991]: 2).

42. R. Craig Malion and Mark V. Kauppi, eds., *The Soviet Impact in Africa* (Lexington, Mass.: Lexington Books, 1984); Michael Clough, ed., *Reassessing the Soviet Challenge in Africa*, Policy Papers in International Affairs no. 25 (Berkeley: Institute of International Studies, 1986); Bruce D. Porter, *The USSR in Third World Conflicts: Soviet Arms and Diplomacy in Local Wars, 1945–80* (Cambridge and New York: Cambridge Univ. Press, 1984), pp. 147–215.

43. See Robert H. Jackson and Carl G. Rosberg, "Sovereignty and Underdevelopment: Juridical Statehood in the African Crisis," *Journal of Modern African Studies* 24, no. 1 (1986): 1–31.

44. Michael Clough, *Free at Last: U.S. Policy toward Africa and the End of the Cold War* (New York: Council on Foreign Relations, 1992).

45. See S. Andreski, *The African Predicament: A Study on the Pathology of Modernisation* (New York: Atherton, 1968), esp. chaps. 1 and 7. See also Dele Olowu, "Bureaucratic Morality in Africa," *International Political Science Review* 9, no. 3 (1988): 215–29.

46. See, particularly, Callaghy, *The State-Society Struggle: Zaire in Comparative Perspective;* Young and Turner, *Rise and Decline of the Zairian State;* Michael G. Schatzberg, *The Dialectics of Oppression in Zaire* (Bloomington and Indianapolis: Indiana Univ. Press, 1988); Nzongola-Ntalaja, *The Crisis in Zaire: Myths and Realities* (Trenton, N.J.: Africa World Press, 1986); Crawford Young, "Zaire: The Unending Crisis," *Foreign Affairs* 57, no. 1 (Fall 1978): 169–85; Jean-Claude Wilhame, "Political Succession in Zaire, or Back to Machiaevelli," *Journal of Modern African Studies* 26, no. 1 (1988): 37–49; "Zaire: Survival Techniques," *Africa Confidential* 29, no. 3 (Feb. 5, 1988): 6–7.

47. World Bank, *Sustainable Growth*, p. 221, table 1.

48. Etienine Tshisekedi, president of the Union for Democracy and Social Progress (UDPS) and "the symbol of opposition," was elected prime minister by the National Conference on Aug. 14, 1992, at the same time when the southern and mineral-rich Sbaba Province threatened succession. See "Zaire: National Conference Decisions," *Africa Research Bulletin, Political, Social, and Cultural Series* 29, no. 8 (Aug. 1992): 10679A–10680A.

49. For background of Zambia's political economy, see William Tordoff, ed., *Politics in Zambia* (Berkeley and Los Angeles: Univ. of California Press, 1974); Doris Jansen Dodge, *Agricultural Policy and Performance in Zambia* (Berkeley, Calif.: Institute of International Studies, 1977); William Tordoff, ed., *Administration in Zambia* (Madison: Univ. of Wisconsin Press, 1980); Cherry Gertzel, Carolyn Baylies, and Morris Szeftel, eds., *The*

The Political Economy of Personal Rule

Dynamics of the One-Party State in Zambia (Manchester: Manchester Univ. Press, 1984); Kenneth Good, "Zambia: Back into the Future," *Third World Quarterly* 10, no. 1 (Jan. 1988): 37–53; Gulhate, *Impasse in Zambia;* Morris Szeftel, "Political Graft and the Spoils System in Zambia: The State as a Resource in Itself," *Review of African Political Economy,* no. 24 (May–Aug. 1982): 4–21.

50. Colin Legum and Marion E. Doro, eds., *Africa Contemporary Record, 1987–88* (New York and London: Africana Publishing Co., 1989), p. B828.

51. "Zambia: An History of Victory," *Africa Research Bulletin: Political Series* 28, no. 11 (Nov. 1991): 10341B–10345B.

52. For background, see John R. Cartwright, *Political Leadership in Sierra Leone* (Toronto and Buffalo: Univ. of Toronto Press, 1978); Christopher Clapham, *Liberia and Sierra Leone: An Essay on Comparative Politics* (Cambridge: Cambridge Univ. Press, 1976); George O. Roberts, *The Anguish of the Third World Independence: The Sierra Leone* (Washington, D.C.: Univ. Press of America, 1982); Fred M. Hayward, "Political Leadership, Power, and the State: Generalizations from the Case of Sierra Leone," *African Studies Review* 27, no. 3 (1984): 19–39.

53. Daniel Fashale Luke and Stephen P. Riley, "The Politics of Economic Decline in Sierra Leone," *Journal of Modern African Studies* 27, no. 1 (1989): 136–37. See also "Sierra Leone Economic Policy and Control Act," *Africa Research Bulletin, Economic Series* 26, no. 12 (Jan. 31, 1990): 9797B–9799C.

54. Luke and Riley, "Sierra Leone," p. 135.

55. Ibid., p. 140.

56. Bankole Timothy, "Sierra Leone: What Next?" *West Africa,* no. 3896 (May 18–24, 1992): 840–41; Peter Da Costa, "Sierra Leone: The Young Guns," *Africa Report* 37, no. 4 (July–Aug. 1992): 36–39.

57. See, particularly, Cherry Gertzel, *The Politics of Independent Kenya, 1963–8* (Evanston, Ill.: Northwestern Univ. Press, 1970); Leys, *Underdevelopment in Kenya;* Joel D. Barkan, ed., *Politics and Public Policy in Kenya and Tanzania,* 2d ed. (New York: Praeger, 1984); Nicola Swainson, *The Development of Corporate Capitalism in Kenya, 1918–1977* (Berkeley and Los Angeles: Univ. of California Press, 1980); Michael G. Schatzberg, ed., *The Political Economy of Kenya* (New York: Praeger, 1987); Peter Anyang' Nyong'o, "State and Society in Kenya: The Disintegration of the Nationalist Coalitions and the Rise of Presidential Authoritarianism, 1963–1978," *African Affairs* 88, no. 351 (April 1989): 229–51.

58. See, specifically, Michael F. Lofchie, *The Policy Factor: Agricultural Performance in Kenya and Tanzania* (Boulder, Colo., and London: Lynne Rienner, 1989), and Robert H. Bates, *Beyond the Miracle of the Market: The Political Economy of Agrarian Development in Kenya* (New York: Cambridge Univ. Press, 1989).

59. David Leonard, *African Successes: Four Public Managers of Kenyan Rural Development* (Berkeley: Univ. of California Press, 1991).

60. See *Africa Confidential* 31, no. 21 (Oct. 26, 1990): 2. It was reported that thirty-two of Kenya's forty-one district commissioners, twenty-one of the thirty-three permanent secretaries, and many high-ranking security officers and government directors of the economy were Kalenjin. See also Jennifer A. Widner, *The Rise of the Party-State in Kenya: From Harambee to Nyayo* (Berkeley: Univ. of California Press, 1992).

61. Jennifer A. Widner, "Kenya's Slow Progress toward Multiparty Politics," *Current History* 91, no. 565 (May 1992): 214–18.

62. See I. William Zartman and Christopher Delgado, eds., *The Political Economy of the Ivory Coast* (New York: Praeger, 1984); Robert M. Hecht, "The Ivory Coast Economic 'Miracle': What Benefits for Peasant Farmers," *Journal of Modern African Studies* 21, no. 1 (1983): 25–53; Dwayne Woods, "State Action and Class Interests in the Ivory Coast," *African Studies Review* 31, no. 1 (1988): 93–116; Richard Crook, "Patrimonialism, Administrative Effectiveness, and Economic Development in Côte d'Ivoire," *African Affairs* 88, no. 351 (April 1989): 205–28.

63. For background to Banda's rule, see Philip Short, *Banda* (London and Boston: Routledge and Kegan Paul, 1974); T. David Williams, *Malawi: The Politics of Despair* (Ithaca, N.Y.: Cornell Univ. Press, 1978); Richard Hodder-Williams, "Dr. Banda's Malawi," *Journal of Commonwealth and Comparative Politics* 12, no. 1 (1974): 91–114.

64. David Hirschmann, "Malawi's Captured Peasantry: An Empirical Analysis," *Journal of Developing Areas* 24, no. 4 (July 1990): 469–75.

65. Ibid., p. 470. See also Jonathan Y. Kydd and Robert E. Christiansen, "Structural Change in Malawi since Independence: Consequences of a Development Strategy Based on Large-Scale Agriculture," *World Development* 10 (May 1982): 367–88.

66. World Bank, *Sustainable Growth*, pp. 222–23.

67. See Robert M. Press, "Malawi Criticized for Rights Violations," *Christian Science Monitor*, Oct. 25, 1990, p. 5.

68. See "Malawi: Dark Side of Success," *African Research Bulletin: Economic Series* 27, no. 3 (April 30, 1990): 9905C–9906AB, and J. Perlez, "Starving Children of Malawi Shatter Leader's Boast of Plenty," *New York Times*, April 3, 1990.

69. *Africa Research Bulletin: Economic Series* 27, no. 3 (April 30, 1990): 9905C–9906B.

70. "Malawi: Riots and Strikes," *African Research Bulletin: Political, Social, and Cultural Series* 29, no. 5 (May 1992): 10585A–10586B.

71. H. H. Gerth and C. Wright Mills, tr. and ed., *From Max Weber: Essays in Sociology* (New York: Galaxy Books, 1958), p. 127.

72. World Bank, *Sustainable Growth*, p. 2.

73. See World Bank, *Accelerated Development in Sub-Saharan Africa*; World Bank, *Toward Sustained Development in Sub-Saharan Africa* (Washington, D.C., 1984); World Bank, *Sustainable Growth*.

74. World Bank, *Sustainable Growth*, p. xii.

CONTRIBUTORS
INDEX

CONTRIBUTORS

David E. Apter, Ph.D., Princeton; Henry J. Heinz II Professor of Political Science, Yale University; former Professor of the University of California, Berkeley and Director of the Institute of International Studies; also has taught at University of Chicago and Northwestern University and at University of Ghana, Université Officielle du Congo Belge, Fondation Nationale des Science Politique, Paris, University of Paris at Nanterre, France, and University of Paris I. Major publications include *The Gold Coast in Transition,* Princeton University Press, 1955; *The Political Kingdom in Uganda: A Study of Bureaucratic Nationalism,* Princeton University Press, 1961; *The Politics of Modernization,* University of Chicago Press, 1965; *Choice and the Politics of Allocation,* Yale University Press, 1973; *An Introduction to Political Analysis,* Winthrop Publishers, 1977; *Against the State: Politics and Social Protest in Japan,* Harvard University Press, 1984; *Rethinking Development,* Sage, 1987; and *Discourse and Power: The Revolutionary Process in Mao's Republic,* co-author Tony Saich, forthcoming.

Carl G. Rosberg, D. Phil., Oxford; Professor Emeritus of Political Science, University of California, Berkeley; former Chairman of the Department of Political Science and Director of the Institute of International Studies; Past President, African Studies Association; also Professor and Head, Department of Political Science, Dar es Salaam, Tanzania, and also taught at Universities of Nairobi and Makerere. Major publications: *The Kenyatta Election: Kenya, 1960–61,* coauthor George Bennett, Oxford University Press, 1961; *African Socialism,* coeditor William Friedland, Stanford University Press, 1964; *Political Parties and National Integration in Tropical Africa,* coeditor James S. Coleman, University of California Press, 1964; *The Myth of "Mau Mau": Nationalism in Kenya,* coauthor John Nottingham, Hoover Institution and Praeger, 1966; *Socialism in Sub-Saharan Africa: A New Assessment,* coeditor Thomas M. Callaghy, Institute of International Studies, University of California, 1979; *The Apartheid Regime: Political Power and Racial Domination,* coeditor Robert M. Price, Institute of International Studies, University of California, 1980; *Personal Rule in Black Africa: Prince,*

Autocrat, Prophet, Tyrant, coauthor Robert H. Jackson, University of California Press, 1982.

Crawford Young, Ph.D., Harvard; Rupert Emerson Professor of Political Science, University of Wisconsin; former Chairman of the Department of Political Science, former Associate Dean of the Graduate School; Past President, African Studies Association; Visiting Professor, Makerere University, Kampala, 1965–66; Dean, Faculty of Social Sciences, Université Nationale du Zaire, Lubumbashi, 1973–75. Major publications: *Politics in the Congo,* Princeton University Press, 1965; *The Politics of Cultural Pluralism* (winner of the Herkovits Award), University of Wisconsin Press, 1976; *Ideology and Development in Africa,* Yale University Press, 1982; *The Rise and Decline of the Zairian State,* coauthor Thomas Turner, University of Wisconsin Press, 1985.

Joel D. Barkan, Ph.D., UCLA; Professor of Political Science, University of Iowa; former Chairman of the Department of Political Science; currently on leave as Regional Governance Advisor, USAID, Nairobi, Kenya, 1992–94; Visiting Senior Lecturer in Political Science, University of Dar es Salaam, Tanzania, 1973–74. Major publications: *An African Dilemma: University Students, Development, and Politics in Ghana, Tanzania, and Uganda,* Oxford University Press, 1975; *The Legislative Connection: The Politics of Representation in Kenya, Korea, and Turkey,* Duke University Press, 1984; coauthors C. L. Kim, Ilter Turan, and Malcom Jewel, *Politics and Public Policy in Kenya and Tanzania,* revised edition, editor, Praeger, 1984; and *Beyond Capitalism versus Socialism in Kenya and Tanzania,* editor, forthcoming, Lynne Rienner Publishers.

Richard L. Sklar, Ph.D., Princeton; Professor of Political Science, UCLA; Past President, African Studies Association; also taught as Lecturer, University of Ibadan, 1963–65; Senior Lecturer, University of Zambia, 1966–68; Visiting Fulbright Professor, University of Zimbabwe, 1984. Major publications: *Nigerian Political Parties: Power in an Emergent Africa Nation,* Princeton University Press, 1963; *Corporate Power in the African State: The Political Impact of Multinational Mining Companies in Zambia,* University of California Press, 1975; *Post-Imperialism: International Capitalism and Development in the Late Twentieth Century,* Lynne Rienner Publications, 1987, with three coauthors; *African Politics and Problems in Development,* coauthor and coeditor C. S. Whitaker, Lynne Rienner Publishers, 1991.

Michael F. Lofchie, Ph.D., University of California, Berkeley; Professor of Political Science, UCLA; former Director of the James S. Coleman African

Studies Center, UCLA; former member of the Board of Directors of the African Studies Association. Major publications: *Zanzibar: Background to Revolution*, Princeton University Press, 1965; ed., *The State of the Nations: Constraints on Development in Independent Africa*, University of California Press, 1971; *Agricultural Development in Africa: Issues of Public Policy*, coeditor Robert H. Bates, Praeger, 1980; *The Political Factor: Agricultural Performance in Kenya and Tanzania*, Lynne Rienner Publishers, 1989.

Thomas M. Callaghy, Ph.D., University of California, Berkeley; Associate Professor of Political Science, University of Pennsylvania; formerly taught at Columbia University and Pennsylvania State University. Major publications: *The State-Society Struggle: Zaire in Comparative Perspective*, Columbia University Press, 1984; ed., *South Africa and Southern Africa: The Intensifying Vortex of Violence*, Praeger, 1985; *Socialism in Sub-Saharan Africa: A New Assessment*, coeditor Carl G. Rosberg, Institute of International Studies, University of California, 1979; *Culture and Politics in Zaire*, Center for Political Studies, University of Michigan, 1988; *Hemmed In: Responses to Africa's Economic Decline*, coeditor John Ravenhill, forthcoming, Columbia University Press, 1993.

Colin Leys, M.A., Oxford; Professor of Political Studies, Queen's University, Kingston, Canada; formerly Fellow and Tutor in Politics at Balliol College, Oxford, and Professor of Politics at the Universities of Sussex and Sheffield, England; also taught in the 1960s at Kivukoni College, Dar es Salaam, Tanzania, Makerere University, Uganda, and the University of Nairobi, Kenya. Major publications: *European Politics in Southern Rhodesia*, Oxford University Press, 1959; *A New Deal in Central Africa*, coauthor R. C. Pratt, Heinemann, 1960; *Politicians and Policies: An Essay on Politics in Acholi, Uganda, 1962–65*, East African Publishing House, 1967; *Underdevelopment in Kenya: The Political Economy of Neocolonialism, 1964–1971*, University of California Press, 1974; currently working with J. S. Saul on *The Two-Edged Sword: Namibia's Liberation Struggle and Its Aftermath*, to be published by James Currey, 1993.

Michael Chege, Ph.D., University of California, Berkeley; Program Officer in Governance and International Affairs for the Ford Foundation in Harare, Zimbabwe; formerly Senior Lecturer in Political Science and Director, Institute of International Studies, University of Nairobi. Major publications: *Democratic Theory and Practice in Africa*, coeditors Walter Oyugi, E. S. Atieno-Odhiombo, and Afrika K. Gitonga, Heinemann, 1988; author of several articles—the most recent, "Remembering Africa," *Foreign Affairs* 21, no. 1 (1992).

CONTRIBUTORS

Robert H. Jackson, Ph.D., University of California, Berkeley; Professor of Political Science, University of British Columbia, Vancouver. Major publications: *Plural Societies and New States,* Institute of International Studies, University of California, Berkeley, 1975; *Personal Rule in Black Africa: Prince, Autocrat, Prophet, Tyrant,* coauthor Carl G. Rosberg, University of California Press, 1982; *Politics and Government in African States, 1960–1985,* coeditor Peter Duignan, Croom-Helm, 1986; *Quasi-States: Sovereignty, International Relations in the Third World,* Cambridge University Press, 1990; *States in a Changing World,* coedited Alan James, forthcoming, Clarendon Press, 1993.

INDEX

Accelerated Development in Sub-Saharan Africa, 146

Accountability: relationship to state, 88, 91; civil society, 92, 109–11; and development, 274

Achebe, Chinua, 185

Addis Ababa, 36

Adjustment Lending Report, 1989, 187

Administration: colonial, 14–16; development, 274–75; independence, 300–302

African Arts, 43

African institutional weakness in contrast to East Asian NICs, 213–15

Africanism, 62; and Lord Hailey, 62

African Management Services Company (AMSCO), 126

African National Congress, 127, 131, 132

Africanness, 1, 4

African socialism, 26, 43

African Socialism and Its Application to Planning in Kenya, 248, 269

African Social Research, 121

African Studies Association, 31, 43

Ake, Claude, 32

Algeria conflict, 14

Algerian 1990 election, defeat of Front de Liberation Nationale, 68

Almond, Gabriel: heuristic functionism, 21; *The Politics of Developing Areas,* 89

Alshain, Armen, 178

Althusser, Louis, 32, 41

American Economic Review, 1960, 161

American political scientists: perspectives and interest, 19–21; behavioralism, 20–21; differences from European colleagues, 20; "evangelical," 61

Amhara, 36

Amin, Idi, president of Uganda (1971–79), 3, 26, 221, 268

Amin, Samir, 32, 220

Amselle, Jean Loup, 79

ANC Freedom Charter, 132

Anderson, Benedict, 71, 79

Angola, 32, 33, 34, 35, 54, 303

Ansari, Javed, 161

Anthropological field studies, 75; "anthropological present," 67

Appiah, Anthony, 41, 43

Apter, David E., 62, 65, 74, 89

Arab-Berber Moors, 26

Arabic-speaking Muslim, 37

Armed Forces Ruling Council, Nigeria, 124

Arusha, 257

Arusha Declaration on Socialism and Self-Reliance, 248

Ashanti, 11, 74

Asia, 70, 159

Austro-Hungarian Empire, 296

Authoritarianism, 24, 39, 90, 247, 300

Authority: decline in Africa, 87; failure of one-party regimes, 89–90

Azikwe, Nnamdi, president of Nigeria (1963–66), 6

Babangida, Major General Ibrahim, president of Nigeria (1985–present), 189, 197–99; political reforms, 124, 125

Bagachwa, M. S. D., 270–71, 276

Balandier, Georges, *Political Anthropology,* 21

Balassa, Bela, 171

Banda, Hasting (Ngwazo Kamuzu), president of Malawi (1964–present), 6, 312, 313

Bangladesh, 259

Barkan, Joel D., 46

Barotseland, 64

Barre, Mohamed Siyad, president of Somalia (1969–91), 26, 36–37

Barth, Fredrik, 78
Barthes, Roland, 41
Bates, Robert, *Markets and States in Tropical Africa*, 32, 40, 146, 147, 151, 152, 153, 154, 156, 157, 158, 159, 171, 177, 188
Battle of Plessey, 10
Baudrillard, Jean, 41–42, 43
Bauer, P. T., 32
Baumol, William J., reasons for the scarcity of entrepreneurship, 176–77
Beekman, Björn, 226, 228
Behavioralism, 20
Belgium, 13; colonial objective, 63; debt cancellation, 234
Benin, 26, 45
Berg, Elliot J., 32, 146, 147, 151, 153, 154, 156, 157, 159, 171, 177
Berghe, Pierre van den, 79
Bettelheim, Charles, 13, 30, 32
Bhagwati, Jagdish, 171
Biyas, Paul, president of Cameroon (1982–present), 26
Blum, Léon, 8
Bochem, Adu, 43
Bohannan, Paul, 43
Bohemians, 293
Bokassa, Jean-Bedel, president of Central African Republic (1965–77), emperor (1977–79), 26
Bonaparte, Louis, 292
Botchevey, Kwesi, 215
Botswana, 45
Bourgeoisie, 29, 30, 31, 121, 230; managerial, 122; petite, 122, 255, 276; ruling class, 205; Kenya's capitalist class, 230, 239; "bureaucratic bourgeoisie," 266
Bratton, Michael, 93; growth of association and capitalist development, 98
Brazil, 222, 225
Britain, 62; capital, 231; colonial rule, empiricism, 9–10; constitutional development, 10–11
British East Indian Company, 10
British Somaliland, 36, 37
Brockway, Fenner, 13
Brookings Institution, 31
Buganda, 74
Bukoba, 257, 271
Bungoma, 256
Burkina Faso, 3, 35, 134, 298

Burundi, 26, 271; as Rwanda-Urundi, 298
Buxton, 10

Cabral, Amilcar, 43, 67
Callaghy, Thomas M., 46–47
Cameroon, 25, 26, 298, 301
Canada, 77, 234
Capitalism, 135; development in Kenya, 231–39; patrimonial, 207–9; predatory, 237
Cardoso, Fernando Enrique, dependency theorist, 225
Cartesianism, 11
Catonism, 281–82
Central Africa, 7, 11, 64
Central African Republic, 25
Central Bank of Tanzania, 273
Césaire, Aimé, 13, 47; theory of negritude, 69
Chad, 25, 34, 37–38
Chagga, 260
Chama Cha Mapinduzi, Tanzania ruling party, 269; formerly Tanzanian African National Union, 248
Chege, Michael, 28, 47, 186
Chenery, Hollis, 161–62, 164, 172, 176, 180
Chikwanda, Alexander, chairman of the Zambia Industrial and Commercial Association, 125
Chile, 213
Chiluha, Frederick, president of Zambia (1991–present), former chairman of Zambia Congress of Trade Unions (ZCTU), 129, 185, 307
China, 33, 89, 122
Chissane, Joaquim, president of Mozambique (1986–present), 36
Christian, 36, 37
CIA, 31
Civil society, 4–5, 87, 92–93, 97, 102, 109–11, 299–300, 310
Civil wars: Angola, 34; Ethiopia, 36; Chad, 37; Liberia, 34–35, 54; Mozambique, 35–36, 72; Nigeria, 34; Sudan, 34; Uganda, 34; Rwanda, 34; Somalia, 36–37
Class formation, weakness in Africa, 29–31, 61, 205, 237
Clientelism, 25, 97, 304

Clifford, James, "ethnographic surrealism," 41; *The Predicament of Culture*, 42
Clive, Robert, 10
Cobban, Alfred, 71
Coffee and tea industry in Kenya, 256–59
Cohen, Sir Andrew, 13
Colbert, Jean (1619–1683), 295, 298
Colclough, Christopher, and James Manor, *States or Markets? Neo-Liberalism and the Development Policy Debate*, 214
Coleman, James Smoot, 61, 89, 145, 291; "development syndrome," 22, 90; contributions to the study of African nationalism, 46, 62, 63, 64, 65, 66, 68, 71, 299; on ethnicity and ethnic consciousness, 72, 75, 76, 77, 81
Coleman, James Smoot, and G. R. D. Halisi, "American Political Science and Tropical Africa: Universalism vs. Relativism," 61, 62, 66, 145
Colonial constitutional development, post–World War II, 10–19, 299
Colonial exports, 297
Colonialism, 6–19; African culture, 12–13; the colonial state, 297–300
Colonial Office, 14, 18, 62
Committee on Comparative Politics of the Social Science Research Council, 21
Committee for the Defense of the Revolution (Burkina Faso), 134
Commonwealth of Independent States, 122
Comparative political economy of Kenya and Tanzania, 247–51
Compradors, 28, 29
Conable, Barker, 314, 315
Confédération Générale des Travail (CGT), 13
Congo, 26, 45
Congress of South African Trade Unions (COSATU), 131, 132
Connor, Walker, 70
Constructionism: conceptualizing of ethnicity, 79–81; Jean-Loup Amselle, 79; Leroy Vail, 80; Peter Ekeh, 80
Contractarianism: Robert H. Bates, 217
Cooper, Frederick, 205, 208
Copperbelt, 128
Coquery-Vidrovitch, Catherine, 67
Corruption, 26, 29, 40, 147, 174, 178, 191, 193, 197, 204, 208, 234, 254, 269, 275, 281, 303, 304, 307, 308
Côte d'Ivoire, 25, 27, 28, 35, 45, 124, 306, 309, 311–12
Coughlin, Peter, 232, 235–36
Council of Foreign Relations, 31
Cowen, Michael, 221–22, 237, 277, 281–82
Critical realism: challenging ethnographic authority, 40, 41; focus on inversionary themes, 41; difficulty of usage, 42
Croatia, 293
Cuba, soldiers, 27, 34; surrogate, 35
Cumings, Bruce, 194–95
Cyprus, 77
Czechoslovakia, 252

Dar es Salaam, 270, 271, 272, 273, 274, 275, 282
Darwinism, 73
Davidson, Basil, 29, 65, 68–69
Deby, Iris, president of Chad (1989–present), 37–38
Decolonization, 13–15, 17–19
Delavignette, Robert, 12
Democracy, 4, 40, 45–46; American political scientists, 19–20; effective government, 87–88; civil society and legitimacy of state authority, 111, 316
Democratic party, 264
Demsetz, Harold, 178
Denmark, 264
Dependency theory, 24, 28–33, 39, 41, 200–201; Kenya, 223, 224–29
Derge, 36
Deutsch, Karl, 22; *Nationalism and Social Communication*, 66
Development: analytical approach, 188–89; role of the state, 177–80; sequence from production to distribution or vice versa, 251–52
Development syndrome, i.e., crisis in political systems, 22, 90–91
Deyo, Frederio, 190, 194; analytical differences between East Asian and Latin American development, 196
Diamond, Larry, 118
Diop, Alioune, and Présence Africaine, 13
Diop, Cheikh Anta, 47, 69
District Development Council (DDC), 101
Djerma-Songhai, 26

Djibouti, 25

Djilas, Milovan, 135

Dodoma, 262, 271

Doe, Samuel, president of Liberia (1980–90), 26, 34–35

Dumont, René, 120

Durkheim, Emile, 20, 73

Dynastic state, 293–97

East Africa, 7, 11, 252, 274; High Commission territories, 64; politics, 282

East African Community, 236, 268

East African Institute of Social Research, 13

East Asia, NICs, 179, 180, 184, 189, 200, 207, 213; comparative perspective with Latin America, 195–97

Eastern Europe, 33, 39, 46, 122, 184, 252; revolution, 1989, 252

Easton, David, notion of the political system, 21

Economic Commission for Africa, 165, 201

Economic Community Monitoring Group (ECOMOG), 35, 40

Economic Community of West African States (ECOWAS), 35, 70

Economic liberation, 171

Education, 12, 118

Ekeh, Peter, 80

Elections, Kenya: competitive one-party elections, 96; multiparty elections, 111

Ellis, Frank, 270

"Embedded liberalism," 212

Emerson, Rupert, 66, 71

"Enabling environment," 123; examples in Africa, 124–26

Engels, Friedrich, 121

Enhanced capacity, 123–24

Entrepreneurship: pessimism, 164–65; scarcity, 176–77; stimulating, 40

Epstein, A. L., 78

Equatorial Guinea, 25, 26

Eritrea, 36; Eritrean People's Liberation Front (EPLF), 36

Ethiopia, 33, 34, 35, 36, 37, 38, 70, 77, 303

Ethiopian People's Revolutionary Democratic Front (EPRDF), 36

Ethnic egalitarianism, 255

Ethnicity, 5, 7, 26, 34, 36–37, 39, 62, 69, 70; "tribalism," 15, 73; Coleman contribution, 75–76; instrumentalism, 72–78; primordialism, 78–79; constructionism, 79–81

Europe, 43, 46, 71; western, 74; Community, 234; central, 293

Evans, Peter: "embedded autonomy," 193, 195, 196; comparing Nigerian development with Brazil, 199

Evans-Pritchard, Sir Edward Evan, 42

Eyadema, Gnassingbé, president of Togo (1967–present), 26

Faller, Lloyd, *Bantu Bureaucracy,* 21

Family Mirror, 279

Fanon, Frantz, *The Wretched of the Earth,* 1, 13, 29, 41, 42, 47, 67

Federal Military Government (Nigeria), 107

Financial Times, 231

Fitch, Bob, 30

Ford-Asilin (Kenya), 264

Formal choice theory, 38–39

Forum for Restoration of Democracy (Ford) (Kenya), 264

Foucault, Michel, 41, 44

France, 7, 39; 1780s, 210; debt cancellation, 234

Frank, André Gunder, 220, 224

Frankfurt School, 33, 41

Free-rider problem, 251

Freetown Creole, 63

Free trade, 172, 173; technological considerations, 173–74; economic considerations, 174; consideration of political economics, 174–76

Frelimo, Mozambique Liberation Front, 35, 36

French colonial rule: assimilationist, revolutionary, and conservative traditions, 7–9, 13, 18–19, 37, 63

French Communist party, 13

French Revolution, 292

French West and Equatorial African territories, 7, 8, 19, 63

Freud, S., 79

Front Islamique de Salut, 68

Functionism, 20, 22, 24, 38, 45

Fundikira, Chief Abdallah, 278

Gabon, 25, 45, 120

The Gambia, 34, 45

Gandhism, 281

Gatundu, 254
Gaulle, Charles de, 27
Geertz, Clifford, 42, 78
Gellner, Ernest, 71–72
German, 231; West German debt cancellation, 234; former East, 252, 293
Gertzel, Cherry, 261
Ghai, Yash P., 261
Ghana, 3, 27, 30, 31, 45, 69, 89, 124, 159, 167, 186, 204, 205, 208, 210, 211, 301, 311
Ghana Trade Union Congress, 134
Gilpin, Robert, "benign mercantilism," 192
Glazer, Nathan, 77
Godfrey, Martin, 232, 233, 238
Gorbachev, Mikhail, myth of Soviet nationality, 74
Governance, 88–89, 91–92, 187, 292, 314
Green, M. M., 12
Green, Reginald H., 32
Grindle, Merilee, 157, 159, 165
Guinea, 3, 7, 27, 32, 70

Habré, Hissene, president of Chad (1982–89), 37–38
Haggard, Stephan, 190; and Chung-in-Moon, 199–200; and Robert Kaufman, 211
Hailey, Lord, 10, 12, 62
Halisi, C. L. R., 61, 62, 66, 145
Hapsburg monarchy, 293–95, 296
Harambee movement: Kenya, 94–103; centralization under Moi, 101–2; character of participation, 98–99; district focus program, 100–101; finance, 99–100; geographic distribution and development, 98; who benefits, 100
Harvard Institute for International Development, 157
Hausa Fulani, 34
Hawiye clan, 37
Haya, 260
Hayes, Carleton, 71
Hegel, G. W. F., 41
Hirschman, Albert O., 161, 251, 254, 256, 268
Hodgkin, Thomas, 9, 10, 29; study of nationalism, 64, 65, 66, 67, 68; ignored ethnicity, 74
Hohenzollern, 293
Hometown Development Association, Nigeria, 103–9; purpose of these urban associations, 103–5; projects and participation, 105–6; leadership, 106–9
Hountondji, Paulin J., *African Philosophy*, 44
Houphouët-Boigny, Félix, president of Côte d'Ivoire (1960–present), 6, 9, 19, 28; presidency, 311–12
Hungary, 252; Hungarians, 293
Hunt, Diana, 233, 239
Huntington, Samuel, 22, 89, 90
Hutu, 34, 36
Hyden, Goran, 200; employment of the term "enabling environment," 123; "uncaptured peasant," 267; incapacity of Tanzania to capture and integrate the peasant into the market, 267; refutation, 271

Ibo, 15, 76; Igbo, 80
Ideological conflict, 34, 38
Imoudu, Michael, Nigerian labor leader, 131
Import substitution, 147–48; reason for failure, 165–69
Independence governmental policy framework, 147–54: administration of foreign exchange rates, 149; bank support for selected industrial sectors, 149–50; control of agricultural prices, 150–51; fixed exchange rates, 148–49; import substitution, 147–48; political rationale of postindependent policies, 151–54; protection, 148; state-owned enterprises, 150
Independents d'Outre-mer (IOM), 1957, renamed Convention Africaine (CA), 9
India, 10, 11, 20, 74, 222, 225
Indonesia, 260
Informal sector, 126–27, 136–37, 209
Institute of Colonial Studies at Oxford, 13
Institut Française Afrique Noir (IFAN), 13
Instrumentalism: ethnicity, 77–78
Interest groups, 154–60
International Coffee Agreement, 256
International Development Agency (IDA), 231
International Finance Corporation, 126
International Labor Organization (ILO), 281
International Monetary Fund (IMF), 170, 186, 187, 189, 195, 198, 200, 201, 203,

International Monetary Fund (IMF) (*cont.*)
204, 212, 213, 214, 227, 231, 232, 233, 235,
267, 273, 291, 305, 306, 307, 308, 312, 313,
315
Intractability of African development, 184–
88
Irele, Abiola, 44
Iringa, 271
Isaacs, Harold, 78
Islam, 36

Jackson, Robert M., 47
Jacobins, 8, 9
Jahn, Janheinz, 43
Jameson, Frederic, 41
Japan, 179, 194, 196, 212, 213; Japanese oc-
cupation, 190–91
Johnson, Chalmers, 193
Jones, Arthur Creech, 13
Joseph, Richard, 206
Juja group, 254

Kagame, Alexis, 43
Kakamega, 257
Kalenjin, 263
Kamana, C. Stanley, 278
Kamarck, Andrew, 32
Kaplinsky, Raphael, 221, 222, 223, 225, 228,
229, 259
Kariuki, J. M., assassinated 1975, 253
Kaunda, Kenneth, president of Zambia
(1964–91), 6, 26, 45, 170, 306, 307, 308;
defeated in presidential election of
1991, 129
Kay, Geoffrey, classical Marxist, 225
Keita, Modibo, president of Mali (1960–68),
6, 8, 9, 26–27
Kenya, 11, 27, 45, 72, 91, 93–103, 190, 247,
253–65, 309–11; debate and the issues,
228–31; economy, 231, 250; decline,
265; foreign capital investments, 231;
industrialization, for export, 233; international capital and the aid community, 234, 235; land reform, 233;
population growth, 232; "predatory
capitalism," 236–37; weakness of the
capitalist class, 237–38
Kenya African Democratic Union, 264, 278,
282
Kenya African National Union, 96, 259, 264,

278; incorporation of the Central Or-
ganization of Trade Unions (COTU)
and National Women's Organization,
but delinked in 1991, 102, 262
Kenya Coffee Growers Association, 257
Kenya debate, 220–22
Kenya Farmers Association (KFA), 97; re-
named Kenya Grain Growers Union,
102
Kenya Independent Schools, 95
Kenya National Assembly, 96
Kenya National Union of Teachers, 261
Kenya Planters Cooperative Union
(KPCU), 257
Kenya Tea Development Authority, 97, 257,
262; weaken the association, 102
Kenyatta, Jomo, president of Kenya (1964–
78), 6, 27, 95, 96, 97; governmental era,
221, 237, 253–54, 255, 261; pursued a
market economy to promote growth,
248, 250; presidency, 279, 281, 309–10
Kerebow, Mathieu, president of Benin
(1972–91), 26
Kericho, 257
Keyes, Charles, 78
Kiambu, 254, 257
Kigoma, 271
Kikuyu, people of Central Province, 95,
221, 230; dominance, 253–54, 255–56,
259–60; Rift Valley massacres, 264
Kilimanjaro, 257
Kilimo cha Kufa na Kupona, 262
Killick, Tony, 213
Kingsley, Mary, 11
Kinyanjui, Kabiru, 277
Kisii, 256
Kitale, 256
Kitching, Gavin, 222, 223, 228, 255, 259
Koffi, Nancy, 44
Kohn, Hans, 71
Korea, 179, 190–95, 197, 198, 212, 214
Korean Central Intelligence Agency, 192
Krueger, Anne O., 171–72; *Liberalization At-
tempts and Consequences,* 172; ideas on
free trade, 172–76

Labor movements, 127; Zambia, 128–29;
Nigeria, 130; South Africa, 131–33; ide-
ology, 133–34; Ghana and Burkina
Faso, 134

Labour party, Britain, 13
Lal, Deepak, 171
Lamine-Gueye, 19
Langdon, Steven, 221, 222, 223, 225, 228, 229
Lari, 254
Latin America, 20, 39, 43, 74, 159, 165, 184, 204, 210, 213, 223; NICs, 189, 200, 207; in comparison with East Asian NIC, 195–97, 200
Leadership: accountability, 91–94; skilled, 308
League of Nations, 296
Leith, J. Clark, 167
Lenin, 2, 77, 133; Leninism, 138; Leninist, 252
Lévi-Strauss, Claude, 41
Levine, Robert, 22
Lewis, Sir W. Arthur, 32, 161, 162, 163, 168
Leys, Colin, 30, 32, 46–47, 72, 222
Liberia, 26, 34–35, 70
Libya, 34, 35, 37, 38, 120
Lindi, 271
Lipton, Michael, 156–57, 158, 159
Lofchie, Michael, 46–47, 257, 266
Loi Cadres, 8; of 1956, 18
Louis XIV, 293
Lugard, Lord, 10; syndrome, 7, 12
Luhya, 254
Luke, David, 308
Luo, 260
Lyotard, Jean-François, 41

Maasai, 254
Macaffey, Janet, 126
Macaulay, 10
McAuslan, J. P. W. B., 261
McClelland, David, 22
Machel, Samora, president of Mozambique (1975–86), 35
Macias, Francisco, president of Equatorial Guinea (1968–79), 26
Mackenzie, W. J. M., 121
Macrosociological and historical crisis of the state and economy, 200–207
Madhupaper International, 260
Madras, 10
Maduka, 262
Maftah, Zakaria, 275
Magende economies, 201
Maine, Henry, 73

Majimbo constitution, 278
Makonnen, T. Ras, 13
Malawi, 268, 309, 312–13
Malaysia, 14, 260
Mali, 9, 26–27, 45, 69
Malime, Professor Kighome, 270
Malinowski, Bronislaw, 20
Maliyamkono, T. L., 270–71, 276
Malthusian crisis, 226; unprecedented population growth, 136
Mannoni, O., 42, 45
Mao, 2; post-, 32
Mariam, Mengistu Haile, head of state of Ethiopia (1977–91), 36; Soviet nationality, 70
Markovitz, Irving, 32
Marx, Karl, relations of class and nationalism, 70, 292
Marxism or Marxist theory, 28, 29, 30, 32, 33, 41, 43, 45, 88, 118, 119, 120, 121, 122, 130, 138, 145, 205, 221, 223, 224, 225, 226, 227, 229, 250, 251, 267, 291
Marxist-Leninist principles, 127
Matatu, 263
Mathew, Gervas, 29
Matiba, Kenneth, 259, 263
Mau Mau, 7, 11, 14, 256, 259
Mauritania, 26
Mazrui, Ali, 44
Mbembe, Achillo, 72
Mbeya, 271
Mboya, Tom, 253, 254, 264
Mecier, Paul, 75
Meek, C. K., 12
Meillassoux, Claude, 32
Mercantilism, 291–92, 311; benign, 212
Mexico, 213
Michaely, Michael, 171
Middle East, 184
Miles, William, 69
Military plot, 273
Military rule, 24, 34–35, 36–38, 305, 308
Mill, James, 10
Miller, Christopher, 11
Miradi, 277
Mises, Ludwig von, 292–95
Mobutu, Sese Seko, president of Zaire (1965–present), 26, 303, 304–5, 306
Modernization paradigm, 21–24; two versions, heuristic functionalism, 21–22,

Modernization paradigm (*cont.*)
  and structural-functionalism, 22–23;
  flaws in the modernization paradigm,
  23–24, 33, 38–39, 45, 66; resurrection of
  modernization theory, 87–91, 109–10,
  224
Mogadishu, 37
Moi, Daniel Arap, president of Kenya
  (1978–present), 238, 254–55; coffee and
  industry, 256–58; government policy
  and opposition, 259–65; government,
  279, 280, 281, 283, 310–11
Mombasa, 236
Momoh, Major General Joseph Saidu, pres-
  ident of Sierra Leone (1985–92), 308
Montesquieu, 25
Moore, Barrington, 280, 281
Moravians, 293
Morgenthau, Ruth Schacter, 65, 67
Morocco, soldiers, 25
Movement for Multiparty Democracy
  (MMD), Zambia, 129, 307
Moynihan, Daniel P., 77
Mozambique, 32, 33, 34, 35–36; Mozam-
  bique Liberation Front (Frelimo), 35
Mreme, Augustine, Tanzania, minister of
  home affairs, 276
Mtikita, Reverend Charles, Full Salvation
  Church, Tanzania, 275
Mudimbe, V. Y., *The Invention of Africa*, 44
Mueller, Suzanne, 266–67
Muge, Bishop Alexander Kipsang, 263
Multinational corporations (MNCs), 227,
  229
Muoroto, Nairobi slum, 263
Muranga, 258
Murilo, Masemde, 263
Museveni's National Resistance Move-
  ment, 236
Muslim, 36, 37
Mwanza, 271
Mwinyi, Al Hassan, president of Tanzania
  (1985–present), 250, 269, 273–77, 282
Mwongozo, 266, 269
Myrdal, Gunnar, 161

Nairobi, 259, 282
Nakuru, 259
Namibia, 46, 67
Nandi, 257

Nation, 64, 65, 71, 72, 73
National Bureau of Economic Research
  (NBER), 171
National Committee for Constitutional
  Reform, 278
National Council of Churches of Kenya,
  94, 102
National Council of Trade Unions
  (NACTU), 132
National Democratic party, 264
Nationalism, colonial protest, 6–7, 14, 20,
  24, 61–72
National Milling Corporation, 271
National Patriotic Front Liberation
  (NPFL), 35
National Price Commission, 273
National Union for the Independence of
  Angola (UNITA), 34, 35
National Union of Mineworkers, 132
Ndiayo, Babacan, president of the African
  Development Bank, 125
Ndjamena, 37
Ndulu, Benno, 250, 273
Neoclassical development theory, 201
Netherlands, 234
Newly Industrial Countries (NICs) of East
  Asia, 179, 180, 189, 195, 196, 197, 200,
  207, 213
New realism, 5, 39, 40, 43, 184, 185, 215
Niger, 26, 31, 45
Nigeria, 7, 31, 45, 62, 63, 70, 91, 189; Biafra
  War of 1967–70, 34; capitalist develop-
  ment, 197–99, 204, 205; economic lib-
  eration, 124; patrimonial capitalism,
  207, 208, 311; trade unions and politi-
  cal action, 130, 190
Nigeria Bar Association, 109
Nigeria Labor Party, 130
Nkrumah, Kwame, president of Ghana
  (1960–66), 2, 3, 6, 13, 30, 43, 47, 65, 69;
  industrialization, 27
Nkrumah's "verandah boys," 138
Nomenklatura (old CCM), 282
North, Douglass, 178, 188
Northern Emirates, 15
Norway, 264
Nurske, Ragnar, 161
Nyanza, 256
Nyayo Tea Zone Development Authority,
  258

Nyerere, Julius, president of Tanzania (1962–85), 6, 25, 43, 65, 170, 277, 282, 314; failure of agrarian socialism, 27, 28; Arusha Declaration of rural socialism, 248–49; policies and government, 261, 262, 266–68, 269, 279, 280; resigned the presidency 1985, 273

Nyong'o, Peter Anyang', 261

Odera, H., 44

Odinga, Oginga, 254, 259, 263, 264

Odinga, Raila, 259

OECD and the European Community, 231

Ogaden Somali, 37

Oppenheimer, Mary, 30

Organization of African Unity (OAU), 27, 70; Lagos Plan of Action, 187, 201

Ossowski, Stanislaw, 119–20

Ottoman Empire, 293, 296

Ouko, Robert, 263

Padmore, George, 13

Pan-Africanism, 63, 65, 70

Parallel market, 268, 272

Parsons, Talcott, structural functionalism, 21

Parti Démocratique de la Côte d'Ivoire (PDCI), 74

Parti Démocratique de Guinée, branch of RDA, 9

Patrimonialism, 300–303; and capitalism, 207–9, and personal rule, 300

Patronage, 25, 97, 205, 209, 301–2

Perham, Margery, 18

Personal rule, 24–28, 88, 191, 300–304, 304–13; Bonapartism, 238

Pinto, Pio Gama, 253

Poland, 252

Poles, 293

Political development, 20, 66, 189

Political dyseconomy, 296–97, 300–301, 314

Political economy, 32, 44, 145; new political economy, 146–47, 188, 214; of Korea—choices and institution, 190–95; comparative development of Kenya and Tanzania, 247–51; historical, 291–92; international involvement, 315–16

Political party system, 67; based on growth and redistribution, 277–79

Popular Liberation Movement of Angola (MPLA), 34

Portuguese dependencies, 7, 13, 35

Poulantzas, Nicos, 32, 41

Prebisch, Raoul, 161

Présence Africaine, 13

Primordialism: ethnicity, 78–79

Princely state, 291–97

Proletariat, 127–34; and labor, 127; trade unions in Zambia, 128–29; Nigeria trade union and politics, 130; labor movements in South Africa, 131–33; ideology, 133–34; Ghana and Burkina Faso experience, 134

Quesnay's maxim, 313

Radcliff Brown, A. R., 20

Rassemblement Démocratique Africaine (RDA), 9

Rattray, R. S., 12

Rawlings, Jerry J., flight lieutenant, chairman of the Provisional National Defense Council of Ghana (1981–92), president (1992–present), 134, 211

Renaissance, 292

Renamo, 35

Rent seeking, 178, 199, 257, 276; ideas of Anne Krueger, 174–76, 177; Rhee Korea, 191, 193–94

Revisionism, 6

Rhee, Syngman, 191

Rhodesia, Southern, 298

Rhodes Livingston Institute, 13

Rift Valley, 256

Riley, Stephen, 308

Rimmer, Douglas, 32

Rocheford, David, 69

Rodney, Walter, 30

Romanov dynasty, 296

Rosberg, Carl G., 47

Rostow, Walt, 225

Royal African Society, 13

Rubia, Charles, 259, 263

Rungwe, 257

Russian Empire, 296

Russian Narodniki, 281

Rwanda, 34, 298

Said, Edward, Orientalism, 42

Samuels, L. H., 32

Sandbrook, Richard, 177

Sankara, Captain Thomas, president of Burkina Faso (1983–87), 134

Santos, José Eduardo dos, president of Angola (1979–present), 34

Sartre, Jean-Paul, 13, 41, 47

Sassou-Nguesso, Denis, president of Congo (1979–92), 26

Saul, John, 30, 32

Savimbi, Jonas, 34, 71

Sawyer, Amos, interim president of Liberia (1990–present), 35, 70

Seers, Dudley, 223–24

Seidman, Ann, 32

Selassie, Haile, emperor of Ethiopia (1930–74), 36

Sender, John, classical Marxist, 225

Senegal, 9, 25, 45, 70

Senghor, Léopold Sédar, president of Senegal (1960–81), 6, 19; theory of negritude, 43; writings of, 65, 69, 170

Seroney, J. M., 263

Shaw, R. Paul, 79

Shaw, Timothy, 32

Shikuku, Martin, 263

Shils, Edward, 29

Shinyanga, 282

Shivji, Issa, 266

Sierra Leone, 26, 63; failure of Momoh to reform, 308; military regime of Strasser, 308–9; parasitic regime of Stevens, 307–8

Singer, Hans, 161

Sklar, Richard, 46, 71, 250–51

Slovaks, 293

Slovenians, 293

Smith, Adam, 253, 291, 292

Smith, Sheila, classical Marxist, 225

Social classes, 29, 31; class formation analysis, 117–21, 131; complementarity and development, 135–38; weakness of class formation, 205

Socialism, failure of, 26, 27, 33, 35, 36, 37, 135; Catholic, 9

Sokoine, Edward, late prime minister of Tanzania, 272, 276

Somali, 36, 37

Somalia, 26, 34, 36–37, 77, 208

Somalia National Movement, 37

Somali Revolutionary Socialist party, 37

South Africa, 34, 46, 67; labor organizations, 131–33; South Africa Defense Force, 35; working-class attitudes, 132–33

South African Communist party, 127

Southall, Aidan, 75

South Asia, 184

Southern African Development Coordination Conference (SADCC), 125

Southern African Economist, Harare, 125

Soviet Union, 33, 34, 35, 36, 39, 40, 43, 46, 74, 89, 90; post-, 228

Spain, 74

Sri Lanka, 77

States, characteristics, 203; European state system, 73; "embedded liberalism," 212–14; patrimonial, 204; problematic and weak, 200–207; role of state in development, 177–80; state formation, 4; weaknesses, 300–304; weaknesses of class formation, 205

States or Markets? Neo-Liberalism and the Development Policy Debate, 214

States and Markets, 214

Stevens, Siaka, president of Sierra Leone (1968–85), 26, 307–8

Strasser, Captain Valentine, president of Sierra Leone (1992–present), 308

Structural adjustment, IMF and World Bank policy, 40, 187, 200, 213, 232, 307, 315

Structural-functionalism, 21, 22–23, 45, 61, 66

Sub-Saharan Africa: From Crisis to Sustainable Growth, 187, 314

Sudan, 7, 34, 77

Suret-Canale, Jean, 13

Swainson, Nicola, 222, 259

Swynnerton, R. J., 256

Taiwan, 179, 190, 194, 212, 251

Tamarken, M., 259

Tanga, 27

Tanzania, 3, 26, 27, 32, 36, 159, 230, 236, 247, 250, 301; comparison with Zaire, 265–66; economic decline and analysis, 266–73; toward liberalization, problems of change and recovery, 273–77

Tanzaphilia, 249

Taylor, Charles, 35

Telli, Diallo, 27

Tempels, Placide R. P., 43, 69

Thailand, 260

Theoretical positions of dependency theory and "classical" Marxism, 224–28
Thiongo, Ngugi wa, 281
Tignor, Robert L., 255
Tigre, 36
Tigre People's Liberation Front, 36
Tocqueville, Alexis de, 70, 91–92
Togo, 26, 124
Tolbert, William, president of Liberia (1971–80), 34
Tönnies, Ferdinand, 73
Tontine, informal credit associations, 127
Touré, Sekou, president of Guinea (1958–84), 2, 3, 6, 8, 9, 12, 32; leaving a legacy of stagnation, 27; view on ethnicity, 73
Trade pessimism, critique, 169–72; identified with development economists, 160–64
Traore, General Moussa, chairman of the Military Committee of National Liberation (1968–79), president of Mali (1979–91), 20, 26
Tribalism, 15, 73
Tripp, Aili Mare, 276
Turkish Empire, 290
Tutsi, 26, 34

Uganda, 26, 34, 230, 236, 271, 298
Ujamaa, failure of Tanzanian socialism, 27, 32, 252, 261, 266, 267, 268, 269, 270, 276, 278, 279, 280, 281, 282
Ulanguzi, 276
Union Minière du Haut Katanga, 31
Union Soudanaise, branch of RDA, 9
United Democratic Front, 138
United Nations, 37, 303
United Nations Development Program, 126
United Nations Human Development Index, 308
United Somali Congress, 37
United States, 31, 34, 36, 37, 40, 74, 227, 231, 234, 238, 303, 305, 313; and Korea, 191–96, 198, 212, 213; policy, 40
Université Cheikh Anta Diop de Dakar, 12
University of Dar es Salaam, 274
Urban bias, 154–57

Vail, Leroy, 80
Vansina, Zan, 206

Vietnam War, 194
Vijijni, 262
Voluntary associations, 93–112

Walker, Connor, 79
Wallerstein, Immanuel, 32, 65, 67, 74
Wanenzi, 120
Wanjigi, Maina, 259
Ward, Barbara, 164, 176
Warren, Bill, *Imperialism: Pioneer of Capitalism,* 225
Weber, Max, 20, 252, 253, 255, 260, 269, 274, 313; influence of historical sociology on modernization theory, 21, 90, 189; patrimonial capitalism, 207, 208
Weekly Review, 260
West African Institute of Social and Economic Research, 13
Wilberforce, 10
Williamson, Oliver, 188
Wilson, Ernst J., III, 125
Wiredu, J. E., 44
Wong, Yuwa, 79
Workers' Defense Committee (Ghana), 134
World Bank, 40, 123, 124, 146, 169, 170, 179, 184, 185, 186, 187, 189, 193, 195, 198, 200, 201, 203, 204, 212, 213, 214, 231, 232, 257, 267, 273, 274, 291, 301, 303, 305, 306, 308, 313, 314, 315; and population growth, 136
World Development Report, 1991, 213–14, 184–85

Yearning, 1; different kinds and consequences of, 2–3
Yoruba, 15
Young, Crawford, 46
Yugoslavia, 77

Zaire, 7, 26, 43, 45, 298, 303, 304–5, 306
Zambia, 26, 45, 75, 120, 121, 128, 129, 130, 185, 301, 305–7, 310
Zambia Congress of Trade Unions (ZCTU), 129
Zambian Public Accounts Committee, 306
Zenawi, Miles, president of Ethiopia (1991–present), 36
Zimbabwe, 11, 36, 67
Zolberg, Aristide, 74